D1789307

Mrs. Oikawa Shiyuko sits among the remains of what was once her home.
Otsuchi, Japan, after the 2011 tsunami.
Photograph: © Alejandro Chaskielberg.

ARCHITECTURE'S ANXIETIES

Kazi Khaleed Ashraf

1

One always arrives at a building, and that perhaps already makes the building an *other*. We are more or less on a slippery slope in our understanding.

Describing a building is a bigger challenge than interpreting one. It's a passage to a deception in which we all participate unwittingly. The process almost always begins outside of that building; it accepts a separation in which a deeply intertwined condition is formatted into conceptual islands. Consciousness and intellect begin when bodies and things are already differentiated and *over there*. Understanding and description simply follow from a splintered world.

Visually legible and easily available objects present themselves as dominant in such a normative reality. And among those things that recede from the horizon of understanding—an irony there—are topography and terrain. That perhaps is the source of architecture's primary anxiety: an uncertain and queasy relationship with location. Architectural thoughts and descriptions need to rescript this topographical counter-predication, and regain the primitive contact with the here.

2

Usually registered as a disjunction, anxieties can be projective and productive in architecture. Rafael Moneo, in his commentary on the work of eight Euro-American architects in *Theoretical Anxiety and Design Strategies* (2004), considers theoretical anxiety a kind of "caustic reflection" and critical discourse, and ultimately generative of design strategies. That the productive capacity of architecture is hinged to wider social disturbances describes the nature of modern architecture. The disquiet over the nineteenth century city, its incapacity to deal with the emerging age led some architects to organize new methods for addressing housing, city frame and social conditions in totally new ways that came to be known as "modern."

In a psychosomatic sense, anxiety is *being modern*, a condition that for W. H. Auden (1948) describes a whole age. Does the "age of anxiety" continue now as an inheritance of the original modernist agitation, or is it more a consequence of a neoliberal world-order, what the sociologist Ulrich Beck describes as a "second modernity"? Is the latter, a "geo-liberated economy," an inherent aspect of *nouveau* middle-class aspirations spurring stresses and strains borne out of unfulfilled desires that lead to more desires and anxieties?

In the rumble-tumble of economic globalization to which all have succumbed, from nation-states to corporations and agencies, and to the individual psyche, and in the furious proliferation of buildings and cities, a single thought haunts us: "What makes for significant architecture?"

3

There are compelling reasons why we should talk about spatial anxieties while addressing architectural significance. In the Portuguese writer José Saramago's novel T*he Stone Raft* (1986), the Iberian Peninsula dislodges itself from the European continent and begins drifting away in the Atlantic Ocean. Disturbances ensue when parameters—coordinates, orientation, position and bearing—that direct our corporeal operations in the lived-world alter. When George Clooney's character Bingham, in the film *Up in the Air*, is asked by a flight attendant on an airborne airplane where he is from, he replies, "Here." Location has a greater human hue; it is more than a simple geographic coordinate.

The Swiss writer Max Frisch, in his novel *Homo Faber* (1954), presents the protagonist Walter Faber as a UNESCO engineer, a quintessential modern man who lives for the service of a purely technological realm, and for whom only the "tangible, calculable, verifiable" exists. As an emblematic figure befitting such a world body as UNESCO, Faber moves from one location to another allowing himself to be uprooted in a liberative way. Frisch, in this existentialist and quasi-ethical novel, charts the enigmatic quandary of such a modern nomad. On a cruise liner —travel being the ubiquitous trope of place-liberation—Faber meets a young woman and falls in love with her consummating the relationship. In a twist reminiscent of Oedipus and his exile from his place of origin and his devastating forgetfulness, Faber finds out that the young woman is actually his daughter. The novel then proceeds towards a tragic Greek destiny.

Sometimes, place remains as it is, but the terms of location changes. In "The Other Side of Silence" (2007), writing about the Indian subcontinent's partition in 1947, Urvashi Butalia recounts her trip from Delhi to Lahore (in Pakistan) to locate an uncle who did not migrate to India with his other Hindu family members following the violence and dislocations of partition. The uncle, Ranamama, opts to stay back in Lahore with his aging mother with the purpose of retaining their ancestral home until the trouble died down. Ranamama promised that he would join the relocated family later but after about 30 years he is still in Lahore, while the other family members live in Delhi. Butalia locates him in the same city that belonged to them for generations, and to which they belonged. Ranamama is in the same house, has converted to Islam, married, raised daughters, and buried his old mother per Muslim customs. Although the uncle has remained in the same spatial coordinates, he himself has become the other.

Mehran Karimi Nasseri's real story positions airport spaces as the most vivid site of modern dislocations. Nasseri, fleeing Iran in 1988 was "stranded" at Charles de Gaulle Airport for more than eleven years while trying to enter France unsuccessfully. While waiting at the airport, he made the terminal his home. Newspapers describe him in the terminal "siting at a table, perhaps smoking a pipe, taking a stroll, stopping to pick up his mail at the post office or lunch at the McDonalds's… he will be looking very much at home."

Being "at home" in this improbable space can now be experienced by those who cannot even imagine such a space. Following Frederick Jameson, in *Postmodernism, or, the Cultural Logic of Late Capitalism* (1991), we can say that this *extruded* or *cleaved open* space —Jameson's "hyperspace"—can now be experienced, and therefore needs to be taken seriously. Many of us will be struggling to look very much at home in this warped world. Jameson thinks that we have not yet developed the "perceptual equipment" to face this spatial convolution, this new hyperspace; in fact, the new conditions require that we "grow new organs to expand our sensoria and our bodies to some new, as yet unimaginable perhaps ultimately impossible dimensions."

4

Would it be a hyperbole to declare that being modern is to be bequeathed with that exhilarating and burdensome nomadism, the promise to transcend the terror of territory but face the terrifying consequence of the Oedipal flight?

The anxiety that we developed with place and location is now thrust on buildings. Modern architecture and its incarnations are bearers of a world-view that architecture need not be encumbered by territory and geography. This was perhaps presented provocatively in Archigram's 1964 architectural vision of literal world mobility, with tentacled mega-machines poised for globe-trotting. Specific places—call them what you may, nation, locality, or region—have taken a bit of a beating to the euphoria offered by new globalization, economization, and more lately, digitization. And what that shares with the old universalist aspiration of modernity is a suspicion of place, or to say it in an obverse way, an unabashed glorification of "placelessness." However, that celebration does not come without its attendant quandary, as the stories of Walter Faber or Nasseri demonstrate.

A basic locational question in architecture begins with: *Where do I work as an architect?* From where do I get my architectural responses, and where do I situate my work. One can design in a situationally independent manner anywhere, but one always builds somewhere. A clever argument could be made that somewhere is anywhere, or nowhere for that matter, or in the voice of Gertrude Stein, that "there is no there there," and so why linger. The first point comes out from the cartography of "free-flow," either the electronic mode of digitization or the fluid capital of globalization, and the latter as an indictment of the sociological and cultural void of the modern city (in Stein's case, Oakland in California). Yet, if one cares to detect, there is a certain wistfulness in Stein's captivating lines. "Where is architecture" is not a question, but it could trigger reflections about the role of architecture in cultural and economic production, and about its situation in the world. In orienting focus away from "what is architecture" to "where," we need to accept that we have been making inordinate demands on the "what," and have left the question of "where" largely unexamined.

Yet, the question of "what" is intimately tied to the matter of "where"—to architecture and its place in the world. "Where" refers to a zone of inevitability, be it geographical or cultural, or some combination of it. Zones and boundaries are never fixed things; their fluidity makes it difficult to maintain a precise overlap of the political, cultural, and geographical, and that is both a charm and challenge. If flux is now the reality, then to what boundedness can architecture respond to?

A reflection on "where is architecture" is either subsumed or found unimportant in the glamorous and spectacular pursuit of the "what." With "where is architecture," the debate may deflect from form to situation, from ideation to sensation, and from the asymptotic present to a phenomenal presence.

5

"The architect's task is more than the manipulation of materials and the molding of space, it is the definition and possession of place," the American architect Charles Moore said more than fifty years ago, and it continues to matter for architectural operations today. While beginning his work at Chandigarh, Le Corbusier's biggest predicament concerned place and territory, on how to begin on that site, and how to relate to the geographic surrounds. Louis Kahn's first meditation on beginning in Dhaka was not quite directed towards cultural associations, but rather toward how the buildings are to take their place there. It is in this taking place that a work of architecture, from Corbusier's Ronchamp to Kahn's Kimbell Art

Corbusier's Ronchamp Chapel in the winter of 2015 (Photo: Saif Ul Haque).

Louis Kahn, Kimbell Art Museum, Fort Worth (Photo: K. Ashraf).

House construction, Honolulu (Photo: K. Ashraf).

Peter Zumthor, Saint Benedict Chapel, Sumvitg, Graubünden, Switzerland (Photo: Saif Ul Haque).

Museum, to speak of grand gestures, or even an anonymous building in Honolulu, literally finds substantiality and significance. Humans are geographic beings; the possessing of place is a basic existential impetus, and has not become passé in the onslaught of new epistemologies and technologies.

Invoking the notion of "place" in the 21st century often has a retrogressive implication, especially with the intonation of romanticism about landscape, of a chauvinism around regional or territorial affiliation, or of something just stable and perennial in the (post)modern world of perpetual flux and denuded fixities. At the same time, the obverse of place —"placelessness"—is increasingly apotheosized as another kind of existent space.

Although *place, culture, region,* and *nation* are often used interchangeably, they are distinct concepts; place does not immediately promote a nationalistic or identity-laden rhetoric, or a cultural foundation. Place and culture, once homological, soon became alter egos, and are now currently at such tangents that we can now pose the phrase: "place versus culture."

With culture becoming portable, malleable, and commodifiable, and the geographic rootedness of culture and community increasingly becoming tenuous, it is possible to question it as a reliable premise for architecture. On the other hand, it is possible that the situatedness of architecture involves comparatively more enduring conditions, or "realities." These "earth-realities"—primarily of a meteorological and terrestrial nature—constitute a place-situation that tacitly and inevitably affects the life and form of architecture there.

6

Identity, with its vexing questions, is the other side of location. An anxiety over identity follows from that of location; it is the locational ontology that conditions the formation of identity and the production of tradition. With tradition now in turmoil, and a fixed pattern of life uncertain, how is the significance of architecture to be considered? Heinrich Hübsch's self-reflection posed in the context of nineteenth century disquiet in Germany —"In what style should we build?"—returns again as a question to any reflective architect embarking on a project.

Framed in the 1980s within a regionalist discourse in architecture, and earlier in the political sphere of the nation, identity remains a stubborn topic, even while stumbling from one kind of articulation to another and encountering newer practices and critiques. While identity may appear as a natural issue for autochthons, it also brings up the question of the other. Transnational exchanges disrupt many of the precepts that have informed regionalist or nationalistic practices. At the same time, an unprecedented wave of migration—intra- and international—creates new definitions of far and near, and ours and theirs, in which identity is constantly being reconstituted.

It is critical for an architect, or a writer or an artist, wherever she or he is geographically, to locate her or his work in this horizon of identity. Czech-born writer Milan Kundera, in his essay "Die Weltliteratur" (2007), considers the place of a work of art in tension between two contexts: On the one hand, a writer, as well as the work, is obligated to the historical process of the nation. Such an emplacement brings up the matter of national identity—as things stand today, one is invariably described/identified within the legal parameter of a nation. Kundera calls this "the small context." On the other hand, the work finds itself placed and categorized in "the supranational history of that art" – what, according to Kundera is the large context, the *weltliteratur.*

The ambiguity of placement is relevant to architecture. Transferring the question of *weltliteratur* to architecture, we wonder: Is Antonin Raymond's elegant ashram in Pondicherry (1936), for example, a European modernist work in India refracted by climate, a Czech-American architect's production inflected by Japan, or by dint of being in India, an Indian work? Similarly, does Chandigarh belong to India, to Le Corbusier, or to European modernism?

Kundera's quandary is a European one: how a work is to be situated within the diverse and porous context of Europe, where there is also a disproportionate status to each nation. How a work is read and positioned on a world stage, whether in the smaller context of a nation or the larger universe of a world art, is still decidedly a Euro-American dispensation. Kundera describes the vexation of writing from Czechoslovakia in the shadow of Europe whence the writer's identity is marked, without the writer's say in the matter, in the small or bigger context, as provincial or worldly. In fact, the politics of placement and the identity of the artist, writer, or architect become particularly fraught outside the Euro-American orbit. In that condition, one has to contend with a more dubious politics of identity categories.

Kundera's double context within which the appreciation of a work of art oscillates is not quite the same as Paul Ricoeur's much discussed dichotomy between a universal civilization and local culture. Consider India, whose nationhood began with a struggle to define cultural identity through the works of artists in Bengal in the late nineteenth century. This was the period when identity arose as a contentious theme as part of and reaction to the colonial system in British India. With art as the site of a nationalist discourse, artists, writers, and intellectuals debated on what constitutes Indian art. While many argued for a nationalist position, the Bengali poet-philosopher Rabindranath Tagore (1861-1941) rejected a nationalist identity for art, and argued more for an individual creativity in the service of a larger humanity. The art critic Benoy Sarkar, writing from Paris in the 1920s, stated that one doesn't produce "Indian" art just by painting in India. Today, in India as in anywhere else, a singular identity is under severe critique and is being replaced by ideologies of hybridity, multiplicity, and fluctuating formations. In shaking up the foundation of a unitary nation, the postcolonial critic Homi Bhabha positions hybridity towards dissolving "coherent identities, conceptual purity and cultural unity." The British-Bangladeshi choreographer Akram Khan's oscillation among various obligations and affiliations, discussed in the next feature here, is a more recent reminder of this ongoing strife.

How to engage this discussion in architecture? With national identity considered suspect, and cultural identity despatialized, the basis of architecture may have to return to something more fundamental and prosaic, such as climate. However, climatic reflections do not excite most social and political scientists engaged in the critique of identity and culture (Bhabha, for example, has nothing to say about it). In that debate, there is no room for weather, and no philosophy of climate.

In the conjunction of climate and architecture, I am not immediately recalling Otto Koenigsberger, Maxwell Fry and Jane Drew, and Victor Olgyay, and their metrics of tropical architecture, as useful as they are, but remembering a lesser known work, the Japanese writer Watsuji Tetsuro's *Climate and Culture: A Philosophical Study* (1961). Notwithstanding controversies around essentialist links between types of climate and the nature of culture, Watsuji's work presents an ineluctable position of climate in our lived experiences, and to our profoundest beings. Place is a surrogate for climate in which the latter is not simply a geographic condition but a particular milieu—literally an environment of molecular continuum in agitation.

In the spectrum of culture and climate, an architectural work remains beholden to the latter. Wherever it is positioned in the interpretive scheme of critique and historiography, an architectural work is still there in a specific locale. And it is to that locational ontology that a work of architecture, unlike a book or painting, or a musical work or performance, or a critique for that matter, must eventually turn to. In fact, interpreted or not, described or otherwise, it is already *there* in that milieu.

7
Poised between disaster and promise, the contemporary city makes architects teeter. A new city is emerging in the landscapes of Asia, Africa, and South America whose contours remain unmapped and whose nature close to being explosive. Powerless to comprehend the scope of the new urban landscape, and unable to figure out a point of entry into the enigma, architects are content in their allocated lots and plots to be ironic or phantasmagoric. Where once architecture and the city formed a twinness, the parameters of one informing the other, there is now a contention. While architects make stunning architecture, the city goes to hell. The production of architecture, thus liberated, seems either unable to deal with the furious city or prescribe ways of negotiations. That remains as a challenge and third anxiety for most architects.

Better understood as economic engines, ecological footprints, and social intensities, cities are poorly comprehended in their humanistic or existential dimensions. Writers and film-makers have done better in drawing the contour of this new city. Whether in the alternative reality of Haruki Murakami's *1Q84*, transnational movement in Wong Kar-Wai's films *Chungking Express* and *2046*, or the ultra-real narrative (of Mumbai) in Gregory David Roberts's *Shantaram* and Suketu Mehta's *Maximum City*, the city once again is the site of new collective consciousness.

In *Memories of Istanbul* (2009), Orhan Pamuk describes the slow but sure disappearance of a deeply sedimented city, lending to Istanbul a melancholia, or *hüzün*, that is particular to that city. But not all cities are shedding their old selves with such wistfulness. Most cities in Asia and South America are transforming with a fury and forwardness in which investment supersedes the environment, and architecture finds itself in an adversarial relationship with the city.

Tokyo provides earlier instances for architecture's edgy relationship with the city. In response to Tokyo's corrugated and discordant morphology, some architects declared their inability to converse with the city and resorted to introverted buildings. Examples are Toyo Ito's U-House (1976) and Tadao Ando's House in Daikanyama (1991). On the other hand, Fumihiko Maki whose work is known for a restrained and elegant language, conceived a dynamic facade for the Spiral

Square in front of the Taj, Mumbai, 2014 (Photo: Amit Ashraf).

Michael Sorkin, Amsterdam Avenue Transformed, New York.

High Line, New York (Photo: K. Ashraf).

Building (1985) as a condensation of the city's ensemble nature. Drawing up a conclusion after analyzing Tokyo, the maverick thinker Kazuo Shinohara (1925-2006) went a step further arguing for a new approach of violent and disjunctional assembly in a manner he called "savage architecture."

When architects do engage the city now, they produce phantasmagorias—edifices of elsewhere in response to the powerful middle-class desires. The "longing for elsewhere" is now embodied in new building configurations that are radically affecting the urban landscape, constituting a new "hyperspace": malls and shopping centers, cineplexes and flyovers, and exclusive apartment and residential complexes.

In writing about the new Indian city ten years ago, I described the mall as urban space par excellence borne out of a transnational exchange that, on the one hand, mimics the shopping culture of America, and on the other hand embodies the surreal city of "elsewhere." "While the American mall is a populist destination, the mall in India and South Asia has taken on a unique and exclusive aura that architecture helps codify. As an alternative to the older streets and bazaars, from where the aspirant class has fled, the mall holds the city at arm's length through a series of barriers—by the curtailed interaction with the surrounding city, by the inevitable motorized access, and by the spectacular security befitting an airport terminal—all of which works towards intimidating people. The residential gated enclaves are similarly policed and truncated from the continuum of the city. The metrosexual citizen can now travel from home to mall, bypassing the rest of India." (2009)

8

Despite a glib consumerism marked by luxury malls and raunchy residences, towards which most architects are understandably rushing to, architecture broadly faces some formidable issues: How best to reconfigure the city, humanistically and ecologically, in the climate of rushed development? What urban types to innovate to meet rising levels of middle-class requirements? How to mobilize the resources of the new economy to raise millions out of poverty, especially in vulnerable regions? And how to rephrase the questions of identity and locality without being parochial or dogmatic?

What, then, makes for significant architecture? It does not have to call out for an ancient name, nor does it have to be abrasively modern to attract attention, as the ancient Indian poet Kalidasa said some 2,000 years ago. To be significant, architecture does not have to be large, monumental, or overwhelming. Some of the finest examples of architecture produced today come from many small-scale projects demonstrating the dense presence of poetics and tectonics even in a low-key situation—for example, the railway Signal Box by Herzog and de Meuron, a quiet courtyard by Anjalendran or Channa Daswatte, a village church by Peter Zumthor, a quirky teahouse by Terunobu Fujimori, a visitors' center in a remote region of Australia by Greg Burgess.

Responding to the anxiety over food and energy security, architecture can be projective of an alternative urban future, as in Michael Sorkin's vegetal plan for feeding Manhattan. Again, architecture does not necessarily have to be urban to be significant, and certainly not the graphical hodge-podge that makes up the metropolitan landscape. Significant architecture need not even be buildings. In an expanded field, architecture now includes the much featured High-Line project, Kongian Yu's ecological park and urban park in Havana. At the same

Konjian Yu, Qiaoyuan Wetland Park, Tianjin City.

Farming carrots in Havana (Photo: Carey Clouse).

Khondaker Hasibul Kabir, Building a Settlement in Satkhira, 2011, Bangladesh.

time, mobilizing a community project in Curitiba or Medellin, building a settlement in a raw landscape in Bangladesh, or restoring of a wetland in Saudi Arabia that receives the Aga Khan Award—all certify as fine works of architecture.

Significance calls for substance. With much of the earlier assurances in tatters—whether the grandiose humanism of modernity or the ethnocentrism of a regional architecture—many architects seek a basis of their work in the fundamental ontology of material formation and site entrenchment, or the reality of lived communities. Whether carried out in a neomodernist or paratraditional vein, making and building are opportunities for architects to create a phenomenal and sensual ensemble, with a social enterprise to support it.

LOCATIONS presents the art of building that demonstrate both the substantiality and sustainability of architecture in an age of new anxieties. Works represented here embody a tectonic clarity, landscape consciousness, humanitarian ethics, constructional elegance, and material sensuality without seeking validation in symbols and signs (even though they may be visually powerful and socially persuasive at times). The works presented or discussed in LOCATIONS invoke neither the tottering certainty of archaism nor the inevitability of excess, but instead the challenge of the assuredness of a *fine built work*. Such acts of building are deployed toward the obligations of habitation and well-being rather than a spectacular presence.

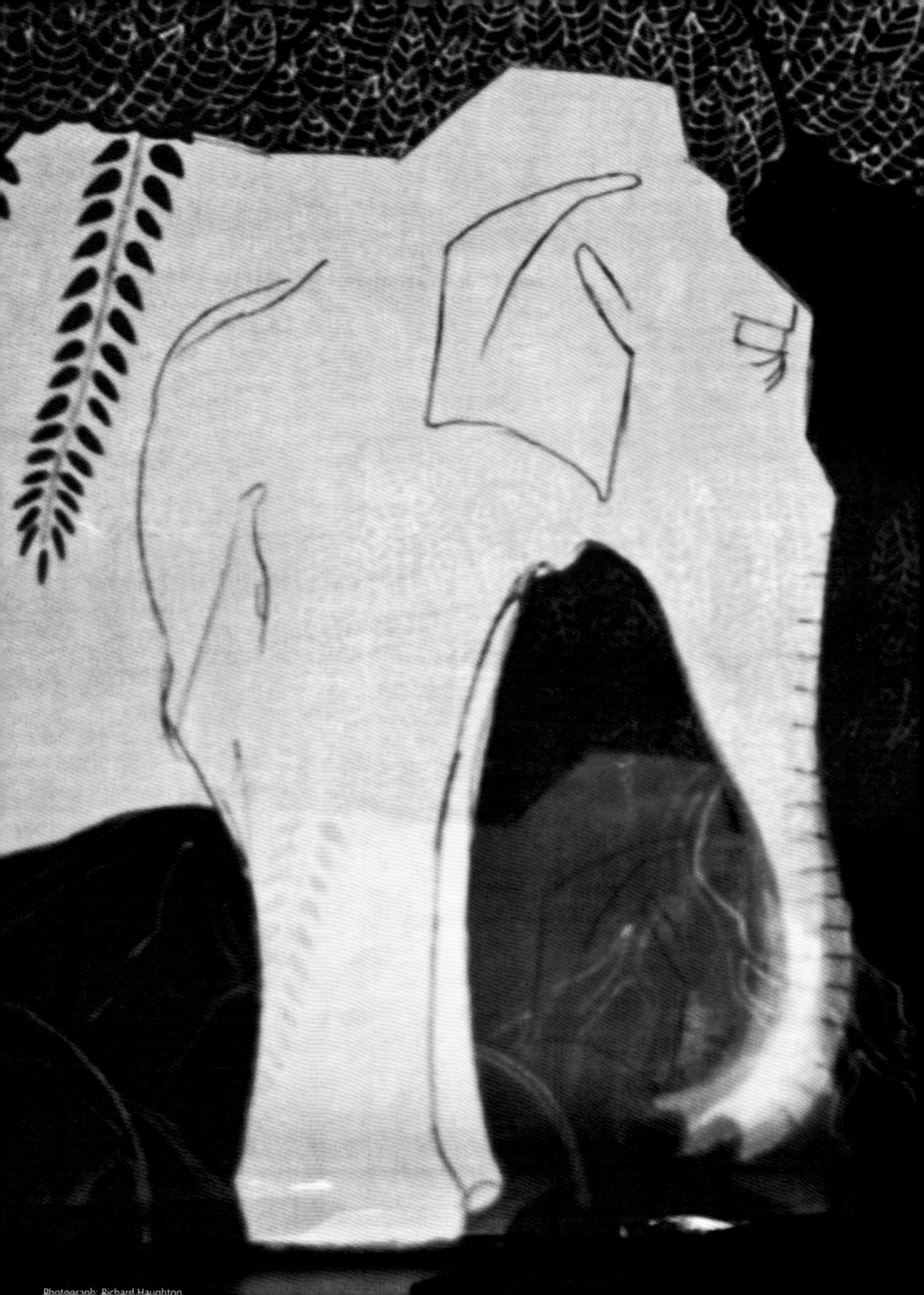

DESH
STAGING THE NATION

DESH
THE AESTHETICS OF STAGING THE NATION

Nayanika Mookherjee

Nayanika Mookherjee is a reader of sociocultural anthropology in Durham University, UK. She has published extensively on her research interests: the anthropology of violence, gendered violence during wars, ethics, and aesthetics. Recent publications include *The Spectral Wound: Sexual Violence, Public Memories and the Bangladesh War of 1971* (Duke University Press, 2015); guest editing the special issue of the *Journal of Material Culture* on "Aesthetics, Politics, Conflict" (2015) and the *Journal of Historical Sociology* on "The Self in South Asia" (2013); and co-editing (with Christopher Pinney) the *Journal of the Royal Anthropological Institute* on "The Aesthetics of Nation" (2011).

Photos provided by Akram Khan Dance Company and Richard Haughton.

On 15 September 2011, celebrated British Bangladeshi choreographer and performer Akram Khan premiered his full-length contemporary solo dance performance *Desh*—translated as the "homeland," or literally "of the land, nation"—in the UK. Billed as his most personal work, the piece draws on "multiple tales of land, nation, resistance and convergence into the body and voice of one man trying to find his balance in an unstable world."[1] In homage to his parent's birth country, Bangladesh, Khan wanted to map the tragedies and comedies that epitomize the motherland. While being a personal and multiple narrative of Khan's discomforting relationship with Bangladesh, *Desh* is also a fictionalized conversation of contestations with his deceased father (as depicted in the performance; Khan's father is alive today). Drawn from Sanskrit, the word *Desh* stands for land, nation, region, essence, and home, while at the same time distinguishing *deshis* (those of the land) from *bideshis* or *bhindeshi* (those not of the land, the foreigner).[2]

The word *desh* is linked to connotations of those who are of the land (Mookherjee 2008)—a connotation that has ironically been the preserve of various British press reviews of Khan's earlier performances. British reviewers of his work have focused predominantly on his being a British Bangladeshi Muslim (Norridge 2010, 30, 31) rather than on his choreography. Contrarily, as Farooq Chaudhry, the producer of the Akram Khan Company points out in a DVD on *Desh* (Khan 2012), the whole point of doing *Desh* was to reestablish Khan's connections to Bangladesh as he was struggling with his identity; he felt he had none. When he was growing up in Wimbledon, London, as Khan notes in the DVD (Khan 2012), his parents' histories did not interest him, and his parents despaired that because their son was not sharing in their experiences, these would be lost. It is telling that when Tim Yip, the visual designer of *Desh* (and of *Crouching Tiger, Hidden Dragon*), asked Khan to do a production based on his "roots," the choreographer responded by saying that he had done enough productions on London and India. Yip asked him to go "deeper" and to create a production on Bangladesh, even as Khan remained uncomfortable with the idea, which was much more of a personal battle.

It is ironic to note that the very reviews by the British press that had conferred an ethnic identity on Khan were done at a time when he was not interested in his deeper—beyond-the-India framework—Bangladeshi history. It is through *Desh* that Khan has explicitly produced a personal account of his own and, above all, his parents' Bangladeshi history. He himself is part of the paraphernalia of British cultural production that has so often collapsed all of South Asia to India without trying to figure out the distinctiveness of other South Asian countries and regions. Khan's mother reminded him that he had been part of various India-related productions but had never done a production for "us Bangladeshi people" distinct from any India-related performance. Farooq Chaudhry's comment that "Akram just needs to go home" sums up the foundational basis for conceptualizing *Desh* (Khan 2012).

Akram goes home: Staging the nation

The performance of Desh is a conversation with the dead father and starts with the funeral rituals. Mapping the weather-marked landscape of Bangladesh, with a haunting music composition by Jocelyn Pook, the performance maps various tropes of land, cloth, memory, democratic resistance, and the war of liberation of 1971. Against the backdrop of audio recordings of boats, traffic, and steamers, shipbreaking and shipyards, the performers overlay the sounds of hammering

Photo: Richard Haughton

on the ground. Viscerally replaying a traffic-crossing scene in a Bangladesh city, the performance also depicts Khan's father's account of the torture of his friend, whose soles of the feet were sliced during the 1971 war by the Pakistani army. The resistance against the Bangladeshi military government through the 1980s and 1990s is seen in the words "Gonotontro mukti pak" (Let democracy be free) graffitied on the back of Noor Hossain, a young political activist shot by the police during protests against the regime of General Ershad in 1987. One of the most magical and surreal aspects of the performance is the interactive animation narrating his parents' story of the boy who likes honey, runs through the fields with grass as high as the sky, and meets crocodiles and elephants. Finally, Khan is confronted with the little boy, who stands in for the future and is poised for great things—a constant potential of endurance and resilience.

Zoe Norridge (Norridge 2010, 20) has pointed out how other intercultural performances similar to *Desh* have been accused of being appropriative, essentializing, reductive, and driven by economic and political rather than aesthetic concerns. But the performance in *Desh* is primarily an aesthetic one and very consciously so. By spatializing speech and movement, Khan embodies a personal and biographical narrative, a poetic and metaphorical language to communicate particularly (according to Khan) to Bangladeshi people. As Norridge notes (Norridge 2010, 31), "Khan's brilliance lies in his use of language with movement—in dancing the conversation." In his journey of a man trying to find himself, Khan suggests that this performance is a journey into his memories; it uncovers what lies hidden and "cuts out the block" that had disallowed him to engage with Bangladesh (Khan 2012). In response to earlier criticism focusing on his identity, Khan attempts a deeper engagement with the specific history and story of Bangladesh rather than a generic performance referencing South Asia or India.

The aesthetics of *Desh*
The history and experiences of Bangladesh are vividly presented in *Desh*, which brings Bangladeshi poetics and sensibilities to a British cultural forum, in which representations of India predominantly stand in for all of South Asia. However, if nations, their conflicts and contested pasts, are to be represented through various aesthetic artifacts (Mookherjee 2011), what multiple senses and feelings does *Desh* evoke and regulate? Kalpana Ram (2011), in exploring the relationship between dance and nationalism in India in the context of the development of Bharatanatyam, has shown how affective engagement of a performance is based on the phenomenology of performance, dance, and spectatorship. She examines how nationalist as well as class forms of identification actually work and in the process focuses on forms of agency, temporality, and affective involvement. The role of spectatorship and the aesthetic sensibilities of *Desh* become even more important to address, given that very little is known about Bangladesh in the UK. In short, what are the allowable affects and emotions in the interstices of performance and spectatorship? Two aspects of *Desh* deserve further critical mention in exploring this relationship.

Leesa Gazi's haunting narration of Shamsur Rahman's poem "Shadhinota" (Independence) in the performance brings to the fore the sacrifices that Bangladesh has gone through to acquire independence. This hard-earned independence had remained an illusive issue to many left-liberal individuals during the military rule from 1975 to the 1990s. Independence is in fact

interrogated darkly by various poets through their examination of the history of rape during 1971. In the following poem, "The Smell of Corpses in the Air," by Shahidullah (1992), the purest form of independence is resurrected from the wreckage of dreams through embodying the horrors of rape:

> Even today I get the smell of corpses in the air,
> Even today I see death's naked dance,
> Even in my drowsiness I hear the desperate scream of the raped woman,
> Has this country forgotten those nightmares, those bloody times? ...
> Independence—that is my family, found by losing all my other dearest ones,
> Independence—that is the priceless harvest bought with the blood of my dearest people,
> The bloody national flag is nothing but my raped sister's saree.

The focus on pro-democracy movements without any reference to the 1980s and 1990s seems to suggest that Bangladesh is currently under an authoritarian rule. Much as one might differ from the various activities of the two major political leaders and the processes of democracy in place in Bangladesh, these leaders were appointed as a result of democratic elections. Hence a suggestion that Bangladesh is currently under authoritarian rule does not reflect the various processes through which the dynamic political processes operate in contemporary Bangladesh. As a result, the beautiful production of *Desh* and its simplistic evocation of the trope of resistance has a tinge of romanticism, since it seems to suggest that Bangladesh as a nation is still caught up in the struggles against authoritarian rule. What is conspicuously absent in the staging of *Desh* is how this political framework also contains an authoritarian presence and the surveillance of indigenous communities by the contemporary Bangladeshi state in the Chittagong Hill Tracts.

More significantly, the absence of the exploration of the Bengali Muslim identity that is intrinsic to being Bangladeshi is a missed opportunity in *Desh*. The only mark of Islam in the staging of the performance is contained in the first funeral scene. This absence leads one to ask questions about the relationship between aesthetics and the politics of spectatorship. Would a deeper portrayal of the Bengali Muslim identity in *Desh* jar a British audience, who already have a limited idea about the "Muslim" country of Bangladesh? Are the participatory pleasures of spectatorship of performances of music and dance reducible to the politics of nationalism, class, and modernity? What are the implications of aesthetics in this? Could we, as in Mahmood Mamdani's argument, locate ourselves as "good" Muslims or "bad" Muslims? And does that require us to chisel out all the markers of Islam? This point might be relevant in a paradox of Khan's identity that emerged in the Olympic ceremony.

While organizing the opening ceremony of the Olympics in 2012, Danny Boyle asked Akram Khan to be the lead dancer-choreographer for a tribute to lives lost, including those during the 7 July 2005 London bombings, as part of that ceremony.[3] Performed poignantly with fifity dancers to Emeli Sandé's "Abide with Me," the segment felt like a fitting tribute to multicultural London's loss on 7 July, with Khan as a most appropriate multicultural icon. The segment, along with showing images of loved ones lost by those in the stadium,

Photo: Richard Haughton

was widely interpreted as a tribute to the fifty-two victims of the bombings in 2005. However, NBC, which was airing the Olympic ceremony in the United States, cut out Khan's segment, which, obviously, made him feel "disheartened and disappointed." NBC explained that it had no indication the segment was a reference to the attacks and felt that the performance was dramatizing "the struggle between life and death using such powerful images of mortality as dust and the setting sun." Khan in turn responded, "It brings to mind the question—but maybe I'm wrong because I don't really know the reason—but it brings to mind a question that maybe it's too truthful, and I think that says it all really." More powerfully he asked, "Is it not accessible enough? Is it not commercial enough?"

The staging of the nation, of one's location, and of one's originary "roots" in Akram Khan's *Desh* brings up various questions of identity in which one's origin may be read differently in different instances. In earlier productions, even while Khan had never portrayed an account of his own Bangladeshi narrative, British reviews primarily focused on his British Bangladeshi Muslim ethnic heritage. In *Desh*, going "deeper" into his roots beyond the India-UK paradigm, Khan chooses to map the history of his parents and of their country of Bangladesh. In doing so, however, he chiseled out any emblem of Islam from the powerful, poignant, and mesmerising performance. Could this choice of the "good Muslim" also be based on what one imagines would be an acceptable affective idiom and aesthetic among the British multicultural audience? Chosen as a multicultural icon to memorialize at the Olympics the London bombings of 7 July 2005, Khan embodied the allowable affects and emotions in the interstices of performance, spectatorship, nationalism, and internationalism linked to 7/7. Yet, ironically, NBC decided to cut away from airing this poignant performance in spite of its international accessibility and commerciality. In the staging of *Desh*, it seems, one can be understood and judged only paradoxically on the basis of one's location, one's *desh*, the land one is from which is always over "there."

Notes

[1] As noted on the website http://www.akramkhancompany.net/html/akram_production.php?productionid=37.
[2] Based on an invited panel discussion with the author of the Olivier Award–winning stage show *Desh*, Karthika Naïr, poet, writer, and dance producer and author of *Desh Diaries: Memories Inherited, Borrowed, Imagined.* Centre for South Asian Studies, Cambridge University, October 2012.
[3] See http://www.bbc.co.uk/news/entertainment-arts-19037588.

References

Khan, Akram. *Homeland: The Making of Desh* (DVD, Drakes Avenue Pictures, 2012).
Mamdani, Mahmood. *Good Muslim, Bad Muslim: America, the Cold War and the Roots of Terror* (Pantheon Books, 2004).
Mookherjee, Nayanika. "Gendered Embodiments: Mapping the Body-Politic of the Raped Woman and the Nation in Bangladesh." In *Feminist Review*, special issue on war, 88: 1 (April 2008): 36–53.
Mookherjee, Nayanika. Introduction to "Aesthetics of Nations: Anthropological and Historical Perspectives." *Journal of the Royal Anthropological Institute* special issue: S1–S20 (2011). Edited by N. Mookherjee and C. Pinney. http://onlinelibrary.wiley.com/doi/10.1111/jrai.2011.17.issue-s1/issuetoc.
Norridge, Z. "Dancing the Multicultural Conversation? Critical Responses to Akram Khan's Work in the Context of Pluralistic Poetics." *Forum for Modern Language Studies* 46, no. 4 (2010): 18–39.
Ram, Kalpana. "Being 'Rasikas': The Affective Pleasures of Music and Dance Spectatorship and Nationhood in Indian Middle Class Modernity." In "Aesthetics of Nations: Anthropological and Historical Perspectives." *Journal of Royal Anthropological Institute* special issue: S159–S175 (2011). Edited by N. Mookherjee and C. Pinney.
Shahidullah, R. Md. *"Batashe Lasher Gondho/Upodruto Upokul" (The Smell of Corpses in the Air). In Rochona Shomogro (Compilation of Essays)* 1, Edited by A. Saha (Dhaka: Bidya Prokash, 1992).

TO KNOW IS NOTHING AT ALL... TO IMAGINE IS EVERYTHING.

Leesa Gazi

Leesa Gazi is an actor, a writer, a TEDx speaker, and the cofounder of Komola Collective. She has developed, written scripts, and performed for a number of productions, including *Birangona: Women of War, Six Seasons,* and *A Golden Age* at the Southbank Centre, and been a script interpreter for *The Tempest* at the 2012 Globe Festival. She has worked as the cultural coordinator and a voice artist for Akram Khan's *Desh*. Gazi is currently directing *Rising Silence*, a feature documentary on the lives of Birangona women, the mass-rape survivors of the Liberation War of Bangladesh.

While working on the production of *Desh*, I came to know Akram Khan closely beyond his artistic persona and discovered him as someone caught in the middle of two cultures. Both are equally precious to him and have defined and made him who he is. I never saw him value or cherish one identity over another. Both flow gently within him, and yet there are subtle ripples here and there that make him create these wonderfully emotive pieces of self-discovery like *Zero Degrees*, *Bahok*, and *Desh*.

People from all walks of life, community, caste, race, and religion have been moved by the themes of distance and dislocation in *Desh*. They have been moved at the most personal level. You don't have to come from Bangladesh or South Asia to realize the pain, joy, struggle, and beauty embodied in *Desh*. The constant displacement of the human condition makes us reach out for *Desh*.

Desh is a search, a journey through which you dare to find yourself. You come to terms with listening to the rhythm of your pulse, in which your past whispers nonstop. That is the reason the performance has touched so many people. People paused for a while to listen to their own inner beings and to its stories. Khan once told me, "My parents' history is in my body." Through *Desh*, he wanted to explore that idea with all of us.

I first started in *Desh* as a voice artist and then found myself translating the script—the Bengali dialogue used in the performance. Gradually I got more involved. I was asked to give my opinion on aspects of the set—things like supervising the Bengali writing on the set, providing historical context at every step of the production, sourcing slogans and poems, sourcing artists for certain roles, prepping my daughter, who played Eshita, the character of Khan's niece, and finally becoming the cultural coordinator. The whole process was quite organic and one of my most precious professional experiences. To be able to work with Akram Khan was an eye-opener for me, both as an artist and as a human being.

I believe Khan confronted himself the most in *Desh*, first, because it is his only solo performance, and second, because it is his most soul-searching production to date. In *Desh*, Khan looked at the young and resilient Bangladesh universally but also microscopically. It was a joy to see the issues that are close to the hearts of Bangladeshis brought into stark relief: topics that excite us, touch us deeply, make us proud, give us a voice, inspire us. He sensed those issues and translated them into his own personal journey of being immersed in and pulled by two different cultures through Bangladesh's national struggles, and also through movements and joy that make them effortlessly relevant to the world.

A touch of humanity and tenderness shines through *Desh*. Khan has a deep sense of connection to humanity and also to nature, which you can experience both as a collaborator working with him and as an audience member watching him perform. For example, Khan finds water fascinating—he connects with it like fish, which is reflected in the fluidity of his movement. Again, he finds people's struggle intensely inspiring; he connects with it like time, and the force of his movement defines that.

This is possible only because Khan truly feels and believes that on one level we are all connected. He does not care much about chance. Everything happens for a reason, and everything has its purpose. He does not cling to one idea. He allows his gut and passion to be the lighthouse for his creative process. When we initially started working on *Desh*, it was about his mother, but during rehearsals he felt it should be about his father, and then later on he found himself deeply bonded with that little boy "who led a street procession during a mass revolt in 1969 in Dhaka, Bangladesh, then East Pakistan."

Because Khan felt the strong connection with the boy protester as a performer, the audience is compelled to feel the same sense of bonding with the boy without even knowing him. When the animated version of that little boy comes on stage and raises his tiny hand and screams with all his might for equality and justice, then a huge part of you wants to chant those slogans with him: "Amader dabi maante hobe, maante hobe" (Our demands must be met). And that is the magic of Akram Khan.

In *Zero Degrees*, when we see the polystyrene "dead man," designed by Antony Gormley, as Akram's co-traveler with Sidi Larbi Cherkaoui, we feel a profound connection between life and death. The model suddenly becomes real to us, and the absurdity of the situation makes us sensitive to the fragility and vulnerability of life. We realize we are all hanging precariously between life, love, and truth.

Akram Khan is a great believer of the beauty and power of the imagination. He would rather imagine than think. He will take a simple everyday story that others might have passed by and his imagination will explore, develop, and see it in a different light and connect it to endless possibilities. Akram Khan believes that "to know is nothing at all … to imagine is everything."

Photo: Richard Haughton

'The Little House' in the morning.

MY FATHER'S HOUSE

Beili Liu

Beili Liu is a multidisciplinary artist. She was born in Jilin, China, moved to the United States in 1995, and now works and lives in Austin, Texas.

Two days before I left Art Farm in Nebraska, in the summer of 2004, I sat in the moonlight—behind me was *The Little House*, near completion, created using handmade adobe bricks. Scaffolding, a tractor, hammers, drills, and empty pallets that once held the bricks surrounded it. In the silence of the night, my memory took me back to years ago, to a small village in the northern province of Jilin in China. Houses there were made of clay and straw; the side of the house looked like the shape of a mountain. We called it the "mountain wall." In one of these houses, I was born to my young parents, who were among the youths sent to rural villages during China's Cultural Revolution. *The Little House* standing on the prairie at the Art Farm is a replica of my parents' hand-built home.

When I received the artist residency brochure from Art Farm in Marquette, Nebraska, one image stood out: a clay mountain more than twenty feet tall. Its caption said, "370 tons of free clay for artists to use." A clay and straw house, like the one I was born in, came to my mind right there and then, after years of carrying its iconic image in my mind subconsciously while I traveled across the globe. I immediately started conversations with my father about building a clay and straw house on the prairie of Art Farm. As an engineer, and having built many houses of this kind in the village, including our own, my father had the knowledge and the experience that were my most valuable resource for *The Little House* project. He taught me the correct ratio in which to mix clay, sand, and straw; drew sketches of traditional wood framework; and instructed me on how to construct a roofing structure and lay thatching on top.

A humble, basic little rectangular house with overhanging eaves traces back to the Neolithic site of Banpo, a Yangshao culture site from approximately 6000 B.C. in northern China. The structures found there already show evidence of the use of mortise and tendon and the use of mud and clay to surround a wooden structure.

Because of the scarcity of materials during dramatic political shifts in China, people in villages depended on whatever humble materials were locally available and easily accessible to build their homes. It is very similar to the pioneers' experience when they first ventured into the Great Plains of America. With no trees to harvest for lumber or stones to collect as building materials, those settlers—in their need for shelter and home—discovered the use of sod. Known as "Nebraska bricks," slabs of soil that were held together by the dense roots of prairie grasses were plowed from the ground in long strips, cut into three-foot-long sections, and then used as bricks for building the sod houses. An early sod house was no bigger than seven by fourteen feet—very close in size to *The Little House* at Art Farm, which is fourteen feet wide, seven feet deep, and ten feet tall. These similarities brought *The Little House* closer to the foreign land it is standing on.

The first six weeks of my two-month artist residency at Art Farm were dedicated to making adobe bricks. Straw was harvested from the neighbor's wheat field, twelve yards of sand were delivered from the Platte River, three miles away, and the brick-making session began—clay, sand, and chopped straw were mixed in a mortar, and then scooped into the brick molds, packed by hand, and released onto the stacked pallets to dry. I soon learned that in their first few days, newly made bricks needed intensive care—direct exposure to sunlight caused cracking; too much wind dried the bricks too rapidly, which caused cracking; too much moisture trapped under the plastic sheets covering the bricks also caused cracking. This meant that

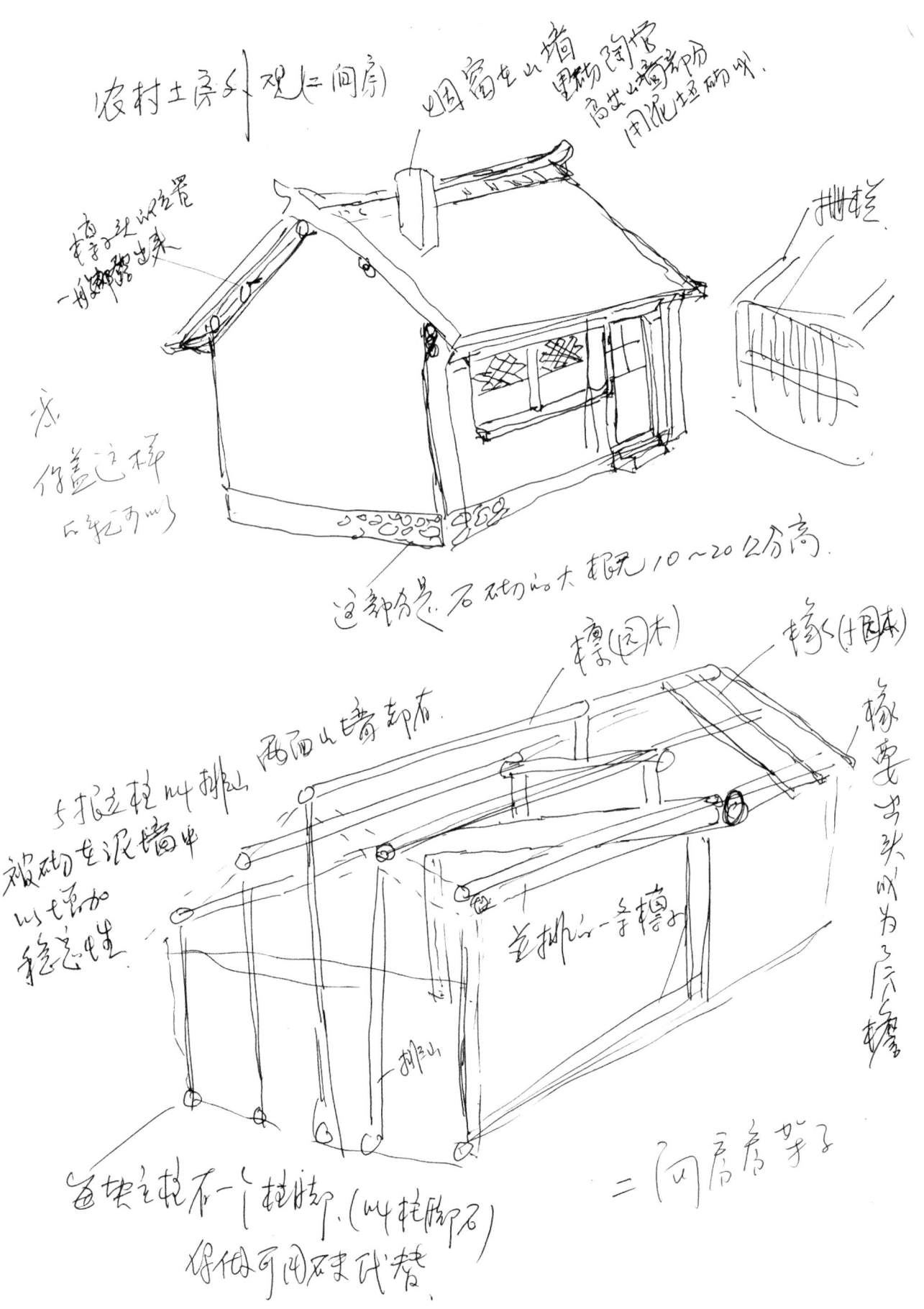

农村土房外观(二间房)

烟窗在山墙

里砌陶管
高出山墙部份
用花土垒砌成.

檩子放在位置
一般都露出来

墙桩

你盖这样
也可以

这部份是石砌的大概10~20公分高.

檩(圆木)   椽(土圆木)

椽要出头以为了疼檐

主挑仓一牵檩

与挑立柱叫排山
被砌在泥墙中
以也加
稳定性

排山

二间房房架子

每架之相不一个柱脚(叫托脚石)
你们可用石矣代替.

all the bricks had to be carefully turned several times during the drying process. I ended each evening with a couple of hours of covering and adjusting the sun shades and the plastic sheets over the newly made bricks as well as the drier bricks, and I started each morning uncovering them and checking to see whether the frequent night rains caused any stress to those precious bricks.

In China's rural villages, the building of a new house is the most celebrated event, a proud result of a family's years of hard work and savings. A new house is usually built for a son of the household, in preparation for his wedding. Young men all around the village are invited to work on building a new house. In a distant land across the ocean, I, a woman and a daughter, was about to build a house of my own.

The building of the house at Art Farm took about two weeks. I learned how to make simple mortise-and-tenon joints using reclaimed lumber and fallen trees at the Art Farm. We laid the foundation using stone from fallen barns and covered the roof with salvaged lath from old houses. Like my parents and ancestors in northern China, I was fortunate to have the help of many—from fellow artists in residence and Art Farm staff to local families and teachers, many whom brought their students.

In rural northern Chinese homes, people paste newspaper as wallpaper to brighten the interior and to prevent dust from falling from the wall surface. Following this tradition, I collected American newspaper articles on China from papers like *the New York Times*, *USA Today*, *the Wall Street Journal*, and local news-papers. The articles give glimpses of how China was viewed by the United States; these will be preserved in the house for as long as it stands on the Nebraska prairie. After pasting these American newspaper articles, I spent my last night at Art Farm in *The Little House*. Moonlight came through the single window and caseted a silver-blue sheet on the platform bed (*kang*), and I was home.

The Little House at Art Farm is the first project of my House Phase Installation Series. In 2006, I had the opportunity work at Djerassi Foundation in Woodside, California, and create *Recall*, a subsequent site-specific installation for the series. *Recall* was made from approximately six hundred hand-stretched wax drips that would shatter upon a light touch. I developed a unique process in the studio that enables me to hand stretch molten paraffin wax in water, into eight- to nine-feet-long strips. These strips are then carefully suspended in the center of a vacant 1900s cattle barn to form a rectangular house structure. *Recall* holds the same dimensions of *The Little House* at Art Farm, and it echoes the angles of the rafters and the roof of the barn. Sunlight falls through the gaps in the decaying roof and projects hundreds of light circles, which glide across the space throughout the day. Seemingly levitating in the center of the space, *Recall* is illuminated and animated by the subtle light shifts and air currents. The simple house form reminds viewers of a familiar domestic space and the comfort it holds. However, the fragility of the material calls for the meditation on trust, shelter, protection, and the permanence of a home.

Simple, double-sloped rectangular houses are found all over the world, from ancient to modern, from east to west. Despite the difference of time, geography, and culture, this basic structure stands as a shelter for people, an archetypal symbol of place—a home. *The Little House* is my home that I created and then left behind, yet it completed my journey from China to America. *The Little House* stands on the prairie at Art Farm as I travel on,

Clay mountain during construction.

Making bricks.

Structure in progress.

Work in progress.

Thatching the roof.

Newspapered wall in the interior.

beginning its approximately thirty-year life span in the weather of the Great Plains as it slowly returns to the earth that it came from.

References

Dick, Everett Newfon. *The Sod-House Frontier* (University of Nebraska Press, 1979).
Knapp, Ronald G. *China's Traditional Rural Architecture* (University of Hawaii Press, Honolulu, 1986).
Knapp, Ronald G. *China's Old Dwellings* (University of Hawaii Press, Honolulu, 2000).
Luebke, Frederick C. *Nebraska: An Illustrated History* (University of Nebraska Press, 1995).

"The Little House" in the winter field.

"The Little House" installed as *Recall*, at the Djerassi Foundation,
Woodside, California (2006).

Patkau Architects, Seabird Island School, Agassiz, Canada (Photo: Patkau Architects).

UNDER THE RADAR

GLOBALIZATION AND THE INCIDENCE OF THE OTHER

Kenneth Frampton

Kenneth Frampton is the Ware Professor of Architecture at the Graduate School of Architecture, Planning and Preservation at Columbia University in New York, and an architect and architectural historian and critic. As author of a number of critical articles, essays and books, Frampton is one of the most influential thinkers in contemporary architectural culture.

Photographs provided by author unless noted otherwise.

"Today, the context is totally different. Today the small can be influential at the large scale as a node in a global network. And the local can break its isolation by being open to the global flow of people, ideas and information. In other words, today we can say that the small is no longer small and a local is no longer local, at least in traditional terms."
- Ezio Manzini (2011)

In a world in which the built environment becomes increasingly barbaric, there also arises, here and there, works of a surprisingly sensitive character. These achievements always seem to entail a certain ambiguous element of "otherness," whether this manifests itself in the form of an unlikely client in terms of normative practice, or the presence of the architect as an "other" in that he, she, or they are working in a context that is totally removed from their everyday lives, or that the whole situation is "other" in that the longstanding division of labour between design and fabrication no longer obtains. Equally "other" is the situation in which the drives of tourism and conspicuous consumption intersect with the basic needs of the subaltern. Again, the "other" is subtly present in the fact that in this digital century a building in the center of London could come to be clad in hand-made bricks from the Forests of Dean. In this way, as Adolf Loos implied in his disconcerting essay, "Ornament and Crime" (1908), men live at the same time in different periods of history. This is condition which yields, on occasion, a fragile beauty wherein both aesthetic form and social function are mutually transcended.

Irrespective of the dubious claims of critical regionalism in recent years, there is a way in which a reciprocal version of this sensibility has come increasingly to the fore, wherein the site and the local material become the primary determinants of the overall form. Although we may contend that this is hardly new, it has become increasingly rare in our spectacular age, particularly if by a site one has in mind not only the topography, but also the availability of local material and the capacity of native labour, along with the exigencies of the climate and the idiosyncratic mores of the vernacular culture.

One of the most surprising and gratifying aspects of contemporary practice over the past two decades has been the way in which accomplished architects from the so-called first world have found themselves building from time to time in the equally eponymous third world. This, in itself, may not be that unusual, but what has been unique of recent times has been the exceptionally refined sensibility and rigor that they have been able to achieve in the indigenous situation, so that one has the uncanny sense that the outcome could not have been more appropriately and poetically achieved if it had been handled by local architects rather than by outsiders.

Perhaps an early instance of a work of this order was the Norwegian architect Jan Olav Jensen's design for a leper colony in India, realized in 1975 in a quasi-Brutalist manner, when the architect was barely eighteen years of age. This isolated project, built in the desert landscape of Lasur in Maharashtra State, was sponsored by the Norwegian Free Evangelical Mission, which no doubt partially accounts for the commission of this young, foreign architect. The building comprises an elongated, single-story compound enclosing an exotic garden and a pool. Access to this green oasis was available to doctors and patients alike, in contradistinction to class and caste systems which still prevail in Indian society. Built of random, rubble stone construction mixed with segments of bonded brickwork, the hospital has a relatively hermetic exterior, the tactile character of which is

Jan Olab Jensen, Leepers Hospital, Kasur, India (Photo: Ram Rahman).

Jan Olab Jensen, Leepers Hospital, Kasur, India (Photo: Ram Rahman).

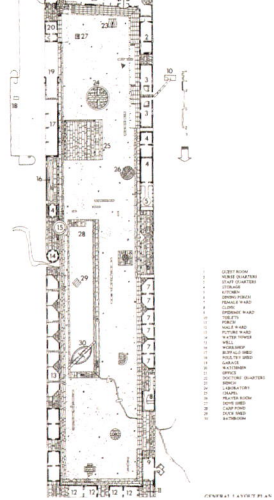

Jan Olab Jensen, Leepers Hospital, Kasur, India (Photo: Ram Rahman).

reinforced by concrete barrel vaulted roofs covered with broken fragments of blue and white tile, in effect, waste ceramic material purchased from a nearby factory. This one-room deep orthogonal compound is subdivided into accommodations for forty patients, staff housing, treatment spaces, a workshop, and a small farm.

Surely one of the most well-known instances of an "other" first world architect intervening in the third world came with the equally young, twenty year old Austrian architect Ann Heringer, who with Eike Roswag collaborated on the design of a school in Rudrapur, Bangladesh (2003), built exclusively out of local materials. This school featured a dramatically cantilevered roof built entirely of rope-bound, bamboo beams and brackets.

An equally remote essay in the Pacific Northwest of the American continent was John and Patricia Patkau's Seabird Island School, built for an Indian band in Agassiz, British Columbia over the years 1988-91. A number of things are notable about this work; in the first instance, it was commissioned by an exceptionally enlightened civil servant from the Canadian ministry of education; in the second, the architects realized that since the band wanted to construct this school themselves, a model would have to be prepared as it was evident that they were unable read architectural drawings, particularly for a work of such geometrical complexity. Apart from the fact that the school is built entirely out of local timber, there are other striking topographic-cum-cultural features present, above all, the fact that the humped- back form of its shingled roof seemed to echo consciously the profile of a nearby mountain. An equally identifying cultural trope is the outriding timber pergola cantilevering over the veranda that extends along the southern elevation of the school. This last alludes to the fish-drying racks that used to be a prominent feature in the front of the native wooden block houses lining the coastline.

A comparably grounded work was built in 1994 for a prominent member of an Australian tribe occupying the Yirrkala area in the Northern Territory of Australia. Designed by Glen Murcutt, the Marika-Alderton House was built for Banduk Marika, who was then a tribal representative in the Australian parliament in Canberra. This two-storey, virtually all timber construction was elevated one metre off the ground in order to avoid flooding and to provide a clear view of the horizon— a traditional defensive feature of import in aboriginal society. Situated 12 ½ degrees south of the equator, where humidity reaches eighty percent, the house had to be capable of being completely opened up so as to maximize cross ventilation. This is the primary reason behind the storey-height, hinged timber shutters which, when raised, also serve as sun shields for the verandah of the house. Since the house is located on sand dunes close to the ocean, it is provided with a slatted timber floor to allow sand to fall through. The main volume of the house was made equally permeable by virtue of pivoting metal roof vents, oriented by weather vanes, so as to align their vents with the prevailing air flow. These devices were installed so as to equalize the pressure within and without when the house is subject to winds of cyclone force, since there is a serious risk under these conditions that internal pressure will blow the house apart. Finally, one should note that the vertical timber "brise soleil" at every structural bay are not only provided for the purposes of sun control, but also to ensure lateral privacy to the various rooms within in accordance with native custom.

As in the case of Seabird Island School, this house makes an

Anna Heringer & Eike Roswag, School in Rudrapur, Bangladesh (Photo: Saif Ul Haque).

Anna Heringer & Eike Roswag, School in Rudrapur, Bangladesh (Photo: Saif Ul Haque).

Markku Komonen, Vila Eilla, Mali (Aga Khan Award).

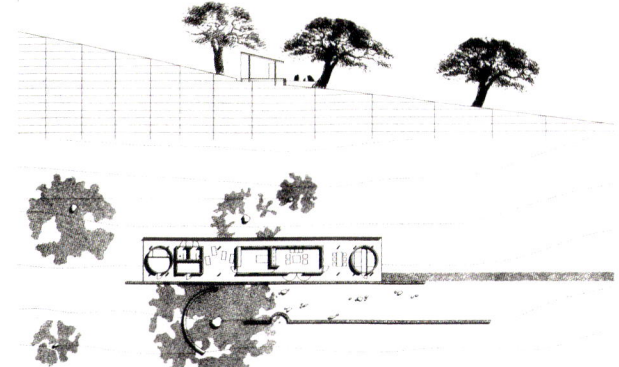

Markku Komonen, Vila Eilla, Mali.

allusion to the native domestic tradition without the slightest attempt to replicate it. With its metal standing seam roof, metal roof vents and tubular metal uprights stiffening its overall timber frame and cladding, it is a virtual translation of a woven native hut into an orthogonal modular form. In this regard, it is important to note that the building was prefabricated in Sydney, trucked overland to Yirrkala in the north, and then reassembled on site. Once realized, this rather unique work has had the effect of establishing a new standard for Australian aboriginal housing in the region. Prior to this, the native populations of the area had been punitively accommodated by the state bureaucracy in inadequately ventilated concrete block houses.

Even more removed from the regularly travelled routes of our globalized world is the Jean-Marie Tjibaou Culture Center built in Noumea, New Caledonia in 1998 to the designs of the Italian architect Renzo Piano. In this case, the most unique feature makes direct reference to the woven fabric of the traditional Kanak hut. This is achieved through the reiteration of monumental louvered timber structures known as "cases", which, circular in plan, range from 20 to 30 meters in height, with their diameter increasing proportionally with respect to their height. These "cases" comprise double-layered shells built out as two concentric rings of horizontal, adjustable timber louvers held in position by curved laminated timber ribs. Entirely made out of exceptionally durable Iroko wood, the resulting conical structures are capped about half-way up by sloping roofs that are either solid or glazed depending upon the program within. The function of the so-called cases varies from dance studios to exhibition spaces and seminar rooms. The aforementioned double-layered louvres are, in effect, adjustable timber membranes that function jointly as wind filters, the angle of the louvers being modifiable according to changing wind conditions. Thus the cases may be totally sealed in storm conditions or left open in fine weather. The remainder of the complex consists of a large flat-roofed, single-storey orthogonal steel structure having the character of a hi-tech "mat-building" which accommodates a large lecture hall and administrative offices. The "cases" are attached like limpets to one side of this structure, thereby serving to symbolize Kanak identity. In so doing they make an allusion to the freedom fighter after which the institution is named.

Another remarkable contribution to aboriginal culture in the post-colonial era was made in the mid '80s under the patronage of a remarkable Finnish woman, Eila Kivekäs, who became involved with a visiting African scholar, the Guinea intellectual Alpha Diallo, who rather inexplicably elected to translate the Finnish national folk epic, The Kalevala, into Fula, the native language of his country. After Diallo's illness and his unexpected death in Finland, Kivekäs arranged for his remains to be returned to Guinea, and soon thereafter came to Guinea herself in order to establish a local craft center, with the additional aim of improving both the status of women in the country and the overall health of the society. To this end, Kivekäs founded the Development Association Indigo in Mali, a small town in Guinea of about 1,000 people. The name of this institution was derived from the traditional indigo blue cloth produced by the women of the region.

Eventually Kivekäs would commission the Finnish architect Markku Komonen to build three works for her in Guinea; her own house in Mali (1989), a Poultry Farming School in Kindia (1990) and a local Health Center. One should note that the

Markku Komonen, Poultry Farming School, Kindia, Mali.

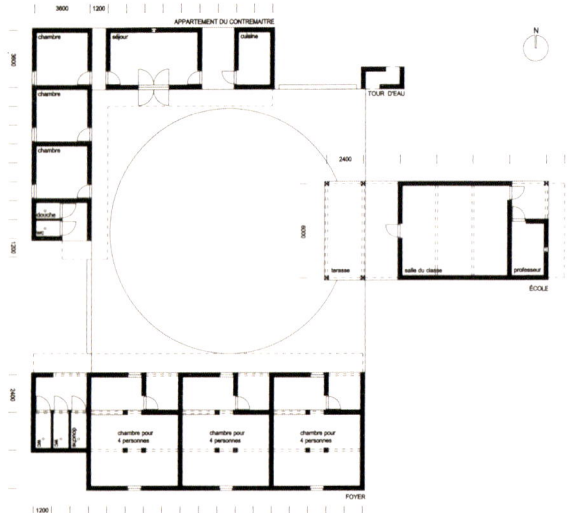

Markku Komonen, Poultry Farming School, Kindia, Mali.

Hollmen, Reuter & Sandman, Womens' Centre, Rufisque, Senegal.

Hollmen, Reuter & Sandman, Womens' Centre, Rufisque, Senegal.

school came into being largely because of Diallo's conviction that for the future well-being of Guinea it was crucial to increase the amount of protein in the daily diet. For him, the least expensive way to do this was to cultivate the art of raising chickens as a matter of national policy. In all three buildings Komonen used inexpensive materials which were readily available, such as bamboo screens, concrete blocks, large bricks made of stabilized earth and roof tiles made of cement, reinforced by glass fiber. In terms of combining these materials for their greatest poetic effect, the simple single-storey Villa Eila is perhaps the most aboriginal building of the three. Here a continuous monopitched, tiled roof and a long woven bamboo screen covering the entirety of the southern face jointly serves to contain the four volumes built of blockwork under a single roof, two of which are cylindrical, plus a single cubic volume and a long rectangular living space divided into two.

By contrast, the poultry farming school is almost classical in its minimalist composition, assembled about a square courtyard. This square is enclosed by two single-storey volumes situated to the South and to the North West corner of the court. These buildings are made out of concrete blocks, the first of which is the permanent dwelling for the instructor/caretaker, while the second, consists of three four-person dormitories for the students. The dominant element situated on axis to the east of the square is the double height lecture hall and preceded by a monumental timber portico. This last is a tectonic tour de force in light weight timber construction. It is made up of transverse beams being elegantly and economically stiffened by wire cables.

Finland was also involved in the realization of a Woman's Center in Senegal, located just outside the city of Rufisque in 1995. This single-storey building, made out of concrete blocks painted bright red, comprises of a simple U-shaped enclosure. It is fitting that this Women's Center should have been designed by three young Finnish women, rigorously trained as architects in Helsinki, namely, Saija Hollmén, Jenni Reuter, and Helena Sandman. The powerfully expressive image of this work stems largely from the protective theatrical form of the enclosure; the red color and perforations here and there within the blockwork.

Needless to say, not all the architects who have worked in the name of the "other" in a globalized world are necessarily outsiders. This applies particularly forcibly to Diébédo Francis Kéré, who represents a unique type of insider-outsider in that he builds in his native country of Burkina Faso, but, at the same time, lives and practices in Berlin, where he was first trained as an architect. Kéré came to worldwide attention in 2001 with the completion of a small, 150-pupil school, built in the village of Gando. This three-classroom, single-story structure is sheltered by a single corrugated-zinc roof, carried on lightweight metal trusses which are fabricated out of welded steel reinforcing rods. Built largely by the villagers themselves under Kéré's supervision, the classroom walls are composed of some 30,000 mechanically hand-pressed bricks. Climatic comfort is ensured not only by the thermal mass of the brick enclosure, but also by the pronounced overhang of the roof, which both shades the facades and protects the building from erosion by the sun and rain.

Equally "hands on architects" may be found in South Asia, where four distinguished architects have recently risen to the fore, designing and realizing works which, while not always dedicated to the sustenance and shelter of the underprivileged "other," have nonetheless worked in such a way as to transform and transcend the received Eurocentric paradigm of modern architecture. I have in mind in this regard the Bangladeshi architects Kashef Mahboob Chowdhury and Marina Tabassum, and the Indian architects Bijoy Jain and Rahul Mehrotra.

Among these, as Kazi Ashraf has remarked, Chowdhury is the quintessential "land architect," so called after Louis Kahn's little known coinage of this term, meaning an architecture whose works have a marked topographic character as is particularly evident in his Friendship Centre, built in 2014 in Gaibandha, some 250 kilometers from Dhaka. With distant typological origins in the Buddhist monasteries of the area, the Friendship Centre is comparable as a heterotopic compound to Jensen's leper hospital in Maharashtra. However, in contrast to the singularity of a hospital, the Friendship Centre is a more programmatically complex institution, housed in a layered matrix in the midst of a floodplain, from which it is protected by a berm on all four sides. While clearly influenced by Kahn as well as by neo-Kahnian Bangladeshi master architect, Muzharul Islam, Chowdhury distances himself from both via his unique feeling for the light and the landscape of the diluvial plains of the Bengal delta.

At once a hostel, a refuge-cum-training facility, and a conference center, the Friendship Centre is run by a non-governmental organization which is particularly active in the remote, economically challenged northern regions of Bangladesh. Its constantly shifting users range from the impoverished, nomadic people of the region, to the presence of foreign consultants and representatives of organizations like the United Nations. Built in a low-lying earthquake zone, it is constructed of brick walls, stabilized here and there by reinforced concrete bracing, and paved throughout in local stone. It is further protected by an earthen embankment, which has proved to be sufficiently stable as to resist the flooding of the surrounding plan. As everywhere in the Bengal delta, water is both a precious resource and a threat. Hence in addition to flood protection, it was necessary both to harvest rainwater in tanks and to implement a complex network of septic tanks and soak wells in order to ensure that sewage cannot mix with floodwater under monsoon conditions.

Equally diluvial is the Panigram Eco-Resort at Jessore, designed by Marina Tabassum. This dispersed clustering of single-storey dwellings, built of mud bricks and thatched roofs, is situated in the very midst of an exceptionally fertile flood plain. A work such as this, despite its "modern" provenance, renders the question of its exact situation within the flow of time nearly impossible to determine. An outsider might well conclude that the project is "other" in a double sense, inasmuch as, while extremely sympathetic to the agrarian way of life to which it is directly related, it also interfaces at every juncture with the "other" of eco-tourism, the clientele that is, who will presumably occupy the residential units which have, in this instance, been elevated on mud brick podia above the flood plain. Both of these architects have recently designed exceptionally sensitive mosques; Chowdhury's Chandgaon Mosque in Chittagong and Tabassum's Bait ur Rauf Mosque in Dhaka. *(see Portfolio:Bangladesh, page - 242)*

Hardly anything could be more "other" than the Hathigaon, built to the designs of Rahul Mehrotra outside of Jaipur in Rajasthan. This totally improbable housing settlement was built to shelter one hundred elephants and their mahouts; that is to say, the beasts themselves, along with their minders and their accompanying families. Built in the foothills of the

Diebedo, Francis Kere, School in Grendo, Burkina Faso.

Rahul Mehrotra Architects, Hathigaon, Amber, India (Photo: RMA).

Rahul Mehrotra Architects, Hathigaon, Amber, India (Photo: RMA).

Kashef Mahbub Chowdhury (Urbana), Friendship Centre, Gaibandha,
Bangladesh (Photo: Wasama Doza).

Marina Tabassum, Panigram Eco Resort, Jessore, Bangladesh.

Amber Palace, the settlement enables the mahouts to live with their charges and their families close to their place of work. Once again, the "other" of tourism is the prime mover lying behind this special economy and unique way of life. The design strategy adopted emphasized from the onset the importance of harvesting rain water, along with the intensive replanting of the devastated, quasi-desert site, the entire enterprise being achieved through local labour and craftsmanship. The built-in bodies of water are absolutely crucial in order to bathe and cool the elephants, not to mention the satiation of their outsized thirsts. The houses, each with an attached stable, are organized in tight communal clusters and built out of locally sourced stone. They are covered by lightweight corrugated metal roofs that double as feed storage for the elephants, which in turn provides additional thermal insulation for the built fabric beneath.

The other Indian architect who has also made a profound contribution to this critical concept of the "other" in a double sense is the Mumbai architect Bijoy Jain. Having been trained in the United States, he has now returned to his native city to create a unique "hands-on" craft-based approach to building culture, as this was once envisaged in the second half of the 19th century by William Morris. Although formally trained as an architect, Jain has become something of a latter-day master builder, having chosen to practice in an exceptionally integrated way both as a designer and as the coordinator of a team of highly versatile Rajasthani carpenters, who have proved just as capable of precise work in steel or ceramics as they are of executing traditional carpentry at the highest possible level. Through this uniquely transgressive approach, Studio Mumbai has demonstrated a mastery not only over the aforementioned crafts, but also of masonry, milled stonework, along with paint and colored plaster. As Peter Wilson has written:

> "Studio Mumbai's locus is in fact not even a building, more a tin-roof held aloft by scaffolding poles—A palm tree nonchalantly grows through the middle. From the roofs hang fans and florescent tubes (working through the night is not unknown, product continues seven days a week). In May the roof gets an extra plastic layer in preparation for the monsoon. Below the canopy is the production stage, open on three sides, with on backdrop wall lined warehouse like with materials—chairs wrapped for shipping, flasks of pigment looking like an arsenal of color awaiting the Indian Holy festival, a tray of hand-made brass switches, logs, slabs of dark uncut wood, ceramic basins, etc. Studio Mumbai is a one-stop shop. They deliver everything, the entire project, worldwide when necessary…Many of the craftsmen are traditional Rajasthanian carpenters, sitting on the pressed-earth floor, holding a piece of wood between their toes, chiseling a precise dovetail joint…Few drawings are produced. Details often evolved on site and in dialogue with the craftsmen entrusted with the realization. Bijoy Jain has issued notebooks bot only to carpenters but also to electricians and other studio collaborators…the architect's role is to select—a surprising reversal of the more familiar hierarchies of invention, description and implementation."

At the same time, one has to recognize that, so far, the output has been somewhat elitist in as much as Studio Mumbai has built a number of exquisitely detailed houses in the state

of Maharashtra, particularly the Tara and Palmyra Houses of 2005 and 2007, respectively. These are without a doubt expensive, high bourgeois residences, which could hardly be more different from the Norwegian mission built in the same state, or from Mehrotra's Hathigaon and Chowdhury's Friendship Centre. All the same, Bijoy Jain has so far overcome the reductive division of labour that has perennially haunted architectural practice both in the past and now in modern times, and in this he has touched, however tangentially, on the possibility of a non-Eurocentric building culture, an escape from the spectacular closure of our commodified, late-capitalist globalized architecture, which can barely free itself for an instant from the reiterative consumption of images and the maximization of profit.

Bijoy Jain (Studio Mumbai), Jamshyd Setna House, India (Photo: Studio Mumbai).

WELCOME HOME, THROUGH THE DOOR

A MORAL PHENOMENOLOGY OF DWELLING

Arindam Chakrabarti

"...man is the relating being who must go on separating... the human being is the being with limits which has no limits. The seclusion of his being-at-home achieved by the door means that man severs a piece from the uninterrupted unity of being in nature. But just as amorphous limitation finds a shape, so man's being limited finds its meaning and its dignity in what is signified by the door—the possibility at any moment of stepping into freedom and out of being limited."
- Georg Simmel, "The Bridge and the Door."

"Do I have a fixed abode...? Of course, and of course not. I do, however, have a "Home Page" on the World Wide Web, which I am constantly building up and playing with... To be homed in cyberspace, therefore, has a double-edged meaning: to be homed and homeless in some sense."
—Susan Leigh Star, "Feminism and the Concept of Home in Cyberspace."

"Make your guest your god... do not despise food one should produce food in abundance... this is a sacred vow, Let a man never deny hospitality to anyone... I am food! I am food! I am food! He alone preserves me who gives me to another. I who am food consume the ungiving consumer of food!"
—Taittiriya Upanishad

"A house is a machine for living in... one can be proud of having a house as serviceable as a type-writer."
—Le Corbusier, *Towards a New Architecture*

Arindam Chakrabarti teaches philosophy at the University of Hawaii at Manoa. After being trained as an analytic philosopher of language at Oxford University, Arindam Chakrabarti spent several years receiving traditional training in Indian logic (Navya Nyaya). Chakrabarti has edited or authored nine books, in English, Sanskrit, and Bengali, including *Denying Existence, Knowing from Words* (with B.K. Matilal) *Universals, Concepts and Qualities* (with Peter Strawson), and has published more than eighty papers and reviews. He also edited the recently published *The Bloomsbury Research Handbook of Indian Aesthetics and the Philosophy of Art*.

Secrets of the Door

Perhaps an Indo-European cognate of the Sanskrit "dvāra," and of the Bengali "dor" and duār," the English word "door," unmistakably drops a clear hint of two-ness (duo/dvā-r), but of which two?

The first pair that comes to mind is the all-pervasive but phenomenologically mysterious "Inside/Outside" dichotomy (and with that comes the concept of the threshold, the in-between). Next, it signifies the duality of strangers versus in-dwellers, public versus private, limited versus unlimited, impersonal versus personal spaces. The door is a separator-connector between both sides of each of these dualities.

Georg Simmel writes: "The human being who first erected a hut, like the first road-builder, revealed the specifically human capacity over against nature, insofar as he or she cut a portion out of the continuity and infinity of space and arranged this into a particular unity in accordance with a single meaning. A piece of space was thereby brought together and separated from the whole remaining world. By virtue of the fact that the door forms, as it were, a linkage between the space of human beings and everything that remains outside it, it transcends the separation between the inner and the outer. Precisely because it can also be opened, its closure provides the feeling of a stronger isolation against everything outside this space than the mere unstructured wall. The latter is mute, but the door speaks. It is absolutely essential for humanity that it set itself a boundary, but with freedom; that is, in such a way that it can also remove this boundary again, that it can place itself outside it." (italics mine)

What could Simmel have meant by this tantalizing phrase "the door speaks"? It could very well be a transposed metaphor. When one speaks, one opens one's mouth. If the other apertures of the body can be compared to sensory-motor windows, the mouth as an exit of words carrying one's belief

Photo : Tazrin Ahmed

and attitudes, entreaties and commands, curses and greetings, is aptly called the "front door" of the face. Reversing the metaphor, one could look upon the door of a house as its speaking mouth. Even when the door is shut, especially with a padlock announcing its inner in-occupation, that silence tells a story. When the door is ajar or wide open, the house beckons us hesitantly or invites us hospitably. And of course, when the door speaks, it begins to be capable of lying. An open door with a curtain obstructing public view can appear to permit the stranger to come in, only to make knocking before coming in impossible, thus setting a trap or test for decency. Open or closed, doors are always telling us to wait. And waiting is one of the most demanding and emotionally complex actions one could be asked to perform.

Both during the day when the outside is brighter than the inside of a home, and during the night when the outside is darker, the doorway remains a twilight zone mediating between the luminosity-binaries.

Socially, the door welcomes the guest to the inner chambers, in acts of obligatory or supererogatory hospitality. But the welcome can turn into a refusal at any point. One can open the door simply to announce that she with whom one has come to visit, is not at home, or would not like to see the visitor. Some traumatizing episodes of ending a relationship can happen at the indecisive space of the door. Contrariwise, a long painful wait of the in-dweller could end with a surprise visit of a much-awaited or long-lost friend, and as the door opens, the heart may open also. With a stammering welcome, the door may be opened ajar, to "get the picture" and then either opened fully dropping all guards, or closed in the face of the suspicious or unwanted guest.

Even the open door, can afford two kinds of traffic, coming in and going out, arrival and departure. While a generous host's doors are open to anyone who is willing to step inside, a more discriminating choosy host may use the door as a check-point. And even an inmate may be "shown the door" in the sense of being driven out.

Visually, the door affords two views: the outsiders' glimpse of the indoors, and the insider's view of the outer world. The most general "architectural meaning" of the door, to use a Kantian expression, seems to be this synthesis of liberty and limitation in social traffic. Some specific types of doors improvise on this generic meaning and makes the door much more than a device for coming in and going out. From the false doors painted on Roman or Turkish walls, to Ghiberti's richly pictorial doors of the Baptistry in Florence, and the gigantic monolithic "Gopurams" of South Indian temples, all the way up to some contemporary non-existent doors in a house with interrupted walls, doors could be used to deconstruct this very bridging-by-separating function that I claimed to be their general shared meaning.

What does the sliding door mean? Unlike the swinging door, the sliding door has the advantage of a changing of the size of the aperture. What does the design of house without a door signify? Just with staggered discontinuous walls, one can create an open space which has enough closure to feel like a room/home, the domestic space can be continuous within and without by virtue of walls becoming discontinuous.

Then of course, there is the matter of the inner as mental and outer as the bodily, and the door as the in-between, marked by the threshold: the private feels of the publicly observable body. The body with its physical openings at the nostrils, eyes, ears, mouth, anus and genitals is called the Nine-Door House in the Bhagavad Gita. In some Buddhist caves in India and in the stone door of the Church of Nativity at Bethlehem, humility of the pilgrim is demanded by the lowness of the door that forces the entrant to crouch and bend one's head. Humility of the upper class elite is required by the low door of the Japanese teahouse.

Doors hold secrets, surprises, and wild wonderings about what lies beyond, from both sides. In *Alice in Wonderland*, we encounter one such mystery-mongering doors. In the much-acclaimed Bengali film from the nineties, *Lal Darja* (The Red Door, 1997) directed and written by Buddhadev Dasgupta, is an allegorical drama about a Kolkata dentist who has a persistent dream of a red door which symbolizes his fear of becoming a cripple. A door in such a recurrent dream could mean the transit from a healthy to a sick stretch of life, a threshold one does not dare to cross. With this "aperitif" of a moral semiotic of the door, let us now get indoors, into the phenomenology of "home."

An Ancient Definition of a Happy Human

One of the first linguistic goofs I made when I arrived in the United States was trying to compliment a warm, efficient, and charming hostess as "a very homely person." "Homely" was a word of praise in India and England. In America, I was told—and I find this suggestive—that it means "physically unattractive." Had that usage been gender-neutral, it would be entirely appropriate to describe Socrates as a rather homely person, though in the Indian/British sense he was not homely at all. He did not live on the street with dogs like Diogenes the cynic, but his life is not known for domestic harmony and peace. And since then, some maladjustment at home and living mostly in taverns, coffeehouses, or symposia have become part of what it takes to be a Western intellectual. Notwithstanding the current stereotype of the homeless, hash-smoking Indian sadhu living in a forest or on a mountaintop, the Vedic sages at the dawn of Indian philosophy, in contrast, would often be responsible parents, teachers, or rulers engaged in domestic rituals. A nonattached householder king would often be wiser in spiritual matters than a homeless wandering monk. A dutiful housewife or a virtuous butcher would teach a conceited ascetic the meaning of dharma.

Home was a good place—a spiritually elevating and materially nurturing place—the temple of both Sarasvatī, the goddess of music, wisdom, and creative speech as well as of Lakṣmi, the goddess of wealth, beauty, and unflaunted virtue.

Yudhiṣṭhira, the all too human moral hero of the *Mahābhārata*, was asked a battery of profound questions (in *Vanaparvan*—the "Book of Wilderness," chap. 267) by a Sphinx-like crane, guarding the water of a lethal lake. One of those simple but deep questions was, who enjoys life? The righteous prince answered: "If someone with no debts to pay back, not living in an alien land, cooks vegetables in one's own home at the end of the day, then such a person enjoys life." Of course both the *ṚgVeda* (10.117) and the *Bhagavadgītā* (3.13) issue strict injunctions against cooking only for oneself or eating alone. So the cooking of this happy-at-home person must be for the sake of sharing food with guests and family.

This minimalist picture of happiness is based on three basic components: lack of economic anxiety, being at home, and contentment at the satisfaction of the basic necessities of life. In spite of being thousands of miles and years away from the place and time of the *Mahābhārata*, it still remains true all around us right now that a combination of all three of these factors is vanishingly rare. Numerous people are homeless in the world now. Many who have a shelter still do not feel that to be their home. Those who have homes are mostly not free from economic anxieties, because, at least in the United States, a typical homeowner does have debts to pay back. Even those lucky or enterprising few who dwell without debt in their own homes tend to suffer from a cultivated discontent—often euphemistically called the drive for growth—a discontent that makes them incapable of enjoying (let alone cooking with their own hands) a simple meal at the end of the day.

The culture of perpetual disappointment with one's durable possessions that has become part of the current consumer behavior is best described in the words of Albert O. Hirschman: "men think they want one thing and then upon getting it, find out to their dismay that they don't want it nearly as much as they thought or don't want it at all and that something else of which they were hardly aware is what they really want."[1]

As a result, perhaps Yudhiṣṭhira's minimalist definition of enjoying life hardly appeals to an average pleasure-seeker in the technologically globalized and economically liberalized, developed and developing societies of the twenty-first century. A cursory look at advertisements for new gadgets shows that invention has become the mother of necessity. One just has to wait till the next new ease-enhancing machine is aggressively marketed in order to realize how badly one has been suffering without it. Yet one seems to look forward to such retrospective knowledge of unmet needs. Faster and wider-ranging telecommunication is valued for its own sake. And because satellite television reaches remote villages of Third World countries faster than literacy, even half-fed children who have never been to a school feel "educated" while watching live coverage of schoolboys in freer countries shooting their classmates and teacher.

Nevertheless, I want to explore one crucial constituent of this ancient and bare definition of human happiness: the concept of "one's own home." The stark simplicity of the meal being cooked by the paradigmatically happy person gestures back to a previous quiz in the same ordeal of wisdom: "By giving up what does one become happy?"[2] Yudhiṣṭhira's laconic reply was: "By giving up greed one becomes happy." One does not need to give up one's work, possessions, or home in order to give up greed or avarice. Indeed, the practice of obligatory hospitality requires possession of a home and yet helps loosen up the grip of greed more than outward renunciation or asceticism. Thomas F. Tierney has argued that the technical culture of convenience spread by such "modern ascetics" as Benjamin Franklin actually owes its origin to the Protestant ethic of using the unrestrained "interest" or drive for moneymaking to curb the passions for spontaneous bodily enjoyment.[3] Though apparently austere, such effort on Poor Richard's part to save time because "time is money" is basically a form of non-hedonistic greed.

But instead of plunging into this complicated economic-psychology of calculative egotistical rationality, recurrent disappointment with current technology, and the postmodern expulsion of happiness from home, first let me state my

argument linking the future of human homes with a certain economically encouraged enslavement to gadgets.

Whether human dwellings are fabricated out of fake timber or fiberglass or aluminum in the future, they will not be "homes" unless they are owned and lived in by hospitable dwellers ready to share their comforts and food with their guests in acts of non-self-seeking non-ostentatious hospitality. A guest is not just a tolerated trespasser or a return invitee or a bribable prospective benefactor. A guest is a hungry or needy other, a chance visitor, a selflessly chosen friend. To echo Emmanuel Levinas, "The possibility for the home to open to the Other is as essential to the essence of the home as closed doors and windows."[4] But opening your door happily to such a guest for face-to-face human communicative practice is not entirely compatible with being preoccupied with attention-absorbing gadgets such as the cellular phone, the entrancing television, the mesmerizing Internet, or even the adolescent CD player with its conversation-effacing headset. Of course, the kitchen and the home space would not be possible or comfortable, in the first place, without the use of some technology. But if a certain Other-forbidding style of consumption of technological products makes the domestic space inhospitable to the unexpected guest and blocks his or her conversation, and if the welcome given to such a guest is the index of the "homehood" of a home, then such enjoyment of gadgets would prevent rather than promote enjoyment of home-life. Because a healthy home-life is, according to the *Mahābhārata*, a necessary condition of human happiness, such a use of technology would lead to unhappiness. Gadgets that are conspicuously consumed by those who can afford to own them advertise themselves as enhancers of domestic comfort and convenience, as if comfort and convenience add up to happiness. That more often than not they ruin domestic happiness should therefore be unobvious.

Not technology itself but a certain routinely self-outdating compulsive use of technology has ruined homes in two distinct ways. In raising the standard of comfort and luxury of one set of people, it has impoverished, displaced, and even liquidated another set of people. But it has also harmed those very homes that it has made incredibly more livable. I shall not talk about the first kind of effect. Building big dams (in contemporary India) like Tehri on Ganga and Sardar Sarovar on Narmada has indeed made thousands of traditional villagers and tribal peoples homeless while apparently promising more electricity to another class of homes and businesses. Instead, I shall concentrate on the more elusive threat that technology poses to those very homes that it perpetually "improves."

But all three legs of my argument above look awfully wobbly. Why should the gadget-friendly person necessarily be "unhomey," unhappy, or inhospitable to guests? Why must a place be hospitable to guests in order to count as a home? Last and most fundamentally, why is it taken for granted that being located at one's own home is such a normatively necessary condition of a good life?

I shall take up these questions in the reverse order. First, I shall consider some serious objections to the very idea of home as a site of value and well-being. Philosophers from Simone de Beauvoir to Luce Irigaray have raised powerful objections against the ideal of home as a haven of fulfillment. My treatment of their critique will be heavily influenced by Iris Young's cautious and critical defense of the value of a

certain kind of home-life in the face of these objections.[5] Second, borrowing insights from Vedic texts and the writings of Emmanuel Levinas, I shall move on to consider the integral relationship between human dwelling and offering food and place to "the Other," which counterbalances the possessive enclosure of the home with an obligatory opening up.

Finally, I shall try to establish that a certain prevalent pattern of marketing and consuming technological products encourages domestic isolation and pride of possession; engenders self-absorption; sows discontent; mechanizes our minds, leaving little room for hosting the unusual; and helps unlearn the simple virtues of face-to-face listening and opening up to other live human faces and bodies. Notice that I am not putting the blame on the gadgets themselves. It is a certain style of getting hooked on them and giving them focal position in domestic lived space that tends to make guests redundant, unwanted, or at best means to exhibitionistic ends. Surely there could be alternative non-isolating, guest-friendly mindful uses of domestic machinery. But it would take ethically vigilant work to steer home dwellers away from such commercially profitable dehumanizing uses to more hospitable uses of those or other technological products.

Given the ubiquity of technology in a modern home and the irresistibility of the worldwide flooding of homes with aggressively marketed entertaining and communication facilitating gadgets, such ethical efforts alone can save those elements of the human home that I argue are well worth saving.

The Grammar of Human Homes

Three cases (*kāraka*-s) from Sanskrit grammar together appear to capture the concept of an abode: the locative, the ablative, and the accusative. At the shallowest level, wherever I am more or less permanently located—my *adhikaraṇa*—counts as my home. At a deeper level, the place I have left, where I am from—the ablative (*apādāna*) gets identified as my home. In an even deeper sense, a morally and materially empowered person regards the intentional terminus or ideal accusative of one's journey—the *karmakāraka*—to be the home one makes or finds. In premodern times, for a traditional wealthy Indian male in an agriculturally based society, all these three might have coincided in a single place. One was located for the most part in that piece of land wherefrom one came and where one wanted to end one's life. But in the fragmented postcolonial times of technological global capitalism, adulthood often entails displacement—a divorce of the locative home from the ablative home and a perpetual receding of the accusative home under the norm of restless repurchase till one dies like the man in Tolstoy's story "How Much Land Does a Man Need?"

In the experience of the diasporic immigrant who left a home to look for another elsewhere, the discontent with the locative home often leads to a fantastic construction of the ablative home endowed with all the desiderata of the ideal accusative home. Wherever one finds oneself seems to fall short of that dreamt dwelling. As a result of or at least along with this disjunction between the where, the wherefrom, and the whereto of living, a fourth sort of conceptualization of home has taken precedence over the other three in our technological times. This is the idea of home as the instrumental case—wherewith—a mere *karaṇa*, a tool to be used and possessed, improved upon, upgraded, jettisoned, and replaced from time to time. Such a dwelling-machine has to be evaluated part

Photo: K. Ashraf

Photo: K. Ashraf

by part on the basis of its efficiency to serve the following purposes:

1. Shelter from environmental and human hazards (hence the durable roof and the sturdy front door with a secure lock)
2. Domination over place: ownership (hence some kind of boundary wall or fencing to mark off territory, with legal documentary support)
3. An address to locate one's life and receive communications (hence the mailbox and the phone line, fax port, and computer terminal)
4. Place to store one's belongings and non-disposable junk (hence the cupboards or lofts or basement or storage space)
5. Room for resting, sleeping, recuperating, healing, and lovemaking (hence the bedroom)
6. Place to cook food and eat it with family (hence the kitchen, the hearth—the center of a household in Vedic, as well as modern, times for many homes)
7. Place to cleanse oneself and perform private bodily functions routinely (hence a hygienic washroom and toilet)

But apart from these seven concrete functions for which the home-machine can be a mere means, there seem to be three more abstract uses of the home space that distinguishes it from a motel or any other accommodation that is a mere commodity. A human home is also expected to be the following:
8. A private secluded place to drop all guards and to experiment with who and what one would like to be: a laboratory of selfhood (It is thus a place that often prepares the dweller to leave that place and go elsewhere. Like a mother it pushes out those lives that it bears in its womb.)
9. A field of nurturing one's link with the past and preserving traditions
10. A place in which to welcome guests

The "inferiority" that these elements make up is to be felt in contrast with two distinct exteriors. Home is indoors compared with the wild out doors of roofless nature, forests, deserts, mountains, fields, rivers, and the ocean. It is also inside contrasted with the outside of the marketplace, the city streets, and the workplace where business is conducted, vehicles run, and people sell goods or services. Domestic interiority is opposed to the openness and solitude of the wilderness and at the same time other than the extroversion of the crowds in the shopping mall. It is supposed to be warm compared with the freezing winds of untamed nature as well as in comparison to the coldness of merely monetary exchange. It is ironic that the adjective "economic" should be derived from the Greek "oikos"—cognate of the Sanskrit "okas"—which means the home, yet the home is one place that is ideally free from economic exchange or bargaining. Perhaps, under the veneer of purely personal nurturing and repose, what goes on in a traditional home is the economic activity of pure and simple exploitation. That suspicion leads me to the first two objections against one of my premises that I shall deal with.

The Dark Insides of Dwellings
Objection A
According to Hannah Arendt, the ancient Greek denigration of the private, domestic life (of women and slaves) sprang from the feeling that the private is literally privative. It amounts to a deprivation from what is best in humans, the intellectual freedom from the demands of the body. The major needs served by dwellings are biological needs like eating, sleeping, reproduction, and evacuation. A life bound to the home is thus

merely bodily existence, not the enriching and ennobling life of the mind that alone distinguishes humans from lower animals. Of course, it is easy to see the holes in this criticism. There is no reason to think that care of the body is a mean job. Indeed, as every Eastern meditative tradition has recognized explicitly, care of the body is completely continuous with "care of the soul." Indeed, the translation of "spiritual" in Sanskrit is the word "adhyatmika" which means "pertaining to the lived body." A home fulfills the demands of the lived body. From this it does not follow that it fulfills nothing but mean animal demands. Even if all we did at home were to eat, sleep, and wash ourselves, the way a human does those things can be and usually are distinctively human. Subhuman animals do not cook or dress. Cooking, eating, and feeding guests can be a sacrifice or worship; taking a bath or dressing up can be a religious or romantic ritual. The human domestic use of the body has nothing beastly about it in that derogatory sense. Indeed, a public nondomestic debate between senators or parliamentarians can resemble a barking match between dogs more than village women privately chopping vegetables at home resembles any subhuman activity. Though Kant must have drawn inspiration from his regular afternoon walks outside his home, he conducted most of his forays into Pure Reason while sitting at home, where, in the evenings, he would often entertain guests. (Kant's butler, who did most of the dirty work, apparently took pride in Kant's literary output.)

Of course, there is no point romanticizing kitchens and valorizing domestic food production. Kitchens traditionally have been small, ill-ventilated, smoky, sooty, damp, dingy places where women have spent most of their lives, resentful and dehumanized. But the traditional—for example, Vedic—ideal home regards the kitchen as the inner sanctum and the cooking fire (gārhapatya agni) as the sacrificial fire to which the first offerings of the day are to be made. The feudal lord, the industrial capitalist, or their ministers and clerks of course never stepped inside the kitchen, let alone performed cooking as a holy ritual. But such architectural and social neglect of the kitchen space, along with pride in an ostentatious drawing room or a luxurious master bedroom, is itself a consequence of the cultural denigration of the process of domestic production and cannot therefore serve to justify such denigration. In a post-Marxist world, with heightened caution against alienation of labor, it should be perfectly possible to make the work areas of the home as livable and respectable as the rooms of leisure. If the home and its sustaining functions causally constitute the very core of its dwellers, then valuing the exterior public life more than the domestic interior would amount to valuing the mask more than the face.

Objection B
Male poets, priests, and philosophers have waxed eloquent about "sweet home," it could be objected, precisely because home is the oldest site of oppression of women. It has always been to the advantage of lazy patriarchs, "busy-in-the-world-at-large" husbands, and spoiled boys to extol the moral and spiritual loftiness of home as a place, because that has been the classic ruse for keeping mothers, wives, and daughters fettered to the hard, uncompensated, uninnovative work of cooking, cleaning, and caregiving.

This objection deserves more serious and elaborate response than I have space for giving in this essay. The recognition of ethical and spiritual superiority of housework that I would like to vindicate (for instance, in my response to objection A,

above) is incompatible with assigning that job to only one half of humanity. Unless one is essentialist enough to believe that cooking or cleaning or caring for children are jobs that males cannot be biologically good at, the age-old transcultural stereotypical marriage between home and the woman is easily seen to be as arbitrary as the stereotypical marriage between lucrative public office and the man. Given that we have been working hard at destroying the latter stereotype, however hard it may die, the former stereotype is also worth breaking. A vocation as morally ambiguous as that of a soldier fighting on battlefields (or in computer-operated warfare) has been traditionally exclusively male. Instead of arguing for abolition of this violent "male" role altogether, empowerment of women has often taken the form of trying to open up that vocation for female volunteers as well. This is because, somehow, society still looks upon that calling as heroic and valorous, and it is well paid. The reason the same move is not made with respect to the hitherto exclusively "female" role of homemaking by opening it up as an empowering role for males as well is because, first, it is not looked upon as a heroic job and, second, it is not paid at all.

The real answer to this objection therefore lies in investigating why domestic caretaking is regarded as unheroic and unglamorous and why such backbreaking and essential work is never remunerated with money. Traditional patriarchy conspired to hide its own singular dependency (for example, through polygamy in certain societies or through the threat of asceticism in others) on home production processes by making those processes invisible in the name of privacy. A double standard worked insidiously behind the patriarchal valorization of and imputation of indignity to "woman's work." Mothering was constructed naturally as a noble and spontaneous human reaction to the vulnerability of the child, the sick, and the tired. While the power of such total control over the private home space was given to the mothers and was announced to be too sacred to be measured by money, the public sphere was regarded as the only real world, and all prestige in the public life was measured by money. With the spread of capitalist individualism, as this money culture started permeating both the private and the public spheres, what was work too highly valued to be bought for money was read as too low to be worth getting good at. The most vital work was regarded as no work at all, while pushing papers or buttons in an office was deemed real productive labor. With such a skewed semiotic of respectability in place, the only way to get equality for the sexes was by equal nonparticipation in the caring, cooking, and cleaning work at home rather than by equal participation. Some feminists have thus suggested that all caring, cooking, and cleaning should ideally be purchasable from common public kitchens or restaurants or from hired helps. Such affluent and "just" individuals of both genders would then live in dwellings like hotels, and the "exploitative" institution of homes would be abolished for them. Because I regard this as an axiological reduction of such a position, belonging to a home's being part of my definition of a fulfilled human being, I think the homes have been used for the common sources of exploitation and discrimination and the capitalist semiotics of "respectable work"—and not because of their being homes as shuch. Homes have also been sites of unthinkable incest, marital rape, and other kinds of abuse. But surely the "homehood" of home cannot consist in its permissiveness to such perversions.

Photo: K. Ashraf

Objection C

Homes are symbols of conservation of the past, treadmills of the habitual, repositories of diurnal repetitive acts, the drudgery of uncreative chores. Housework is cruelly boring and perceived as dehumanizing. That is why most creative artists and revolutionaries and spiritual leaders leave home and break from tradition and habitual ways of living and thinking. Simone de Beauvoir expresses this complaint most eloquently: "Few tasks are more like the torture of Sisyphus than housework, with its endless repetition: the clean becomes soiled, the soiled is made clean, over and over, day after day. The housewife wears herself out marking time: she makes nothing, simply perpetuates the present. She never senses conquest of a positive Good, but rather indefinite struggle against negative Evil....Eating, sleeping, cleaning—the years no longer rise up toward heaven, they lie spread out ahead, grey and identical. The battle against dust and dirt is never won."[6]

My answer to this would be a much needed defense of routine, action, of ritual as celebration and ceremony, and—more radically—of the creativity of the habitual.[7] Many will agree with me that novelty is highly overrated for totally market-economic purposes. Humans need to rediscover the joys of everyday familiar things and events, to recognize a routine, plain dinner to be as much of a gift as the "lucky old sun" or the same concerted chirping of birds at every daybreak. Just as it is sick to resent them as boring, it is sick to hate one's home because it lacks surprises. The surprises one can look forward to within a fortunately monotonous home are the unexpected visitors, the unprecedented turns of human interactions inside and outside the family. It is only the worst sort of novelty that comes from tragic attempts at daily change of lodgings or from frenetic refurnishing of the home space.

Objection D

The home idea has been hallowed by colonizing cultures at the expense of slaves and colonies, as in Victorian England. Edward Said, through his reading of Jane Austen's *Mansfield Park*, argues that the British sense of settled bourgeois home depended on empire building in the colonies. For Said, that which assures the domestic tranquility and harmonious attractiveness of one is the disciplined productivity of the other.

But of course it would be a mistake to overgeneralize from this that homebuilding is necessarily a privilege of the colonial bourgeois. For the nineteenth-century, colonized Indian middle class, as well as for a large number of dispossessed women in Bangladesh who took loans from Grameen Bank to build cheap dwellings of their own, a community of homes was precisely the foothold from where an identity of resisting colonization and oppression was constructed. Iris Young quotes Bell Hooks here: "Historically African American people believed that a construction of a home-place however fragile or tenuous has a radical political dimension.... [O]ne's home-place was one site where one could ... resist."[8]

Objection E

Valorizing "own home" as a value leads to nationalism at the collective level and encourages territorial pride and regionalism with imaginary homogenized pasts. As Bonnie Honig writes forcefully: "The dream of home is dangerous, particularly in postcolonial settings, because it animates and exacerbates the inability of constituted subjects—or nations—to accept their own internal divisions, and it engenders zealotry, the will to bring the dream of unitariness or home into being. It leads the subject to project its internal differences onto external Others and then to rage against them for standing in the way of its dream—both at home and elsewhere."[9]

My response is this: If we pay attention to the eighth and tenth functions of the home listed above, then we shall see that the home idea need not be a homogenizing idea. The domestic site could be a space for experimental self-criticism and negotiation, a nourishing of differences. Ramakrishna, a nineteenth-century Hindu mystic, used to tell the story of the discriminating mother who cooks different soups for different children with different digestive capacities. It is part of good caring that it does not use the same recipe for all its charges. The welcoming of guests and letting the guest take up and modify the domestic space that a traditional hospitable home permits also breaks its regimentation. The past-preserving function of a home is syncopated by these welcome ruptures of continuity from within and without.

Objection F
The root of home is in the male desire to go back to the security of the womb. Nostalgia is fed by separation anxiety.

In spite of these negative historical or psychological associations, Iris Young recognizes home as critical value because it provides a feeling of safety, individuation, privacy, and meaning preservation through linking up with a constantly renegotiated narrative of one's past.[10]

Thus, great positive value for the concept of home can be salvaged from the oppressive and escapist political psychology that clings to its history. While welcoming available technology within our own homeplace, we need to preserve the human character of that lived space by eschewing those isolating uses of technology that make us Other-blind and averse to face-to-face human contact. Like our own wonderful but not fully understood bodies, our amazing tools can be enabling as well as separating. When we touch each other or listen to the voice of god, we do not need a cellular phone and we must make sure to stop the noise of the Net or of satellite television.

A Transcendental Deduction of Hospitality
Dwelling is our mortal way of being on the earth. A home is where a human being typically lives from and retires back to. But humans live well through a dialectical process of making and unmaking, learning and forgetting, controlling and letting be, with technological interventions and with a search for raw, ungroomed nature, claiming to know and confessing ignorance. Human dwelling is also governed by this rhythm of contrariety. Physically, a dwelling is an enclosed place with walls and a roof, yet it is not a dwelling unless it has doors and windows or other openings into unenclosed space like a yard because life without a lanai is not worth living. To be at home is not to be boxed in a windowless chamber.

At a deeper psychosocial level, privacy and ownership, which make a home out of a house, need to be relieved by the contrary currents of sharing with family and friends and hospitality in order for a place to really count as one's own. A secret lonesome hideout or a solitary cell is not a home. One does not want visitors to squat and take over one's place, but one likes occasionally to be able to invite others whose home it is not and say to them: "Please feel free here and make yourself at home."

A place cannot become a home unless it is open to the needy or friendly other. Unshared consumption of food or space is comparable to an allegedly private use of language or a solipsistic placement of semantic conventions, must as such one-person languages are not languages, such egotistical usurping of space is also not dwelling. As Rosemary L. Haughton has shown beautifully,[11] the host's readiness to make common, at least temporarily, what is legally private breaks down the barriers of ownership, reminding us that private possession is after all a conventional fiction. Thus, as Haughton puts it: "The ability to welcome others into the home ensures that home does not become isolation. Hospitality means a letting go of certainty and control—and paradoxically it's only this letting go that allows the richness of growth and change that makes real and not pretended continuity possible."[12]

The hymn on gift in the RgVeda (10.117) opens with the warning that starvation alone is not death. Ungiving consumption is also tantamount to not living. To live as humans is to consume after one has ritually given the first share of food to guests and needy neighbors. If in developed countries the architecture of human habitats does not permit hosting needy neighbors or hungry guests anymore, the concept of hospitality has to be extended to include the distant hungry in other parts of the world as one's guests and neighbors. This is not supererogatory charity. It is an obligatory gift without which the nourishment turns into one's own death, being eaten by one's own food.

Of course the microwave and the pressure cooker help being hospitable locally, and the Internet and telecommunication help in hosting distant neighbors globally. But if the marketing technique of some gadgets requires that one's egotistical calculations are fanned by invitations to buy fifty times more for oneself than for others, then the existence of this sort of gadget itself is threatening to the Other-sensitive, sacrificial living and the "owning by acknowledgment of owing" that I am proposing to make our ideal. If it is possible to make and use gadgets that would not totally consume us as we consume them, then technology can actually coexist with and even help a hospitable way of living and hence a flourishing home dwelling life.

Just as the first home of a human child is usually a home not belonging to him or her but a home to which he or she belongs, the ownership over one's own home remains different from the ownership over other material possessions such as gadgets and jewelry. Levinas' project of finding even the meaning of sensory proximity or contact in "taking care of others' need," in a giving vulnerability, and in "welcoming the wretched into your house" has striking echoes in the Vedic idea that eating—and, by Upanishadic extension, any sensory consumption—is futile if it is solitary, that speech originates in spilling over of loving friendship, and that the guest is to be worshiped as God. This deification of the guest is not only an ancient Indian idea. Here is what David Appelbaum writes in his illuminating chapter on houseguests:

Listen to Eumaeus as he greets the raggedy tramp at his gate: "My conscience would not let me turn away a stranger in worse state even than yourself, for strangers and beggars all come in Zeus's name, and a gift from folk like us is none the less welcome for being small."

It is his lord that he greets. For this reason in holier times, hospitality was universal sacred law.... Take the humble couple of Ovid's *Metamorphoses*, *Baucis* and *Philemon*. A pair of ruffians appears one stormy night at their front door. The hut is rude, their cupboard poor.... But the hosting spirit is strong upon them. They feel no shame for their belongings, or their condition, which is an inner plenitude. Their only need is to obey an impulse to host.... The guests are no men but gods. Zeus and Hermes are testing the law of hospitality. For receiving the strangers, Baucis and his wife reap rich rewards.[13] The Indian epic *Mahābhārata* is replete with such awe-inspiring stories of self-effacing hospitality as exemplars of ideal domesticity.

Egotistic Techno-fetishism and the New Gyges' Ring
One cannot attribute the gradual attrition of the virtue of hospitableness in a society entirely to technology. But technological culture—insofar as it has any moral predilections at all—has a pull toward an egoistic Ayn Rand type of ethics. The great communication revolution has smudged the distinction between home and the world, but its chief lure has been controlled self exposure, seeing remote things without being seen, watching famine in Africa or flood in Bangladesh on CNN from one's dinner table without one's gluttony being seen by the malnourished homeless. Virtual conversation thus preserves human separateness about which Emmanuel Levinas remarks: "Gyges' ring symbolizes separation. Gyges plays a double game, a presence to others and an absence, speaking to 'others' and evading speech; Gyges is the very condition of man, the possibility of injustice and radical egoism, the possibility of accepting the rules of the game but cheating."[14]

A communication that is faceless and empty-handed is also not even proper language, because to speak properly is to be ready to relinquish the ownership of an idea for the sake of a wholly unknown mind behind the listening ears of the other.

Three aspects of the phenomenology of home technology can go against hospitality. The first, distraction and absorption with the telephone, television, or the Internet create a false sense of companionship with a distant cyber chatter or a caller on the phone, or the sheer exhilaration of keeping impressively busy. No room is left in one's life for un-self-interested leisurely conversation with a visitor. The common sight of a piano in a middle-class household, to be played by or for the guest, is gradually replaced by stereo music systems or multimedia computers, which provide for passive entertainment. No guests are welcome when *Downtown Abbey* is on! Chronic attention deficit, psychologists say, goes hand in hand with obsessive behavior. The information highway runs right across our dining space and our sitting room; we are in the world always but never there at home to usher in our friends and neighbors.

Second, jealous exhibitionism and an unsharing, possessive pride are also fostered by certain kinds of gadget use. It is interesting that what is increasingly more valued than personal "warmth" in people and house-holds is "being cool"—a certain dazzling fashionableness that is to be envied rather than enjoyed. Even hospitality turns into an act of showing off when one is immersed in the consumer culture of perpetual renewal of technological belongings. The guest is made to feel wowed rather than welcomed. This is essentially the fault not of new technology but of the way it is marketed, even though there is reason to believe that the speed of constant improvement depends upon this kind of competition and greed breeding.

Gadgets are items of conspicuous consumption, and they are used as status symbols in a society of class climbers. A home becomes a replaceable possession with a price tag with which to compete against your guests. Through CNN you can also peep through a pornographic display of world-wide poverty while sitting in your basement home theater in front of a gargantuan TV screen that makes all the homeless workers of the world unite in front of your plush couch.

Finally, the craze for increasing speed and convenience leads to devaluation of one's own current home space as needing constant technical "improvement," thus losing the meaning-preserving aspect of home dwelling.

My moral worries are not about home technology as such. They are about homeplaces turning into marketplaces, about food and company becoming another purchasable commodity, about hotel customers being the only guests, and about dwellings becoming only perpetually upgradeable machinery.

Housing Human Beings
A characteristic remark that Wittgenstein would make when referring to someone who was notably generous or kind or honest was "He is a human being." The first time that he presented himself as a lodger at a house in Wales, the lady of the house inquired whether he would like a cup of tea. Her husband called to her from another room: "Do not ask; give!" Wittgenstein would relate this incident and remark, "That was a human being."

Unbridled greed for purposelessly progressing technology can ruin those very homes that it promises to enrich, besides promoting dehumanizing inequality of resources across society. The culture of discontent and control-hungry impatience that the producers and sellers of gadgets thrive on is sure to render hospitality, at the individual, transnational, and transcultural level obsolete, except perhaps at hotels, casinos, brothels, and business or political promotional feasts. Such a world-wide-web of instant communicators and speedy travelers will be an awfully lonely place where perhaps all humans would be Net-using nomads. Neither Yudhiṣṭhira nor Wittgenstein would deem them happy humans.

Notes

[1] Albert O. Hirschman, *Shifting Involvements* (Princeton: Princeton University Press, 1982), 21.
[2] Mahabbarata, *Vanaparvan*, 267.71.
[3] Thomas F. Tierney, *The Value of Convenience: Genealogy of Technical Culture* (Albany: State University of New York Press, 1993).
[4] Emmanuel Levinas, *Totality and Infinity* (Pittsburgh: Duquesne University Press, 1969), 173.
[5] Iris M. Young, *Intersecting Voices: Dilemmas of Gender, Political Philosophy, and Policy* (Princeton: Princeton University Press, 1997), chap. 7.
[6] Simone de Beauvoir, *The Second Sex*, trans, and ed. H. M. Parshley (New York: Vintage Books, 1974), 504.
[7] My student Brian Bruya has done good work on this by comparing Dewey's notion of habit with the Confucian notion of yi-infused li, or propriety-infused ritual conduct.
[8] Young, *Intersecting Voices*, 160.
[9] Bonnie Honig, "Difference, Dilemmas, and the Politics of Home," Social Research 61.3 (fall 1994): 585.
[10] Young, *Intersecting Voices*, 147-156.
[11] Rosemary L. Haughton, "Hospitality: Home as the Integration of Privacy and Community," in The Longing for Home, ed. Leroy Rouner (Notre Dame, Ind.: University of Notre Dame Press, 1996), 204-216.
[12] Ibid., 214.
[13] David Appelbaum, *Everyday Spirits* (Albany: State University of New York Press, 1993), 5*-
[14] Levinas, *Totality and Infinity*, 173.

THE REAL WILDERNESS IS OUTSIDE

TROPICAL ISLANDS RESORT IN GERMANY

A.-Chr. Engels-Schwarzpaul

In the *Punch* cartoon of the Great Exhibition in London (1851), a "European rider with a spiked helmet" races closely "behind the African elephant and next to an American Indian" *(Kaiser 2006)*. They waste no time on noticing each other but scramble furiously toward the finishing line. Meanwhile, some contemporaries nurtured pious hopes that intercultural encounters at the exhibition would further mutual understanding and world peace. Thus, Sigfried Giedion remarked, "To take a turn about this place ... is literally to travel around the world, for all nations have come here; enemies are coexisting in peace" (in *Benjamin 1999*, 175–76).

In 2006, the Tropical Village at the Tropical Islands resort in Germany featured several houses from the tropics, a Samoan fale in their midst. Set on an oval, elevated platform, the fale signals the South Seas' eternal sun and balmy breezes. Its handcrafted pandanus mats, carved posts, weaving, and lashing details tell of an imaginary place where time moves at a different pace. As part of the €70 million themed resort, the fale is sheltered by the former Cargo Lifter hangar's 360-meter-long steel dome at Brand, 60 kilometers southeast of Berlin. Set up by the Chinese Malaysian multimillionaire investor Colin Au, Tropical Islands is to satisfy a Germanic yearning for sun—unmatched by expendable incomes and geographical location.

Both scenarios stage notions of progress, nostalgia, and exoticism. Both combine labor and leisure in peculiar ways. Giedion observed how enemies coexisted in peace, and someone at Tropical Islands Resort labeled the Tropical Village a "one-world-village" (*Eine-Welt-Dorf*).

These tropes orient experience, shape perception, and activate knowledge. But which knowledge? Both the *Punch* cartoonist and Giedion registered competitive conflict and peaceful coexistence at the 1851 exhibition. And some disagreement also accompanied the Tropical Islands resort's establishment, despite Au's assertion that he knows the German character: "I've done my research and I know how the Germans tick" (in *Connolly, 2004*).

I visited Tropical Islands Resort three times between January 2006 and November 2008. Even in 2006, little was visible about the fale's origins, and what little there was had disappeared in 2008. By then, the previously almost inaccessible fale had been renamed Kalmoa Cocktail Lounge (associating it vaguely with Indonesia) and served as a public smoking lounge—with about the same attractiveness and integrity as a run-down airport smoking lounge. Visitors hardly notice the fale as a building in its own right; of 15 randomly addressed visitors on 8 November 2008, only 2 thought they had a vague idea of where "the Samoan house" might be found—and they were wrong. There isn't much that could help people make a connection with Samoa: the fact that it was once a German colony has disappeared from national consciousness. From a historical perspective, this is a strange dissociation.

The French philosopher Jacques Rancière (born 1940) and the German philosopher Walter Benjamin (1892–1940) share an interest in the relationships between art and politics, the creation of pictures of the world in perception and language, and the productive potential of conflict to open up new spaces of visibility. They may offer pointers regarding Tropical Islands' potential to aid or prevent the appearance of certain forms of relationships.

Dr. Tina Engels-Schwarzpaul is a professor in spatial design and postgraduate studies at AUT University—Te Wananga Aronui o Tamaki Makau Rau, in Auckland, Aotearoa/New Zealand. Selected publications include "A warm grey fabric lined on the inside with the most lustrous and colourful of silks': Dreams of Airships and Tropical Islands" (2007); "Restless Containers: Thinking Interior Space—Across Cultures" (2011); "Access/Arrival: Welcoming Difference" (2012); "Globalised Desk-top Skirmishes? Reporting from the Colonies" (2012); Of Other Thoughts: Non-traditional Ways to the Doctorate—a Guidebook for Candidates and Supervisors (with M.A. Peters (2013); and The Offerings of Fringe Figures and Migrants (2014).

THE GREAT DERBY RACE FOR EIGHTEEN HUNDRED AND FIFTY-ONE.

Punch 20 (1851), page 208

Eine Welt Dorf (Photo: Author).

When the sky is creased and the horizon limited: Regimes of visibility

As Beatrice von Mangoldt noted (2013) during a weeklong sojourn at Tropical Islands as a waitress for the TV documentary *7 days … German Tropics*, it is difficult to imagine how people take these tropics as real, given the creases in the sky and the limited horizon on the painted canvas over the South Seas (a large swimming pool). She suggests that a shared reality arises from the needs and desires of all those gathered in the resort (those who come on holiday and those who work), in which chlorine replaces cholera and everything, including the weather, becomes predictable. Tropical Islands is as big as eight football fields and accommodates 6,000 people. Some spend days and weeks here, in a holiday world without disgusting smells, street vendors, mosquitos, and begging children.[1] There is no rain or storm, the temperature is steady, and one can pay (via electronic chips) in euros. This interior world is secure and, for that, one can perhaps forget about not only limited horizons but also the 14,000 tons of steel overhead—they can disappear from perception.

For Rancière, aesthetics is precisely the experience of perception and an intrinsic dimension of knowledge (rather than a theory of the beautiful contrasting or complementing knowledge). Aesthetics derives from *aisthesis*: the appearance of that which shows itself, of itself, and is perceived by feeling. When it suspends the accustomed coordinates of space and time that shape our "specific sensorium" (2005), it is intrinsically political. Rancière believes that the disruptive potential of aesthetic experience can enable different ways of seeing (2006, 2): "Spectacles which disassociate the gaze from the hand and transform the worker into an aesthete" (2006, 9) can disrupt the consensus of an established order. He calls the established order, or the administrative apparatus defining appropriate "ways of being, doing, and saying" (2004, 6), the police. Its opposite is politics, which entails calling into question existing divisions between, for example, common and private, or visible and invisible. Politics happens through disagreement over the "configuration of the sensible," that is, the "visibilities of … places and abilities of the body in those places, … about the very configuration of the visible and the relation of the visible to what can be said about it" (2003a, S5).

Benjamin similarly wagers on disruption against consensus as a way of changing the status quo of a continuous state of emergency (Benjamin, 1940, Suhrkamp Verlag/1969, 257). For him, conflict between what is and is not (or can and cannot be) is the very energy driving renewal (1969a, 320; 1923/1969, 79). In translations, for example, conflict is part of the vital relationship between original and translation. Changed and non-identical, the latter represents and expresses "the central reciprocal relationship between languages" (72) and releases in a different language what remained repressed in the original (1969b, 80). Different languages configure the experience of perception in different ways, because sensory perception (taste, touch, hearing, seeing, smell) relates to symbol systems like language, which configure differently what can be said about the sensible. In aesthetics, similarly, historically specific modes of visibility and intelligibility, not just of art, are established. These modes of visibility are impacted by politics when it creates theatrical spaces for new and disparate things to appear, setting up a stage where previously unrelated things may be connected. Real or metaphorical displacement may shift a community's perception of "the relation between a situation and the forms of visibility and capacities of thought attached to it" (Rancière 2006, 9) so that new objects become visible and thereby available to thinking. When such shifts are reintegrated into a "generally accessible mode of reasoning or form of language," a collective creative reconfiguration of the common world of experience becomes possible (Rancière, 2000a, 116).

Tropical Islands' status with respect to both aesthetics and politics is uncertain. Obviously, there is no connection with high art here, something that applies also to traditional Samoan art. The work of the tufuga (master builders) has, like that of many non-European art forms, long been denied the status of art by Western experts. On the other hand, claims to the status of art are increasingly made in the entertainment industries, for example when the designer of the video game The Mark of Kri asserts that "video games … are pieces of art" (2003). It would be impractical and elitist to rule out the possibility that some phenomena at Tropical Islands may qualify as art. It is likely that they shape a specific sensorium, suspend the ordinary coordinates of space and time, open up new ways of seeing, and reconfigure a common world. Do they, however, lend themselves to politics? Does Tropical Islands afford potential for creative reconfigurations through conflict or disagreement?

According to Rancière, a controversial world can be polemically framed within the given one as long as there is debate about what can or cannot be expressed. Consensus, by contrast, far from simply being an agreement between political or social partners about shared interests, "properly means the dismissal of the 'aesthetics of politics'" (Rancière, 2003b) by suppressing efforts, usually of outsiders, to create "another way of seeing than that which oppresses them" (Rancière, 2006, 3).

The wilderness stays outside: From World Exhibition to Theme Park
Consensus, like politics, is not a given, but produced. During the heyday of imperialism, for instance, states deliberately created internal consensus by appealing to pride in national progress and technological achievements. French national and municipal bodies, for example, gave workers hundreds of thousands of free tickets for World Exhibitions, and French workers' delegations were officially sent to the 1851 London World Exhibition (Benjamin, 1999, 186). To Benjamin, the exhibitions were training schools in which the masses "learned empathy with exchange value. 'Look at everything; touch nothing'" (Benjamin, 1999, 201). Consensus arose when, on arrival, they were enthralled by the phantasmagoria of an interior "universe of commodities" (Benjamin 1999, 8). The commodity performed "as an actor on a phantom stage" (182), with which the visitors empathized. Alienated from themselves and others (Benjamin 1999, 7), they surrendered to and even enjoyed manipulations that affected their perception as much as their thinking, which adjusted reality to the masses and the masses to reality (Benjamin 1969b, 223).

Lost from perception was, then, that the 1851 Crystal Palace's interior, an exhibition of the world in a village (see Kaiser, 2006) for a global public from diverse classes and countries, was less inclusive than might be expected. What was staged in the village were predominantly English and French industrial products—contrasted with performances of the simple "native" life in the colonies. This strategy would be employed ad nauseum at later world exhibitions. Exotic displays, compensating for a widely felt loss of authentic tradition in Europe, played out as a series of spatial tropes (DiPaola 2004,

328–31), which structured the experience of the strange and changed European perceptions of self and other. A trope, of course, is a rhetorical device. From the Greek "a turn," it shifts our perception and the way we make sense of the world. Thus, in the 19th-century German literature of Samoa, a strange exterior space, exotic and abundant nature, morphs into an interior space (a zoological or botanical garden) to be filled with homely elements and commonplace exotic images. In a strange cultural space, childlike, happy, and naive noble savages wait to be civilized. These tropes are overlaid and interlaced by a space of erotic power where fragments of the strange woman blend with fruit and flowers, and the strange colonial territory is appropriated metaphorically through the sexual act between colonizer and native woman.[2] At Tropical Islands Resort, too, the world is brought into a vast interior. Signs like "Welcome to the One-World-Village" and "Peace Camp" make reference to global unity and peace. Exterior and interior morph in the resort's promotion as an "Island of eternal summer" (Allmaier, 2004). Village, islands, or world suggest topographies organized by different thresholds of inside and outside—but all contained by the resort's huge dome: Bali lagoon and South Sea, rain forest, waterfalls, rivers, and spa pools, "several islands plus a sandy beach" (Eames, 2006b). In a strangely familiar strange exterior space, visitors stroll along "1.2 km of jungle pathways … and enjoy cultural shows by 160 performers from the six indigenous areas" (dpa 2004). Which those indigenous areas are, however, remains unclear, and a general multicultural confusion prevails.

In the 2005 show "Call of the South Seas," more than eighty "indigenous" performers further confused the strange cultural space when the all-Samoan troupe purported to represent all Pacific Islands. The scenario was staged by the Samoan Tourism Authority (STA) general manager Lesaisaea Reupena Matafeo, who convinced the organizers that it was unnecessary to involve several smaller groups from different Pacific Islands. Matafeo claimed that the Samoan troupe was able to perform all their dances: "We all know that our island dances differ slightly from each other and we don't look too different from each other" (in Leaupepe, 2005). It is not that the effects of visibility do not matter to the STA: while rather generous on the multicultural side, the organizers ensured that only performers with a history of "good conduct" represented Samoa by asking for "reference letters from their pastors" (Leaupepe, 2005). However, their efforts to control regimes of visibility from a Samoan perspective, namely to have their culture portrayed in accordance with their own values (while excluding other Pacific cultures), was frustrated by the Tropical Islands website designers' creation of a space of erotic power: The video "Holiday and Night" exposes fragments of strange women from a mix of cultures, a topless glimpse included—all to the soundtrack of "Pacific" music. Many Samoan contributors or observers would be dismayed to hear "cultural" shows staged at Tropical Islands described as extravaganzas with "feathery headdresses, spangly bikinis and bottoms like J.Lo" (Eames, 2006b).

Rancière's notion of the "partition of the sensible" (Rancière 2000b, 8) refers to the historically and geographically specific modes of distributing time and space, and of visibility and intelligibility, that prevail in social situations. Aesthetics provides in its image-spaces a degree of freedom from normal conditions and images of the possible. However, as long as particular objects and subjects are missing from the stages of globalized and virtualized theatrical spaces (from 19th-century world exhibitions to contemporary theme parks);

Entrance flanked by X-ray machines (Photo: Author, 2006).

Bali Gate (Photo: Author, 2006).

as long as disagreement cannot take place, the question of whether or not enemies coexist in peace is a mute question. The hangar's membrane not only separates a freezing outside and a balmy inside in winter; it divides and connects two different types of wilderness year-round. That wilderness inside (palms, rain forest, and exotic architectures) is safe. The real wilderness stays outside. Perceptible in the ruined buildings with Russian graffiti along the road—which once housed the administration of the largest military airbase outside the Soviet Union—conflicting histories mark the region surrounding Tropical Islands Resort. They introduced a great deal of third world in the first. Successive and different imperialisms placed the hangar housing the resort, like an alien spaceship, in the territory of what was formerly the largest military airbase outside the Soviet Union. Inside, with hardly anyone noticing, a former German colony makes an appearance; to Germans, Samoa today seems just like any other tropical island—if they can place it at all. The resort itself is located only an hour's drive away from the reestablished German metropolis, Berlin, but it is in many ways light-years and worlds removed. The 1990s economic restructuring following German "reunification" has left the region crippled and, as Europe is restructured within a global context, unemployment in Brandenburg soared to around twenty-one percent. Xenophobia is rampant. In the current order of consensus, foreigners are regularly attacked by neo-Nazis in its surrounds, often at bus or railway stations; meanwhile the resort's employees are trained to welcome visitors with smiles. There is plenty of dissenting politics outside, visible and audible. Consensus prevails inside.

Strangely, on a late mid-winter afternoon in 2006, the entrance area gave precisely the impression of an oversize railway station. As in airports, X-ray machines guarded access to the theme park proper; Rancière's police employed technologies of counting and discounting. Visitors' experiences are monitored and controlled in advance: upon entering, they are equipped with electronic chips on wristbands.

In 2006, it took only minutes to travel around the tropics: from the Balinese Gate, where the Tropical Village begins, to the Bali Pavilion, the Borneo Longhouse, the Thai House, the Samoan fale, and from there to African and Amazon huts. Then and now, two stages provide near-constant entertainment and glimpses of exotic worlds, featuring, for example, Pacific, Brazilian, Cuban, and Caribbean shows. Only glimpses though: What was invisible to the sun-searching Germans the performers entertained during the show "Call of the South Seas" was that the Samoans were freezing in a climate they were neither accustomed to nor properly equipped for. Working exceedingly long hours, unable to leave the compound or their hotel, they eventually did not even earn enough to travel in Germany. All that the visitors could see in the resort's image space were projections of their own desires. Samoan visibility faded even more after the performers' contract ended. The intelligibility of the fragments of their show in the website's video has since diminished even further, and so has that of the fale.

While the fale's physical presence remains, the way in which it is staged obscures its historical and geopolitical context. On the website, it is described as a "typical Polynesian straw hut," "a sort of community house for several villages." "It is particularly large and each of the 28 beautifully carved wooden posts represents one of the participating extended families" (Tropical Island Management GmbH 2005a). The reference to harmonious community life is as unmistakable as the nostalgic flavor in the description of the Tropical Village's architecture: it was "built with authentic houses from 6 tropical regions of the world. They were constructed on site at Tropical Islands by craftsmen from their respective home countries" (2005c). Claims to authenticity are often paired with representational realism.[3] Similarly, bad translations often adhere to excessive accuracy. However, as Benjamin remarks, a translation must not try to resemble the original; it must instead "incorporate the original's mode of signification, thus making both the original and the translation recognizable as fragments of a greater language." (Benjamin, 1923/1969, 78). To preserve the state in which a translator's language happens to be is a principal mistake (Pannwitz quoted in Benjamin, 1923/1969, 81), for the potential that lies between the lines of the original text cannot be recognized when reverence for one's own language and culture is greater than that for the "spirit of the foreign," or when the desire to control and contain is greater that the willingness to abandon oneself to the other (82). "Allowing his language to be powerfully affected by the foreign tongue," a translator must "expand and deepen his language by means of the foreign language" (81).

While realism suggests correspondence with the world, certainty of representation relies on the "difference in time and displacement in space" that separate "the representation from the real thing" (Mitchell, 2002, 501). This distance is preserved in the distance an exhibition places between observer and object. The logic of consensus, of a global community in which, "unfortunately, some groups or individuals still stay behind or accidentally fall astray, as traditional forms of social bonding tend to loosen or vanish" (Rancière, 2005), is likely to reinforce the division between what counts as in and what as out. The outsiders, nevertheless, are then drawn into the production of phantasmagoric appearances of cultural reality, which both extend and numb the senses through technical manipulation (Buck-Morss, 1992, 22). Objects and performances are "real enough" at Tropical Islands, but their setting-into-scene requires enormous logistics of construction, engineering, transport, environmental and operational control, media presence, and finance. To let viewers forget about the background of the display, to make a narcotic out of reality itself,[4] labor occurs backstage, as it were, while the performance appears joyful. Thus, the audience (seated for dinner along the South Sea's sandy beach) watches the evening show on the island across the water, while technicians, cooks, and cleaners discreetly serve in the shadows.

Ultimately, simulated encounters with the exotic, and the fascination with commodified leisure or experience, are likely to disappoint. Rancière notes that, for Benjamin, "the arcade of outdated commodities holds the promise of the future" only if it is closed, "made unavailable, in order that the promise may be kept" (2002). A world of total visibility leaves no room for appearance to occur, to "produce its divisive, fragmenting effects" (Rancière 1999, 104). When everything is on display and up for grabs, a visitor is "called on to live out all his fantasies in a world of total exhibition," in which everything seems possible but ultimately doomed to disappoint (120). There is a price to be paid for bringing the distant too close without a willing to go beyond ourselves (Taussig, 1992, 23ff). Productive distance is obliterated, and the conflict between what can and cannot be said suppressed.

Yet, Tropical Islands is not all about consensus, even though disagreement usually takes place offstage, out of sight. Thus,

some of the carefully selected Samoan performers had to be recalled home following "constant disorderly and drunken behaviour" (Sio, 2005). On the one hand, this behavior might have been induced by the "24/7 of fun" environment at the resort (Tropical Island Management GmbH 2005b); on the other hand, by their living and working conditions.[5] Turned into objects of European fantasies, some Samoan performers may have preferred to clearly disagree, at the price of their disappearance.

When can disagreement take place? Taking a turn.
Tropes, turns, travels … what they share are changing vistas and aspects, which will always be perceived in different ways. Travel in Tropical Islands is not really to travel around the world. Not all who have come here coexist in peace, but neither are they enemies. There is no apparent consensus about a common world, but neither is there obvious disagreement. If experiences are the "sensible configuration of [a] lived common wor[l]d" (2003a, S4), then the common world seems out of joint here. Disputes about what one sees and feels, "how it can be told and discussed, who is able to name it and argue about it" (S4), could lead to a common reconfiguration of the sensible but do not take place. Insofar as the Tropical Village, the Samoan fale, and the show "Call of the South Seas" are translations of a foreign original into a local idiom, they could express what remains repressed in Samoan contexts. However, the resorts prevailing configurations tend to obscure the common world rather than make it visible.

Rancière's perspective is distinctively philosophical and, to an extent, Eurocentric. It cannot account for "cases of intercultural différend, for which there would never be a common scene of interlocution" (2004, 81), and translation cannot even begin. In such situations, those not counted (remaining invisible and inaudible) not only have to accept the discursive norms of the "virtual community" they are confronting and explain themselves by them. They must also divide the sensible according to rules or laws that are alien to them (87). Disagreement seems impossible, almost by definition, with an exotic Other whom one loves to briefly visit and look at, but with whom one does not want to be lastingly involved (Beuchelt, 1987, 100).

Further, we tend to assume that everyone wants to be part of our community of disagreement. What if some prefer not to? When discussing Tropical Islands resort in Samoa, I sometimes had a distinct sense of withdrawal: rather than disagreeing with Tropical Islands management's handling of contracts or the use of the fale, two interviewees (from quite different positions within a range of opinions) placed responsibility with the resort's management but preferred not to elaborate. On the other hand, Colin Au, who believed Tropical Islands would be successful because he knew how Germans tick, sought little involvement with locals of the Brandenburg region to understand its context. Many Germans hunger for the tropical sun, but they may not care about cultural specifics and are likely to be less interested in authenticity than Au believed. Visitors' interest in exotic cultures, beyond fleeting allusion, was not strong enough to sustain the resort as a viable business venture. At the end of 2006, Tropical Islands was restructured. While the notion of the world in a village was maintained, the village and the fale are diminished next to the children's fun park and now look like an assembly of props. The restructuring was evidently based on a better understanding of the target market and predictably led to an environment that would be familiar

Samoan fale (Photo: Sylvia Henrich, 2007).

Samoan fale in the Tropical Village (Photo: Author 2007).

to many Germans from saunas on the outskirts of cities: factory halls filled with plasterboard and pathetic trompe l'oeil—as well as tons of hygienic tiles. While people have always participated at Tropical Islands to different degrees and in different roles, there are now only few foreign "villagers" with whom visitors could agree or disagree. One Samoan, who stayed in Germany because he fell in love and still works as a barkeeper at Tropical Islands, clearly recognizes how his appearance contributes to an impression of authenticity, just like the palms. However, at least in front of a camera, he shows no disagreement (in von Mangoldt and Gromes, 2013).

Not surprisingly, Rancière and Benjamin were also interested in theater and the stage, given their interest in art and politics, perception and language, and the potential of ruptures and conflict to open spaces of visibility. Rancière even defined politics as a theatrical performance involving the gap, the difference between places where a demos exists and those where it doesn't.

> Politics consists in playing or acting out this relationship, which means first setting it up as theatre, inventing the argument, in the double logical and dramatic sense of the term, connecting the unconnected (Rancière, 1999, 88).

Similarly, Benjamin conjures the appearance of fleeing actors in the final scene. Brought to a standstill by the realization of their appearance on stage, they enter into "the visual field of nonparticipating and truly impartial persons," which "allows the harassed to draw breath, bathes them in new air." Correspondingly, claims Benjamin, there must be "a place, a light, a footlight glare, in which our flight through life may be likewise sheltered in the presence of onlooking strangers" (1934/1986, 91). Because they never wholly identify with spectacle, onlookers can actively and knowingly engage with it, drawing on their own experiences from a critical distance (Hallward 2006, §13). The stage and its power at Tropical Islands resort are very different at the moment. Closeness and distance, degrees of engagement and reflection, would be important ingredients in the creation of conditions under which disagreement becomes possible and the partition of the sensible might change.

References

Allmaier, M. *Palmen fürs Volk*. Retrieved 12 May 2006 from http://zeus.zeit.de/text/2004/52/Tropical_Island.

Benjamin, W. "One-Way-Street." Translated by E. Jephcott. In *Walter Benjamin: Reflections. Essays, Aphorisms, Autobiographical Writings*, edited by P. Demetz, 61–96 (New York: Schocken Books, 1934/1986).

Benjamin, W. "The Task of the Translator." In *Illuminations*, edited by H. Arendt, 69–82. New York: Schocken (original work published 1923, 1969).

Benjamin, W. "Theses on the Philosophy of History." In *Illuminations*, edited by H. Arendt, 253–64. New York: Schocken Books (original work published 1940, Suhrkamp Verlag, 1969).

Benjamin, W. "The Work of Art in the Age of Mechanical Reproduction." In *Illuminations*, edited by H. Arendt, 217–51 (New York: Schocken, 1969b).

Beuchelt, E. "Zur Rezeption der Völkerausstellungen um 1900." In *Exotische Welten. Europäische Phantasien*, edited by H. Pollig, S. Schlichtenmayer, and G. Baur-Burkarth, 98–105. (Stuttgart: Institut für Auslandsbeziehungen and Württembergischer Kunstverein, 1987).

Buck-Morss, S. "Aesthetics and Anaesthetics: Walter Benjamin's Artwork Essay Reconsidered." *October*, 62 (Autumn, 1992): 3–41.

Connolly, K. "Germans Get Taste of Tropics an Hour's Drive from Berlin" (2004). http://travelvideo.tv/news/more.php?id=A3758_0_1_0_M.

Déotte, J.-L. "The Differences between Rancière's *Mésentente* (Political

Disagreement) and Lyotard's *Différend*." SubStance: *A Review of Theory and Literary Criticism* 33(1) (2004): 77–90.

DiPaola, K. *Samoa— ‚Perle' der deutschen Kolonien? ‚Bilder' des exotischen Anderen in Geschichte(n) des 20. Jahrhunderts* (doctor of philosophy) (University of Maryland, College Park, 2004). https://drum.umd.edu/dspace/handle/1903/241.

dpa. "World's Largest Indoor Rainforest Gets the Nod" (2004). Retrieved 3 March 2006 from http://www.skyscrapercity.com/showthread.php?t=88305.

Eames, A. "Welcome to Germany's Pleasure Dome" (2006). Retrieved 6 September 2006 from http://travel.timesonline.co.uk/article/0,,10290-2187529,00.html.

Goldmann, S. "Zur Rezeption der Völkerausstellungen um 1900." In *Exotische Welten: Europäische Phantasien*, edited by H. Pollig, S. Schlichtenmayer, and G. Baur-Burkarth, 88–93 (Stuttgart: Institut für Auslandsbeziehungen and Württembergischer Kunstverein, 1987).

Hallward, P. "Staging Equality: On Rancière's Theatrocracy." *New Left Review* 37 (January–February, 2006): 109–29.

Hendry, J. *The Orient Strikes Back: A Global View of Cultural Display* (Oxford: Berg, 2000).

Kaiser, W. *World Exhibition 1851: The Rat-Race for Progress* (2006). Retrieved 12 December 2013 from http://zis.uibk.ac.at/quellen/weltausstellungen/Kaiser_punch.html.

Leaupepe, J.N. "Dancing All the Way to Germany" (19 February, 2005). Retrieved 2 May 2006 from http://www.samoaobserver.ws/news/local/ln0205/1905ln007.htm.

The Mark of Kri on Playstation 2—Long Read. (2003, August 2004). Retrieved 5 September 2004 from http://www.aocafe.com/forums/viewtopic.

Mitchell, W.J.T. "Orientalism and the Exhibitionary Order." In *The Visual Culture Reader*, edited by N. Mirzoeff, 495–505 (London: Routledge, 2002).

Rancière, J. *Disagreement. Politics and Philosophy*. Translated by J. Rose (Minneapolis: University of Minnesota Press, 1999).

Rancière, J. "Dissenting Words: A Conversation with Jacques Rancière." *Diacritics* 30(2) (2000a), 113–26.

Rancière, J. "Literature, Politics, Aesthetics: Approaches to Democratic Disagreement." Interview with Solange Guénoun and James H. Kavanagh. *SubStance* 29(2) (2000b), 3–24.

Rancière, J. "The Aesthetic Revolution and Its Outcomes: Emplotments of Autonomy and Heteronomy." *New Left Review* 14 (March–April, 2002).

Rancière, J. *The Politics of Aesthetics* (2003b). Retrieved 13 December 2005 from http://theater.kein.org/node/99.

Rancière, J. "Introducing Disagreement." *Angelaki: Journal of the Theoretical Humanities* 9(3 December, 2004): 3–9.

Rancière, J. "Statement on the Occasion of the Panel Discussion: "Artists and Cultural Producers as Political Subjects. Opposition, Intervention, Participation, Emancipation in Times of Neo-liberal Globalisation." *Klartext*. Symposium conducted at the meeting "Der Status des Politischen in Aktueller Kunst und Kultur," (Künstlerhaus Bethanien und Volksbühne am Rosa-Luxemburg-Platz, Berlin, 2005). Retrieved from http://www.klartext-konferenz.net/teiln_30.html.

Rancière, J. "Thinking between Disciplines: An Aesthetics of knowledge." *Parrhesia* 1 (2006): 1–12.

Schlehe, J. "Themenparks: Globale Kulturrepräsentation, Nation Building oder Freizeitvergnügen?" In *Blick nach vorn: Festgabe für Gerd Spittler,* edited by K. Beck, T. Förster, and H. P. Hahn, 298–310 (Köln: Rüdiger Koppe, 2004).

Sio, M. "2 Dancers Being Sent Home from Germany (25 May, 2005). Retrieved 13 May 2006 from http://www.samoaobserver.ws/news/local/ln0505/2505ln004.htm.

Steffen-Schrade, J. "Exkurs: Samoaner im Frankfurter Zoo [Tropical Islands]." In *Talofa! Samoa, Südsee—Ansichten und Einsichten,* edited by G. Kroeber-Wolf and P. Mesenhöller, 368–87 (Frankfurt: Museum für Völkerkunde, 1998).

Taussig, M. "Physiognomic Aspects of Visual Worlds." *Visual Anthropology Review* 8(1) (1992): 15–28.

Tropical Island Management GmbH. "Samoa Fale: Open Houses for Living in the South Seas" (2005a). Retrieved 12 November 2005 from http://www.my-tropical-islands.com/village/samoa-fale-e.htm.

Tropical Island Management GmbH. "The Tropical Village" (2005c) Retrieved 12 November 2005 from http://www.my-tropical-islands.com/village/index-e.htm.

von Mangoldt, B., and Gromes, S. 7 Tage … *deutsche Tropen* (2013) Germany. Retrieved from http://www.n-joy.de/leben/siebentage1149.ebentage1149.html.

Notes

[1] CEO Jan Janssen told the German news magazine *Tagesthemen* on March 22, 2015, that each time there are warnings of natural or social catastrophes, visitor numbers immediately go up.

[2] These tropes (described by DiPaola for German literature of the time) appear, for instance, at the 1896 Samoan Show at the *Zoologischer* Garten in Frankfurt (see Steffen-Schrade, 1998) and survive into current tourism marketing. 19th century zoological gardens were, along with dioramas and panoptica, preferred venues for the exhibition of exotic natives. Their performances, choreographed with elaborate dramaturgic effects, were inserted into exotic dreamscapes, and the zoos' architectures increasingly alluded to the animals' places of origin, for instance in Berlin during the 1870s.

[3] Excessive realism in representation, and the will to control and contain, characterised the Egyptian exhibit at the 1869 Paris world exhibition. A street made to resemble Cairo, it was painfully rendered in medieval decay and chaos, with even the façades made dirty. The streets were crowded, not only with make-believe Orientals, but fifty imported Egyptian donkeys. The mosque, like the whole street, was built as a façade. "As for the interior, it had been set up as a coffee house, where Egyptian girls performed dances with young males, and dervishes whirled" (Muhammad Amin Fikri in 1892, quoted in Mitchell, 2002: 497). Benjamin noted that during the 1867 Paris World Exhibition, "the 'oriental quarter' was the center of attraction" (see Benjamin, 2002: 189-90).

[4] They may have suffered a similar degradation to that of the Egyptians in Paris, 1869, which "seemed as necessary to these spectacles as the scaffolded facades or the curious crowds of onlookers. The facades, the onlookers, and the degradation seemed all to belong to the organizing of an exhibit, to a particularly European concern with rendering the world up to be viewed" (Mitchell, 2002: 497).

[5] Translation slightly altered.

TERUNOBU FUJIMORI

TERUNOBU FUJIMORI MASTER OF THE TEAHOUSE

Izumi Kuroishi

The architectural historian Terunobu Fujimori has presented unique readings of modern architectural history in Japan and suggested alternative readings and interpretations of the city. Since the 1980s, he has organized an urban survey group called the Street Observation Society, which discovers odd objects and their ephemeral conditions that suggest more site-specific urban context and unconsciously formulated everyday space. Since the 1990s, he has designed more than twenty projects, of which his teahouses are particularly appreciated in Japan and recognized worldwide.

Jin Chokan Moriya Historical Museum

In Nagano, the Jin Chokan Moriya Historical Museum is Fujimori's first major work. He admits that he first tried to find another architect for the building's client, but when he realized that no one would have a better understanding of or a closer connection to the project's local ethnography and geography, he hesitantly agreed to do the work himself, despite his lack of design experience. As he presumed, the general critique of this project was at first rather severe, but after finishing several projects, including his own house and houses for friends, his design skills were in full swing.

The Jin Chokan Moriya Historical Museum commemorates the history of the Moriya family, priests of Suwa Great Shrine, one of Japan's oldest shrines that involved worshipping a deity from the Stone Age. Located under the Mishaguchi shrine and taking the flow of the mystic chi by standing between the mountain and the everyday world, the building appears to have grown from the soil.

Fujimori consciously avoided imitating traditional domestic buildings for the museum's design. Instead, he was inspired by the description of mud houses as being the origin of architecture from the Mongolian plateau by the Japanese architect Takamasa Yoshizaka, one of Le Corbusier's pupils. The museum's exterior wooden-shingle wall has turned black with mold, and the roof is covered with platy andesite. It has no symbolic elements of Shinto architecture and is also different from the typical history museum exhibiting paintings and documents. Fujimori revived the ancient ritual of the Suwa Shrine based on historical texts and displayed it on the main wall as is. The interior wall is covered with earth-colored stucco, whose short pieces of straw express a tactile materiality in the space. Since his grandfather was a master carpenter, Fujimori was familiar with construction sites from an early age. He intuitively knows that a building is a direct representation of a locality and is associated with its community and the formation that community's identity. In his *What Is Architecture? (Kenchiku to wa nanika,* 2011), Fujimori explains that he follows two rules in his design practice: First, don't imitate anyone's buildings, no matter the period, whether historical or contemporary, or the architectural style; and second, use natural materials or plants to harmonize the buildings with nature. Within these rules, Fujimori expresses his free spirit in creating buildings using traditional materials and technologies in harmony with the local landscape.

Teahouse Tetsu

Located in Kiyoharu Art Village, Teahouse Tetsu is one of the Fujimori's freestanding teahouses. Kiyoharu, built on the site of a former elementary school in the mountain area of Nagano prefecture, is the realization of a dream of the Shirakaba-ha artists. Its founder, Chozo Yoshimi, who is one of Japan's most well-known art dealers and well acquainted with Shirakaba-

Izumi Kuroishi is a professor at Aoyama Gakuin University in Tokyo. She studied at Tokyo University and received her Ph.D. in architectural theory from the University of Pennsylvania. Kuroishi conducted cross-cultural workshops on social spaces in Japan and abroad and has curated the exhibitions "Kon Wajiro Retrospective" in Japan, "Design and Disaster" at Parsons in New York, and "Sea, Mountain and Family," about everyday culture, photographs, and community, in Tokyo after the 2011 tsunami. Her recent book is *Constructing the Colonized Land: Entwined Perspectives in the East Asia during World War II.* She was a visiting research fellow of the Canadian Centre for Architecture in 2015.

Photographs by Akihisa Masuda, except Jinchokan Moriya Historical Museum and Beetle's House, courtesy of Atelier Fujimori.

ha artists, asked Fujimori to design the teahouse as an art object. The teahouse stands as a "one leg scarecrow" beside a fragment of Eiffel Tower and museums by Tadao Ando and Yoshio Taniguchi.

To enter the teahouse, one has to ascend a tree trunk to a platform and then climb a ladder to a small entrance strung with gold. The structure shakes along with the movement of the visitor, as the building is an extension of the tree—or, as Fujimori puts it, the "space [is] nestled in the ribs coming out of the spine." The teahouse is the same height as the surrounding cherry blossoms in spring, offering visitors a feeling of oneness with nature. Noh player Hideo Kanze described it as "a space to return [to] oneself by unifying with nature away from the emotional distress in this world and [one's] disabled body," suggesting that it represents the essential spirit of the tea ceremony as well as the utopian idea of Shirakaba-ha.

The teahouse is only 2.5 square meters wide, but it feels unexpectedly spacious, thanks to its conical shape and wide corner window. The roof's hand-rolled copper plate, the handblown window glass, a window opening assembled only by inserting sticks, a small furnace placed casually, and the grass-mat floor covering are among the building's rustic handmade details. The handmade glass of the windows provides a distorted view of the outside, representing Fujimori's resistance to the popular contemporary notion of transparency realized through mechanical technology. The teahouse's peaceful and intimate atmosphere is more like that of a children's tree house than a formal conventional teahouse—showing Fujimori's interest in aligning Teahouse Tetsu with the origin of a primitive hut.

The unique idea of Fujimori's teahouses
The Japanese teahouse is a place for meditation, intimate conversation, and appreciating the highly sophisticated aesthetics of objects. Symbolic and philosophical meanings are often implied in the detail, arrangement, materials, and size of the space; the way various materials are used in the design demand visitors to have intellectual ability and knowledge of manners of bodily movement. In studies of Japanese architecture, tea master Senno Rikyu's So-an (glass cottage) style has been recognized as having the most highly elaborate architectural representation, with a sensitive and naturalistic philosophy of Zen, even though Rikyu himself kept challenging and deconstructing tradition. Fujimori examined Japanese teahouses' construction and social context, the psychological and sensory aspects of their design, and their intended spatial use. Additionally, he studied the functions of teahouse in each period of history, including the lost meanings and arbitrary nature of their design. Then, with the Teahouse Tetsu, Fujimori threw (ucchari) teahouse theories overboard. He criticized, relativized, and rearranged the rules, aesthetics, and meanings of teahouse design and replaced them with his idea of the origin of architecture.

Fujimori's works and words are favorites of the public, who appreciate his buildings' sensuous and spontaneous aspects. Two recent teahouses, Takasugi-an, or Too-Tall Cottage (Nagano, 2004), standing in his parents' farmland near the Jin Chokan Moriya Historical Museum, and Soratobu Dorobune, or Flying Mud Boat (Nagano, 2010), pique people's curiosity, with their unusual shapes and settings. As later Irikawa-tei (Taiwan, 2010) stands on five bamboo trees, Takasugi-an stands on two very tall and thin tree trunks, its ephemeral construction an

extreme expression of instability. It sways with the wind and the movement of its visitors, whose sense of fear may be sharpened along with their sense of liberation from the earth. Fujimori said in an interview, "Finally, I am able to do whatever I want," which makes one wonder whether he had wished to design such buildings from the beginning. The Flying Mud Boat, which hangs by cables from four poles and has a cocoon shape, especially appeals to our sympathies and playful imaginations.

Fujimori's projects are constructed with the help of volunteers, including students and locals, which brings an aspect of familiarity to visitors and viewers. Starting with the Jin Chokan Moriya Historical Museum, many of his designs have been finished with the assistance of Jomon Architectural Team, a group consisting of his students and friends. He does not attempt to hide the roughness in the molding or in the ornamental details but instead exposes the design framework and the arbitrariness of the natural materials. The Chocolate House is a teahouse that protrudes from the main residence. Entirely covered with hand-rolled copper plate and reached by a staircase from a tall, open space, the teahouse looks like a fortress from the outside. But its interior is human-scale and covered in smooth stucco with decorations of grilled twigs. The simple crafting and playful construction by Jomon Architectural Team add a homey, tactile impression to the house as a shelter. On the other hand, the Beetle House (London, 2010), constructed in the Gallery of Medieval and Renaissance at the Victoria and Albert Museum in London as part of the exhibit "1:1—Architects Build Small Spaces," was created with the help of volunteers from the Royal College of Art's Architecture and Sculpture Departments. The house has four legs and is clad in black-charred pine beams, which Fujimori adapts from traditional wooden building's technique to extend the building's lifespan. He said in an interview that his design methods are to use natural material and to integrate real grasses and trees, and that his main theme is to return the act of living to the primitive state before civilization. For his English version of the Japanese teahouse, he researched ancient structures in the UK, such as those from the Stone Age, and tried to create a small, secluded space with a fire.

The ultimate smallness of his teahouses is based on the idea of Rikyu's Joan in Kyoto, but expresses different sense of *sabi* (solitariness) as in the Ichiya-tei (One Night Teahouse). Designed for former prime minister Morihiro Hosokawa's house, it is constructed on a small hill in the garden of the house. Reached by small stairs. It shows a humoristic and warm distance from the everyday life.

Fujimori's works unify avant-garde and primitive ideas of architecture and challenge our conventional understanding of architecture based on the ideas of function, beauty, and strength. At the same time, in his design and construction, Fujimori keeps questioning the meaning of architecture in its most basic sense of materiality, physical sensation, and means of manufacturing a building as a place of playful and joyous experience.

Jinchokan Moriya Historical Museum, Chino-city, Nagano (1991).

Ichiya-an (One Night Teahouse), Ashihara-shimo-gun, Kanagawa (2003).

Exterior and interior view of Chocolate House, Kokubunji-city, Tokyo (2009).

Interior and exterior view of Beetle's House, London, UK (2010).

Interior and exterior view of Irisen-Tei, Hsinchu, Taiwan (2010).

Interior and exterior view of Soratobu Dorobune (Flying Mudboat),
Chino-city, Nagano (2010).

Interior and exterior view of Takasugi-tei (Too Tall House), Chino-city, Nagano (2004).

Interior and exterior view of Chashistu tetsu, Kitamori City, Yamanashi (2005).

Hayman Island House (Photo: Anthony Browell).

KERRY
HILL

AN EQUAL MUSIC

THE ARCHITECTURE OF KERRY HILL

Philip Goad

Philip Goad is Chair of Architecture and Redmond Barry Distinguished Professor in the Melbourne School of Design at the University of Melbourne, where he teaches design and architectural history. He is the author of *New Directions in Australian Architecture* (2001), co-author of *New Directions in Tropical Asian Architecture* (2005), and co-editor of *The Encyclopedia of Australian Architecture* (2012). He has lectured on contemporary Australian architecture in London, Beijing, Bogota, Dhaka, Kuala Lumpur, and Mexico City, and has been published in *A+U* (Japan), *Architecture Australia*, *Architectural Record* (USA), *Baumeister* (Germany), *Casabella* (Italy), *Monument* (Australia), and *World Architecture* (UK). In 2014, he was co-curator of the exhibit, "Augmented Australia, 1914-2014" at the Australian Pavilion at the Venice International Architecture Biennale.

To know a building by Kerry Hill is to experience a carefully orchestrated sequence of spatial moments. Collectively, these moments—and there are many—some fleeting, some extended like the passage of a long corridor, amount to a gradual transformation of mood. You become sensitized. You become calm. It's not too pompous even to suggest that the experience is transcendent. This is a bold claim but the evidence resides in the work itself—work that is spread across diverse continents, cities and landscapes. There are few architects today whose buildings, at the same time, speak so eloquently of their place. Hill has no qualms about looking directly at local materials, forms and construction practices for his language. The poetry of his making speaks across cultures, not in any way demanding a hegemonic reading but instead allowing visitors to slow down, to pace themselves to what Vikram Seth described in his romantic novel of eponymous title as "an equal music."[1] This is a term, which I have purloined and applied to the point at where the haptic and optic in architecture coalesce.

It would be hard to identify another Western architect who has practised for more than forty years in an Asian setting and achieved the same level of reconciliation of spatial and material cultures and still adhered to precepts of the modern. One thinks of architects like Antonin Raymond whose practice and work spanned across Japan, India, and the United States or Joseph Allen Stein who practised and worked in California and India.[2] Both these architects were modest and deeply respectful of the cultures in which they found themselves. But they also recognized the inherent modernity of traditional architectures and deployed, to their advantage, what might be described as the classical tendencies of either a timeless vernacular or a pedigreed architecture of pedigreed patronage for ultimately rational ends. It is no surprise therefore to learn of Kerry Hill's respect and influence for what might be described as the "wholeness" of Balinese and Japanese culture and their respective architectural traditions where refined craft is intrinsic not just to utility but symbolizes an elevated intellectual plane.[3] It is also no surprise that the influence of Louis Kahn and Mies van der Rohe are invoked and that Hill's exquisite plans begin life as hand-drawn abstract shapes in blue pencil.[4] His practice continues to hold dear the connection between mind, eye, and hand. As in most works of music, someone has to string the notes together. Hill is not ready to abdicate intention.

With the exception of Armitage Hill in Sri Lanka, a place of personal preoccupation for Kerry Hill since 1992, the collection of work featured in this volume dates from the last ten years of his largely Singapore-based practice.[5] The buildings are located in Singapore, India, Bhutan, Thailand, Jordan, and Hill's native Australia. They include hotels, houses, and a theater: places of dwelling and public gathering. They are also places that become at certain times, sites of intense individual reflection. It's revealing then to consider the hotel, a building type with which Kerry Hill has had a long and venerable association since his early blooding with the type at the Bali Hyatt for Palmer and Turner in 1972.[6] Unlike the bucolic informality of the tropical hotels of Geoffrey Bawa and Peter Muller, two architects whom Hill counts as friends and mentors, Hill's hotels translate the concept of resort into the utopian setting of the Cistercian or Buddhist monastery. Each of those monastic communities contains a series of buildings where the movement through courtyards of different size, serial repetition whether via column, window, or doorway, serial passage along colonnade and cloister, and embracing protective roofs all combine to offer places for public ritual or private prayer. In the case of the hotel, it is public and private escape from an external sensory maelstrom. Hill subverts the idea of the brash bustling international hotel for the transcendent experience of individual contemplation. Thus at The Chedi in Chiang Mai, the guestroom corridor has an ascetic quiet made lyrical by dappled shade. At Amankora Paro in Bhutan, vernacular farmhouses become habitable temples. At ITC Sonar Bangla, the center is not a cloister but a spreading bagh (water garden): the palace and monastery merge. At the Aman in New Delhi, residential slabs become mute, defining walls, elegant bastions against the noise of the city beyond.

For Hill, the house also becomes another community of buildings: a monastery, temple, or palace but in miniature. The living room of the Ogilvie House is an open pavilion framed by two "walls" with the ocean resplendent as a framed view. At Hayman Island, the dining terrace is a double height, stretched bale, monumental in the greater landscape but intimate from within a guest bedroom. These are pleasure pavilions certainly, but they also convey a pervasive, almost aristocratic sense of eremitic tranquility. Even in the high-rise block of Martin No. 38 in Singapore, the one-bedroom apartments of the low-rise towers have a treasured separateness from the elevated public landscape of gymnasium and pool. The exception in this collection is the State Theatre Centre in Perth. However, here the complex becomes a secular temple to the senses. The ceiling of the main foyer is hung with a forest of golden metal tubes, a chorus of sheer visual delight before hushed silence is demanded in the auditorium's timber-lined drum in readiness for performance by others. Materiality is deployed here like the episodic progression of a symphony. The complex at Armitage Hill is a combination of all three: house, hotel (or rather a place for receiving guests), and theater (or rather a landscape for the rituals of relaxation). This is Hill's version of Bawa's Lunuganga[7] but a place where the orchestration of new buildings and new terraced landscapes is like an ongoing and unfolding dream.

In each of these buildings, Kerry Hill has refined his notational elements and from this tectonic language, three elements stand out. The filigreed screen crosses cultures as a veil to ensure modesty and privacy, a mechanism to see and not be seen, a light diffuser, a ventilating grille, an ornamental device—the jali of Mughal princes—and a moderator of climate. Water becomes a new ground plane of reflection, a garden where the earth is see-through, a perfect bath to cleanse the body, a cooling device to take advantage of any zephyr of breeze, and if moving, creating an aural shift in key, defining ambience. Walls, always orthogonal, speak of the place: rammed earth in Bhutan; terra cotta in Kolkata; Gangapur sandstone in New Delhi; local Jordanian stone in Dibeen. Connecting these elements—screen, water, and wall—in an ever-changing hymn is the diurnal passing of shadows. Kerry Hill's buildings make physical a contemporary reading of Junichiro Tanizaki's In Praise of Shadows where the subtle gradation of darkness illuminating the texture of wood grain or the lustre of gold leaf is played off against the brightness of light.[8] Like Tanizaki's masterwork, Hill's architecture is an ode to the act of not forgetting the shadows of time and tradition while still embracing the light of modernity. To each, Hill plays an equal music.

The Architecture and Design of Antonin and Noemi Raymond (New York: Princeton Architectural Press, 2006). Stephen White, Building in the Garden: The Architecture of Joseph Allen Stein in India and California (Delhi, New York: Oxford University Press, 1993).
[3] Geoffrey London, "The Nature of a Practice," in Oscar Riera Ojeda (ed.), Kerry Hill: Crafting Modernism (London: Thames and Hudson, 2013), 20-24.
[4] London, "The Nature of a Practice", 17.
[5] Kerry Hill has two offices, one in Singapore, the other in Fremantle in Western Australia.
[6] Philip Goad and Patrick Bingham-Hall, Architecture Bali: Architectures of Welcome (Balmain, NSW: Pesaro Publishing, 2000), 18.
[7] Geoffrey Bawa's estate at Lunuganga was the Sri Lankan architect's country home from 1946. He added and altered buildings and landscapes on the property until his death in 1998. See Geoffrey Bawa, Christoph Bon, and Dominic Sansoni, Lunuganga (Singapore: Times Editions, 1990).
[8] Junichiro Tanizaki, In Praise of Shadows (1933) was first translated into English by Thomas J Harper and Edward Seidensticker in 1977 and published by Leete's Island Books.

Notes

[1] Vikram Seth, An Equal Music (London: Orion, 1999).
[2] Kurt G.F. Helfrich and William Whitaker (eds.), Crafting a Modern World:

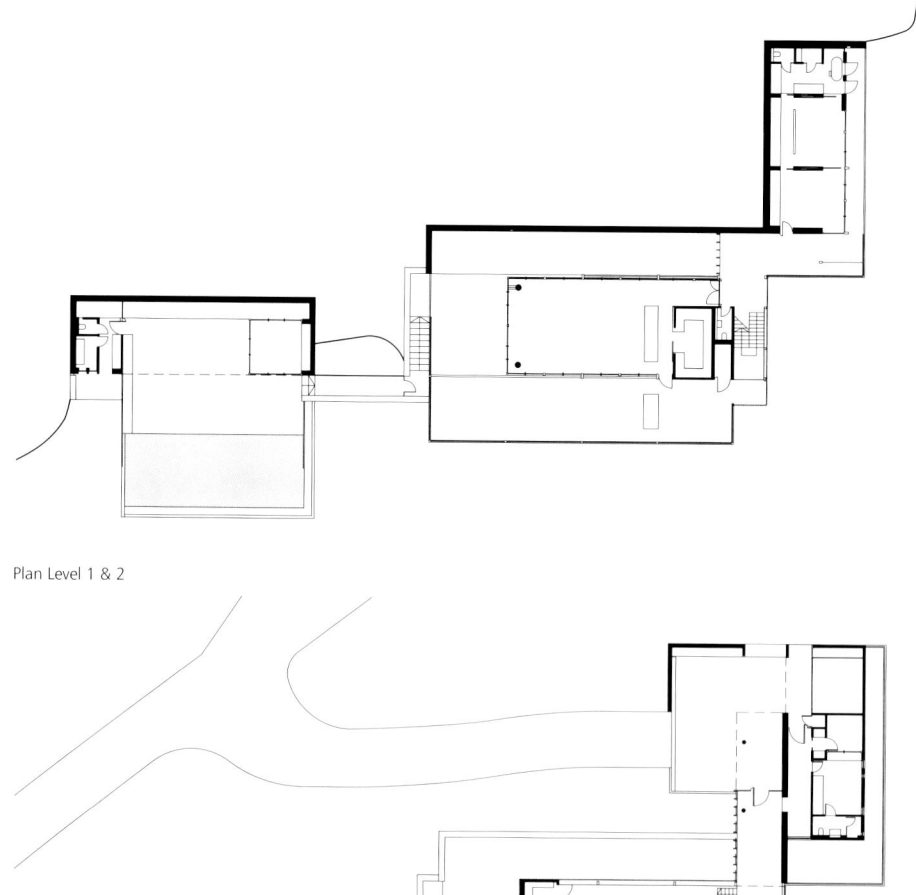

Plan Level 1 & 2

Plan Level 3

Hayman Island House
Hayman Island, QLD, Australia, 2011

Hayman is one of seventy-four Whitsunday Islands situated in the northeast coast of Queensland, Australia, beside the Great Barrier Reef. Perched on the hillside of this island are eight exclusive residences known as the Hayman Island House, each on a 4,000 sq. m. (43,056 sq. ft.) plot, consisting of a four-bedroom house with a private pool ranging from 8,000 to 11,000 sq. ft. The layout of the house is flexible so the homeowners can customise their place. They can add rooms or enlarge others according their lifestyle needs. During the whale season from July to September, the residents will have an optimum view of the Pacific Ocean and can witness the annual migration of the whales and their calves as they pass through the Whitsunday Islands.

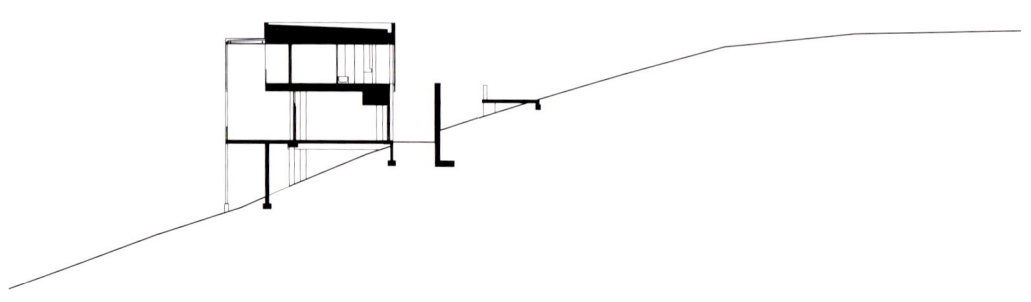

Photo: Dean Adams

Section

Elevation

Photo: Angus Martin

Photo: Anthony Browell

ITC Sonar Bangla Hotel
Kolkata, West Bengal, India, 2003

The ITC Sonar Bangla Hotel in Kolkata exemplifies the city's blend of the modern and the traditional. It is an original interpretation of the deltaic landscape of Bengal. By integrating an existing waterbody into the public areas and hotel guest rooms of the hotel, Hill brings about the aquatic, flood-prone impression of the region. Due to the hot-humid climate, Bengal engages the use of perforated pavilions and open-to-sky courtyards, which have been incorporated within the design of this complex in a vernacular-minimalist yet modernist tone. Within these fragmented building masses, there are spaces for restaurants, a health club with swimming pool, mini golf course, 600 parking spaces and 240 deluxe rooms, all connected through courtyards and colonnades along the water edge spaces. The tea pavilion floats on a 120 meter long waterway that forms the core of the complex.

Local glass-reinforced concrete louvres pigmented with brick dust, have been used to create a rustic quality. Kerry Hill says, "They are not precise, adding to a feeling of hand crafted building technique. They express a balanced juxtaposition of heavy and lightweight elements that feels just right." The building is cladded with beige Gangapur stone and the authentically reproduced sculptures from the Bengal's Pala period have been used to adorn the façade.

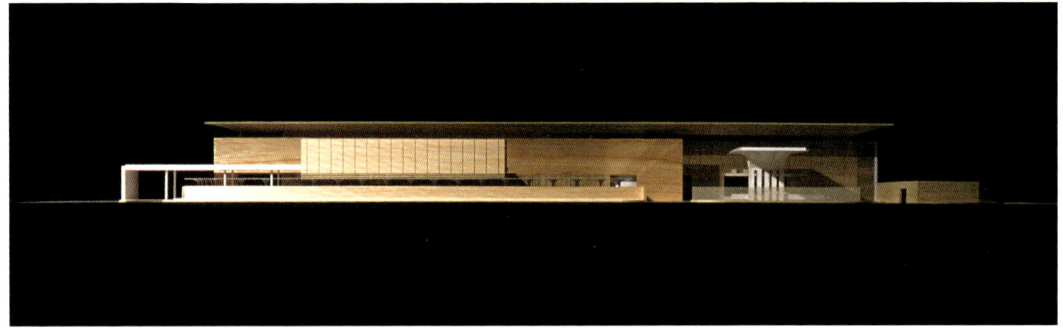

All Photos: Albert Lim K.S.

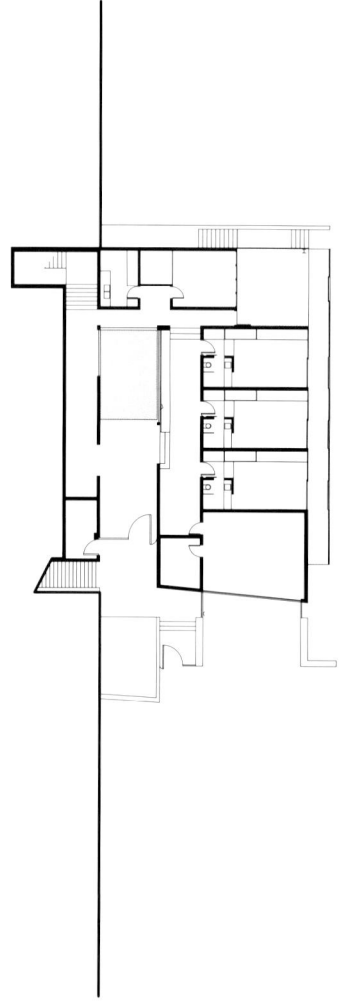

Plan lower level

Ogilvie House
Sunshine Coast, QLD, Australia, 2002

The design of this single-family residence came as a direct response to remarkable view of the Noosa National Park and Sunshine Beach. Located on the top of a headland, the building is sensibly positioned within the site so that it may provide proper climatic protection from the prevailing south-easterly winds and sufficient privacy from the neighbours. At the lower level, there is water court with a gallery that houses the extensive Ogilvie family's art collection at the entrance of the house, followed by gymnasium and guest accommodation. On the upper level, there is an enclosed living, dining, and kitchen space which is sandwiched between a double height courtyard that is also a reflection pond and a flexible semi-open living space, containing an infinity pool, a covered terrace, a deck, and a garden overlooking the ocean.

The horizontally-layered timber-screen façade frames the view of ocean and moderates the climate while juxtaposed texture is accomplished with the glass panels and solid concrete block walls. The colour scheme is rendered in a soft earthy tone tinged with olive, all skilfully defined by brittle white bandings.

Photo: Jon Linkins

Photo: Jon Linkins

Photo: Reiner Blunck

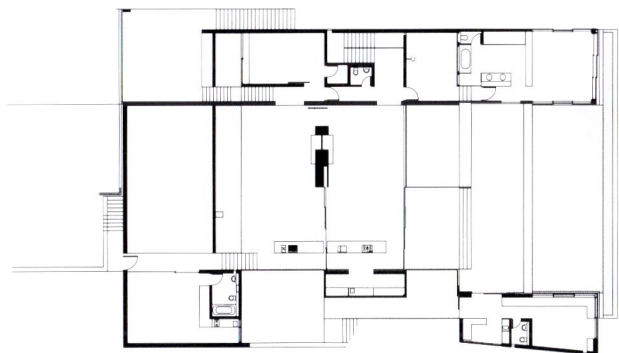

Plan upper level

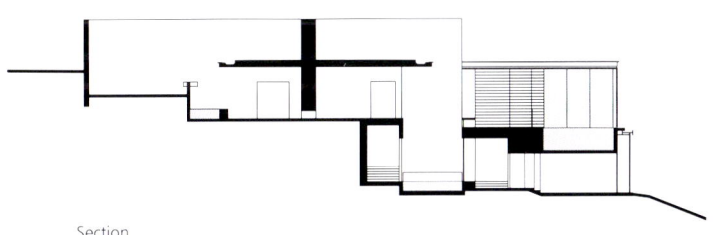

Section

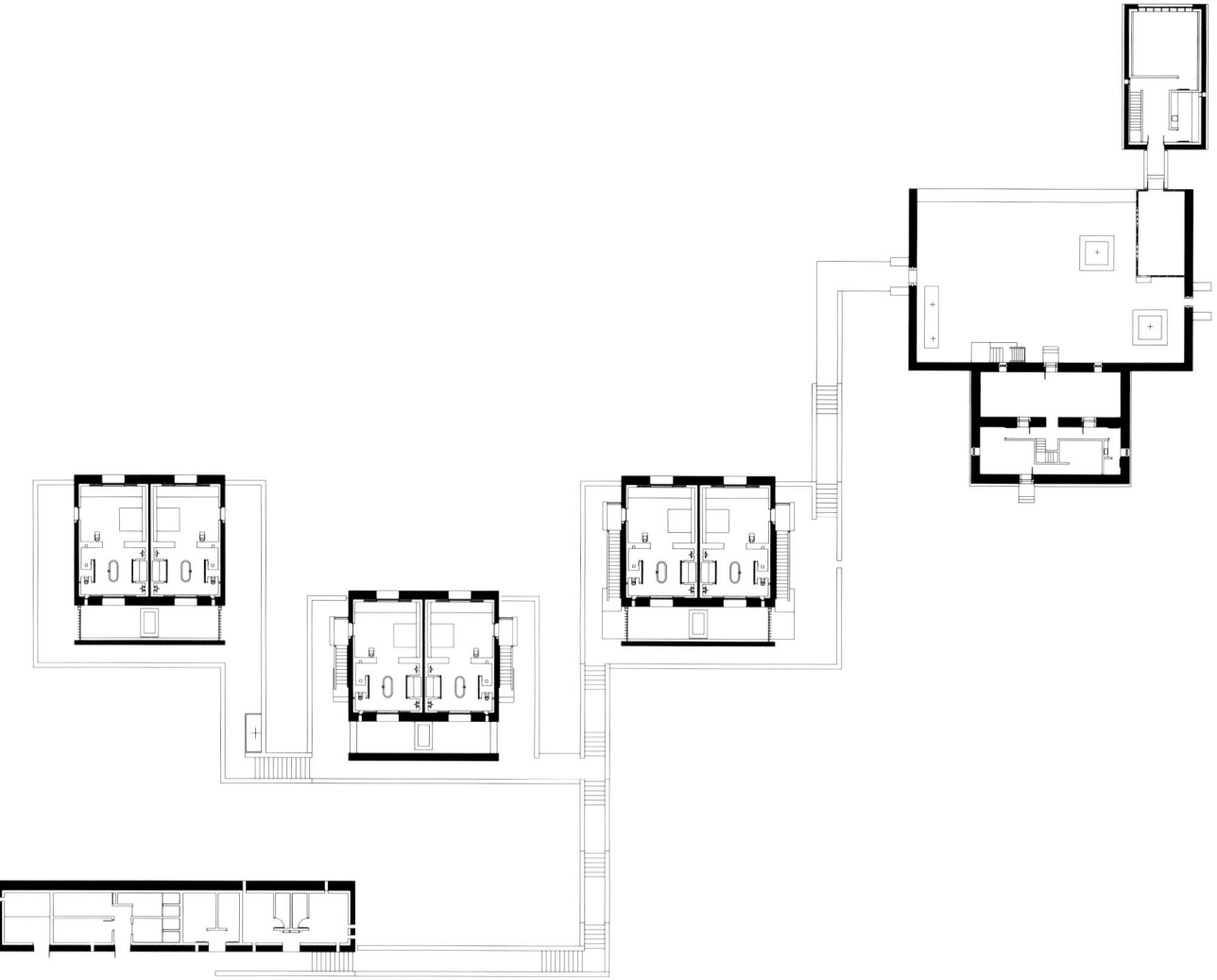

Amankora Punakha, Plan

Amankora
Thimphu, Punakha, and Paro in Bhutan,2007

Bhutanese in form, materiality, and spirit, these innovative and regionally sensitive designs are resort projects situated in cities of Paro, Punakha, and Thimpu within the Himalayan kingdom of Bhutan. The building form and proportion are conversant with traditional Bhutanese architecture with references to indigenous weaving and dying processes.

The outer shell of these buildings are constructed with a refined indigenous mud building technique. Traditionally, earth is compacted in a timber framework manually with wooden hammers and white lime is plastered to prevent it from deteriorating over time. However, at the Amankora buildings, earth was poured into a metal framework and compacted mechanically in layers. The earth mixture had a percentage of cement and waterproofing additive while the exterior façade was treated with waterproofing sealant. Structurally, local timber was used for all the walls and ceilings and solid timber boards were used as floor finishes.

Photo: Shinkenchiku-sha

Photo: Shinkenchiku-sha

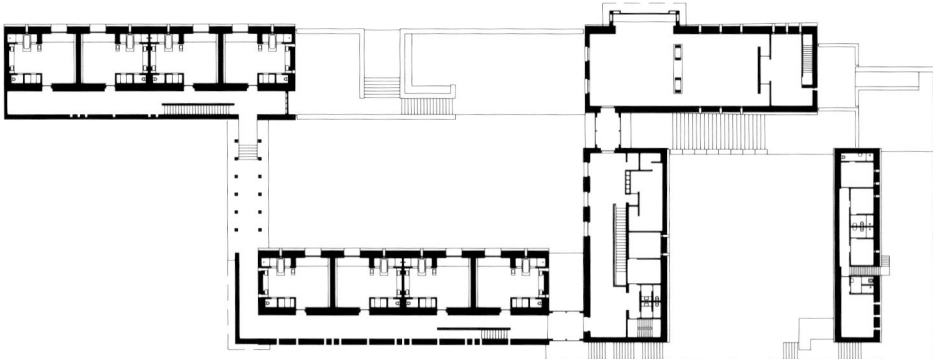

Amankora Thimpu, Plan level 2

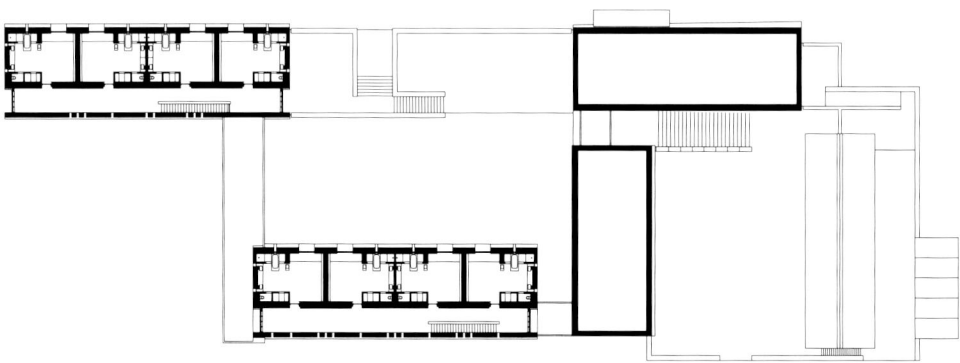

Amankora Thimpu, Plan level 3

Photo: Shinkenchiku-sha

Photo: Shinkenchiku-sha

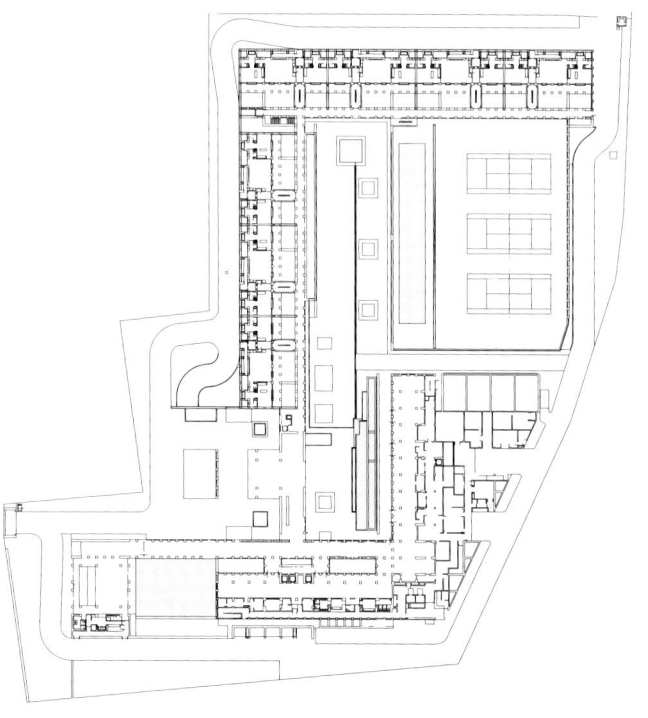

Plan level 1

The Aman New Delhi
New Delhi, Delhi, India, 2009

Arising from the functional demand for a luxurious contemporary city hotel, the Aman New Delhi (renamed The Lodhi) provides exclusivity to the guests through varied public and private facilities. It accommodates a salon, a recreation center, fitness center, spa and sauna room, a library, a cigar lounge, and a business center on premises.

The design philosophy for this hotel emerged from being located near the center of New Delhi, a short distance from Humayun's Tomb, the sixteenth century Mughal monument and hence "traditional design is referenced through suggestion and association rather than replication and through the reinterpretation of indigenous building forms as opposed to mimicry." Mughal architecture is embedded in a simple and direct way through the idea of columns and courtyards. The central space is composed of a long courtyard with lawn, reflection pools, and mature trees while private spaces have extensive verandas, courtyards, and plunge pools enclosed with a semi-open double-height volume. Unification of the interior and exterior space is achieved through cladding Gangapur both inside and outside as well as placing columns in central spaces. Moulded from glass reinforced cement and fixed with stainless steel brackets, the contemporary interpretation of "Jaalis" or perforated masonry are placed between the columns in a drifting expression, flitering sunlight and giving privacy. These intricate screens cast animated shadows onto the building surfaces during the day and have the effect of a lantern at night. By restraining the palette in dark stained timber panelling, olive hued Rajasthani Khareda stone and handmade carpets, the resonances of luxury is accomplished through detailed finishes rather expensive materials.

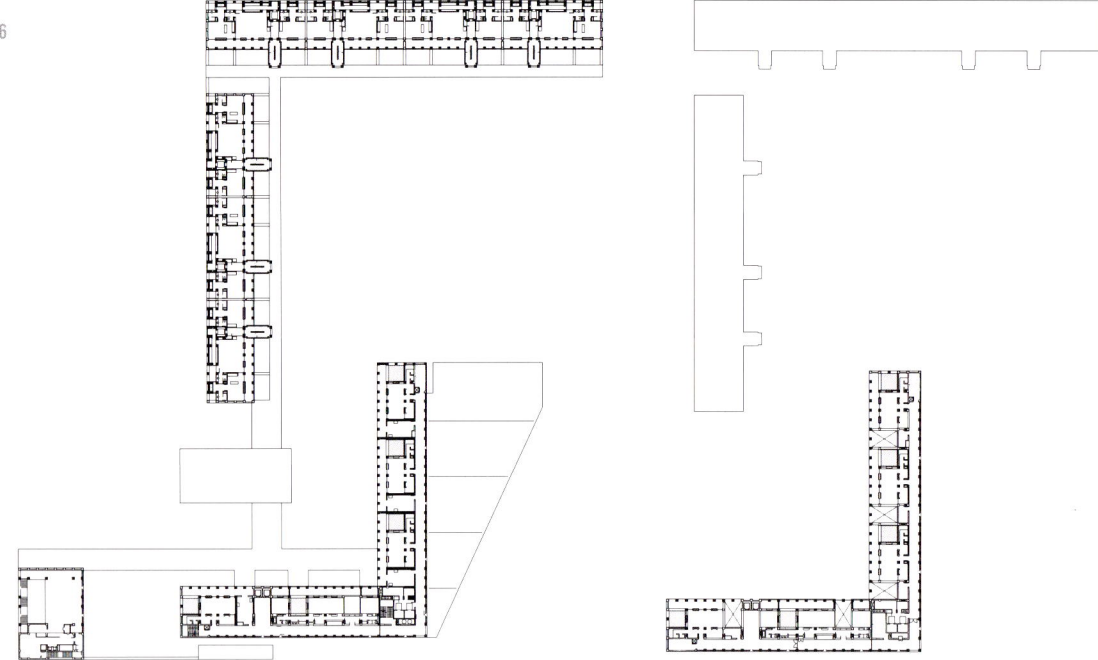

Plan level 2 Plan level 6

All photos: Albert Lim K.S.

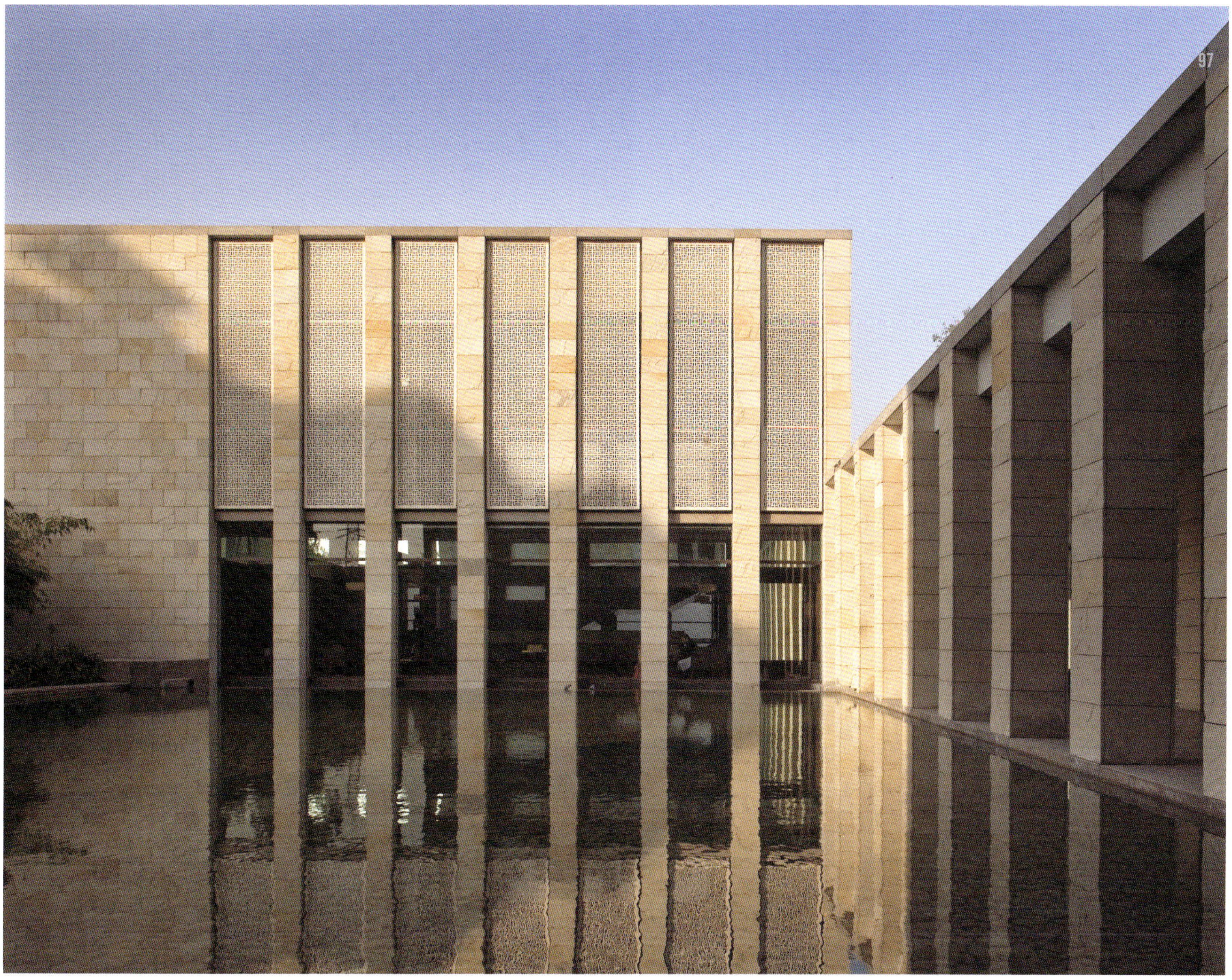

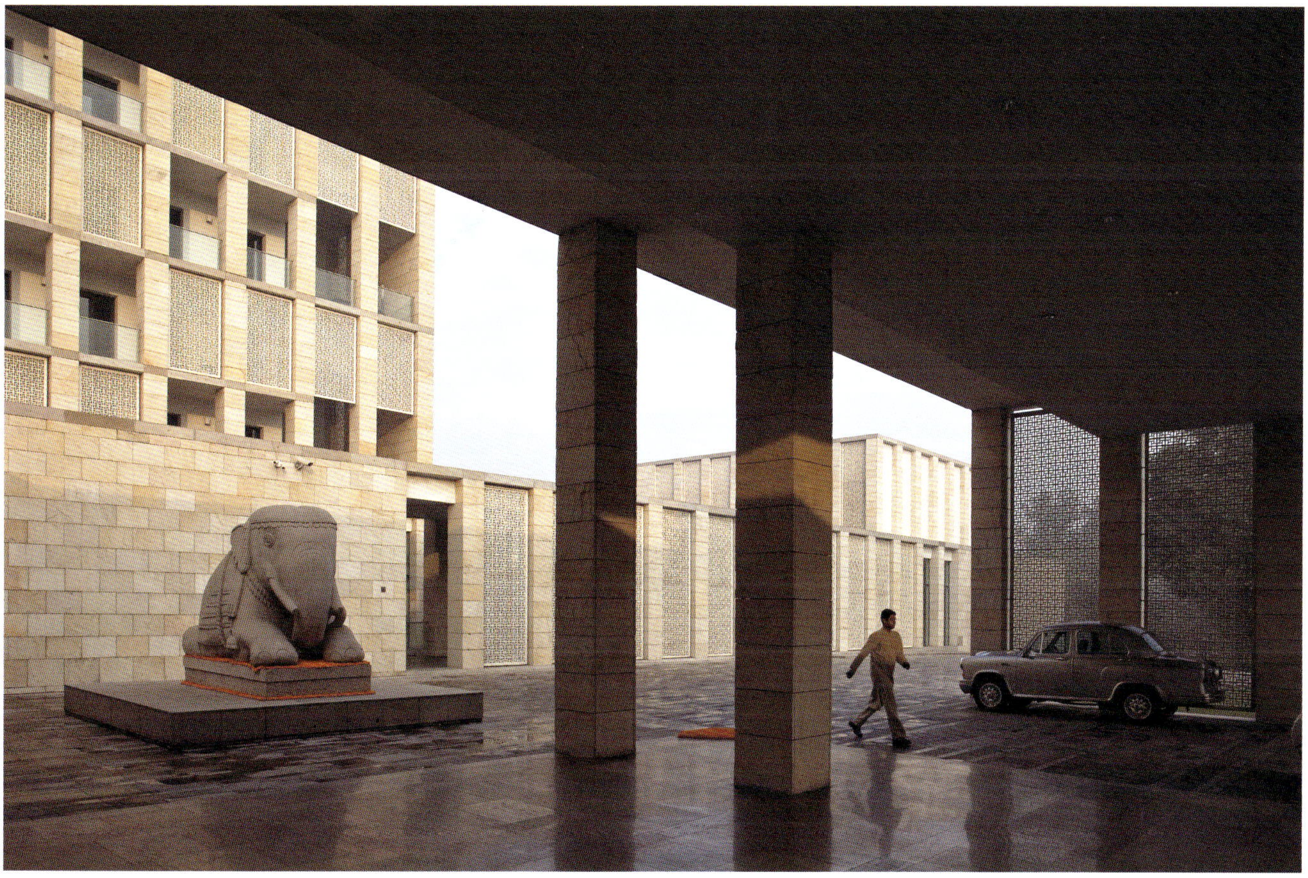

Photo: Adrian Lambert—Acorn Photo Agency

State Theatre Centre
Perth, WA, Australia, 2010

Kerry Hill Architects won this new center through a design competition in November 2005 and the construction began in 2006. This 100 million dollar center facilitates 575-seat Heath Ledger Theatre, a 200+ seat flexible performance space known as Studio Underground, a multi-purpose outdoor space, associated rehearsal rooms, and public foyer spaces as well as state-of-the-art theater equipment. The concept for this building arises from an interchange of opposite forces, a sensation between darkness and light, an expression between mass and transparency, and a language between robust and delicate. It intends to convey the spatial drama associated with the experience of attending a theatrical performance.

The foyer space is multi-levelled and features dramatic metallic finishes. Studio Underground is clad in black metal. Each of the theaters within the center are vertically stacked, creating space for the outdoor performance area. The practice describes its design as deliberately contemporary in expression, with spaces articulated by form and material.

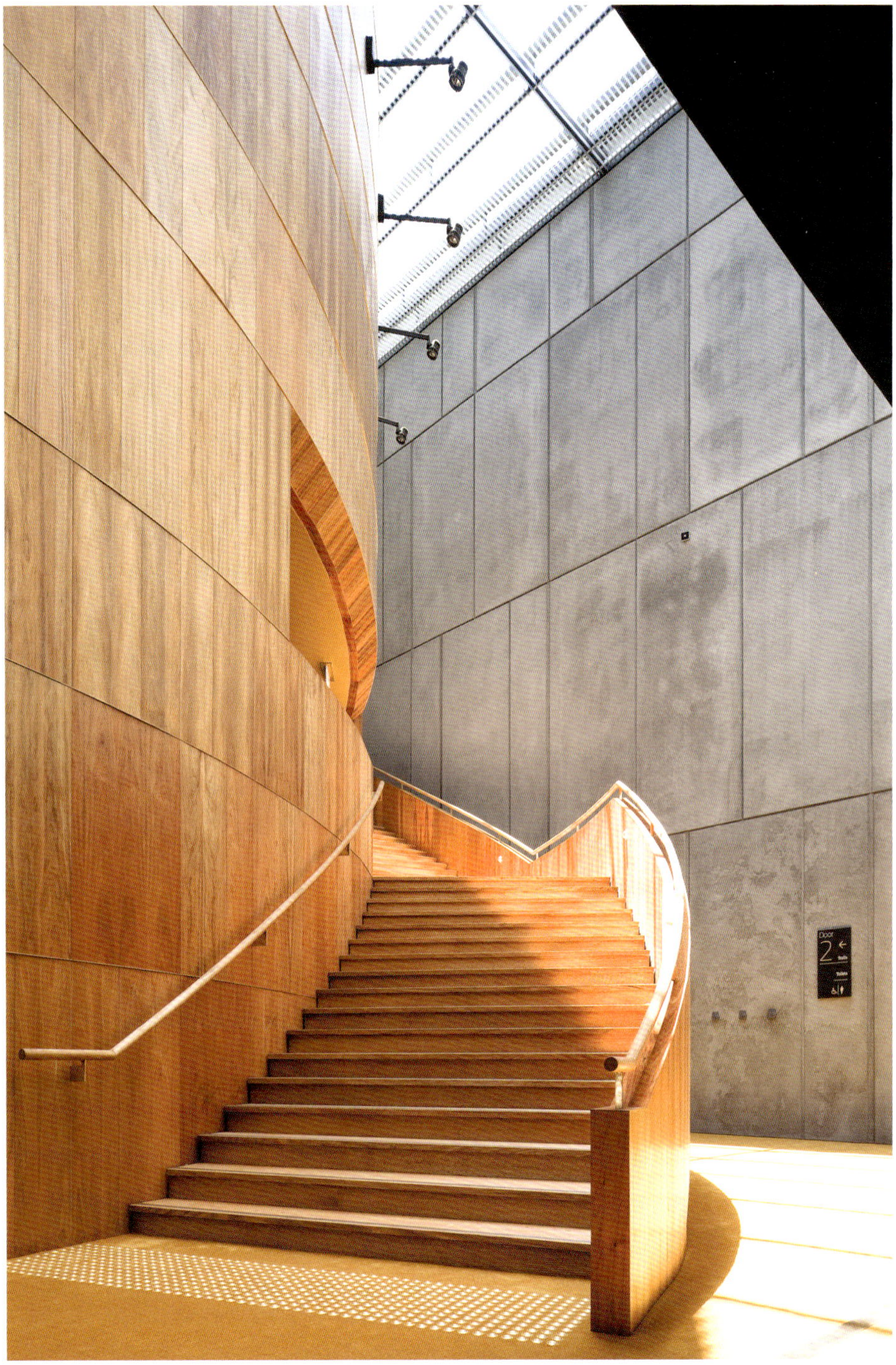

Photo: Robert Frith—Acorn Photo Agency

Photo: Luke Bartholomew Tan

Photo: Adrian Lambert—Acorn Photo Agency

THE PLEASURE OF ARCHITECTURE

THE A. S. HOOK ADDRESS

Kerry Hill

The A. S. Hook Address has most often delivered a critical, sometimes philosophical message to the profession; it is rarely used as a platform for showing the architect's work. This seems a little odd, presuming most recipients were selected because of their buildings. So I am going to try and do both. The message will be short, the slides will take longer.

I think we all know that practising architecture can be euphoric and, at times, it can be desperate and dark. Tonight, I would rather dwell on the bright side, the pleasure of architecture. I would also like to talk about some of the principles that inform our work. These ideas are not prescriptive, nor are they intended to align with a particular school of thought. Of course you can pin a label on us if you want to, but I prefer to think of our work as simply building appropriately. Our aim is to emphasize the importance of sensual experience and an intuitive approach over theoretical speculation. I do not think you can find a reason for everything you make.

Like previous medal winners I have also spent time reading what other medal winners have had to say. Twenty of them in fact, back to 1983, when Gil Nicol and Ross Chisholm were the last Western Australians to receive this award. You should all do it sometime—it is comforting to read how little has changed, which confirms my belief that much of what we say and do as architects has preceded us.

I am reminded of an old Chinese proverb: "The future is only the past again—entered through another gate." I am often asked how different practice in Asia is to that in Australia. In fact there is little difference, providing architecture with a capital "A" remains the center of focus. Building, however, leaves no room for doubt, which, unfortunately for architects, often means making a statement in the face of the risk of being wrong. So for me, working at the coalface of building in Asia has really meant just "doing it." Little time has been spent reviewing the process. What I have found in the labyrinth of socioeconomic, geopolitical, and multicultural layers that form the diversity of places in which we build is that problems arise when an architect allows peripheral issues to cloud or absorb one's thinking—issues that assume undue importance because they are foreign (sometimes exotic), often fascinating, and therefore distracting.

One is too easily led into the trap of local politics and social agendas. These may involve important issues but few architects, if any, are equipped to deal with such matters. We are trained to design and build, and I have found in my thirty-five years of working in Asia (and now elsewhere) that there is a need to act single-mindedly and to exclude all things peripheral to our central aim of making good, and hopefully, appropriate buildings.

For example, building in India—a country beset by problems that only India can resolve (and they are presently doing a pretty good job of it). India has its own way of doing almost everything. No foreigner can change that and it is naive to imagine you might. They have their own building delivery systems, at times confusing and almost always frustrating, which you must view with tolerant amusement or you won't succeed.

Indians also have a profound respect for architecture—not just the educated elite but also the poor and humble (perhaps even more so). There is great pride in India's architectural heritage, both ancient and modern.

Armitage Hill Hotel, Galle, Sri Lanka (1992)

Armitage Hill Hotel, Galle, Sri Lanka (1992).

Armitage Hill Hotel, Galle, Sri Lanka (1992).

Where differences do exist, it is not in the practice of architecture so much as in the attitude of the industry that commissions and builds it. I have found that, generally, serious architects make good buildings wherever they are.

Architecture, in its making, necessarily becomes part of the physical world. Its form can manifest in diverse ways, but ultimately each building needs to tell its own story—it can belong to a family of precedents but it must speak for itself. Just as every person has a life of his or her own, each work of architecture has an absolute value all to itself. This is especially brought to focus in today's world where many of us live and work in multicultural societies in which the ideas of what is local and what is universal are intermixing.

A line from Lewis Mumford, written in 1941, is fitting in this regard, "It would be useful if we formed the habit of never using the word regional without mentally adding to it the idea of the universal – as the problem of regionalism is ultimately how to live in a world of particular interests without ceasing to sustain mankind as a whole." I have found that spending time in another culture makes one aware of both the similarities and the differences. This is beautifully put by the Mexican poet Octavio Paz: "The only way to know ourselves is to recognize the otherness in others." Much of what we think of as architecture is represented by physical form while, in essence, architecture speaks to the senses—it cannot rely on image alone. The experiential quality of architecture embodies the intangible aspects of light, air, sound, and touch. It is about how a place feels; it places intuition before intellect.

There is a need to find in architecture those abstractions that approach the essence —"the felt structure of reality."

In this respect, working without the base of consistent cultural or locational conditions poses a unique set of architectural challenges, for if architecture is perceived as image only, in the context of regional response, it is very easy to fall into a state of mind in which tradition takes over from innovation, or worse, innovation denies tradition. The regeneration of building forms or literal variants of past models—no matter how well they are crafted—can only stagnate the operational idea of tradition and, at worst, debase both itself and its past. In that sense, it fails to address the concerns of contemporary architecture. Equally, an architecture that denies its past is at risk of being skin deep: architecture that is at home everywhere and nowhere.

More than any other art, architecture takes time. Through affinity we align ourselves with ideas to which we aspire. They are the necessary points of reference that shape one's thinking on the long journey of architecture, during which we are required to accept, reject, adjust, and react to the diverse web of ideas that combine to influence our collective and individual design attitudes.

So how might an architect approach this delicate balance?

In my practice of architecture I have chosen a middle ground and have purposefully allowed a reciprocal influence to exist between my allegiance to selected Modernist principles and the experience of living and working in Asia. I have also limited the theoretical ambitions of our practice to a few qualities I have come to admire in architecture. One of these is exactitude, another is authenticity.

Exactitude is attributed to any object that is constructed with precision, with the right pieces, which has neither too much or too little of anything, and within which one material pays respect to another. It is tangible, clearly evident when attained, and should not be confused with minimalism in which a formula towards spareness is rigorously pursued.

Authenticity is not so easily read; it has to do with the genuineness of origins. It is felt as much as it is seen and it evolves through intuition as much as through critical observation. For me, it is the ability of a work of architecture to feel comfortable in its own skin, to look forward and backwards with ease. There is no formula for achieving this state—one can only address the conditions within which it is felt to exist.

Inherent in our idea of authenticity is a desire to localize or ground each project. However, the problems of localization are compounded when working in different countries and different cultures at the same time. In addition, it is not only about extending the valid character of a place, but also the creation of new places. It involves a response to the tangible and current realities of a situation, of site, climate, technology, tradition, and the human values of a place. It is building with a sense of belonging and I believe it is here, in one's response to place, that the operational idea of tradition lies, and within which, cultural continuity can exist.

Sara Caples elegantly addresses this idea while writing about African-American culture and the issue of, "How to proclaim pride in the unfolding present without overwhelming the quiet history of the past." Within our search for authenticity, we allow each project to clearly identify itself through place, purpose, and material, in the hope that, in Asia at least, our modernist approach might be enriched by accommodating the traditions of the East.

We have no formal design methodology, but strategies have emerged through an informal process that wanders between observation, analysis, and intuition, between local and universal ideas. We allow the uniqueness of each situation to influence our decisions but we are not constrained by it.

With hindsight, perhaps the most unifying strategy in our work is the plan. The parameters for each project are brought to order in the plan, which I see as a mode for distilling elements into a clear diagram; a key to the scheme. Plans are abstract cross-sections which reflect the functional organization of a building. They are the basic plane upon which a spatial experience develops but they offer few clues for our understanding of variations in form and volume. Our plans have their roots in modernism on the one hand (I was educated in Perth in the sixties) and in Asian precedents on the other, where the plan is often derived from an idealized diagram of spatial order. At times, there is a perceptible shift between the plan and the building. If plans are an abstraction of the ordering of a building, the embodiment of our buildings in three dimensions is layered with climatic, construction, and material devices that help give the building its character.

Climate is an immutable part of our architecture, the mainstream for much of its form, as is the site, though I don't believe in the dictum that "the solution lies in the site." The site is a premise; the solution is in your head.

Materials can be fundamental in connecting the past with the present, and where possible we use materials common to the place of each project, but we like to rethink our understanding of how that material might be used. I prefer working with natural materials for their generic compatibility: Dubrovnik (where we are now building) is stone; Bhutan is mud (or stone); Kyoto was timber. In these places this seems the natural way to build.

We reference past building traditions through suggestion and association rather than replication, and through the reinterpretation of indigenous building forms as opposed to mimicry. We prefer to build upon what is there and to contemporize our understanding of what it can be. I think of it as being current, but filtered through a sieve of traditional values. In this way it is familiar to people, but not quite the same. It is new, but connected to the past—hopefully in spirit, at least.

In recognition of this, we have resisted the development of a "house style." Pressure of practice, however, increasingly necessitates the reuse of tried and tested components. We have developed a "loose fit" kit of parts—an inventory of materials and strategies, the purpose of which is not to consolidate a language, but of learning to master a set of tools, because only in doing this can an architect arrive at the degree of freedom required to turn his or her work into something creative.

This will, of course, have some bearing on the work, as common building materials and their way of joining may suggest common origins, perhaps even a style; but hopefully a place-based style reinvented through the use of modernist principles and free of cultural encrustations.

This may suppress regional sensitivity, but I hope not.

While preparing this talk it became apparent that two streams have emerged in our work. One alludes to the vernacular in places such as Bhutan and Sri Lanka where sufficient building tradition remains intact as to be influential. The other is more abstract and includes our buildings in Singapore, Bangkok, and Dubai—cities that have been reinvented.

Perhaps it is as simple as the form of a roof or the size of a window opening that informs this difference. It may also demonstrate the pervasive force in continuing tradition.

Working with these ideas we hope to particularize our buildings according to the special character of each place by bringing together functionality and geometry, place and technique, space and materials, in compositions that are fundamentally "quiet."

For the "show and tell" aspect of the talk that follows I have selected a snap shot of projects from the past ten years, mindful that the resonance of buildings cannot be seen, it can only be experienced.

As the 2006 RAIA Gold Medallist, Kerry Hill delivered the A.S. Hook Address at School of Architecture and Fine Arts, University of Western Australia, on October 25, 2006. This is an abridged version.

Pachacamac House (Photo: Cholon Photography)

LUIS
LONGHI

IN SEARCH OF A CONTEMPORARY MACHU PICCHU

THE PROJECT OF LUIS LONGHI

Maya Ishizawa

Maya Ishizawa is a Peruvian architect with a degree from the School of Architecture and Urbanism at the Ricardo Palma University, Lima, and experience in architectural design, construction, stage design, and art direction. In 2007, she received the Monbukagakusho scholarship from the Japanese government for research on cultural landscapes in the Andes region. In 2009, she obtained a master's degree in media and governance at Keio University in Tokyo, after which she did an internship at the UNESCO World Heritage Centre in Paris. In 2014, she received a Ph.D. in heritage studies from the International Graduate School at BTU Cottbus-Senftemberg, Germany. Currently, she works as a researcher in the World Heritage Studies Program at the University of Tsukuba in Japan, where she focuses on landscape studies and nature-culture linkages in heritage conservation.

In 1911, the American explorer Hiram Bingham came upon the most emblematic Inca complex ever, Machu Picchu. While this event has been called a "discovery," the locals who guided Bingham to its location had cultivated the stone terraces of the site, built during the 15th century, for 100 years before Spaniards reached the Inca land. Fortunately, Machu Picchu was not found by Spanish colonizers and remained conserved under the vegetation that had covered it for nearly 500 years.

When Bingham revealed the importance of Machu Picchu, the topic of identity was becoming central in the discourse on nation-state building in Peru, which is still ongoing. Machu Picchu and other Inca archaeological sites of the Urubamba River valley were chosen as symbols for this new nation. While Inca architecture became one of the most exploited symbols for the creation of a Peruvian identity, indigenous peoples, inheritors of the Inca civilization and their traditions, were treated with disdain during the 286 years of colonization and evangelization. Nevertheless, the resilient Andean communities could safeguard their worldview and the traditional knowledge represented at Machu Picchu.

Contemporary architecture in Peru suffers from a particular paradox. Despite the country's having such magnificent examples of architecture that converse with the environment and site, there is a discontinuity between Inca building tradition and contemporary Peruvian architecture. The latter, fueled by a capitalist market, is seen as the soulless and uninspired production of buildings. The "colonial style" that has been constructed over pre-Hispanic foundations has been copied in neo-colonial architecture, and the "chicha style" has invaded Peruvian cities. Peru's architecture is the reflection of a society that has been traumatized by a colonial past and later integrated into a global civilization without being healed of those traumas.

It is in this context that Luis Longhi operates as an architect in Peru. Longhi's architecture is a reflection on the identity of Peruvian culture and conversations with Incan architecture. Born in 1954 in the city of Puno, next to Lake Titicaca, the sacred lake of the Peruvian Altiplano, where the Incas are thought to have originated, Longhi feels very close to this landscape. Of Italian descent, he was raised among Quechua and Aymara people, who connected him emotionally with their indigenous ancestors and their traditions, which were undermined by the hegemonic Western culture imposed over the Andean world. After studying and living outside Peru for fifteen years (in the United States and India), Longhi felt compelled to return to his homeland to recover its architectural essence and to create a contemporary Inca architecture.

Longhi graduated from the Ricardo Palma University in Lima, where he studied under Juvenal Baracco for four years and worked for additional two, before going to the United States for postgraduate studies. He completed his master's degree in architectural design and sculpture at the University of Pennsylvania and further studies at the Harvard Graduate School of Design in Boston. He worked with recognized architects like B.V. Doshi, Adele Santos, David Slovic, John Bower, and Marshall D. Meyers. He taught at his alma mater the Ricardo Palma University and also at the Peruvian University of Applied Sciences (UPC) in Lima and the University of Hawaii at Manoa.

Longhi searches for an original architecture through a communication with place, a feel for local materials, and an ability to play with light. He feels a kinship with Louis Kahn, Isamu Noguchi, Peter Zumthor, Carlo Scarpa, and, of course, his pre-hispanic architect ancestors, through their works at the waka of Puruchuco, the Temple of the Moon in Machu Picchu, and the Tiahuanaco Gate of the Sun.

At the same time, as an artist-sculptor and architect, Longhi listens to his instincts at moments of creation. He has also developed principles that he elaborates through his practice. First, he understands nature as a divine creation from which he derives a respect for the environment and place. Second, he considers the work of an architect as the translation of a divine creation. By accepting the intepretation of the word design as being formed by de, meaning "divine," and signum, meaning "sign," Longhi defines design as the act of taking divine decisions that would give the architect the huge responsibility of being the "guardian of the planet." It is through this parameter that Longhi understands how to recognize good architecture—the kind that can move emotions. Third, Longhi uses Louis Kahn's notion of an "architecture with soul" as inspiration. Fourth, he considers himself as having been, like Luis Barragán, "touched" by beauty. And finally, he admires the labor of Inca architects who honored their gods through their work. Hence, Longhi's search for an architecture translates as work that is responsible to the environment and the cultural space, charged with a soul that can elicit emotions in its dwellers and visitors, and that connects the present with the past, especially in the context of Peru through the regeneration of Inca design principles.

Longhi enjoys not only working in the natural landscape, as evidenced by his beach houses, but also establishing deep relationships with old buildings in ruin. Both his Yuyanapaq and Municipal Theater projects connect memories with buildings. In Yuyanapaq, housed in the decaying Casa Riva Agüero, which was ransacked during the Pacific War in the 19th century, he connects memories and buildings and confronts the more recent Peruvian terrorism and war (1980–92), the effects of which have been borne primarily by the inheritors of the Inca, the Andean peasant communities. For six months, through pictures and recordings, the victims of the war became the dwellers of this house in ruins, achieving a poetic metaphor between the country and the house.

The Municipal Theater, partly consumed by a fire in 1998, was adapted by Longhi to be a setting for Shakespeare's King Lear. Longhi transformed the audience floor into the stage, connecting the old decaying theater through a platform that later became the stage for several other plays. In this intervention, Longhi tried to respect the building and its wounds, leaving them until it was restored.

The Pachacamac Hill House is Longhi's most emblematic work. A residence for a distinguished intellectual couple, the house captures all the principles that guide Longhi's practice: recovering pre-Hispanic symbols and traces and masterfully expressing the deep interrelations between art, architecture, and place. Working with local materials found on-site, he created land art between the sea and the hills of the Andes.

These are only the first stones of a contemporary Machu Picchu in Longhi's vision. But knowing Machu Picchu was not the task of a single architect, Longhi, as an educator, aims to nurture a new generation of Peruvian architects who will respect the environment, the place, and the culture and who are ready to add new stones in the edifice of a contemporary Machu Pichu.

Photo: Veronica Schereibeis

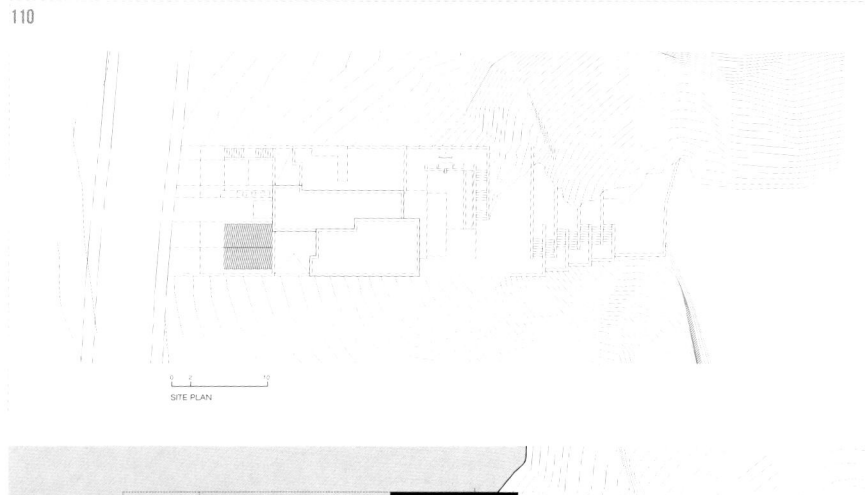

SITE PLAN

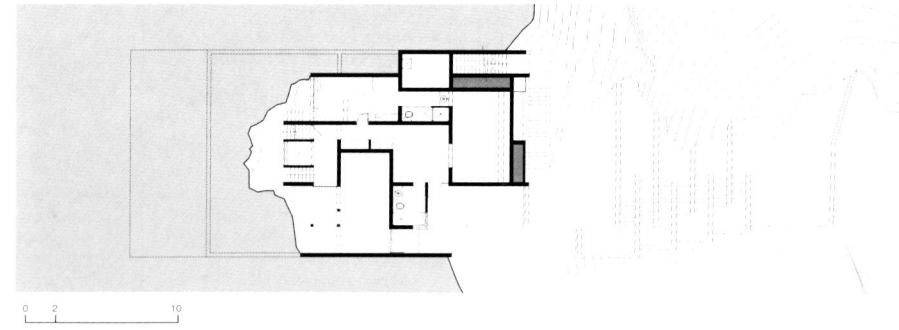

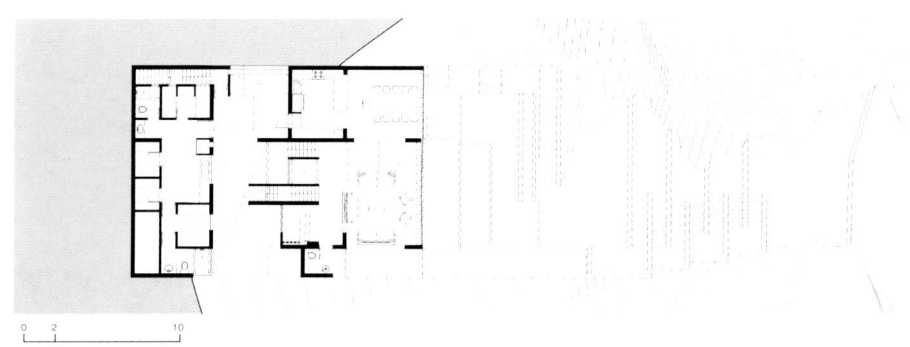

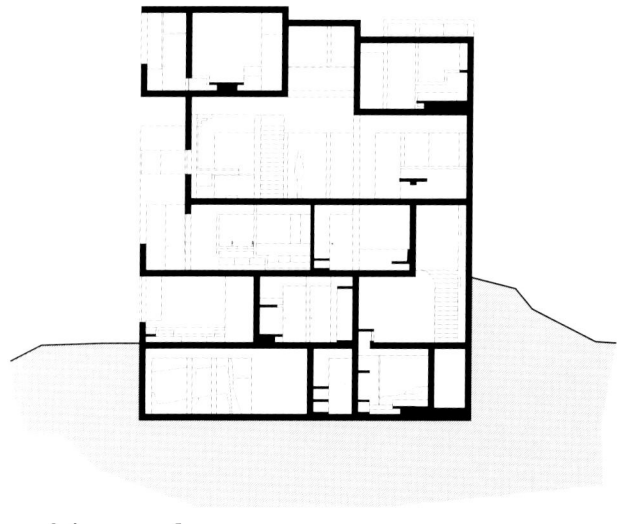

"Touching the Ocean"
Alvarez House
Misterio Beach, Lima, Peru, 2010

Located at a cliff of Playa Misterio in a gated beach community 117 km south of Lima, this beach house was the answer to a specific program requirement given by the client a successful surgeon with a large family. It has a vehicular and pedestrian access at approximately 40m over sea level. The social area of the house was required near the entry occupying two levels while accommodations for children and parents were organized in two parts: two levels above socials area were designated for the boys and their guests and three levels below social area for parents, girls, and their guests. Swimming pool and recreational facilities were located at lower levels occupying a series of terraces designed to connect the house with the ocean.

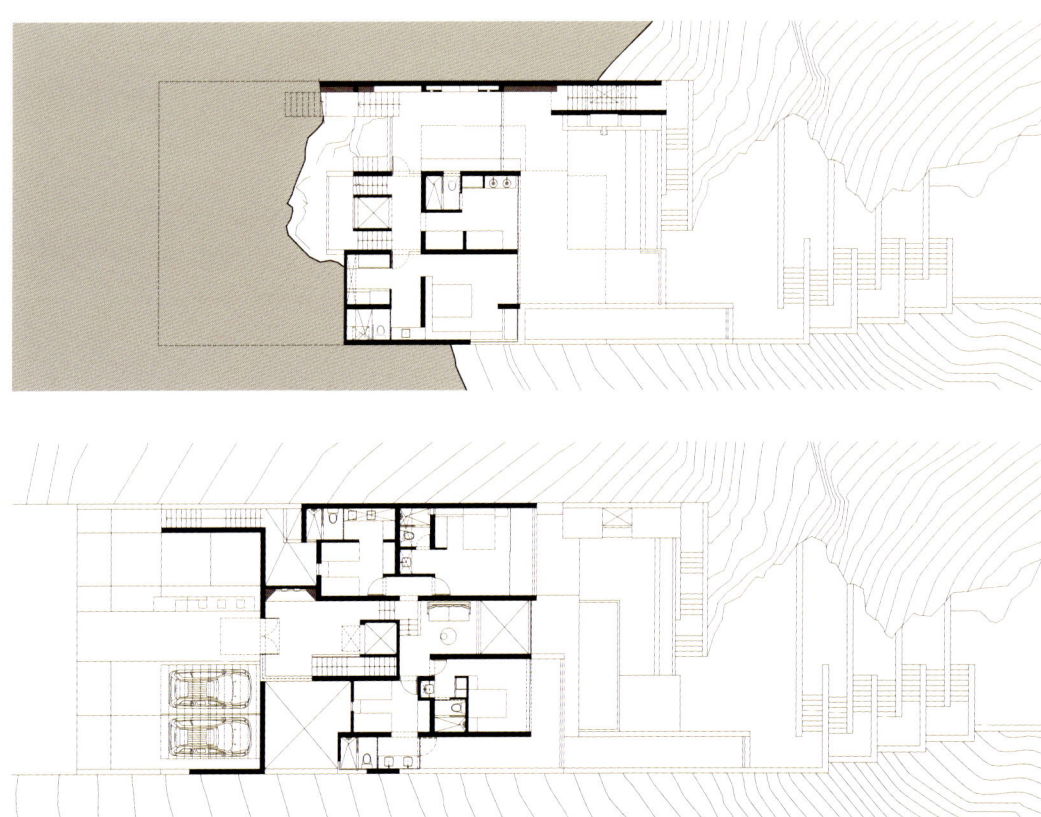

All photos: Juan Solano

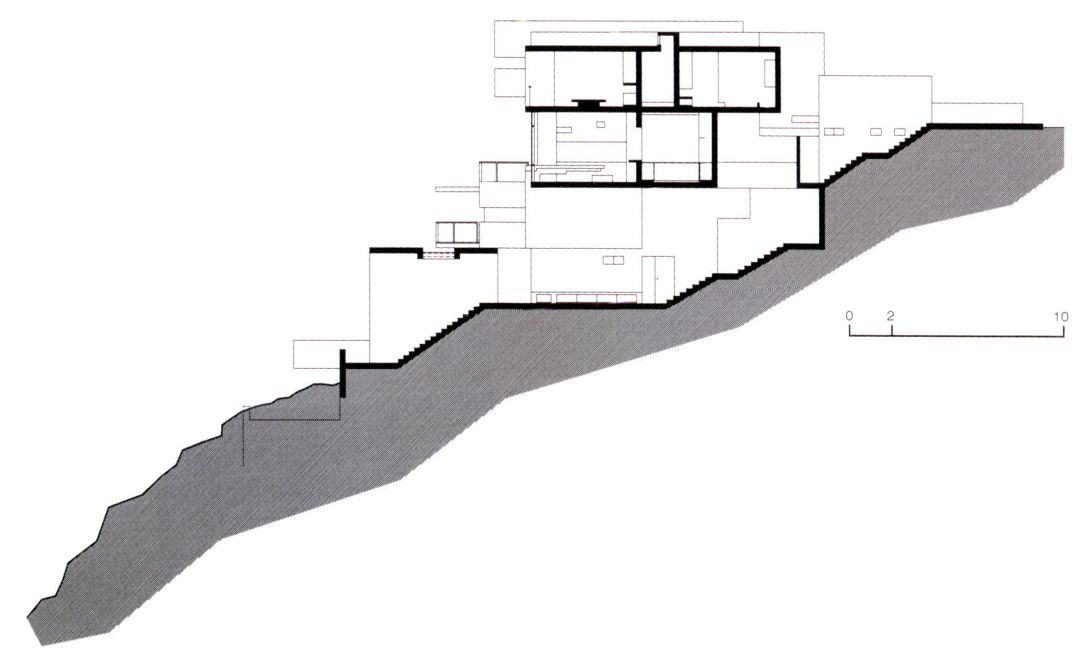

0 2 10

"Floating in the Desert"
Beach House Q
Playa Misterio, Lima, Peru, 2010

Infinite rolling dunes from the desert to the East and rocky Pacific Ocean cliffs used by fishermen to the West converge on the site of Beach House Q; creating a unique natural environment. Beach House Q is the first residence built in one of the areas not yet occupied at the Beach Club Misterio located 117 kilometers south of Lima, Peru. Challenging the stillness of the surroundings, Beach House Q materializes the dreams of a young couple in a "floating volume" which embodies the spaces for a future family. The volume is supported by circular columns placed by intuition, as a dance, instead of forcibly in a grid. The dancing columns are accompanied by sliding glass panels that define the common area of the house; living-dining and terrace are integrated or separated by the option to open or close the glass panels depending on social and weather conditions. The rest of the house—guest rooms, kitchen, and services—are tastefully secluded at the back of the sloped site thus providing visual contrast with a volume of water in the front which has been unearthed for the enjoyment of swimming. Each view in the house connects to the infinite of the horizon.

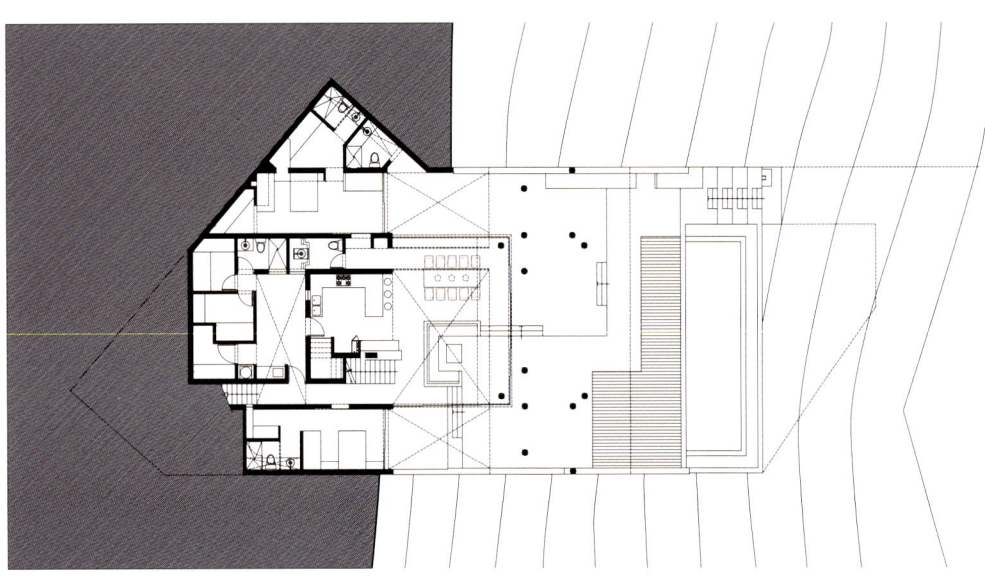

Photo: Cholon Photography

0   5   15

Photo: Juan Solano

Photo: Juan Solano

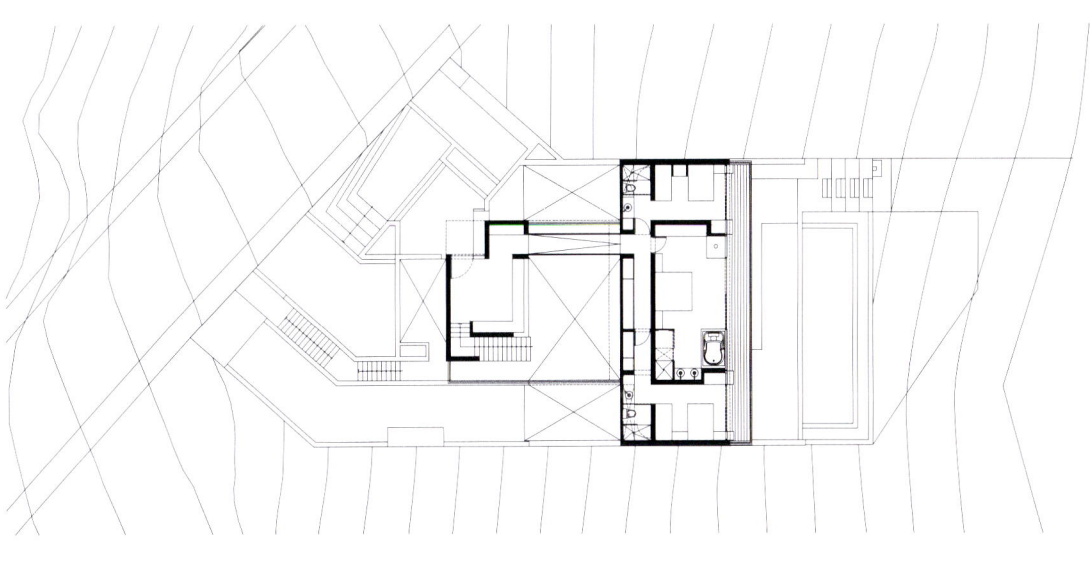

0   5   15

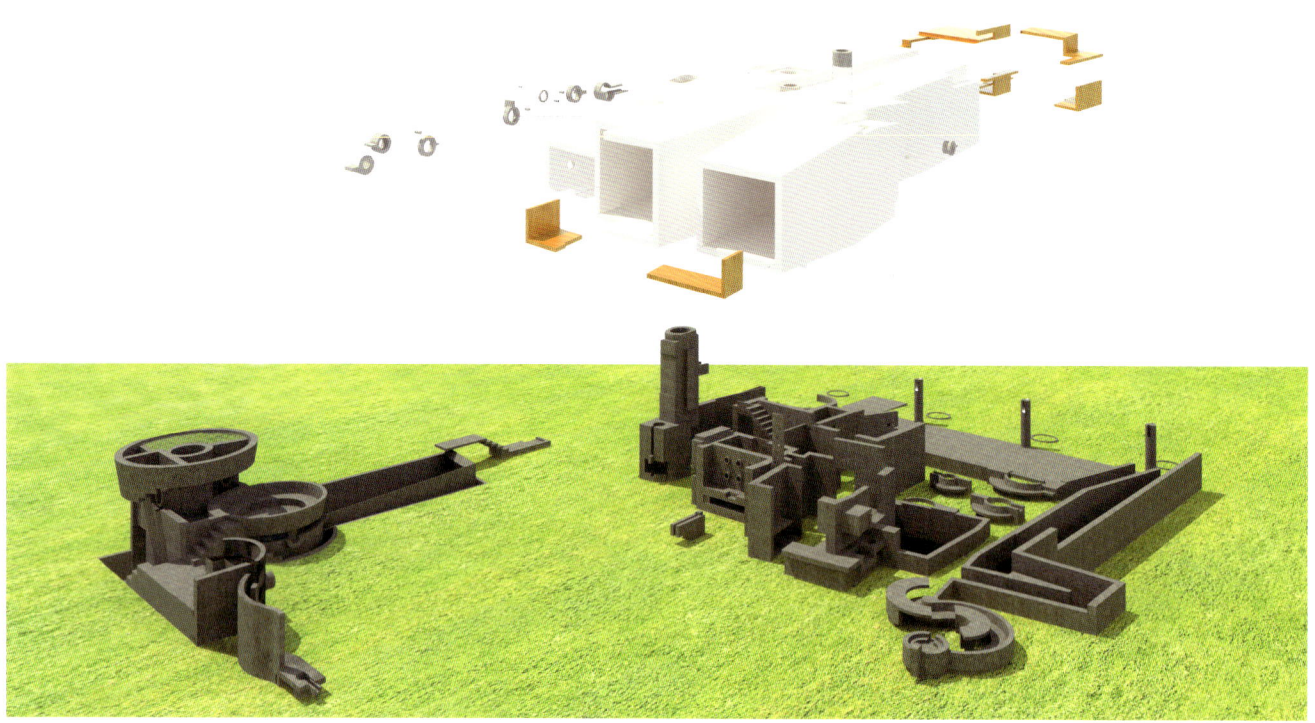

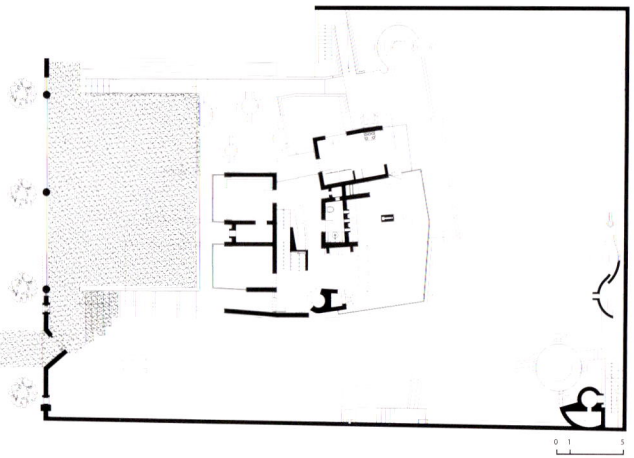
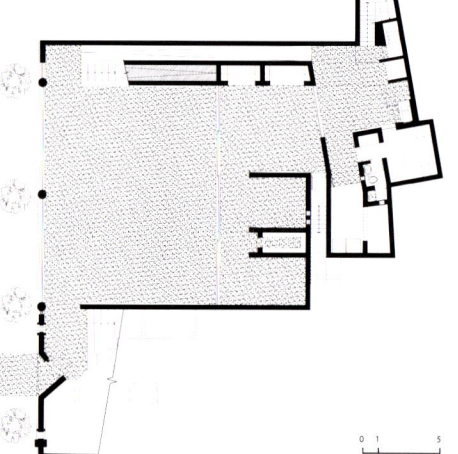

Veronica Beach House
Pucusana District, Peru, 2013

Veronica house was an exploration for Peruvian architecture that is better related with the international style. The 40m pool and the staircase
accessing different levels is combined within natural rock site to form an
integration between the artificial and the natural. Carved into the hill,
the terrace and swimming pool is the social area of the building. The
private spaces have been accommodated into a volume of two levels
that "float" above the terrace space. The natural colors tones are a
derivative from the rocky surroundings.

Photo: Juan Solano

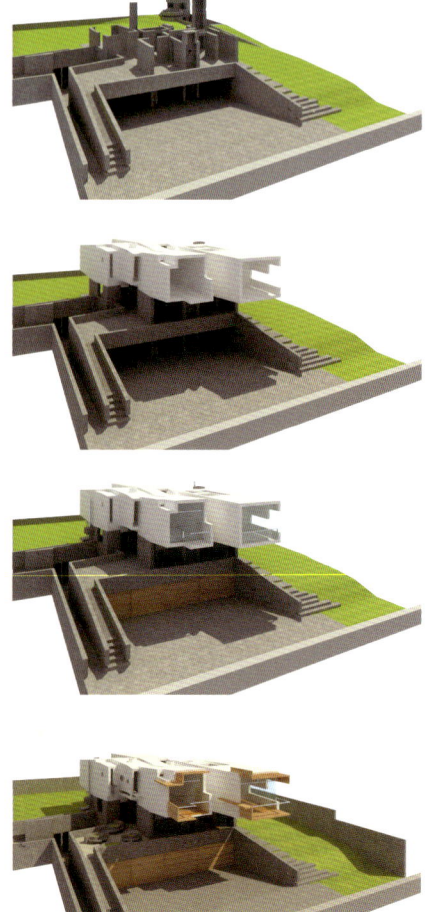

Photo: Juan Solano

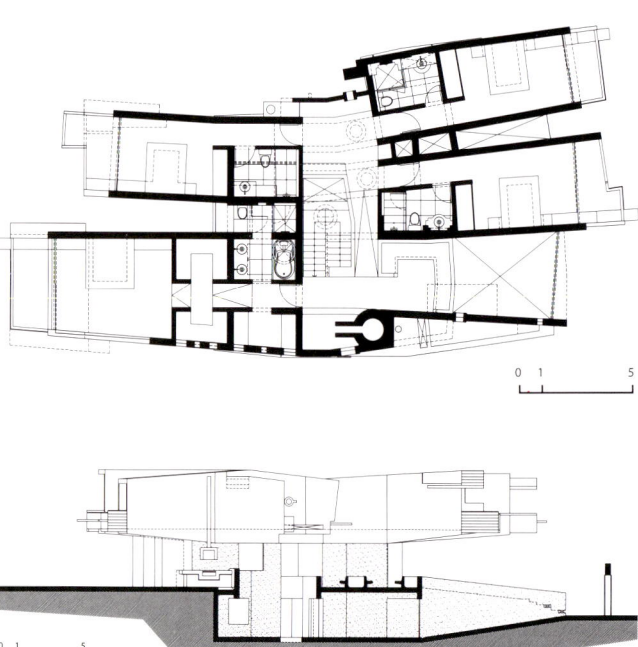

Photo: Cholon Photography

Photo: Cholon Photography

Photo: Juan Solano

Photo: Juan Solano

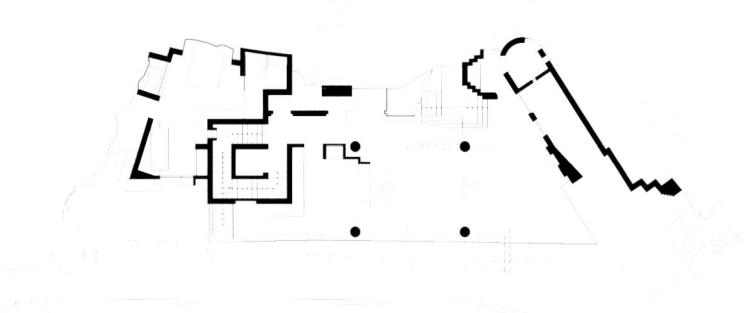

0 1   5

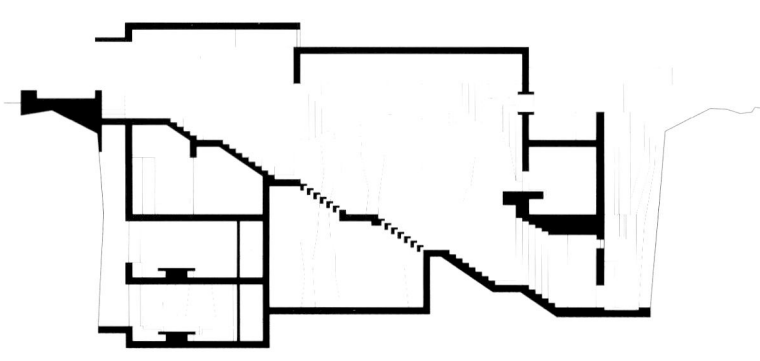

0 1   5

"Volume with gender"
Casa CN
Playa Misterio, Lima, Peru, 2011

Casa CN flat house belongs to a pediatrician, a gynecologist, and their two children. When interpreting their dream for a life of summer, the project was conceived as three independent volumes, but together form one house. The house is a composition of three, separated by open spaces, which allow the entry of natural light and ventilation to all private spaces of the house. This also provides vertical and horizontal circulations articulated through sculptural elements in concrete volumes seeking a continuous communication with the sun during different times of the day. The largest volume belongs to the couple and is facing south-west with spectacular sea views. The second floor has a master bedroom and a private terrace roof. The volume under the social area is connected to a large terrace and infinity pool. Smaller volumes for both children have a north-east orientation and spectacular sea views. The rooms and bathrooms are open within double height volumes. Beds and closets were built on the site, providing privacy without losing the feeling of spaciousness.

Photo: Juan Solano

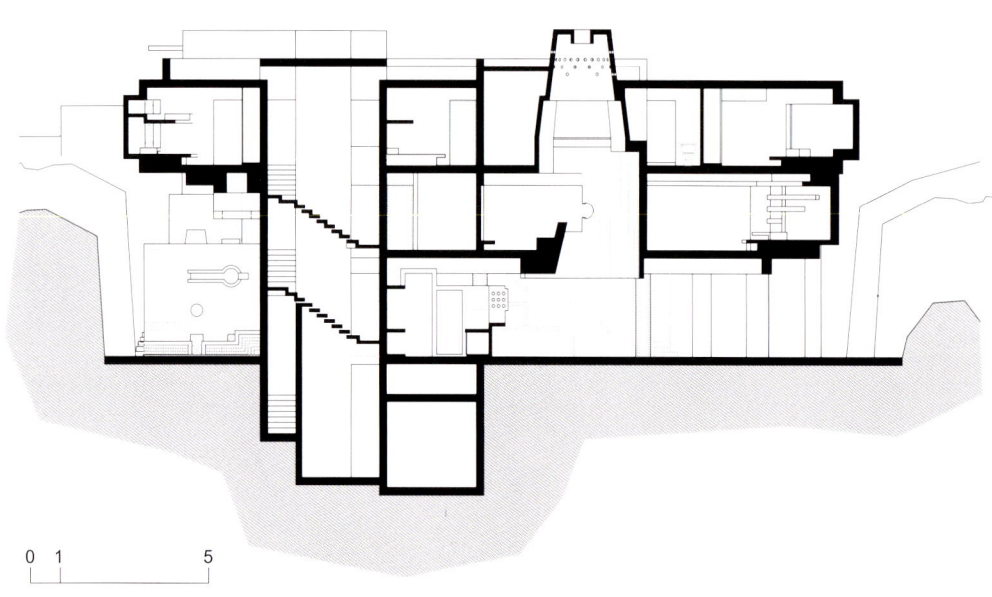

0 1   5

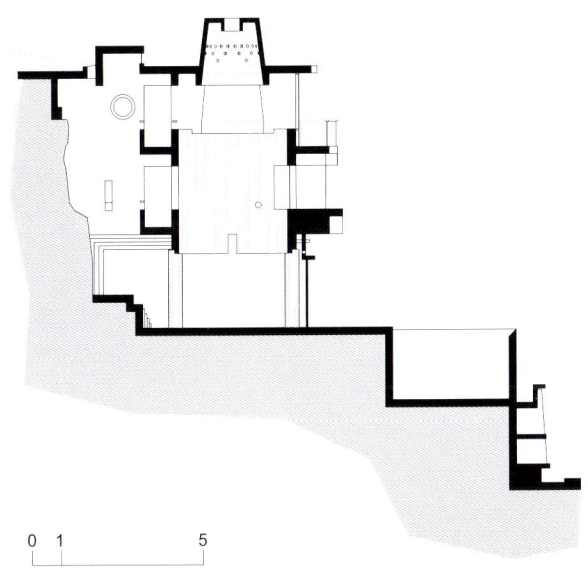

0 1   5

All photos: Juan Solano

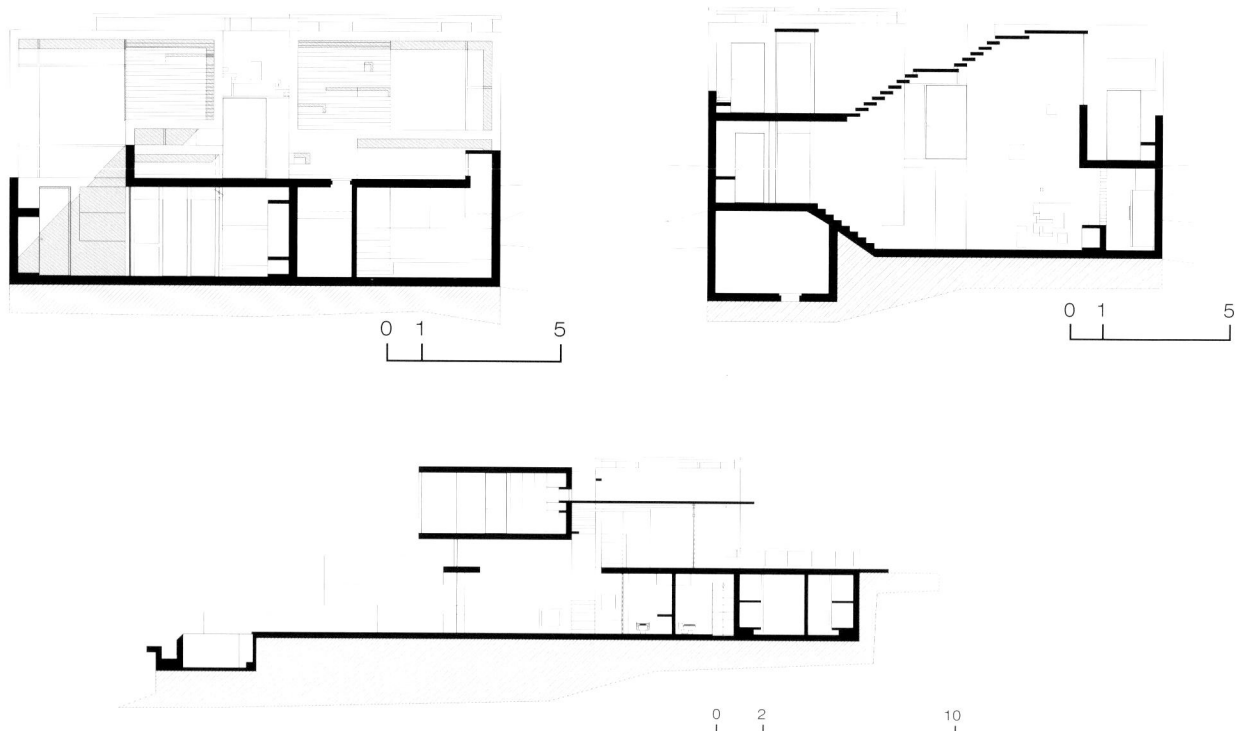

0 1   5

0 1   5

0   2   10

"A House Forever"
Casa Para Siempre
La planicie, La Molina, Perú, 2013

When a young couple came to my office to commission the design and construction of a house where they would live forever, I knew I had in my hands a great opportunity to continue in my search of ancestral contemporary architecture. In that moment, I was ready to dedicate exclusive time to interpret their dreams in order to create a "container of life."

My vision for a special house was confirmed when I went to the site for the first time and realized that it was already occupied by an old house where the couple was living with their two children. Then, the task was to demolish the material but keep the spirit, in order to replace the old construction for a "House Forever."

The metaphor for the design was to imagine that a big ancestral rock was found in the site and needed to be carved in order to accommodate the living spaces.

This "black carved stone" would be occupied by a 4 car garage, service patio, maid's quarters, and pool baths in the basement; kitchen, dining, and living spaces on the first floor. The carving of the spaces would generate interesting "built in" furniture with strong texture to be assorted with other natural and artificial materials in order for the allegory stone to remain as natural as possible to eventually be perceived as part of the owner's desired garden.

To complete the composition, the black stone base supports four cantilever volumes containing the intimate rooms, as the "white floating stones."

L.L.

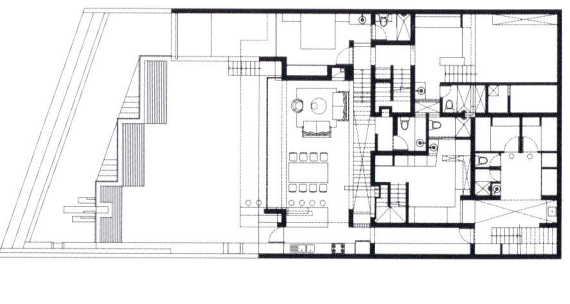

0 2   10

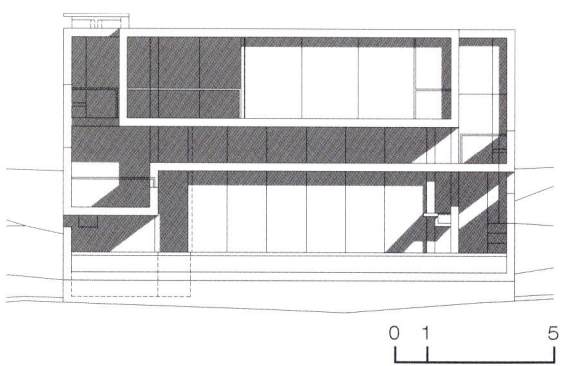

0 1   5

All photos: Juan Solano

Pachacamac House
Lomas de Jatosisa, Pachacamac, Lima, Peru, 2009

In the olden days of Peru, the selection of the site for a specific Inca building (use) was the most important action to be taken. Only when the right site was found would they follow-up with the intervention, which usually was minimal in order to produce a great building (Temple of the Sun and Temple of the Moon in Machu Picchu).

In our days, people seldom follow that order as usually the "need" comes first and later the search of the site. In the case of Pachacamac house, I knew the order was there as the clients fell in love with the site, and then thought of doing something afterwards. They realized that it would be the place to spend their last days and also understood the magnitude of their decision.

Only 40km south of Lima at an undeveloped region near pre-Inca remains, there is a small hill surrounded by bigger mountains, a perfect site if we follow the Peruvian tradition to always look for a protector or "Apu" in the surroundings. The lack of electricity and water sewage systems in the area helped the visitor find other types of energy transmitted by the place itself, which is evident when one walks and feels a special communication with it. This fascinating communication with the earth and its components was a constant guide for the development of the project.

The job of an architect is to interpret the dreams of the client. When an architect finds themselves interpreting philosophy, the results are transformed in a fascinating and unexpected way. It becomes an architecture that is difficult to plan before building begins; one in which many design decisions take place during construction.

The development of this "process" occurs only when the client allows the architect the freedom to design and build. The clients for the Pachacamac house are a couple who are philosophers now discovering spaces in their house which can transport them to their memories both from their past and from their future.

The intervention in untouched environment at the coast of Peru has helped me understand that in order to achieve successful architecture in natural sites, it is fundamental to listen to the environment and establish a relationship with it. This relationship is similar to any other type of relationships between humans, be it direct, sophisticated, romantic, respectful, sane, or insane.

The response to the site was to bury the house inside the hill, trying to create a balanced dialogue between architecture and landscape, where inside / outside becomes a constant interpretation of materiality with a strong sense of protection and appreciation of the dark and the light. A glass box sticks out of the hill symbolizing architectural intervention on untouched nature.

Photo: Juan Solano

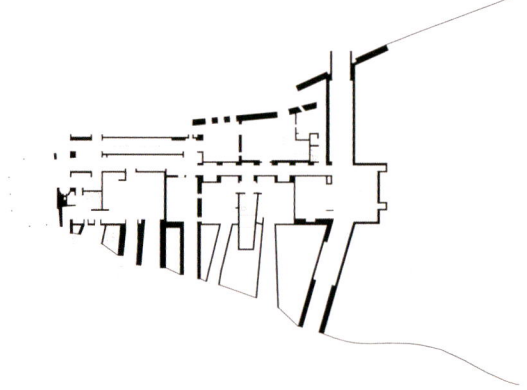

Photo: Elsa Ramirez

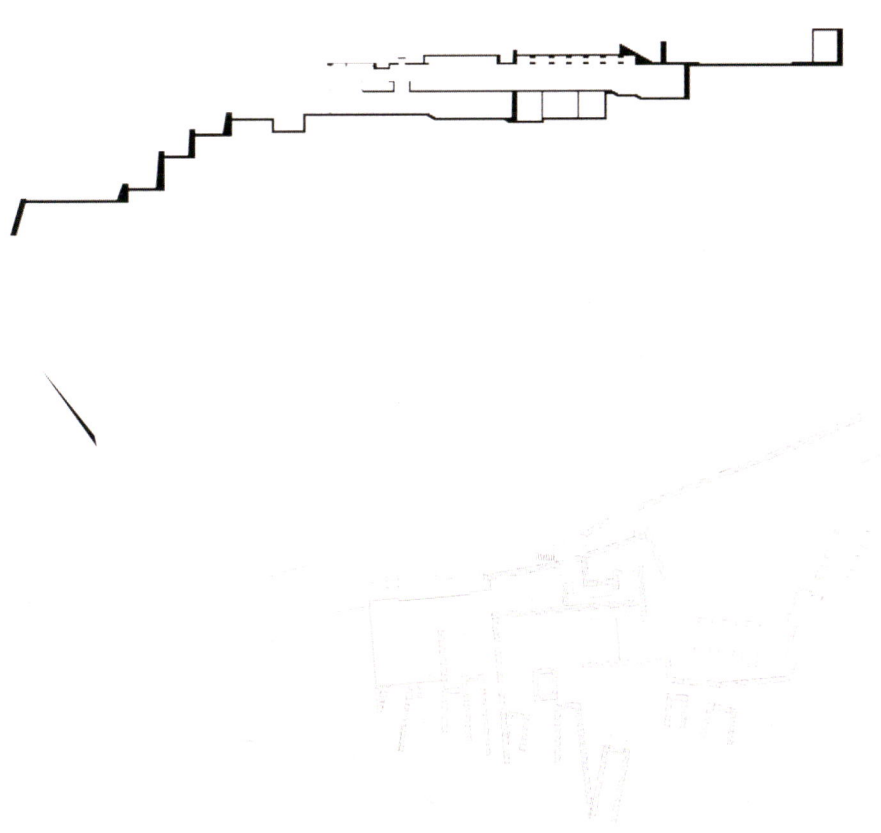

Courtyard in the rain, Home Office, Battaramulla.

C. ANJALENDRAN

MUCH MORE FROM A LOT LESS

THE ARCHITECTURE OF C. ANJALENDRAN

David Robson

Anjalendran occupies a pivotal position in the evolution of contemporary Sri Lankan architecture. He was born immediately after Sri Lanka gained its independence and grew up in a world of apparent harmony and tolerance, a world which was shattered by the anti-Tamil riots of 1983 and the subsequent decades of civil war.

Having worked briefly in the office of master architect Geoffrey Bawa at the end of the 1970s he developed his own practice during the 1980s against a background of rising communal discord. He was younger than the early generation of Bawa associates—such as Raheem, Ratnavibushana, and Jacobsen who had worked with Bawa during the 1960s and early 1970s—and older than the generation of Jayatilleke, de Mel, and Daswatte, his own former assistants, who worked with Bawa during the 1990s. However, throughout the 1980s he acted as Bawa's unpaid personal assistant and took on the role of link between these different groups.

Anjalendran studiously avoided the "contemporary vernacular" mode which characterised Bawa's work of the 1960s, and his designs respond to Minnette de Silva's call for a regional modern approach (de Silva, 1953, 1965) which was later adopted and developed by Bawa during the 1970s. Anjalendran's projects use local materials and technologies to make affordable buildings that are robust and easy to maintain—more with less. Like Bawa before him he exhibits a sensibility to space and the scenographic dimension of architecture but he places greater emphasis on surface texture and materiality. Whilst Bawa remains his acknowledged guru, Anjalendran has never imitated him, preferring to develop his own preoccupations. And he exhibits his own special qualities—a clarity of purpose, a simple directness, a preoccupation with the social implications of spatial hierarchies, and the use of color to amplify intentions.

A member of the minority Tamil community, Anjalendran still regards himself, first and foremost, as Sri Lankan. He watched in despair as many of his friends and relatives left the island, but he resolved to stay, and today he is one of the very small number of Tamils who are active in the architectural profession. At once an outsider and an insider, his work is undeniably Sri Lankan in spirit though it is enlivened by Tamil nuances.

Anjalendran was born in Colombo in 1951 into a family that had originated in Jaffna's Nallur district and had prospered as civil servants under Dutch and British rule. His maternal grandfather was Suntharalingam, a famous mathematician and politician who was an early advocate of a separate Tamil state, and his father, Chelvadurai, was a successful engineer. Nominally Hindu, the family was western in outlook and spoke English in their bungalow home.

Anjalendran studied at Colombo's elite Royal College, but during his teens he trained as a dancer and was the most promising male exponent of Bharata Natyam of his generation, a fact which probably contributed to his strong awareness of space. Soon after his coming-out dance, however, his father made him give up dancing to concentrate on academic studies. In 1970 he was offered a place to study engineering at the University of Moratuwa but later switched to the newly opened architecture course in the University of Colombo and gained his degree in 1973. He then transferred to the Bartlett in London and completed his diploma in 1976 before joining Bill Hillier's "Space Syntax" course where he obtained an M.Sc. in 1979.

After graduating at University College London, David Robson spent three years in Sri Lanka helping to establish a new School of Architecture in the University of Colombo. Between 1974 and 1979 he was the Principal Housing Architect in Washington New Town in the UK where a number of his designs won national awards. In the early 1980s, he worked as a planning adviser on the Sri Lankan government's "100,000 Houses Programme." He has been Professor of Architecture in the University of Brighton and a Visiting Professor in the National University of Singapore and in the Technical University of Brno. He is the author of books on low-cost aided-self-help housing and housing for the elderly as well monographs on Sri Lankan architects Geoffrey Bawa (2002) and C. Anjalendran (2009). His most recent books include The *New Sri Lankan House* (with Robert Powell, 2015) and *The Architectural Heritage of Sri Lanka* (with C. Anjalendran and Dominic Sansoni, 2015).

Back in Colombo, Anjalendran worked briefly with Geoffrey Bawa at a time when the master architect was developing designs for the Sri Lanka Parliament and the Ruhunu University Campus. However, it soon became clear that he did not fit into the office environment, and with Bawa's help and encouragement, he started his own office on his mother's veranda in 1981. But the two remained friends, and Anjalendran acted as Bawa's unpaid assistant and amanuensis during the next decade. Indeed he was largely responsible, behind the scenes, for putting together Bawa's so-called "White Book" which was published in 1986 (Taylor, 1986), and helped to organise the exhibition which was shown first at the RIBA in London and which later travelled to Brazil, Australia and Singapore.

Anjalendran's practice has always been small. For ten years it operated on his mother's veranda in Cinnamon Gardens and was folded away at night. Since 1991 it has occupied a veranda on one side of the courtyard of his own home-office in the outer suburb of Battaramulla. He owns neither car nor mobile phone, and has never employed a secretary. He claims that he can survive by building one project per year, while two will also support a tour of India, and three will fund a trip to Europe.

One early project was "given" to Anjalendran by Geoffrey Bawa and involved the insertion of an advertising agency into an existing bungalow. Anjalendran insists that Bawa also supplied the initial ideas, but the project helped to launch his practice and strengthened the bond between them. It coincided with his design of a compact courtyard house for the historian Senake Bandaranayake and his wife Manel Fonseka (1980). In many ways this can be viewed as a scaled-down version of Bawa's Ena de Silva House, though it occupies one third of the land. It suggests that Anjalendran began with a desire to emulate the master while making his ideas more accessible.

More houses followed: several, such as the Alagaratnam House (1991) and the Lilani de Silva House (1992), explored ways of creating viable town houses on ever smaller plots. The latter occupied a mere seven perches (175 sqm.) but managed to pack in three bedrooms, servants' quarters, three courtyards, and two roof terraces, all enjoying light, air, and privacy. Non-housing projects of the same period included an office building for Milco (1987), and an astonishing gem factory in Nugeguda (1992).

In 1983, Anjalendran completed a social center in Nuwara Eliya for SOS Children's Villages. This led to his becoming the organisation's sole architect over the next fourteen years during which time he created a series of schools, social centers, and orphanages. These projects demonstrated his ability to create places of great beauty out of simple materials with minimal budgets and allowed him to develop the ideas which had been passed on to him by Bill Hillier in London.

Later projects included a series of estate bungalows: a coconut estate bungalow at Dankotuwa (1997), a cinnamon estate bungalow at Mirissa (2002), and, more recently, a tea estate bungalow at Deniyaya (2013). These enabled him to experiment with ways of connecting buildings to landscape.

Soon after starting his own office he began teaching, first in the University of Moratuwa and later in the Colombo School of Architecture. His office has remained small and almost all of his assistants have been intermediate or graduate students from one or other of the two schools. As a result, a large number of today's practicing architects are his former students or assistants.

Often the boundary between his office and his teaching studio became blurred. In 1983, he had helped Barbara Sansoni and Ronald Lewcock put together the set of measured drawings of old Sri Lankan buildings which would later be published as Architecture of an Island (Lewcock, 1998). This inspired him to embark on his own measured drawing project using both his assistants and his students. Measuring old buildings gave his students a feel for history and honed their surveying and drawing skills, but the results also augmented a growing archive of important records and highlighted the need to protect Sri Lanka's heritage.

Anjalendran is an obsessive collector and it comes as no surprise to learn that his favourite poem is Pablo Neruda's "Ode to Things." He now owns one of the most comprehensive collections of contemporary Sri Lankan paintings as well as representative collections of carved Portuguese saints, bronze Hindu gods, Ena de Silva batiks, and Barbara Sansoni handlooms. However, it is his vast library of dossiers on all the leading architects and artists of his day which is the most noteworthy. This has enabled him to write with authority on a range of topics and publish widely across the sub-continent.

The following selected projects illustrate a number of different typologies and cover each decade of Anjalendran's practice.

Bibliography

Anjalendran C. "The Architecture of SOS Children's Villages," in Sri Lanka Architect Vol. 100 No. 5 (Colombo: Sept-Nov, 1989).
Anjalendran C. "Offices for Milco, Narahenpita," in Mimar No. 34 (Singapore: March, 1990a).
Anjalendran, C. "The Hermann-Gmeiner School, Piliyandela," in Mimar No. 34 (Singapore: March, 1990b).
Anjalendran C. (with Rajiv Wanasundara). "Trends and Transitions," in Architecture and Design (Delhi: March-April, 1990c).
Anjalendran C. "Current Architecture in Sri Lanka," in Mimar No. 42 (London: March, 1992).
Anjalendran C. (with Channa Daswatte). "Recent Architecture in Sri Lanka, 1991-1993," in Architecture and Design (Delhi: July-August, 1994).
Bawa, Geoffrey. "Ceylon – A Philosophy for Building," in Architects' Journal (15 Oct, 1969).
de Silva, Minnette. "A House in Kandy," in Marg Vol. vi, no. 3 (Bombay: June 1953).
de Silva, Minnette. "Experiments in Modern Regional Architecture in Ceylon," in Journal of the Ceylon Institute of Architects (Colombo: 1965-66).
Lewcock, Ronald, Barbara Sansoni & Laki Senanayake. The Architecture of an Island (Colombo: Barefoot, 1998).
Lim, William and Tan Hock Ben. Contemporary Vernacular (Singapore: Select Books, 1998).
Robson, David. "Three Villages in Sri Lanka," in Mimar No. 43 (June, 1992).
Robson, David. Bawa: The Complete Works (London: Thames and Hudson, 2002).
Robson, David. Beyond Bawa: Modern Masterpieces of Monsoon Asia (London: Thames and Hudson, 2007).
Robson, David. Anjalendran: Architect of Sri Lanka (Singapore: Tuttle, 2009).
Sansoni, Barbara. Vihares and Verandahs (Colombo: Barefoot Pvt Ltd., 1978).
Taylor, Brian B. et al. Geoffrey Bawa (Singapore: Concept Media, 1986. Colombo: Icomos, 1996).

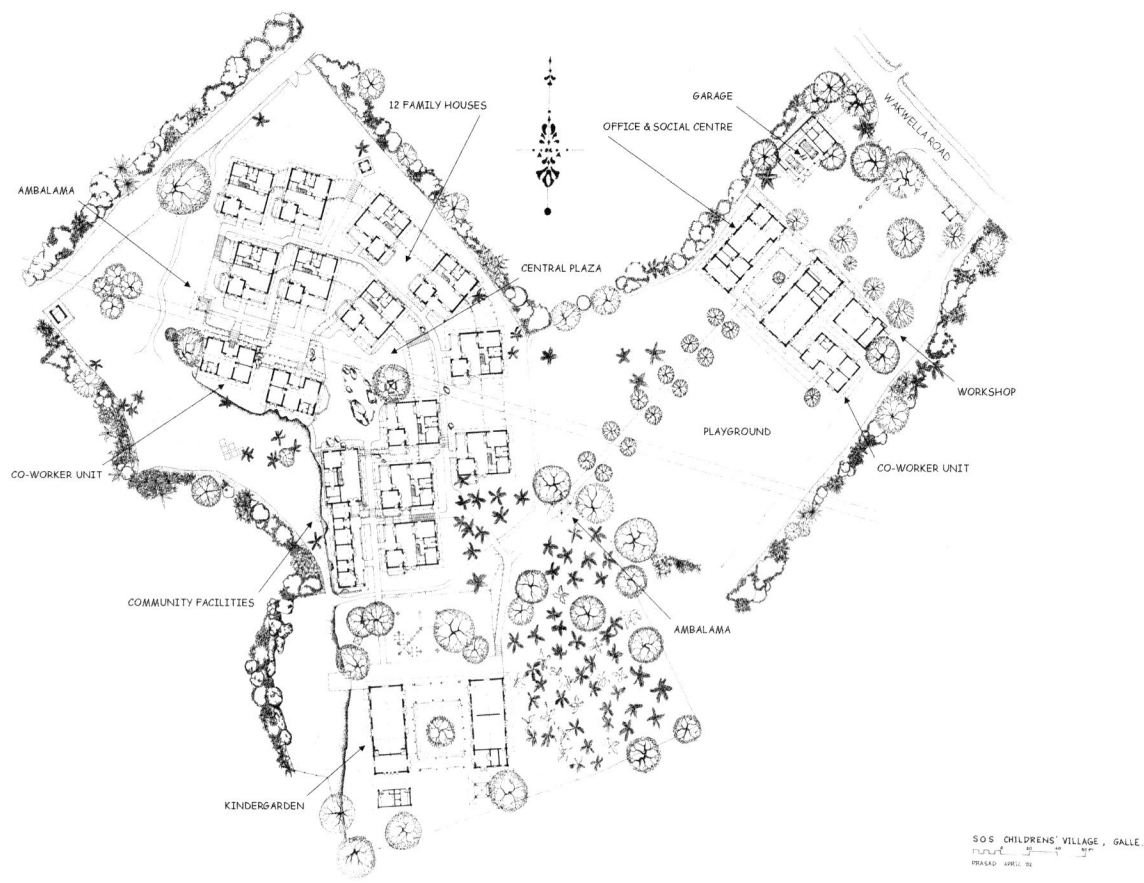

12 FAMILY HOUSES

AMBALAMA

GARAGE

OFFICE & SOCIAL CENTRE

WAKWELLA ROAD

CENTRAL PLAZA

WORKSHOP

PLAYGROUND

CO-WORKER UNIT

CO-WORKER UNIT

COMMUNITY FACILITIES

AMBALAMA

KINDERGARDEN

SOS CHILDRENS' VILLAGE, GALLE.
PRASAD APRIL 92

SOS Children's Village
Galle, Sri Lanka, 1987-94

In the early 1980s the Austrian charity SOS Childern's Villages International employed an Indian firm of architects to build their first village in Sri Lanka at Piliyandela near Colombo. Soon after this Anjalendran was commissioned to build a second village in Nuwara Eliya as well as a school in Piliyandela. The Piliyandela school was built using locally available materials with a unit cost of less than half that of the adjacent village. Subsequently Anjalendran became the main SOS architect in Sri Lanka and over the next fourteen years went on to design two more villages, several schools, social centers, and a home for retired mothers.

The Galle SOS Village is located on the northern edge of the town. Anjalendran's plan placed the administrative buildings next to the road and relegated the village and its associated primary school to a wooded hillside at the back of the site. This had the advantage of leaving a large flat area free for a playing field, but also allowed the houses to benefit from the improved ventilation and tree-shade of the hillside.

Visitors enter the enclosed courtyard of the reception building and then cross the playing field along an avenue of aralia trees. This terminates in a small pavilion in the form of a traditional ambalama that marks the boundary between the school and the village, the two being separated by a generously equipped play space. The plan of the school echoes that of the administrative building: two parallel pavilions are linked by covered arcades around a courtyard.

The village itself contains a dozen family houses, each home to ten children with their surrogate mother, and four staff houses which are

arranged along the contours in such a way as to create two principal routes, a central village square, and a number of cross-alleyways. The houses are split-level to accommodate the slope. An entrance veranda leads into the double height main living room from which half-stairs connect up and down to the bedroom floors. Flouting tradition, Anjalendran placed the kitchen at the front so that it could serve as the eye of the house and enable the house-mother to look after her charges.

Walls are built of a combination of black granite and honey coloured "kudugal" and roofs are of clay "Calicut" tiles. Bright colors are applied to the concrete frame and the woodwork to add interest and identity, and the utilitarian cement floors are punctuated with brightly colored tiles. The buildings were cheap to build, but, equally important, they are robust and have been easy to maintain. After twenty years they look as good as new.

In Galle, Anjalendran strikes a fine balance between order, accident, unity, and variety. The strong sense of community is tempered by the autonomy of the individual parts and the logical pattern of the layout is broken to accommodate the vagaries of the landscape. The spaces between the buildings are every bit as important as the buildings themselves and every pocket of ground is made to work: boulders are incorporated into the landscape and trees offer shade and protection.

Entrance to the village.

SOS CHILDREN'S VILLAGE - GALLE
FAMILY HOUSE - SECTION & ELEVATIONS

DEEPALI / FEBRUARY '91.

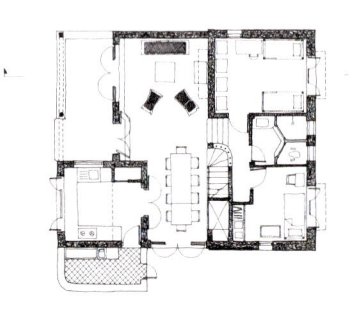

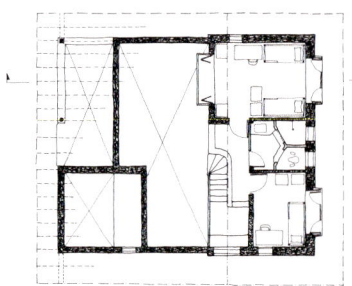

SOS CHILDREN'S VILLAGE - GALLE
FAMILY HOUSE - PLANS

DEEPALI / FEBRUARY '91

Typical house veranda.

The Aralia Avenue.

The Village Center.

Anjalendran's Home-Office
Battaramulla, Sri Lanka, 1991-93

Anjalendran quit his mother's home in 1992 and moved to the new suburb of Battaramulla. The house that he built for himself functions as his home, his office, the library for his huge collection of books and his private art gallery. It occupies a tiny plot of ten perches (250 sqm.) and sits at the heart of a small enclave of houses that he has designed for friends and relatives.

It consists of two pavilions which face each other across a small garden court. The main pavilion is on two floors: above are two bedrooms and a bathroom; below are the kitchen, the carport/entrance which doubles an overflow drawing office and the large double-height space which functions as sitting room, dining room, office, and conference room. In the second pavilion are the main bedroom and the veranda drawing office.

The idea of the house can be traced back to le Corbusier's Maison Citrohan and may have been inspired by the modernist houses which Bawa and his associate Ulrik Plesner built in Colombo at the beginning of the 1960s, but its pragmatic no-nonsense approach is uniquely that of Anjalendran.

The palette of materials is simple—a concrete frame painted in subtle colors, plain white plastered walls on the inside and rubble walls outside, a roof of round clay tiles laid on corrugated cement sheet. Overhanging eaves shield the interior from tropical sun and monsoon rain while the steeply sloping ceilings encourage cooling drafts. The most important single element is the central courtyard: a sea of crushed red kabook under a single tree. This acts as the lung of the house and registers the passage of time and the changing pattern of the weather.

The house serves as a prototype for low-energy, high-density living. It turns its back on the congested chaos of the burgeoning city and creates an oasis of tranquillity. Water is drawn from a well, soil waste is disposed of in a septic tank, storm water runs into a soak-away, natural stack ventilation removes the need for air-conditioning. Multiplied by two it became a generous town house for Anjalendran's friends Dharmavasan and Julie; divided by two it became a compact and affordable self-built house for their nanny.

Courtyard towards the office veranda.

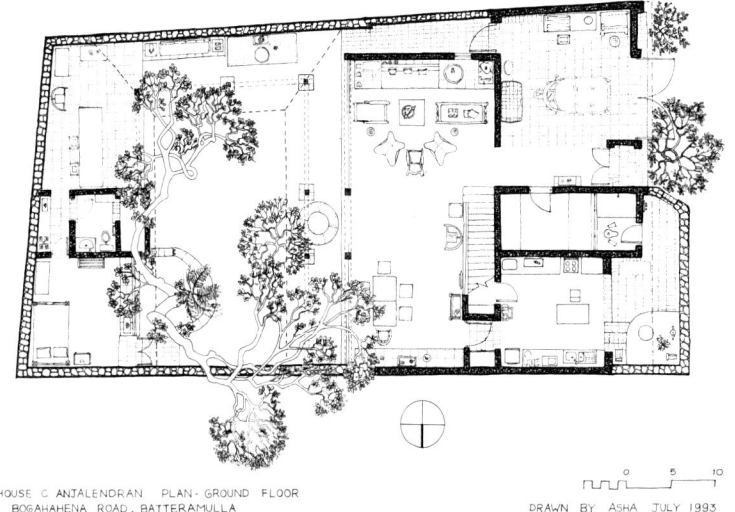

OWN HOUSE C ANJALENDRAN   PLAN - GROUND FLOOR
60/8 BOGAHAHENA ROAD, BATTERAMULLA

DRAWN BY ASHA JULY 1993

0   5   10

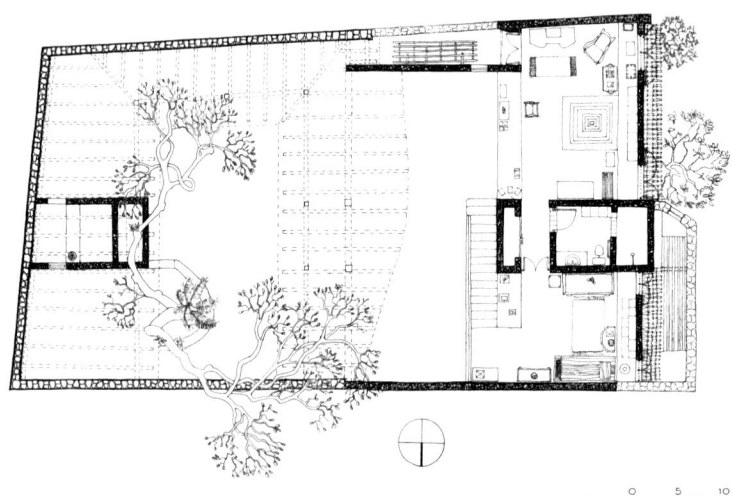

OWN HOUSE C ANJALENDRAN   PLAN - UPPER   FLOOR
60/8 BOGAHAHENA ROAD, BATTERAMULLA

DRAWN BY ASHA JULY 1993

0   5   10

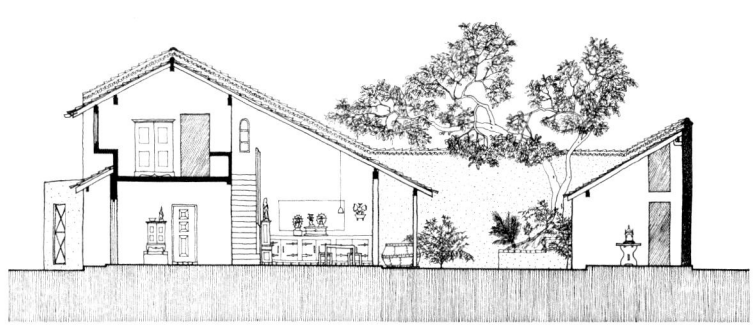

OWN HOUSE C ANJALENDRAN - SECTION
60/8 BOGAHAHENA ROAD, BATTERAMULLA

DRAWN BY MOHAN NOV 1995

0   5   10

View from the sitting room.

From multi table to courtyard.

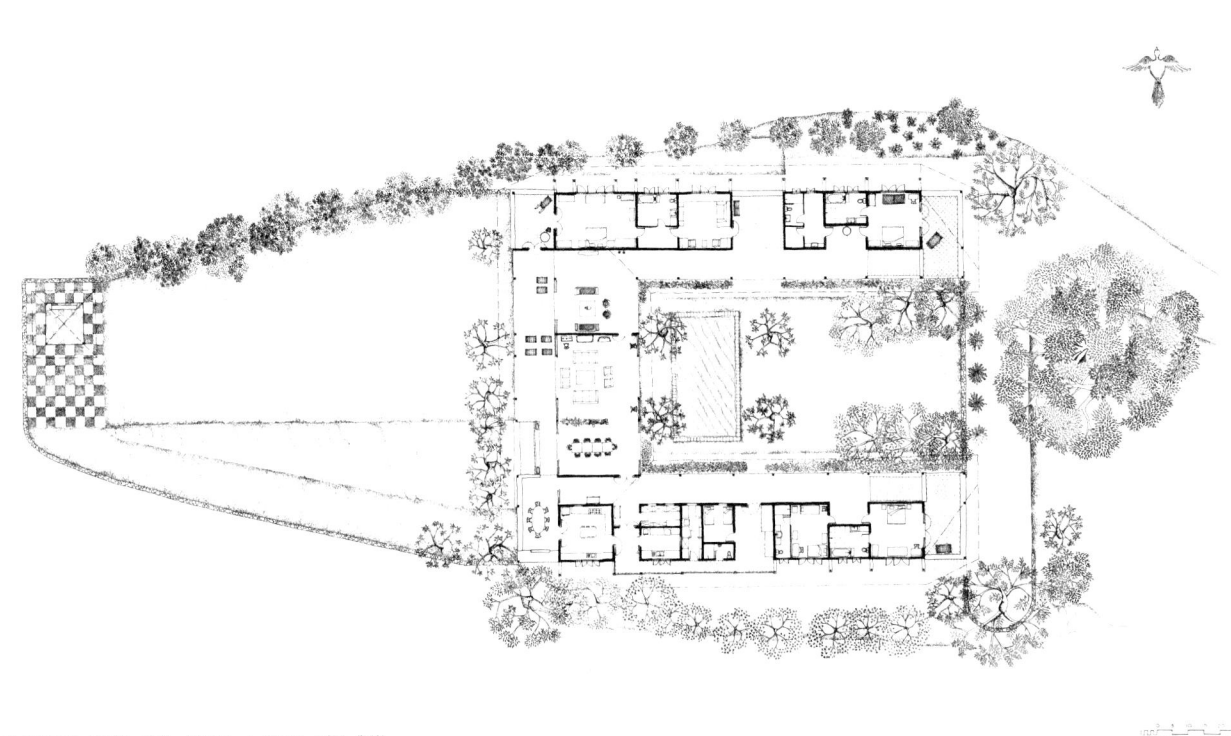

CLIENT OCCASION, MIRISSA HILLS, MIRISSA | GROUND FLOOR PLAN

Cinnamon Hills,
Mirissa, Sri Lanka, 2002-2011

In 2001 Anjalendran was asked to design a new bungalow for a hilltop cinnamon estate near Weligama Bay on the south coast of Sri Lanka. The owner, Miles Young, was the CEO of a Hong Kong based advertising company. Anjalendran was initially reluctant to get involved with a complex project for an expatriate client, but he was won over by the challenge of the site and he and Young became firm friends.

The estate lacked any form of habitation and Anjalendran's first move was to persuade Young to buy a plot of land close to the foot of the hill on which was an elegant but dilapidated colonial bungalow. This was remodelled to serve first as a temporary residence and later as a supplementary guest house. Meanwhile a new principal bungalow was taking shape on the top of the hill in a position which commanded magnificent views south-westwards over the Indian Ocean and north-wards towards the Southern Highlands. The main body of the house was raised to the very summit and took the form of two parallel wings connected by an open sitting and dining rooms to form a courtyard and swimming pool. The sitting room opens to a deep veranda that looks out across a sculpted lawn to a small roofed pavilion which punctuates the view across the bay towards the setting sun. On the lower level the south wing has been fashioned into an arcade that serves as a sculpture gallery, while the north wing houses the car-port and entrance.

Although spatially generous, the buildings are of simple construction, designed to withstand the buffeting of the monsoons. Miles Young, like Anjalendran, is a collector, and together they have filled the spaces with paintings and sculptures, as well as carefully chosen pieces of antique and contemporary furniture. Pride of place goes to the metal sculpture, commissioned from artist Laki Senanayake, which forms a

screen between the sitting and dining rooms, to the large Ena de Silva batiks which hang on the walls of the Visitor Centre and to the wayside shrine dedicated to Patini, the goddess revered by cinnamon peelers.

Young's requirements evolved as the project progressed and over the past decade a number of other buildings have been added to the estate. His enthusiasm for cinnamon has led him to create a visitor center which incorporates a museum, a demonstration kitchen, a restaurant, and budget-priced guest accommodation. This is located on a shelf of land below the summit and occupies a formal two storey pavilion with a central courtyard. The cinnamon peelers are seasonal workers who belong to a particular caste and live apart from the local villagers. Anjalendran designed a special structure to provide them with temporary accommodation above cinnamon workshops and stores. In another corner he has built a small hamlet of farm cottages for the permanent workforce.

The various buildings have been conceived as events within an organised landscape and plans are now afoot to create a circuit of pathways through the cinnamon plantation, much after the manner of an 18th century English landscaped garden or, indeed, of Geoffrey Bawa's garden at Lunuganga.

This whole project has cost little more than the price of a single house in Central London. It celebrates the mysteries of cinnamon while adding a new chapter in the long history of estate bungalows.

From multi table to courtyard.

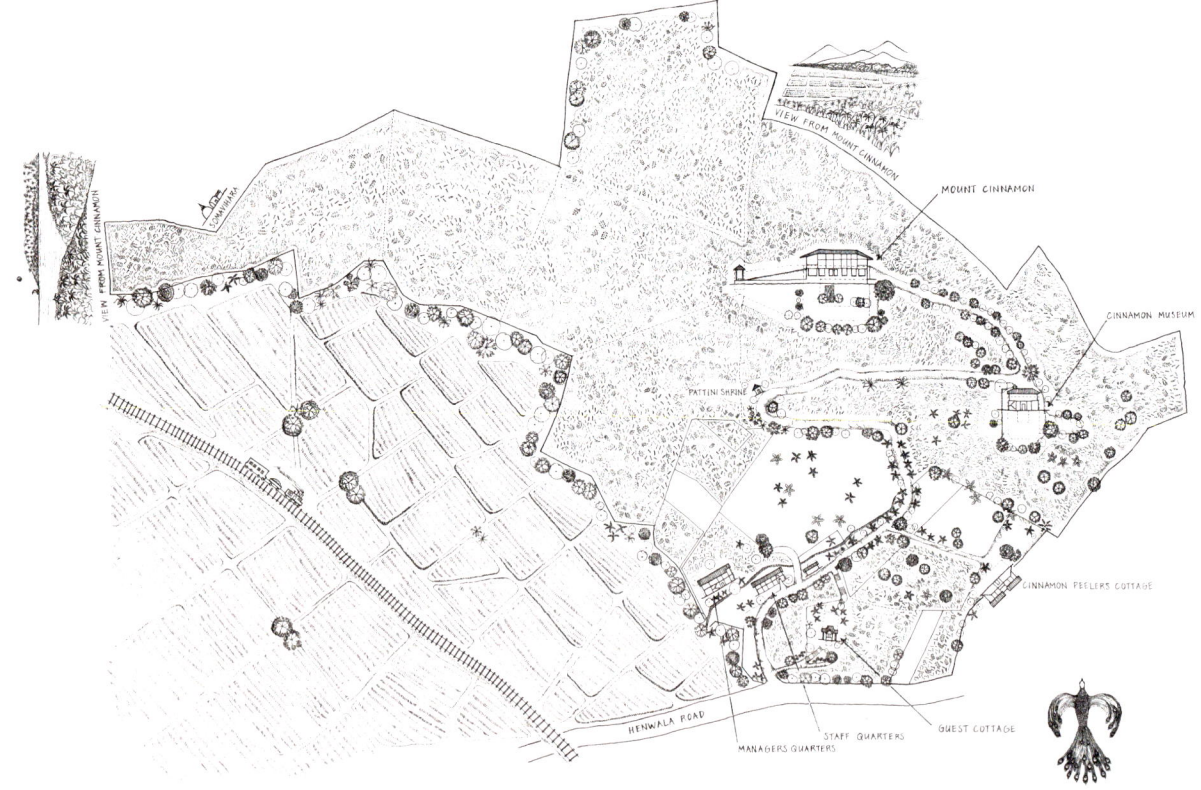

LOCATION PLAN
MIRISSA HILLS, HENWALA ROAD, WELIGAMA, MATARA.

The Patini shrine.

View across the lawn.

Pool court and veranda.

The breakfast balcony.

View towards the Ambalama.

View across the lawn.

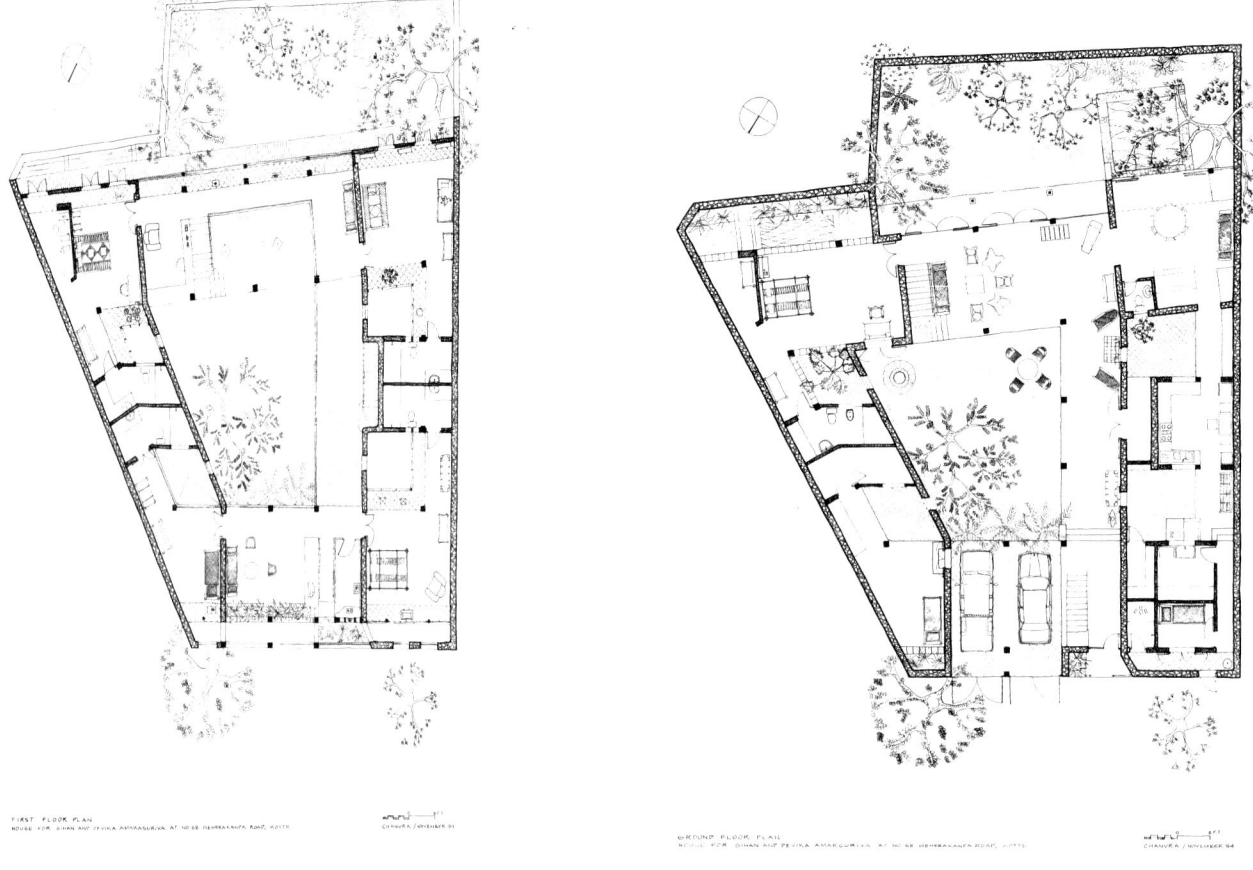

FIRST FLOOR PLAN
HOUSE FOR GIHAN AND DEVIKA AMARASURIYA AT NO 68 DEHIWAKANTA ROAD, KOTTE   CHANURA / DECEMBER 94

GROUND FLOOR PLAN
HOUSE FOR GIHAN AND DEVIKA AMARASURIYA AT NO 68 DEHIWAKANTA ROAD, KOTTE   CHANURA / NOVEMBER 94

Amarasuriya House
Kotte, Sri Lanka, 1989-91

Which is the more astonishing: that Anjalendran conceived of such a bizarre house or that his client went ahead and built it? Gihan Amarasuriya's family owns tea estates in the south of Sri Lanka and Anjalendran had already built a compact estate bungalow for him near Galle in 1985. Now married, he wanted to build a town house for his future family, a house for elaborate parties with plenty of room for overnight guests. His site lay in Kotte close to the ruins of the medieval citadel of Sri Jayawardenepura. Perhaps these inspired Anjalendran to build what is in effect a small urban fortress, but he may also have been led on by his passion for crusader castles.

The house is completely enclosed by a high rubble wall, which is only broken to make way for the car-port and entrance. The rooms are arranged in a cordon that surrounds a single stone-faced courtyard, a cordon that is pierced by vertical shafts which bring light and air to the kitchen and the bathrooms. On the ground floor there's a bedroom wing to the left and the kitchen and servant's wing to the right while beyond a closure wing contains the double-height sitting room and the dining room. On the first floor are more bedrooms as well as a study balcony, a family sitting room and a Buddhist shrine. A final stone stair winds up to the roof which takes the form of a continuous paved terrace with two roofed pavilions and a perimeter of continuous raised planter beds. The large planter beds at the four corners occupy what might have been artillery emplacements but contain flowers instead of guns.

Courtyard and the sitting room.

152

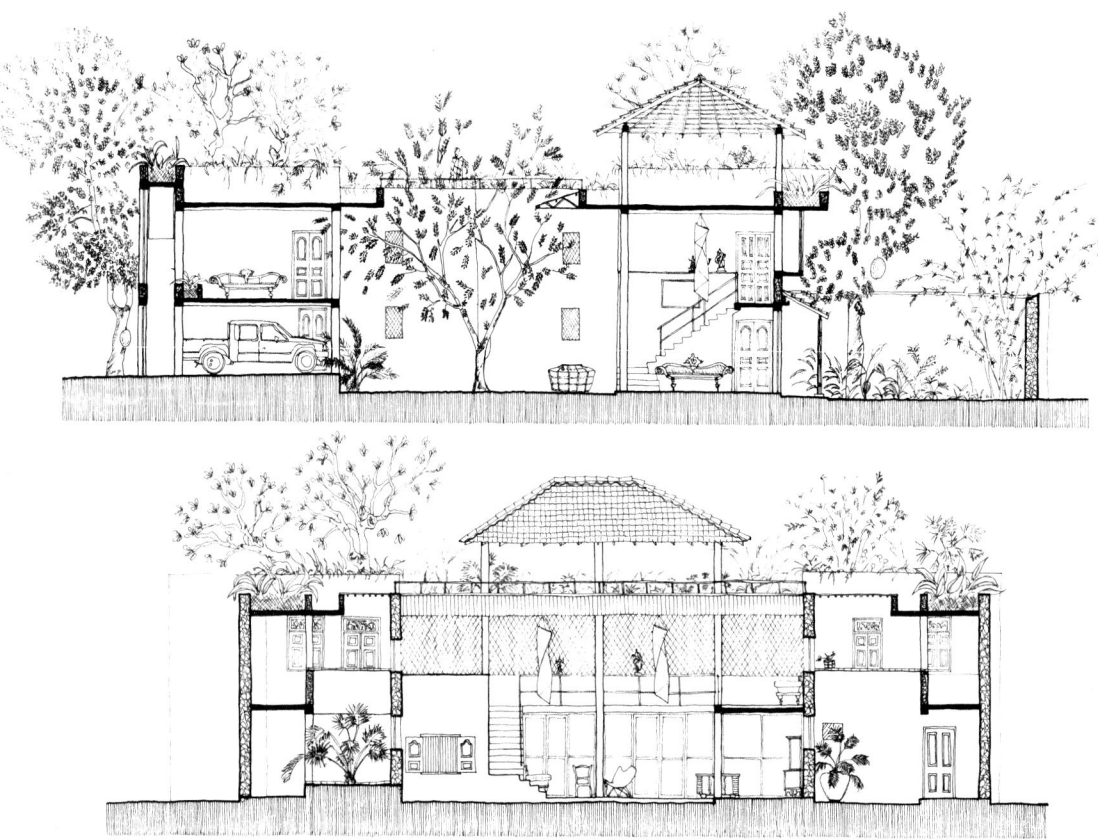

CHANUKA / NOVEMBER 04

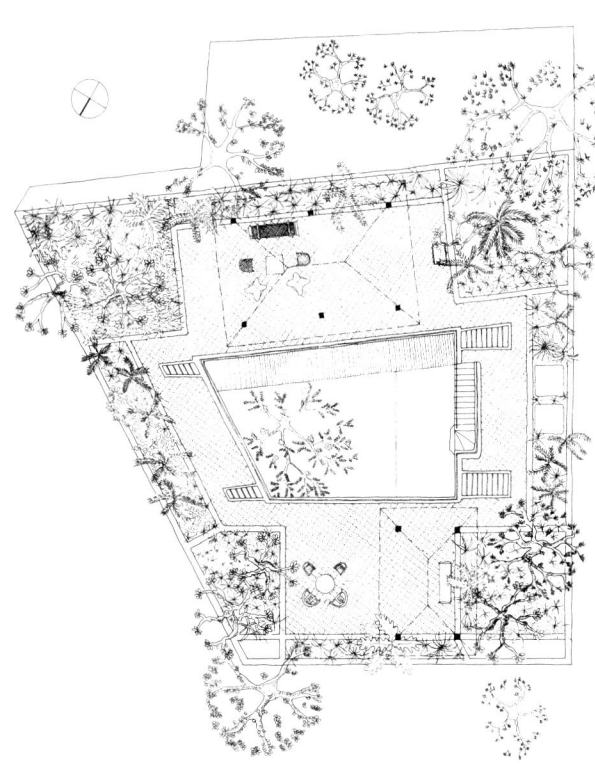

Stair to the roof level.

The stair and the mezzanine study.

Courtyard.

Uluru-Kata Tjuta Cultural Centre (Photo: Jimmy Yang).

GREGORY BURGESS

TO CALL MY TRUE LOVE TO DANCE[1]

FIVE BUILDINGS BY GREGORY BURGESS

Conrad Hamann

Conrad Hamann is associate professor in Architectural History in the School of Architecture and Design, RMIT University, Melbourne. Earlier, he studied architectural history at Columbia and then Yale Universities on a Harkness fellowship. At RMIT he teaches Australian architecture, twentieth century architecture, and the general history of urban form. He is completing a book on Gregory Burgess' architecture since 1968, and a second book on the engineer Bill Irwin, both for URO Publishing. With Philip Goad and Geoffrey London, he is completing *An Unfinished Experiment in Living: Australian Architects and the Detached House, 1950-1965*, for the University of Western Australia Press. He has also published a book on the Australian architects Maggie Edmond and Peter Corrigan (Oxford, 1993; revised and expanded for Thames and Hudson, 2012). He has written and published 120 articles, essays, and commentaries for publishers in Australia, Britain, Germany, and Japan. For nine years he worked with Lovell Chen, architecture and heritage consultants; he completed over 150 surveys for them and became a senior associate there.

Gregory Burgess has been active as an Australian architect since the 1970s, and since the 1990s his designs have gained increasing attention in Asia and Europe. His Hackford house in eastern Victoria (1980-81), burnt down in a forest fire, was on the cover of the London *Architectural Review*'s 1985 issue on Australian architecture, and his Uluru Kata-Tjuta cultural center in Central Australia was on the cover of Tokyo's *A+U* in 1996. Peter Davey, reviewing the world's architectural hopes in 1997, saw Burgess as one of a few clear prospects as his architectural forms, not determined by market concerns, engaged both nature and the spirit. Along with Ralph Erskine and Frank Gehry, two of Davey's other nominees, Burgess shares a pluralist approach to architecture, with a constant response to the details and circumstances of context, built as well as natural. Burgess and Gehry developed their approaches initially in responding to largely suburban context in their respective cities, Melbourne and Los Angeles. At the same time, Burgess' celebration of the spiritual and the natural in form and materials led to his being seen as "Sydney" (Glenn Murcutt, Richard Le Plastrier, Peter Stutchbury) and so outside of Melbourne's often aggressively inner urban, industrial, and grit-based architectural thinking. But as with Gehry, Burgess has shown an ability to straddle the gulf between architectural pluralism and its predominantly urban and suburban engagement, and a consciously anti-material, anti-consumerist stance, with architecture marked by a consistent environmental concern.

Gregory Burgess's architectural direction showed early. His student designs stressed recycling and careful intervention in an existing inner suburbs, warts and all, at a time when the University of Melbourne expected its final year students to flatten such surroundings for high-rise replacements. His earlier solo practice designs, though broadly characteristic of the early and mid 1970s with window chamfers, rounded return stairs, bursts of bright color and earthy-finished materials, but showed a spatial and thematic complexity quite distinct from most contemporary Australian work. Burgess soon showed an acute sense of newer directions, generated in part from his awareness of palpably transgressive architects overseas, including Paolo Portoghesi, Ralph Erskine, Bruce Goff, Hans Scharoun, and much earlier, Rudolf Steiner.

A marked shift in Burgess's architecture also developed around 1977-1982. This was stimulated by meditation and shows in his journey into the sweeping lines and tension of expressed movement and the pauses and episodic repose offered by symbolic geometry. These parallel forms resonate with Theosophy's emphasis on eurythmia; they also recall the German Expressionists' fascination with polygonal and crystalline shapes, and the way these could act as lenses for the spirit and varied contexts of surrounding cities through their vision of the Stadtkrone or "urban crown." This links him also with Walter Burley Griffin, Marion Mahony and their circle in Australia earlier. As with the Griffins, Burgess also brings an acutely narrative, sequential sense to his plan shapes and expressed themes. The architectural consequence of narratives, with episode and encounter, finds expression and exploration in a significant chain of Australian architects recurring over the last century. Designs of Gregory Burgess bring back something of the cultural ferment of the 1900s when Australia was breaking free from the Victorian order through Free Style architecture, the Arts and Crafts Movement, and their own engagement with early modernism.

There is, besides, the continued parallel with often forgotten details and imagery from the half-vernacular, half-architected tradition of other architecture in Melbourne suburbs and in Victoria's regional buildings. The sheet-panels and battens on Burgess's Mendelson house (1995, 2007) and in the bedroom wings of his Burraworrin (1998) and Stone House (2005), the casual timber planking on the outer walls of his Eltham Library and Community Centre (1994), or the similarly planked side walls of his Brambuk Living Cultural Centre (1990), are the stock of innumerable, everyday Australian buildings of the period 1900-1950. Brambuk, which for a moment around its entrance leads you in among the storage buildings and side streets of many of Victoria's country towns, speaks of building since modernity, but of its more casual, taken-for granted byways rather than its heroic moments.

And yet Burgess's architecture has a continual sense of the heroic and the monumental. By monumental I mean compressed assemblages of forms redolent with meaning, rather than the more broadly accepted view of monumental as beyond human scale, with massive form and conspicuously enduring materials. The monumentality of action has been a recurring characteristic of Australia's most interesting architecture, and at several points has fused between building genres. In Australia's Federation period (1890-1915), for example, suburban houses came to embody so much force they could notionally be sited on central city street corners and still hold their own. This arguably also true of Gregory Burgess buildings: numbers of his houses and highway rests could be transplanted to inner city corners and work there in sheer architectural energy. This is in part why they have a heroic demeanour. But heroism in Gregory Burgess buildings also stems from their sheer delight in embracing complex tasks and reflecting that complexity,

Yet, these Burgess buildings would be difficult places to inhabit if there was no separation in scale and movement sense, in compression of meaning, between interior and exterior. Their monumental or heroic sense would only be sounding brass or tinkling cymbal unless balanced with an abiding affection for the details of life and task inside each building. Inside, the continuing sense of occasion and event in his buildings is now sustained by narrative events – the revelation of light through moveable skylights, and his continually layered stairwells; the renewed use of the corridor, often curving out of sight or broadening into unexpected living space. This has evolved into two main themes that interweave constantly with each other. The first is the projection of movement in the imagery; the second is the sense of episodes or destination-places in each of his buildings, reinforced by either a symmetrical shape or an orchestration of light and concentric layers at a central point.

Melbourne's red brick provided his designs with an early link to surrounding imagery and context, best seen in his Johnson house in Camberwell (1984), or his Northcote Health Center, begun the same year. Brick dominates various of his later Melbourne designs, as with his Box Hill Community Arts center (1985-90) and his Catholic Theological College in East Melbourne (1999). Familiar with the Ballarat and Stawell region, Burgess harnessed the rich bricks of quarries in western Victoria, employing them on his Horsham Catholic Church of 1988 When Victoria's bricks became expensive after 1995, he switched to other forms that could generate a similar vividness and texture, and still be harnessed to the projection of movement. These included powder-coated steel, color-washed concrete, rammed earth and wider and less customary use of timber, ceramics, and glass. A series of buildings reflect this: notably the Space Science center at Strathmore, Melbourne, the High Country Visitor Center at rural Mansfield (both 2006), the Burrunja Cultural center at Upwey in Melbourne's eastern hills (2011), and the Institute of Koorie (aboriginal) Education, Deakin University in Geelong (2012). Many Australian buildings reflect this recent material change. But Burgess's usage is essentially his own: close-grained, changeful, as Ruskin would have it, and again, as Ruskin urged, lined with the colors and imagery of nature.

Notes

[1] From Tomorrow Shall be my Dancing Day, traditional (fourteenth century?) in William Sandys' *Christmas Carols Ancient and Modern* (London, 1833).
[2] Notably the Metal Workers' Union building in Kreuzberg, Berlin,1921-24, and the Park Synagogue, Cleveland Heights Ohio, 1948-50.

De Young Centre for Performing Arts
Carey Baptist Grammar School
Barkers Road Kew, Australia, 2010

Named after a former principal, the performing arts center and music school is Carey's first notable architecture since its original building, alongside the school's first building, Urangeline, formerly a private house by Reed, Henderson, and Barnes, completed in 1884. Urangeline was among Australia's first forays into Queen Anne-inflected free style, and the center acknowledges this in its use of a similar hue to the old building's red brick, flecked with the black, gold and some green flashes. The red-brown colors, and some of the actual brick, continue the building it replaced, Laycock House (1926), a stolidly proportioned dormitory that was later converted to science classrooms, with a hipped roof and symmetrical composition otherwise carrying typically mid-1920s neo-Georgian suggestions. This shared the new building's site with a pair of tennis courts so the previous imagery was of solidity on one hand and open space on the other.

In the new building this duality is suggested, but now shivered into facets of changeful episodes, in flashes of open window-walled "voids," lit like lanterns at night, and with other facets of solid surfacing closing over at intervals, like shutters in the flashing images of a zootrope. With zigzagging skyline, an outgrowth of the earlier fan forms of Burgess houses such as Windhover are used on the center (1981). The main stair, squeezed through the office walls, is another embodiment of Scharoun and Aalto displacement in mass, marks the boundary not only between the auditorium and the smaller classroom areas, but also between the inherently rectilinear geometry of the music school

rooms and their necessary closure, and the large and celebratory auditorium which bows outward as if in response to the envisaged action inside. The juxtaposition of these geometries reworks Aalto: the free, even billowing form of Aalto's church naves, as at Imatra, and his auditoria, as at Helsinki's House of Culture, and the tighter geometry of necessarily rectilinear room grouping, as with the House of Culture's office wing, the Imatra Church vestry and the encircling city wall around Rovaniemi Cultural Centre. But the sense of sculpture in this building is altogether different from the Aalto designs, if not wholly distant from the changeful and almost haptic sense in Scharoun's school and hall exteriors. The exterior reads in waves, in gusts, as music is so often experienced. At its edges the timber awning braces recall the necks and bows of stringed instruments, cellos, and bases. Scharoun's extraordinary section in his 1957-62 Berlin Philharmonie, where the auditorium becomes almost a bird's nest set on oblique strut-poles, is recalled here, especially in the building's rearing mass as it sits against the main road outside.

But Burgess' design is also figured in scales and textures that are undeniably local and of attenuated proportions, echoing both his considerable contact with Australian inland and with lightly built, circumstantial structures on the one hand, and the bulk of his sites in Melbourne suburbs, with there materiality and often unexpected ranks of plate-glass and aluminium-framed windows. There is something in this design of sticks for balusters and lean-to poles for columns. The

CLEARANCE 2.3m

Photo: John Gollings

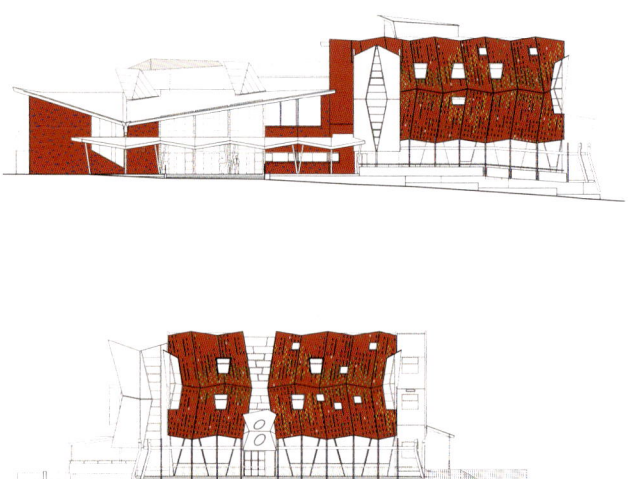

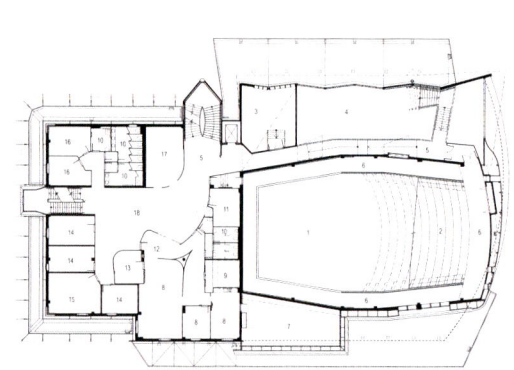

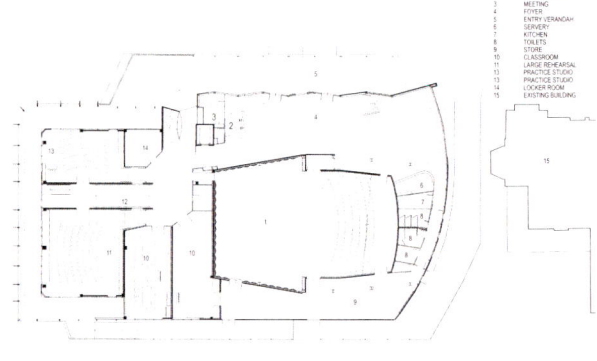

iris-window, first explored in Burgess' public housing of the early 1980s, recurs in the projection of winding stairs on the western entry to the classrooms, the oculus windows now squeezed off-center by the sheer force of movement around them. So too with the leaning balusters on the main stair, back-staggered for a time as if catching breath before the final push to the top, or the breaths implicit in so much music. The stair hall is clearly grown from the CTC center in East Melbourne (1999), but is now a crush area rather than a central core, and the vistas and the climb of the stairs themselves are geared to make it an intermediate space, encountered on our way to the conclusive dramas in the auditorium and the music rooms, but infusing Carey's audience with a flashed encounter with expanding and free space.

In both legacy and image Carey's new music center sustains the heroism in plurality, and the sheer sense of occasion, of other smallish institutional buildings in Melbourne's middle-range of suburbs, as with Edmond and Corrigan's Ringwood Library (1995) and Burgess' own Community Arts centre at Box Hill (1990), Eltham Library (1992) and Community Health Center at Northcote (1984-7). It also reminds one that Burgess is very much an architect within Melbourne suburbs, as much as he works in rural settings.

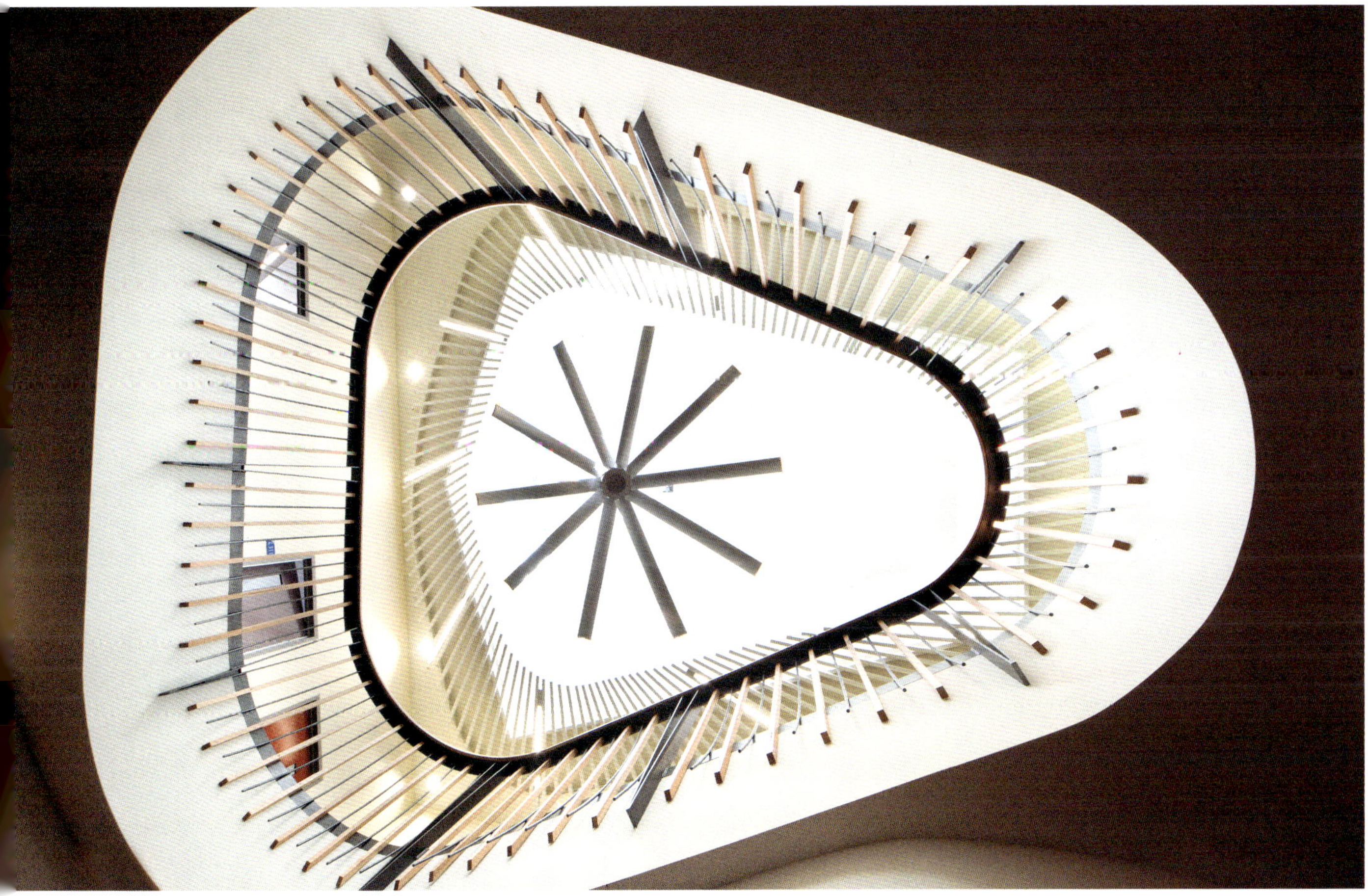

All photos: John Gollings

Moorooduc Estate Winery and Restaurant
Mornington, Victoria, Australia, 2001

Winemaking has developed on the peninsula south of Melbourne, and, as elsewhere in Australia, is reflected in growing numbers of winery-restaurant buildings. Moorooduc was among the first, and shows the balance between simple rectangular service and servant spaces, and Burgess' commitment to representing an order of movement. This is now concentrated in a channel of canted, splayed, and seemingly displaced areas in a run through the center of the design, with the core vesica pisces reiterated (almost) in a central vestibule. Externally this shows as a set of bays, each expressed with a coved roof, while the more mobile spaces around the kitchen and wet areas are shown as a double-height bay set off-center, surmounted by a lookout tower with a wing-form cantilevered roof. As with Burraworrin and Burgess' other more recent Peninsula houses, the winery and restaurant use rammed earth or pise extensively, both for thermal advantage and in answer to the new expense of clay brick. The coved interiors, the lightly columned verandah and the look-out tower have varied precursors around the peninsula and in central Victoria, and they give the building a faciality,

a human countenance, seen at several points in the Carey Performing Arts Centre. But they also, interestingly, evoke the luminous first wave of great public architecture in Victoria. With Moorooduc, much of the grace and arcaded movement embodied in, say, JJ Clark's Old Melbourne Treasury (1857-1862), and the mixture of solemnity and whimsy seen in William Wardell's Melbourne Gothic Bank (1883-1885). The wrought steel balustrade, seen in other Burgess designs, mirrors the coved roofing above. This dance of line, in turn ascribing a split vesica pisces, recalls the mirror imaging swoop and sinew in the balconies of his earlier Hackford house of 1980-81.

Photo: John Gollings

Photo: John Gollings

Photo: Gregory Burgess

Photo: John Gollings

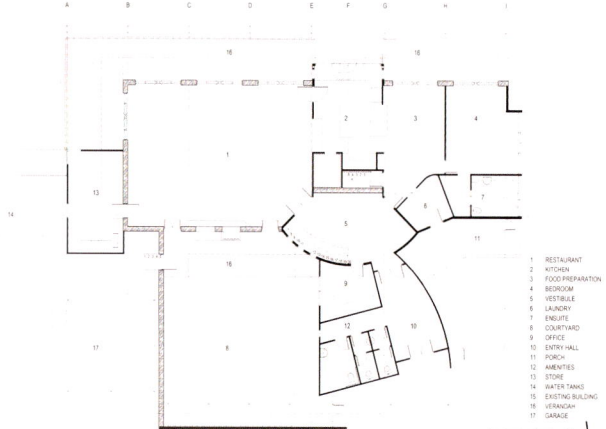

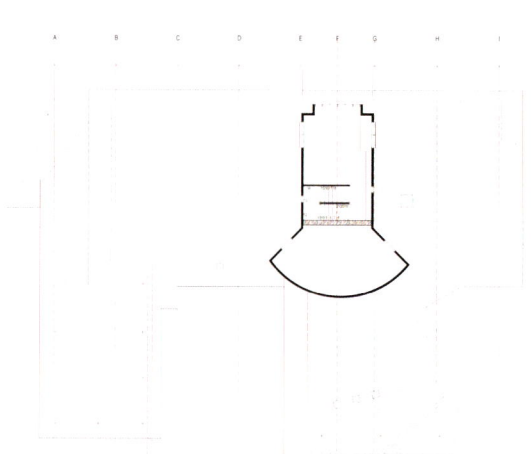

1   RESTAURANT
2   KITCHEN
3   FOOD PREPARATION
4   BEDROOM
5   VESTIBULE
6   LAUNDRY
7   ENSUITE
8   COURTYARD
9   OFFICE
10   ENTRY HALL
11   PORCH
12   AMENITIES
13   STORE
14   WATER TANKS
15   EXISTING BUILDING
16   VERANDAH
17   GARAGE

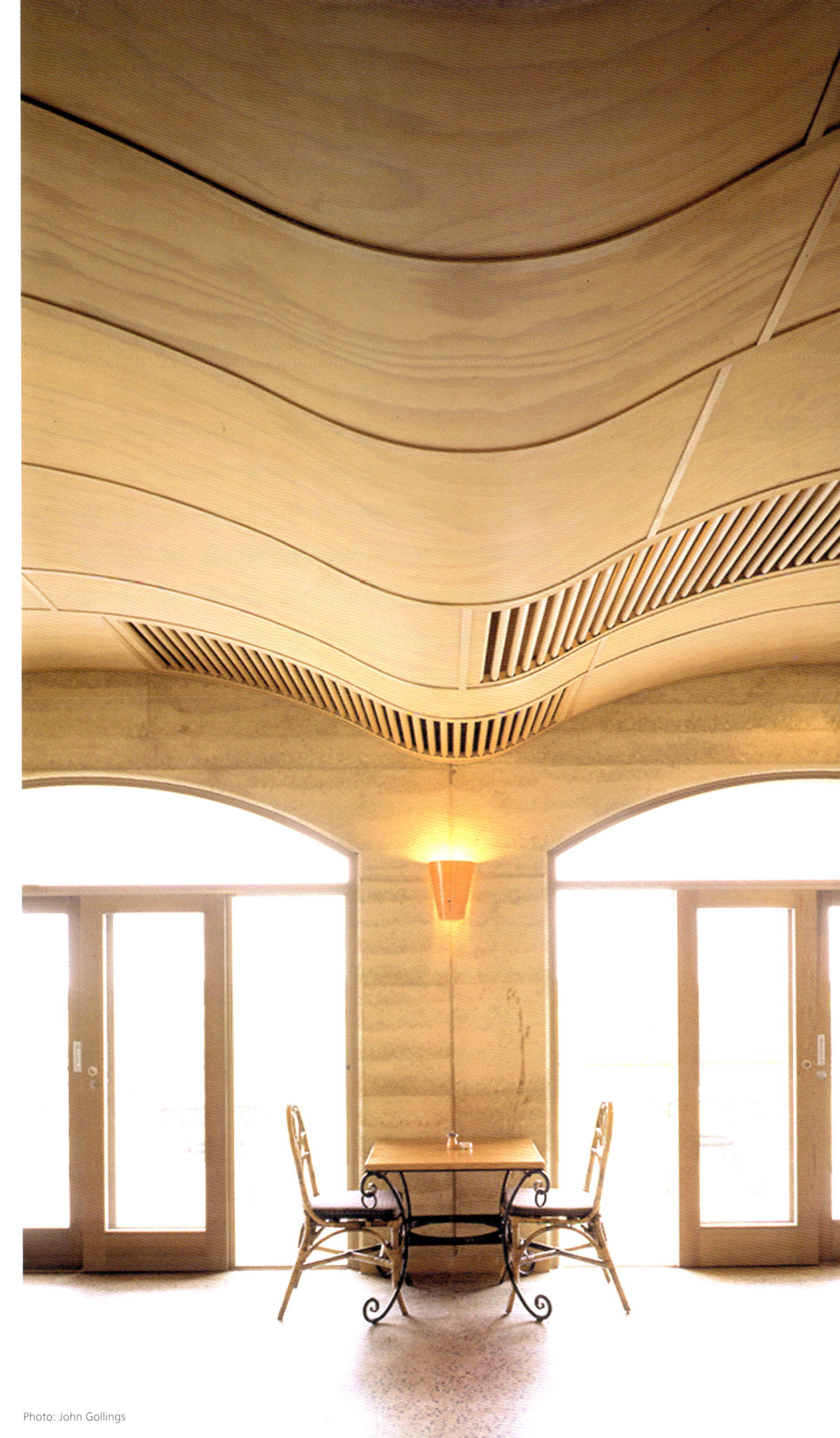

Burraworrin, Castan House
Shoreham, Victoria, Australia, 1998

Burraworrin was the first of four large family houses to Burgess' design at Shoreham on the eastern side of the Mornington Peninsula, south of Melbourne. Here, the family was of a notable lawyer who had argued successfully for Aboriginal land rights over twenty years. The house is placed at the crest of a knoll overlooking the deep blue of Westernport Bay. The building reads in profile as a large yacht or a small ship, with a forward-staggered conning tower and "front" decking, and small port-hole-like openings and pergola "rear" decking like the marquee decks of old clippers and earlier resort ships. This profile had been seen in numbers of Mornington Peninsula houses from the 1930s on, though much more literal than in this design. But at the same time, Burraworrin has the irregularly trimmed planking suggestive of the bundled branches of east coast aboriginal shelter. In plan and in its sensations of entry, the house furls walls around itself as if reminding visitors it is a compound and a family house, holding itself aloof to a degree from its immediate surroundings, and gazing resolutely out over the bay. The approach paths, however, ascribe a eurhythmic dance, the drive and orchard path are split into weaving and intersecting lines, ribbons that sweep back and forth on the way to the house, like trailing ribbons. This airy movement and being is reinstated at the core of the house, where the lightest cantilevered stair, linked to a ceiling by stretched newels, greets

a five-faced lattice ceiling "rose" that seems to rotate in time to the stair's upward spiral. Around it is a half-ceiling, blue as the sky, and above that a light plywood-sheathed upper dome, its portholes now reading as occuli, and re-using a time-honoured basic walling material seen in countless small holiday houses in this region. This light-filled realm extends into the colors and scales of the dining area. The living area, spreading under a slow coved ceiling, looks almost manorial, but is saved at the last moment from this state by the simultaneous recall of a ship's interior, and the low coved ceilings seen, again, in crucial early holiday houses, again, of Roy Grounds and others in the 1930s, when suburban Melbourne first came to really holiday here. The exteriors, closer up, lose their ship-like line and demeanour, fanning out into bundles and fans of paling timber and matchstick slats, and the portholes around the pergola join this texture as well, becoming smaller-grained slat screens, patches set against the perimeter palings.

In plan, the house fronts the bay with two semi-ellipses, each recalling the vesica pisces or fish bladder, a shape formed from the fusion of circles, a component of sacred geometry linked to the outset of Christianity and a recurring signature through many Burgess designs. The images are not exclusively Christian however: they also encompass,

Photo: John Gollings

All photos: John Gollings

quite literally, the arm and hand movement of dance, and the circling of individuals in dance. They are also header masses, drawing a chain of smaller bedroom spaces after them, again through a spine-pas-sage of muted plywood sheeting and battens, pausing only to project curving decks or an open living space where the occasion needs it. The swirling plan, tightening and loosening like a forming reef knot, is a free, more physical recasting of the Erich Mendelsohn splay and linking curve seen in a series of his buildings in the 1920s and 1930s.[1] But the sense is freer here: knocked from symmetry. Burgess always does this. The symmetrical is potentially there, in the wind, but few if any of his projects are ever finally in symmetry. And what drives them away from symmetry, invariably, is Burgess's determination to record and celebrate the specifics of narrative and circumstance. The half-elliptical patio at Burraworrin can never exactly balance the similarly shaped living room, because it is not the same. No area of action within a building is the same, though they may be related. The symbolic and the representation of grouped function always draws his designs away from duplication or repetition.

This is a paradox, because, for all his admiration of Louis Kahn, Burgess is for the particularity of circumstance and the moment in his buildings, recorded in their shape for posterity rather than being generalised and relating to changing functions that can occur in a generalised space, as Kahn and for that matter the Venturis would have it. Burgess' real architectural affinity is with Hans Scharoun's post World War II designs and through him, Hugo Haering in the 1920s, and Haering's idea of neues Bauen, where each function was to receive its own sculptural and symbolic expression. In Haering's thinking, if a component had to be repeated, it still has an obligation to variety in external form and in our spatial experience inside. This meshes with Burgess' perceptions in architecture: he sees social and spiritual alienation lying at the core of modern, industrialised, architectural repetition.

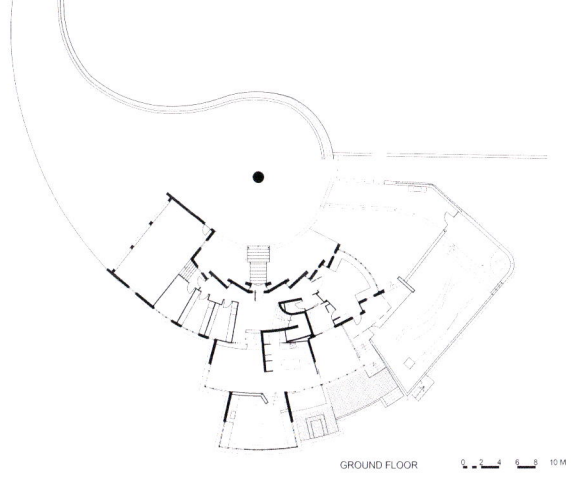

GROUND FLOOR   0 2 4 6 8 10 M

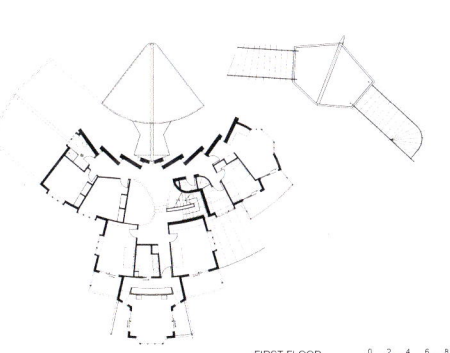

FIRST FLOOR   0 2 4 6 8 10 M

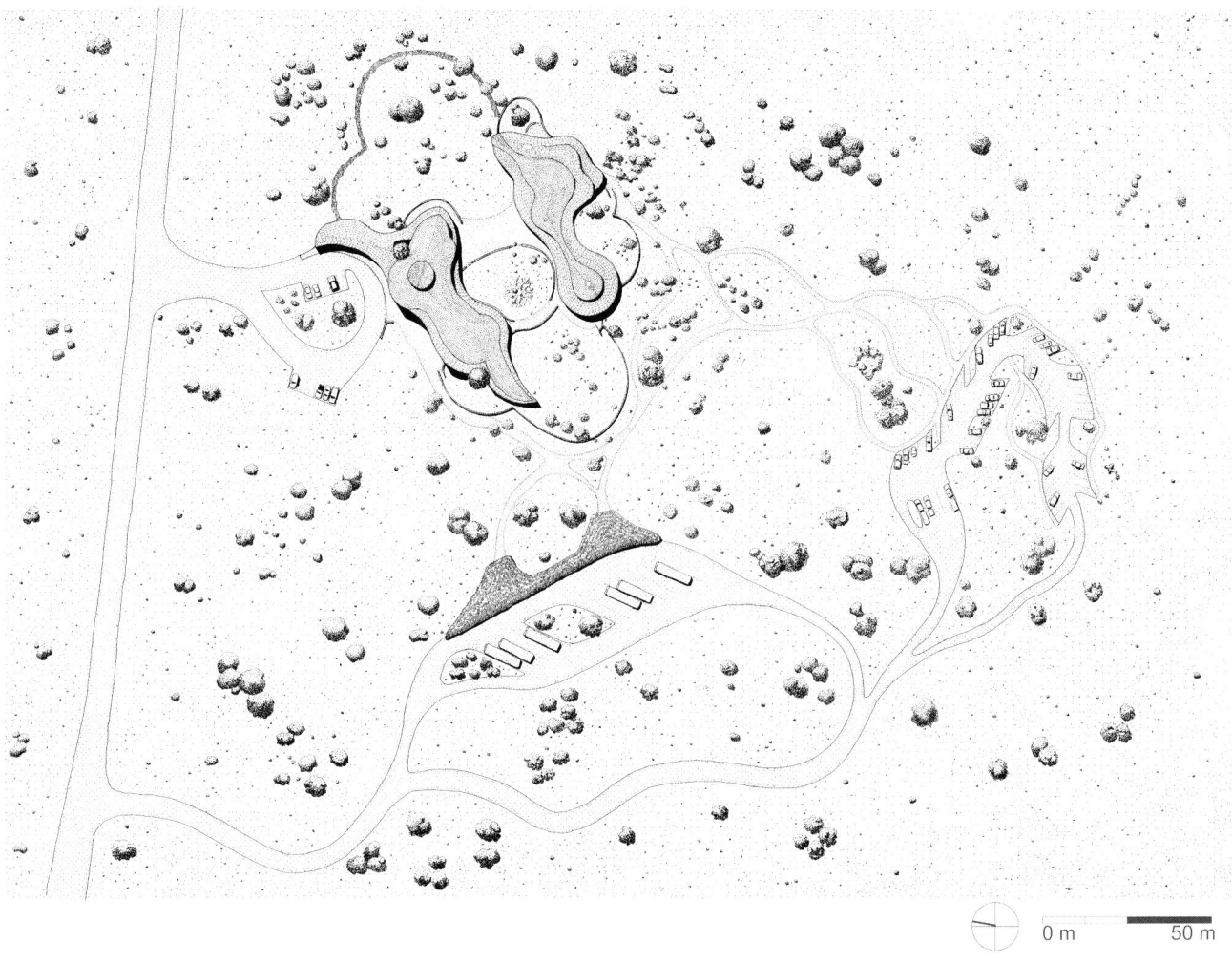

0 m   50 m

Uluru-Kata Tjuta Cultural Centre
Uluru, Northern Territory, Australia, 1995

Appearing on the cover of Tokyo's *A+U* in 1996, Uluru-Kata Tjuta
Cultural Centre reflected Greg Burgess' growing reputation outside
Australia. Seen from the air, the center resembled two weathering
leaves that have fluttered to the red land surface, connected by curving
stems, which, as in the ageing leaf-roots, have turned gold, silver,
umber, and olive. The forms themselves were related to paintings and
sand drawings the Angangu people had done, while Burgess and his
assistants had spent time with them in a period of study and co-living.
Light is guided into the center's interior through undulating eyebrow
dormers, a little like the one HH Richardson pioneered in his Ames Gate
Lodge and his New England libraries of around 1880. And the center
buildings, hugging the land surface under a blasting inland sun with
the stone-grained sting of a wasp by day and often near freezing at
night, are locked in a projection of survival, accord, communion, and
shelter. The roofing glows with the enchanted light of Bruce Goff's
houses in America's Southwestern prairie, but with a new immensity of
scale and spread, rising and climbing low hills. Inside, the desert light
is guided down into the shady core through conical skylights set inside
arrowhead and herringbone-pattered spline-columns, and the roofs and
ceilings are linked to the internal columns like the branches and leaves
of saving trees. Crucial in the community's ritual and gathering are the
trees kept on the site, and the new buildings were intended to extend
the pattern and movement of the people's gathering and contact under
a permanent roof.

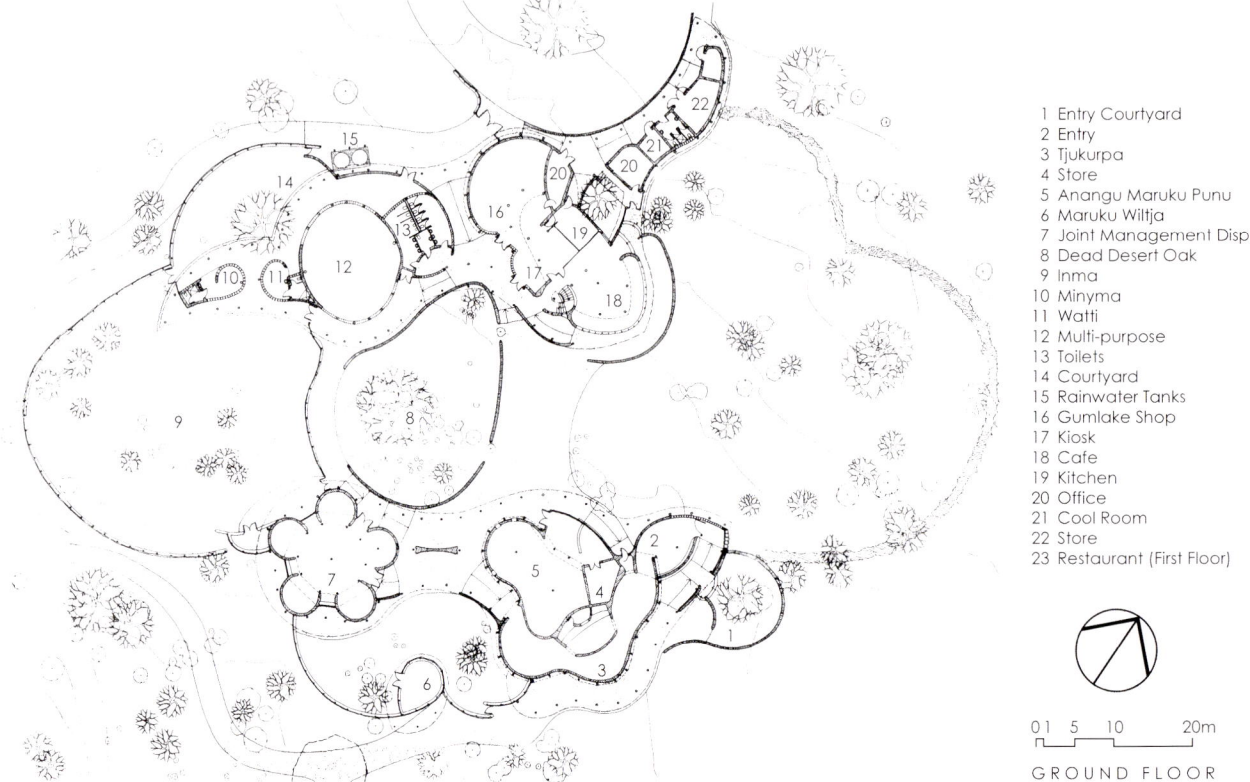

Photo: Craig Lamotte

1 Entry Courtyard
2 Entry
3 Tjukurpa
4 Store
5 Anangu Maruku Punu
6 Maruku Wiltja
7 Joint Management Display
8 Dead Desert Oak
9 Inma
10 Minyma
11 Watti
12 Multi-purpose
13 Toilets
14 Courtyard
15 Rainwater Tanks
16 Gumlake Shop
17 Kiosk
18 Cafe
19 Kitchen
20 Office
21 Cool Room
22 Store
23 Restaurant (First Floor)

01 5   10   20m

GROUND FLOOR

Photo: Gerry Musse

Photo: Tim Webster

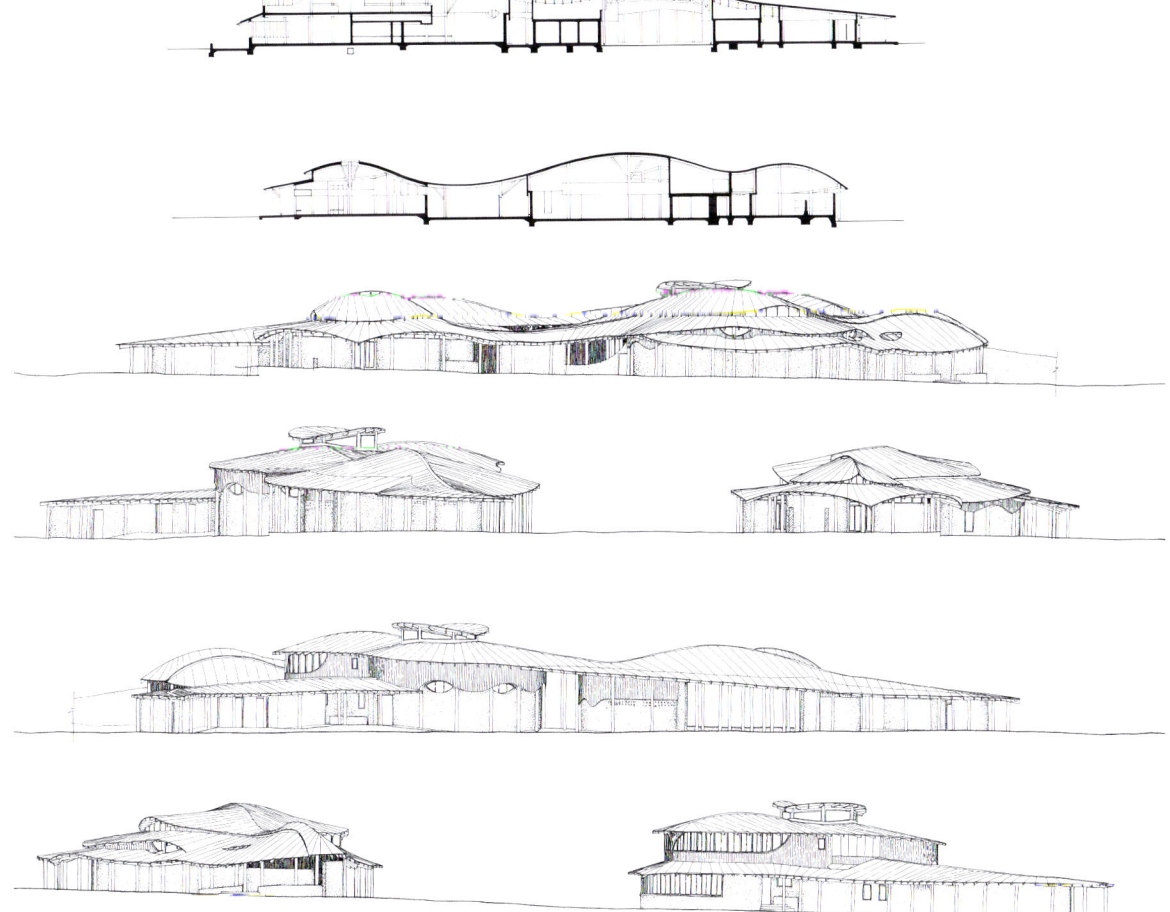

Twelve Apostles Visitor Amenities Building
Port Campbell, Victoria, 2001

The Twelve Apostles are resilient rock formations that have survived
pounding sea off Victoria's south coast (one collapsed recently);
they are a traditional image and symbol of Victoria, much as
Sydney's Harbour Bridge and Opera House "stand" for New South
Wales. Burgess developed this project in conjunction with another
interpretative pavilion, unbuilt, for Loch Ard Gorge in the same region,
a major shipwreck site, and an information center built at Lorne, a
resort town in the region. The Twelve Apostles building is a broadly
vesica pisces shape in plan, with a smaller vesica pisces lantern at
its core. But with ribbed walling, the building gains a "thorax" and
cephalon "head" that suggests a primeval trilobite. The building was
conceived as part of a swirling landscaping pattern that was to shape
car park and lay-by areas on both sides of the south coast road. Not
all that work was completed, but the Visitors' Center was, and in a
surprisingly intimate relation to the road. As with Burraworrin, the
pavilion appears to take off in flight, with two soaring spur-roofs above
each entrance, and the front on it seems to grow wings in a sweeping
bird form. The roof is set above a set of floor to ceiling windows and
wing walls. In this way, though the building is a basic single-storey
structure with a sloping monopitch roof, it gains monumental presence,
leaping towards the sea carrying its lantern upwards at an angle with it,
sharpened in contrast with the land behind as it sits beneath a coastal
range of tall hills. Inside, the building is surprisingly enclosed and
sheltering, given how open it is in elevations, and how airy the roof is. It
is figured in a powder-coated steel decking of blue and the palest gray,
like the scudding clouds on that coast.

Moonee Ponds Creek

Train Tracks

Service

Courtyard

Courtyard

Classrooms

Entry

Forecourt

Library

Classrooms

Context Plan

5   15   25 M

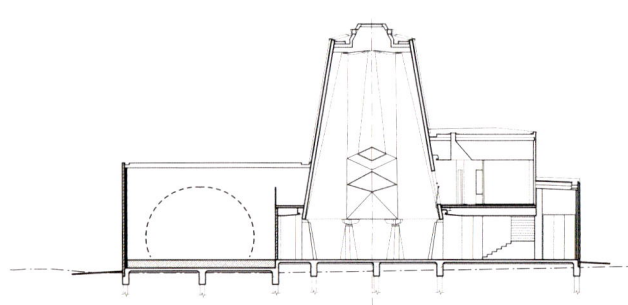

Photos: John Gollings

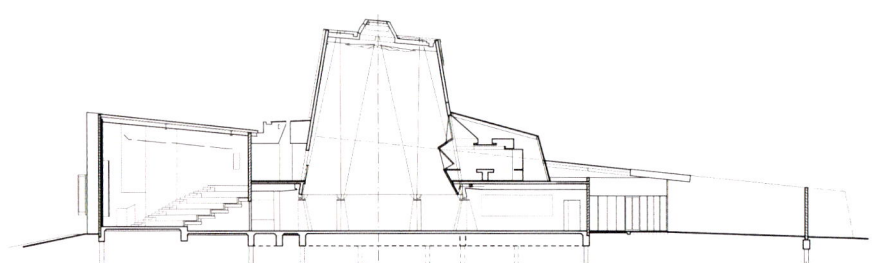

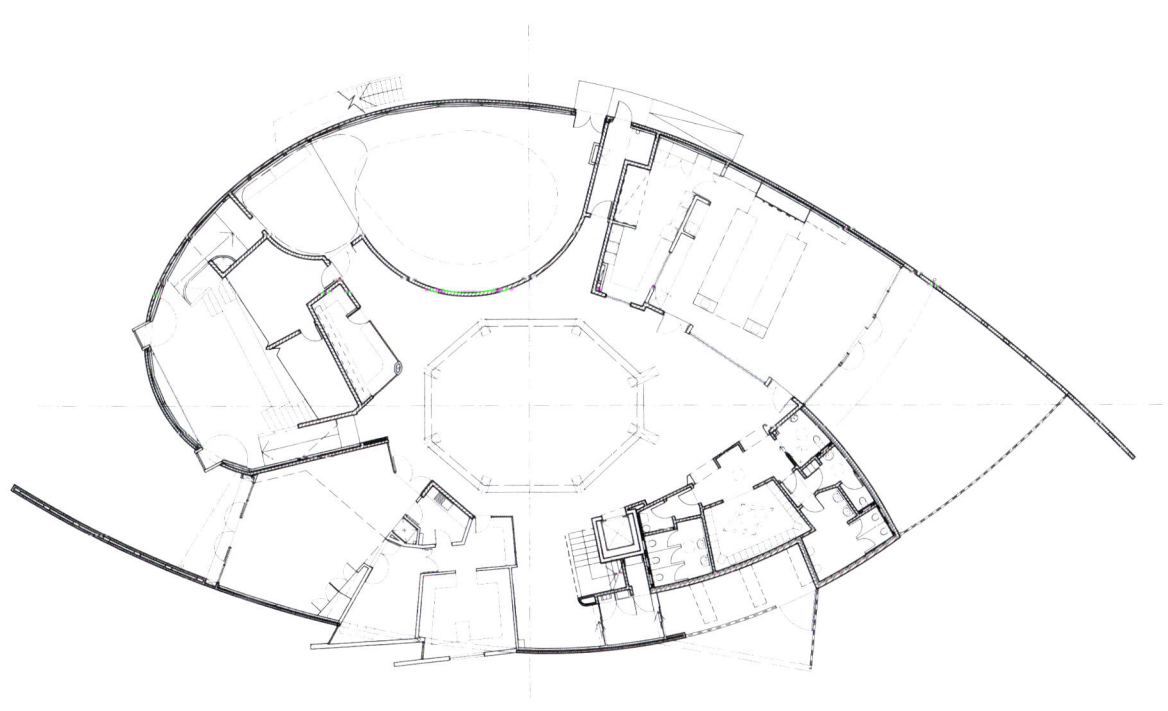

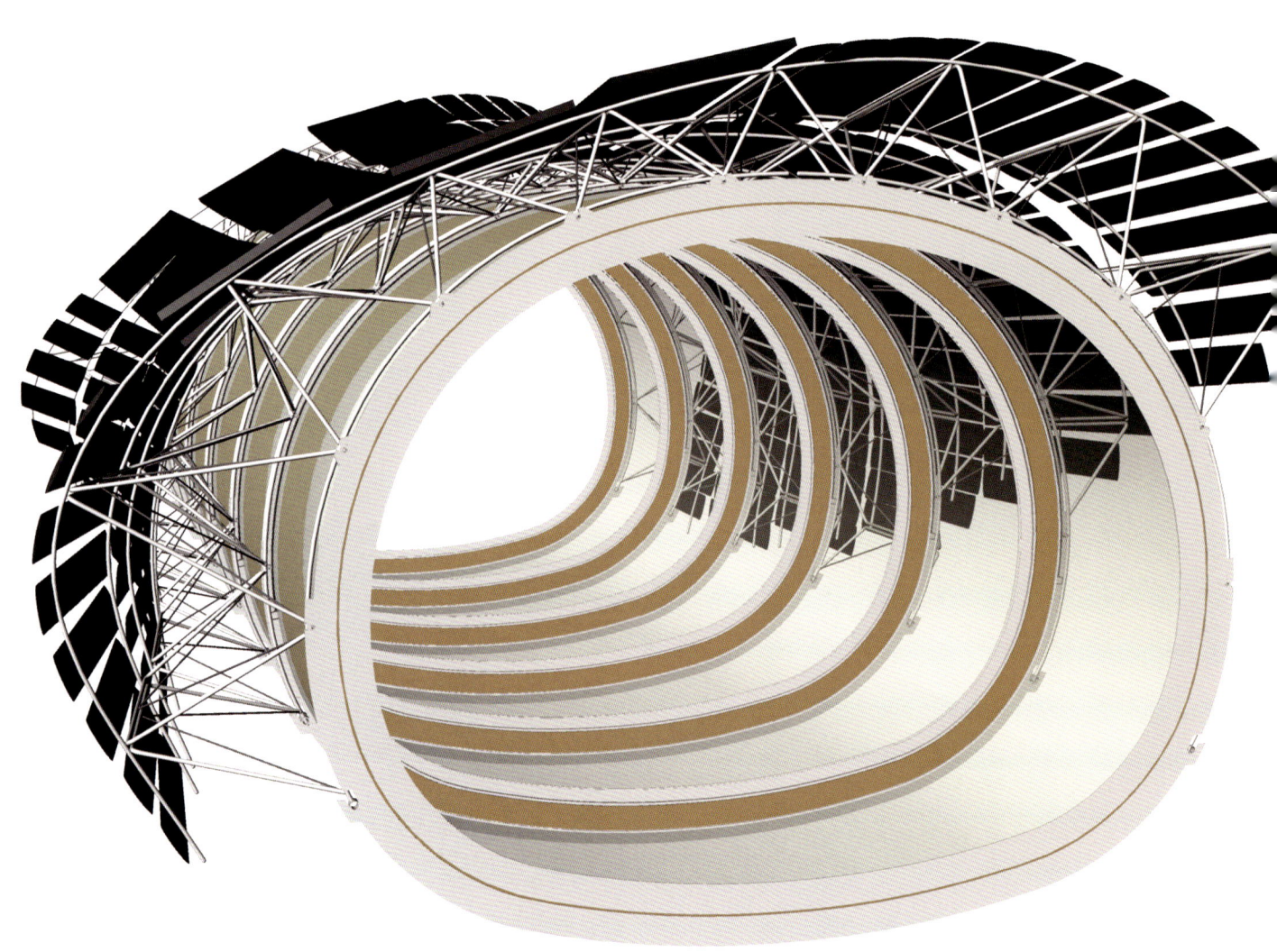

REINVENTING THE TROPICAL HOUSE

David Rockwood

David Rockwood is Professor, Director of the Construction Process Innovation Lab, and Co-Director of the Urbanism Research Lab at the University of Hawaii at Manoa. Exhibitions of Rockwood's work include the Buenos Aires Biennial, Princeton University, The Storefront for Art and Architecture, The Smithsonian Institution's Archives for American Art, and the National Building Museum. His work has been published in R.I.B.A Journal, Architectural Design, Civil Engineering, Domus, Engineering News Record, GA Houses, GA Houses - Project, Ottagono, Progressive Architecture, and American Masterworks: The 20th Century House. Rockwood's book Bamboo Gridshells was published in 2015 (Routledge). Rockwood's research is focused on building materials, methods, structural systems, and urban transport. Rockwood led University of Hawaii's U.S. Department of Energy's 2011 Solar Decathlon competition. In 2014 he was named a Fulbright Specialist and received a Fulbright award for urban planning in Danang, Vietnam.

Why reinvent the tropical house? Despite the growing trend towards urbanization, many people in the tropics still live in predominantly rural areas. Most contemporary rural houses have gravitated away from indigenous materials and forms, as the traditional natural materials are no longer available, and the craft skills to make them have been lost. Unfortunately, the new tropical houses do not often incorporate traditional wisdom as to siting, orientation, shading, and ventilation, and do not provide an optimal fit with social and cultural practices. Houses and structures in the city also lack innovations as far as tropical building wisdom is concerned. Certainly, additional design and research is needed to develop more appropriate tropical housing.

Around mid-century, a number of architects and researchers began investigations of tropical housing, hoping to more appropriately address region specific design issues. A primary focus was given to providing human thermal comfort through the application of scientific techniques. Maxwell Fry's and Jane Drew's *Tropical Architecture in Humid Zone* (1956) was an important early text in this movement. The book collected knowledge from their extensive work in India and West Africa, as well as work of other architects, with the intent to explicate design best practices. Koenigsberger's *Manual of Tropical Housing and Building: Part 1 Climatic Design* (1973) offered specific analytic techniques to guide passive high performance building system design. Victor Olygay's *Design with Climate: Bioclimatic Approach to Architectural Regionalism* (1963), and *Solar Control and Shading and Devices* (1957) offer rigorous methods to design climate responsive buildings.

Starting earlier in the 20th century, architects began experimenting with prefabrication building techniques in an effort to lower cost, increase quality, and speed construction. Famous prefab examples include Le Corbusier's Dom-ino house (1915) and Roq et Rob (1949), Gropius' and Wachsmann's General Panel System (1941), and the various projects of Jean Prouve, including his La Maison Tropicale (1949).

The University of Hawaii was selected as one of twenty university teams from around 100 entries internationally to compete in the U.S. Department of Energy Solar Decathlon 2011. The design for the team's competition house sought to reconnect with indigenous traditions, while integrating appropriate modern materials and technologies. The competition challenged twenty university teams to design, build, and operate a net-zero solar powered house. The house was named "Hale Pilihonua," which in the Hawaiian language means "one with the land," and the design began with the question of how to best adapt traditional tropical house design practices to account for the current conditions of climate, culture, and environmental stewardship, and thereby serve as a model for a new and higher performing tropical house.

Traditional tropical houses—despite variations—typically have a number common primary features. Perhaps foremost is the large roof that protects from monsoon rains and the harsh midday sun. Columns are used in lieu of walls to maximize openings for natural ventilation. The floor is typically raised to protect the occupants from ground moisture and flooding. Such features were instrumental in formulating the overall diagram of the house, and informed specific elements which were reinterpreted as was felt appropriate for the contemporary context.

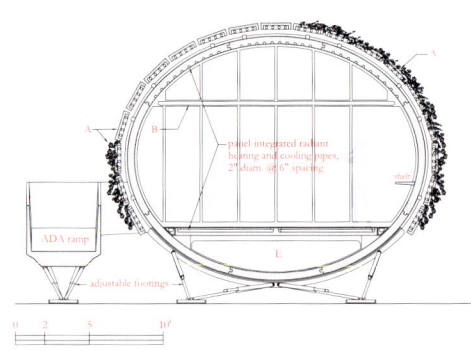

Looking forward, we see the trend toward smaller families, a desire to live simply—albeit with some modern conveniences—and to connect more closely with the natural environment. Also seen is a desire for greater self-sufficiency using renewable resources and lessening dependence on aging infrastructure and fossil fuels.

The vernacular sheltering roof was reinterpreted as a "second skin" that provides adjustable daylighting/shading, and that harvests solar energy.

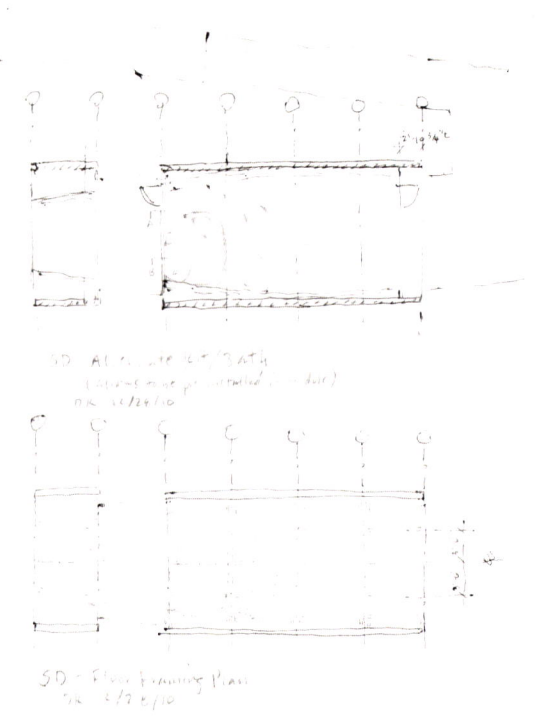

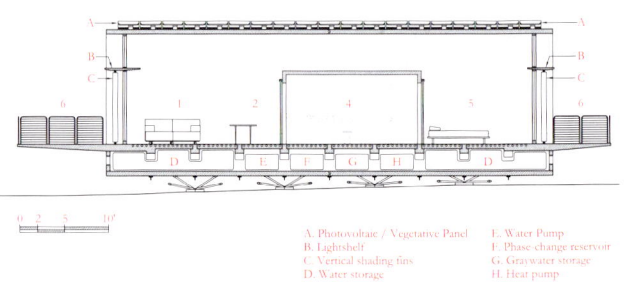

A. Photovoltaic / Vegetative Panel   E. Water Pump
B. Lightshelf   F. Phase-change reservoir
C. Vertical shading fins   G. Graywater storage
D. Water storage   H. Heat pump

To respond to the smaller family living simply, the house was made diminutive with an open flexible plan.

A composite "space frame" foundation was used for adjustment to varied terrain and support the monocoque composite sandwich shell enclosure.

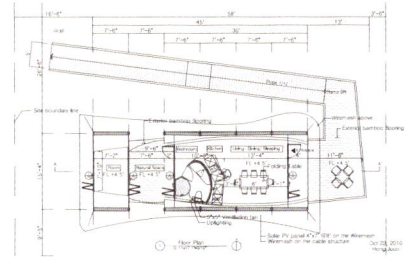

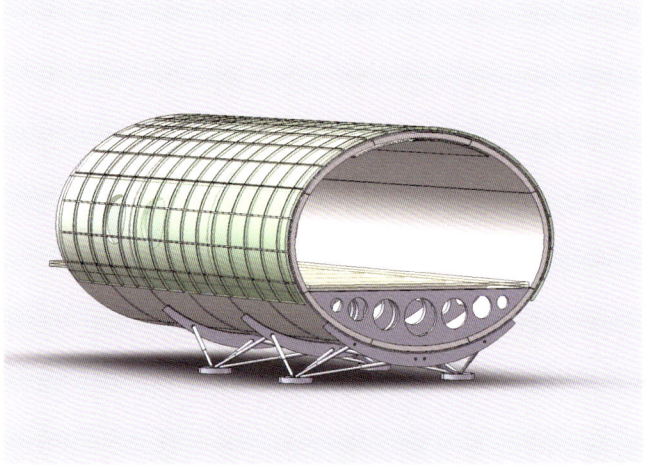

The house can be fully opened for ventilation and to connect with the outside environment and is raised to increase airflow and protect from ground moisture.

The shell was comprised of "staves" to allow compact transport and be tensioned together on site

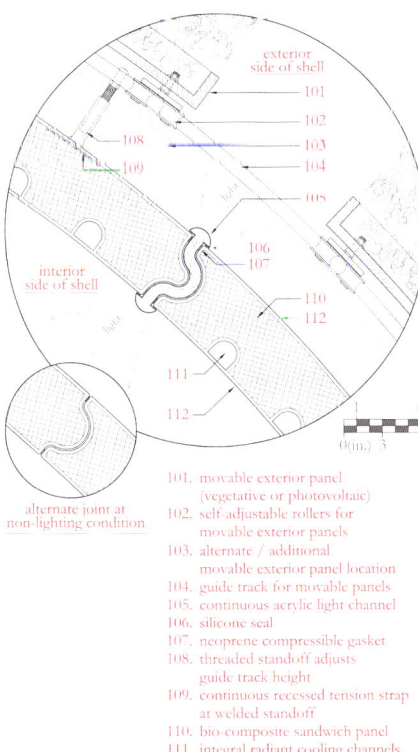

101. movable exterior panel
(vegetative or photovoltaic)
102. self-adjustable rollers for
movable exterior panels
103. alternate / additional
movable exterior panel location
104. guide track for movable panels
105. continuous acrylic light channel
106. silicone seal
107. neoprene compressible gasket
108. threaded standoff adjusts
guide track height
109. continuous recessed tension strap
at welded standoff
110. bio-composite sandwich panel
111. integral radiant cooling channels
112. interior / exterior face of shell
(cloth /resin)

alternate joint at
non-lighting condition

The round cross section allowed use of radial post-tensioning, and greater freedom in placing openings, while decreasing the weight of the structure.

Translucent FRP shell skins with aerogel cavity insulation were proposed for thermal resistance and to provide abundant daylighting.

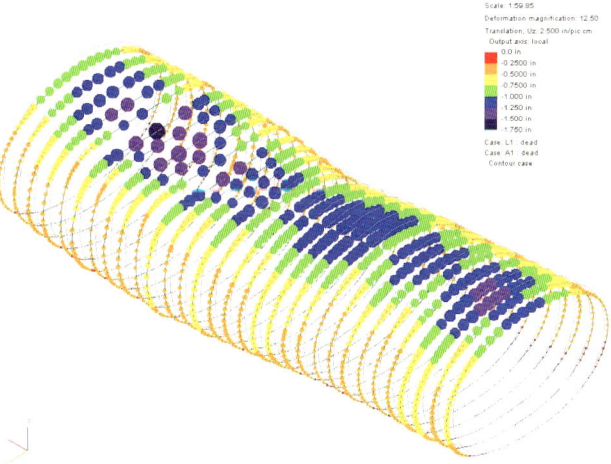

In a next iteration, the shell was reshaped to increase airflow and offer greater spatial variety. A structural solution for this shell geometry was found after considerable effort.

Molded acrylic light channel bars were positioned between abutting staves to bring natural light deeper into the interior.

The composite monocoque shell required third part testing to meet code requirements.

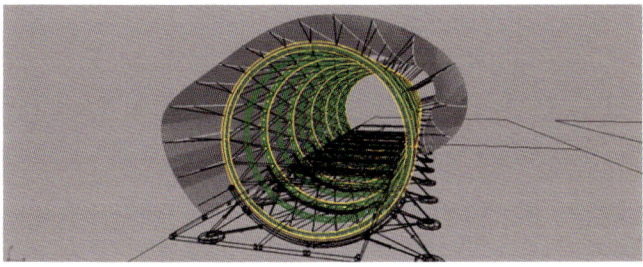

To shorten development time, a semi-monocoque shell was then proposed.

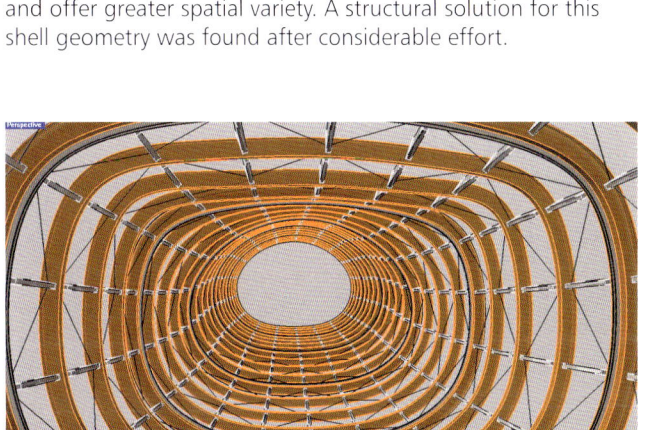

The doubly curved shell required too many unique parts and was therefore abandoned due to time constraints.

In the final scheme a straight extruded form was proposed to simplify the shell and keep the project on schedule.

Layers of interior bamboo plywood were studied as a way to further modify the light effects and shape the interior space.

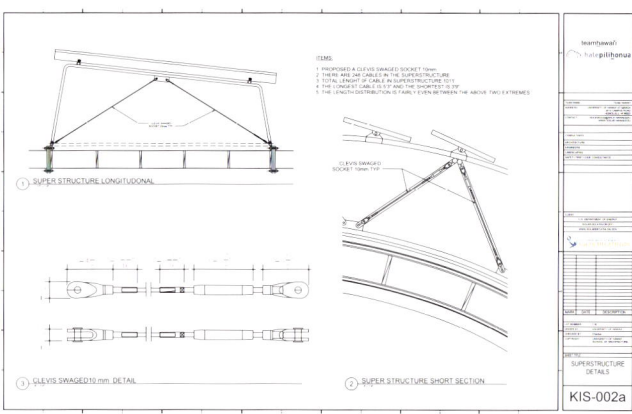

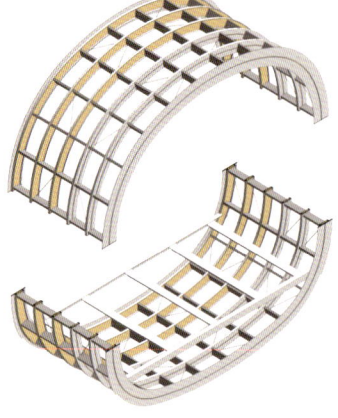

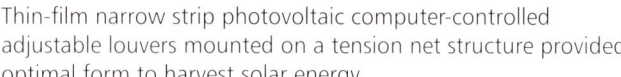

The house was designed as a series of modules that could be prefabricated and connected end-to-end on site to allow construction to be completed in 7 days.

Thin-film narrow strip photovoltaic computer-controlled adjustable louvers mounted on a tension net structure provided optimal form to harvest solar energy.

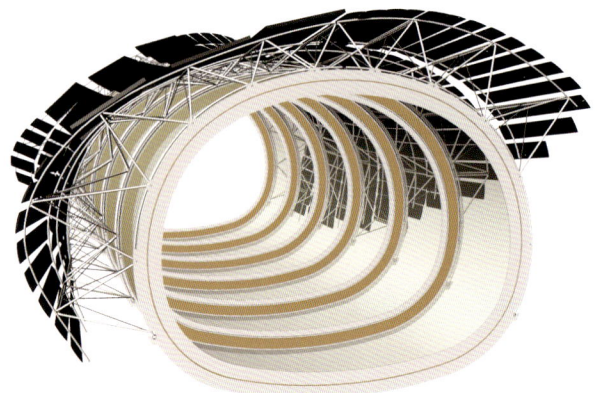

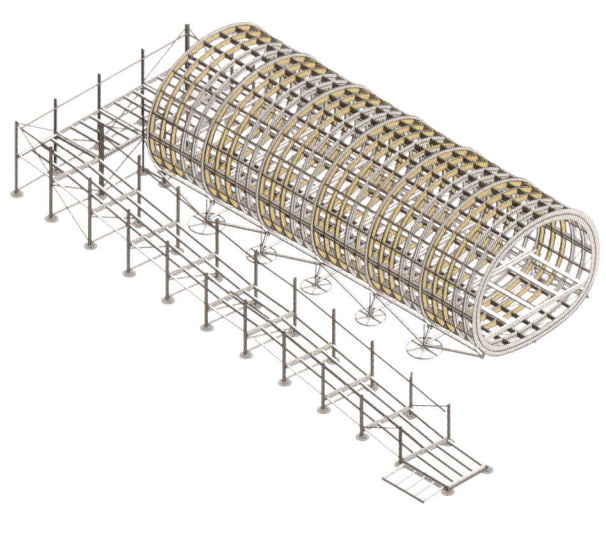

The second skin tension net was transformed into a series of trusses clipped to the shell such to fit container shipping requirements and speed on site assembly.

Conventionally sized panels were substituted for the thin strip photovoltaic panels that became unavailable. This required adjustments to the design of the second skin surface.

In sum, the project allowed exploration of new materials and technologies to provide human comfort and energy harvesting, while providing appropriate solutions for tropical climatic response. While the house was designed for rural conditions, many of the design strategies and technologies may be transferred to urban housing. This is an important next step in design research, and would contribute to improved living conditions in rapidly growing tropical cities. A guiding image of the design was of a couple having tea seated in a bamboo forest. Around them would be the wind, with the sun dappled over them and the ground, ever changing. Firmness and commodity are nothing, if there is not also delight.

Liljestrand House, Tantalus Drive, Honolulu (1952).

LEARNING FROM HAWAIIAN MODERNISM

FIVE DESIGN THEMES OF VLADIMIR OSSIPOFF

Dean Sakamoto

Dean Sakamoto, FAIA, is an educator and practicing architect. For many years, he served on the faculty of the Yale University School of Architecture and is currently associate affiliate faculty at the University of Hawaii at Manoa Department of Urban and Regional Planning. His New Haven and Honolulu based firm, Dean Sakamoto Architects is known for its environmentally sensitive and culturally specific designs of buildings and places. He is the editor of the award-winning book, *Hawaiian Modern: The Architecture of Vladimir Ossipoff* (Honolulu Museum of Art and Yale University Press, 2007 and 2015), and curator of the exhibition of the same title.

Vladimir Ossipoff (1907-1998) played a key role in developing a distinctive form of modern architecture in Hawaii. In his seven decades of practice, he combined local and global influences in his work at a time of swift political and social change in the 50th State. Today, the lessons of Ossipoff's diverse body of work are not only relevant to the Asia-Pacific region, but also provide models for architects who value stewardship of the land and the reconciliation of disparate cultural legacies. Yet neither Ossipoff's designs, nor the evolution of modern architecture in Hawaii are well known outside the islands. Today, we can learn much from this important figure and a forgotten strain of twentieth century regional Modernism.

Ossipoff saw architecture as a way to reinforce local identity, while also being expressive of the larger world he inhabited and being respectful of nature. In 1978, he articulated environmental concerns as a responsibility of architects: "The design of buildings will be oriented to energy conservation. The emphasis will be not in overcoming nature's heat and cold by enormous mechanical means but in rolling with nature's punches by absorbing or repelling them with design."[1] This shrewd outlook informed Ossipoff's approach. His straightforward yet elegant vision provided Modern architectural responses rooted in each site, available local resources, and specific conditions set by his clients. He did not seek to make a signature architectural statement, but rather found ways to express key design themes.

Ossipoff was a cosmopolitan figure, who combined a sharp wit with a critical design eye. Born in Vladivostok, Russia, he grew up in Japan because his father was assigned to a diplomatic post in Tokyo. He lived there until he was fifteen years old, when, in the wake of the Great Kanto Earthquake of 1923, his family migrated to California. After earning an architectural degree from University of California, Berkeley in 1931, he boarded a steamship to Honolulu where he began his career. By the time of the Pearl Harbor bombing, he had already designed several buildings in a Modern idiom and, within several years after the war's end had gained recognition locally and internationally. Upon taking office as president of the American Institute of Architects Hawaii Chapter in 1964, Ossipoff declared a "War on Ugliness," focusing on what he considered as mediocre and uncontrolled development in the burgeoning Waikiki tourist district. He was just as zealous, though more diplomatic, with his clients, ever insisting, "You will like it when you see it."[2]

His projects were published widely and his firm garnered numerous design awards for commissions from the more intimate houses, schools, and churches to larger commissions for office buildings, hospitals, and airports, most of which remain in use today. Ossipoff was deemed "the dean of Hawaiian architecture"[3] for his rich designs that are sympathetic to the land, fusing western modernism with Japanese elements and other island vernaculars. The resulting architecture is delightfully particular to its place and has proven durable over time.

Hawaiian Modernism

Architects in Hawaii designed modern buildings in the late 1930s by adapting formal strategies to the island's geographic isolation and unique physical and social conditions. By the end of the World War II, Ossipoff was a leader within a group of young architects who included Alfred Preis, Allen Johnson, Philip Fisk, and Thomas Perkins. They would proceed to design modern buildings during the decade of rapid development that followed statehood in 1959, the same year in which jet travel to the islands began.

IBM Building, Honolulu (1962).

Tourism and the military drove this economic expansion as the islands shifted from a Territorial oligarchy to its status as a Democratic, multi-cultural state in 1962.[4] It was during this era of social change that local architects reached beyond the Territorial Style—which during its golden era of the 1920s, produced landmark adaptations of Neoclassical and Mediterranean Revival styles—toward the work inspired by Modern architects such as Le Corbusier, Mies van der Rohe, and Frank Lloyd Wright. Hawaiian modernism reached its pinnacle in the 1970s, marked by the completion of John Carl Warnecke's futuristic Hawaii State Capitol (1969) and Ossipoff's modernization of the Honolulu International Airport (1970-1978). This architectural vanguard was celebrated in a local exhibition and publication, *A Decade of Design*, which featured later work by Ossipoff, his colleagues, and internationally known designers who also realized important buildings in the islands, such as Warnecke, I.M. Pei, and Minoru Yamasaki.[5]

As modern architecture's critique began by Robert Venturi and others during the 1960s, as symbolized by events such as the devastating fire at the Paul Rudolph's Yale Art & Architecture Building in 1969, Ossipoff and his peers continued to regionalize the modern idiom in the islands through the late 1970s. For Hawaii, modern architecture not only represented post-war optimism like it did elsewhere, but it reinforced the socio-political transition from a Territorial oligarchy to a democratic State. Ironically, the post-modern approach among many of Hawaii's architects after two decades of Statehood was a return to the Territorial Style as epitomized by the design of the Hawaii State Convention Center in 1998, the year of Ossipoff's death.

The opening of the exhibition, *Hawaiian Modern: The Architecture of Vladimir Ossipoff* at the Honolulu Academy of Arts and publication of its accompanying catalogue in 2007, effectively disseminated the story of modernism in these remote islands through this unforgettable man's work. Since then, architectural design preference in Hawaii has returned to the modern style. However, to attain a basic understanding of Ossipoff's genius, one must first learn from a few of his thematic tendencies.

Five Design Themes

Although Ossipoff did not theorize upon or document his architectural principles, in retrospect, a number of recurrent themes are evident through the close reading of his drawings and experience of his buildings. Fundamentally, one may argue that the following five themes prevail in his best work: "Revealing Site" presents buildings integrated with their sites in compelling ways; "Hawaiian and Modern" displays the range of Ossipoff's design sensibility; "Darkness and Air" reflects upon his artful juxtaposition of shade and natural ventilation to create comfort and intrigue in his buildings; "Native Materials and Modern Tectonics" illustrates Ossipoff's uses of local resources as well as new building technologies; and "The Living Lanai" examines Ossipoff's transformation of the ubiquitous Hawaiian lanai—a freestanding, open-sided, flat-roofed indigenous structure—into a building type in itself.

Revealing Site

Vladimir Ossipoff was a master at creating a resonant alliance between a building and its site. Often, his designs thoughtfully unfold aspects of both the structure and its environment as the visitor moves through them. Proceeding from a typically discreet entrance farther into an interior may reveal a grand vista or an intimate view. A fundamental aspect of Ossipoff's site design strategy was the careful placement of a building: rather than reshaping the landscape. Ossipoff designed buildings to respond to the characteristics of the terrain. Enhancing the connection between interior and exterior, between building and landscape, he slowly reveals the small and grand characteristics of each

His most poetic work in this regard is the Robert Shipman Thurston, Jr. Memorial Chapel at Punahou School (1967), in Honolulu. The chapel sits in quiet repose in a district called Manoa Valley, linking the grounds of the Punahou School—a prestigious independent school originally founded by Congregational missionaries in 1841, which the New York architect Bertram Goodhue master-planned in 1917—with the natural spring and pond after which the school was named. According to legend, an elderly Hawaiian couple who lived in the verdant Manoa Valley prayed for water and were instructed in a dream to uproot the stump of a hala tree. In doing so, they uncovered a spring of clear, sweet water, which they called *Ka Punahou* (the new spring).[6]

A courtyard around the spring creates and intimacy that continues inside the chapel, where subdued lighting has a calming effect on the high energy of youthful churchgoers. Entering the building, one passes through impressive doors made of koa, a handsomely grained and dramatically colored native hardwood, into the narthex, where more koa grillwork serves as a sanctuary screen. The main sanctuary floor slopes gently downward, coming to rest at the level of the pond, which actually enters the chapel. Bands of brilliantly illuminated stained glass, all cast shafts of colored light out across the water. Ossipoff designed rows of koa-wood pews to follow the floor's descending angle towards a coral stone altar. Although the chapel seats 500 people, no seat is farther than forty feet from the altar. The acoustics are remarkably clear within the voluminous space.

Thurston Chapel is an archetype of Ossipoff's vision. It is at once Hawaiian, Modern, and a timeless solution that cannot be traced to any other precedent. The result is rich in formal expression and materiality, and inextricable from its site and the legend that resides there.

Hawaiian and Modern

Although Vladimir Ossipoff was educated in the Beaux Arts tradition at Berkeley, he embraced modernism, and he developed new aesthetics and technologies in Hawaii. Many elements of his designs incorporated modernism's abstraction of form, efficiency of structure, and minimal ornamentation. And yet, Ossipoff's approach was pluralistic: he did not deny the inclusion of Hawaiian customs, indigenous materials, and influences of the sub-tropical climate on shelter. His commercial structures, in particular, thoughtfully merged local conditions with international sophistication, resulting in a style that affirmed modern architecture as the architecture of Hawaii's statehood years.

The Hawaiian Life Insurance Building was at the forefront of a new brand of corporate architecture similar to, yet ahead of, that of Connecticut General by Skidmore, Owings & Merrill (1956). The six-story structure was Hawaii's tallest new building and Ossipoff's largest project. Situated about a mile away from Honolulu's downtown financial district, Hawaiian Life was designed to take into account both suburbanization (the home and life insurance businesses increased alongside the develop ment of single-family housing in Honolulu's hinterlands) and its employees' daily commute by automobile. The L-shaped building footprint accords with its corner site and allows efficient movement from parking lots on either side of the building to the elevator lobby and strategically placed internal and external stairways. Although the two legs of the plan appear to be perpendicular, the lower, two-story wing is splayed in conformance to the irregularly shaped site. This obtuse angle expands the space for the surface parking lot fronting the busy boulevard, while still allowing a second employees' lot at the south side of the building.

Ossipoff was always concerned with optimizing natural light and conserving energy. Hawaiian Life was praised in the January 1955 issue of *Architectural Record* for its "glareless daylighting," which the architect achieved by shielding the north-south-oriented high-rise wing with vertical and horizontal louvers and glass-block fenestration.[7] This feature allowed greater quantities of daylight inside and reduced the use of artificial light while reducing solar heat gain. The northeast and southwest wings of the building shelter both the elevator lobby and the storefront entries from the prevailing winds and direct sunlight.

The Hawaiian Life Building, an early public statement of modernity in a new Hawaii, exemplifies Ossipoff's attention to both environmental conditions and the growth of post-war Honolulu.

Darkness and Air
Ossipoff often remarked that the traditional Japanese house— with its thin walls, dark interior, and natural ventilation—is better suited to Hawaii than Japan.[8] The Japanese author Jun'ichiro Tanizaki notes that "the beauty of the Japanese room depends on a variation of shadows, heavy shadows against light shadows."[9] Working within a culture that blends Pan-Asian values with a balmier climate, Ossipoff's residential interiors artfully manage low levels of filtered daylight cast upon natural surfaces to create elegant, mysterious spaces, both for comfort and aesthetics. This subtle articulation of shade and air was a balancing act of allowing permeability to the trade winds, yet providing protection from rain and sunlight—all while preserving views with carefully placed windows

The Goodsill residence, an intimately scaled house designed for a young lawyer and his family in a new suburban tract on the southeastern slope of Diamond Head in Honolulu (1952), illustrates this theme well.

A compact jewel box of surprises within nautilu-like shape, the residence is fragmented into three parts: curling around a garden tucked in its center are separate wings for living and dining, a master bedroom, and children's rooms. To enter each wing requires a brief step outside, as there are no enclosed halls but only a roof overhead. Finding the main entrance is a discovery. Since his clients left most of the design decisions up to him, Ossipoff's primary constraints were imposed by the need to provide weather protection and shade, while also conforming to a small, sloping lot. The house responds to its site in an unusual but elegant way, maintaining intimate scale, a familiar palette of materials, and subtle spatial and daylighting dynamics.

Inside, the intimate scale continues, enhanced by warm wood

finishes and low lighting rich in shading that recalls Tanizaki's statement. Ossipoff created the effect by deploying a series of side-lighting strategies. The living room is illuminated primarily by floor-to-ceiling, glass-and-screen sliding doors, which are, in turn, sheltered by the large eaves over the walkway leading to the lanai. The courtyard lawn and acid-stained concrete walk reflect significant amounts of light into the living room. To lessen glare, Ossipoff designed a high, narrow ribbon window opposite the large glass doors to admit direct morning light and soften the strong, reflected afternoon sun. The late-afternoon reflections lend the illusion of an additional few feet of height to the modestly scaled room. The master bedroom has the same intimacy in its long and narrow plan, with a bed at the center; an assertive, built-in, boomerang-shaped desk at the far end; and a room-length wardrobe that blends with the lime-washed redwood walls. With the bedroom's only window-wall facing north, the available daylight is absorbed by both walls and high ceiling, transmitting a muted light.

In this modest house, Ossipoff artfully conceived the qualities of shade, ventilation, and daylight, resulting in a quiet atmosphere that belies its sophisticated positioning, spatial organization, and climatic response.

Native Materials and Modern Tectonics
Vladimir Ossipoff combined an artist's eye with an interest in technical innovations. He recognized the importance of connecting a building to its context by using local materials, while applying the most advanced engineering and construction techniques that his clients could afford. Inside, he often used native koa and ohia woods to add appeal to both residential and commercial buildings. He also mixed local volcanic rock and sandstone from the shoreline into his buildings' structural concrete and various surfaces. Working closely with Honolulu-based engineers Alfred Yee and K.D. Park, Ossipoff designed several innovative structures built of site-cast and pre-cast reinforced concrete. For example, his Diamond Head Apartments was the first fully prestressed concrete high-rise in the world.[10] Two of Ossipoff's best-known commercial buildings in Honolulu-the McInerny Waikiki Store (1957) and the IBM Building (1962), illustrate contrasting approaches to the challenge of modern design that expresses a local sensibility

The IBM Building is a Honolulu landmark that brought cutting-edge reinforced concrete technology to a prominent urban site. Ossipoff had hoped to portray IBM's international image as a leader in computer technology, while still creating a Hawaiian sensibility. He designed a simple, reinforced-concrete frame structure and, to protect the building's floor-to-ceiling glass curtain-wall from the blazing sun, overlaid it with a sculpturally distinctive, precast concrete grille, a screen that is practical yet abstract.

The balance of these elements lies in the grille's 1,360-part design, which not only functions to reduce glare, but "gives the building the distinction that the company wanted."[11] Ossipoff singled out this project as one that needed to express both the global character of his client's business and the local context through design. In a news article he wrote about IBM, Ossipoff stated: "Not only does the systematic, rather repetitious pattern of the concrete grille express the computer-world character of the IBM Corp., but [it] also gives the building a sense of belonging in the sun. The deep shadows of the grillwork become as significant a part of the architecture as any part of the structure itself."[12] Ossipoff further emphasized that his grille

A view of Honululu from mountains (Photo: Vicky Sambunaris).

Honolulu International Airport Terminal (1970s).

Outrigger Canoe Club, Honolulu.

Blanche Hill House, Honolulu (1961) (photo: Robert Wenkam, courtesy Ossipoff Snyder Rowland Architects).

Liljestrand House, Tantalus Drive, Honolulu (1952).

Liljestrand House, Tantalus Drive, Honolulu (1952).

was custom-made to address other problems: designed to be self-cleaning, it was angled to keep pigeons from nesting in it. Less than three miles away, the tourist district of Waikiki—historically a low-scale residential area with a handful of mid-rise hotels—had been evolving into a high-density resort zone. In 1956, McInerny's, a local clothing retailer, commissioned Ossipoff to design a new store fronting the historic Royal Hawaiian Hotel—a startling pink, beachside art-deco era extravaganza—at the heart of Kalakaua Avenue, the district's rapidly changing main thoroughfare. Ossipoff proposed a scheme based on terms he felt suitable for the area, both in his use of materials and in urban design.

As opposed to the tectonic expression of the later IBM Building, at McInerny's, Ossipoff concealed the structural steel framing under a palette of natural materials. A textured beige sandstone veneer from Waianae (a western coastal district on Oahu) was used for the façade and inlaid in the concrete slab walkways. The stone evoked the primacy of Polynesia, and provided a dramatic contrast to the large plate glass windows. Redwood infill panels and concrete blocks were patterned with perforations for light and ventilation. The diagonally laid, standing-seam copper roof added a dynamic dimension to the earth-toned body of the building. The overall effect of McInerny's material palette was that of a large house clad in local stone and edged in glass, and further enlivened by a lush, landscaped perimeter. Despite its popularity among tourists and locals alike, the McInerny's building lived a short life. It was razed in the late 1970s to make way for a larger retail complex which was the result of a local design competition for which Ossipoff acted as lead juror.

The Living Lanai
Ossipoff's most innovative contribution to modern architecture was the transformation of the indigenous lanai into a building type unique to the islands. Recognizing the potential of this open-sided, freestanding, and lightly roofed structure to serve as the primary living area of a home, or as an inviting public space in a larger structure, Ossipoff created and perfected a sort of non-building. When protected from the trade winds and rain, the lanai creates an ideal indoor-outdoor space that is minimal both structurally and in terms of its visual impact. It has a low profile roof line, while being buffered from the weather by service or private structures, such as kitchens or bedroom wings. In projects that presented opportunities for merging interior and exterior, Ossipoff explored the possibilities of the lanai as a total structure, eventually transforming it into large-scale complexes.

Ossipoff designed Blanche Hill's home on the Kahala beachfront like a lanai, in order to be as informal and open to the environment as possible. Although it was demolished in the 1980s, the Hill residence, built in 1961, was a finely situated complex of small interior rooms linked by expansive exterior spaces. To maximize openness, Ossipoff concealed the header beams inside the ceiling assembly above the wide openings across the lanai and living area, allowing three layers of floor-to-ceiling sliding and bi-folding panels—wood shutters and glass-and-screen doors—to open or close completely to the outdoors. With much of the building's structural support concealed, the home offered exceptional unobstructed views. The overall effect was one of delight, structural ambiguity, and seamless indoor-outdoor living

Nestled in abundant foliage and dwarfed by neighboring high-rises, the Outrigger Canoe Club complex is almost invisible from the street. The structure becomes comprehensible only upon one's passage through it, as it unveils its spectacular beachside site. Except for service areas, offices, locker rooms, and restrooms, all of the interior spaces are open air, shade, daylight, intimate gardens, and views of the shoreline and ocean penetrate a grid of concrete and coral piers that support a horizontal trelliswork above. All public spaces in the complex—the reception area, bar, terrace, and dining areas—are, in most instances, an extensive hau, a native climbing plant arbor.

Ossipoff's design strategy for the Outrigger is clear: to consolidate or completely suppress vertical architectural enclosures, and make all public spaces as open to the environment as possible. The dominant architectural feature of the Club, its simple arbor structure, is set on a fourteen-foot-square grid. Numerous two-foot-square coral and concrete columns support the matrix of painted concrete girders and unfinished redwood beams overhead, which span more than sixty percent of the main building's footprint. The kitchen, offices, and locker-room facilities are packed around the mauka or "towards the mountains" end of the property, occupying both ground and basement levels, and allowing most of the beachfront to be occupied by the lanai structure. The support structures of the club serve both as partitions to shelter open spaces and as enclosures in their own right, as they do at the Blanche Hill residence. The wall at the entry, for example, is perceived as simply that, though it conceals administrative offices behind it.

It was through the evolution of the lanai that Ossipoff contributed most profoundly to the Hawaiian built environment. By combining the logic of an indigenous vernacular typology with twentieth-century Modern precedents and a Japanese sensitivity toward nature, he established a timeless and original building form possible only in the tropics.

196

Goodsill Residence, Honolulu (1952).

Blanche Hill House, Honolulu (1961) (photo: Robert Wenkam, courtesy Ossipoff Snyder Rowland Architects).

Thurston Chapel, Punahou School, Honolulu (1967).

Notes

[1] Vladimir Ossipoff, "Energy Molds Future," *Honolulu Advertiser*, Apr. 7, 1978.

[2] Quoted in George Johnson, "Vladimir Ossipoff: An Architect's Architect," Spectrum Hawai`i, Hawai`i Public Television, 1988.

[3] Rod Ohira, "Vladimir Ossipoff, Dean of Hawai`i Architects, Dies," *Honolulu Star-Bulletin*, Oct. 2, 1998.

[4] The end of the war catalyzed a social upheaval that empowered the rising class of Americans of Japanese ancestry (AJAs), whose ethnic solidarity helped them achieve majority control of the Territorial Legislature in 1954 and elect John A. Burns as the state's first Democratic governor, in 1962.

[5] *A Decade of Design: Hawai`i Chapter AIA and State Foundation on Culture and the Arts* (Honolulu: Hawai`i Society AIA/SFCA, 1969).

[6] Punahou School, "About Punahou," www.punahou.edu.

[7] "Glareless Daylighting in Hawai`i," *Architectural Record* (Jan. 1955), 155–58.

[8] Vladimir Ossipoff, "The Japanese House," *Hawai`i Architect* (March 1986),5.

[9] Jun'ichiro Tanizaki, *In Praise of Shadows,* trans. Thomas Harper (New Haven: Leetes Island, 1977), 18.

[10] "The 50th State: Back Seat to No One," *This Earth*, company flyer (Oakland: Permanente Cement, 1959).

[11] Mary Adamski, "Grilles Make Comeback in Honolulu Architecture," *Honolulu Advertiser* (n.d.), news clipping from Ossipoff family scrapbooks, collection of Xandra Ossipoff, Honolulu.

[12] Vladimir Ossipoff, "Building Designed for the Sun," *Sunday Star-Bulletin and Advertiser* (Feb. 6, 1966).

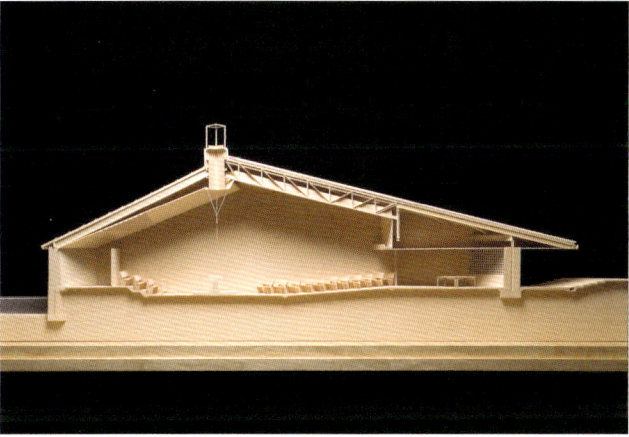

Thurston Chapel (Sectional Model)

LEGACIES THAT WE LEAVE BEHIND

AN INTERVIEW WITH BALKRISHNA DOSHI

Kazi Khaleed Ashraf

We met in front of the Cave, the now ubiquitously known Husain-Doshi Gufa in Ahmedabad, designed and made as a gallery for the work of the artist M.F. Husain. It was the day just before the Cave Gallery was to be inaugurated. There was no lofty portal to ascend, no pilotis to go around, just a gash in the body of the earth marked by a short series of steps that led directly down into the womb of the Cave. We sat on the floor, Balkrishna Doshi and I. Some workers were still scampering about doing last-minute work for the opening next day. Doshi had brought a cassette of Boléro for one of the workers. It played as we conversed on Kahn, Dhaka, and other things that last and things that disappear. At that time, I thought I would title this piece "The Rsi, the Cave, and Ravel."

Kazi Khaleed Ashraf: *You have talked about your experiences with Le Corbusier and Kahn many times before. It is still an incredible story. I think we can return to this topic with each passage of time.*

Balkrishna Doshi: Let me first make it clear that I worked with Le Corbusier first. I do not know how, but I was fascinated by his work. It is the kind of work, which is always trying to break the rule: very lyrical, very Mediterranean with moving, flowing spaces...

I did not know that before I joined Corbusier, but I learned it over time. Even when I went to the Acropolis after four years in Corbusier's office, I did not understand what he was saying about Acropolis. You see, I was a novice in this, but there is something called inner sensibility which occurs, comes out slowly, and begins to discover what you saw somewhere and which you experienced through someone's building: the juxtapositions, counterpoints, strengths of rhythm, surfaces, and whatnot.

Then, in 1958, when I got the Graham Fellowship, a friend took me to Kahn's office for the first time. Never had I seen such a humble man. He came out; he met me; he showed me slides of Richards Medical Building. There was a model of Salk Institute. The towers of Richards Medical Center stood totally different from what one saw as a tower: sketches of towers rising, stacks rising, and the glass, glances of the trees, and the geometry with minimum columns.

Then, he took us out to dinner. That time, he borrowed money from his secretary. A busy man, all of a sudden, meets a stranger. He saw my work. I showed him the housing that I had designed after leaving Corbusier's office, the ATIRA housing for Vikram Sarabhai. He talked about its primitive expression. He said, "how did you do this; this is really strong."

After that, I taught at Washington University and, later, went to Philadelphia to give a lecture, and again, I met him. Then, I went to teach in Philadelphia in 1961 for several weeks. I met him frequently then. My introduction to Kahn was gradual. I was introduced to him as being a young architect from India but more so for my work with Corbusier. He was always asking about Corbusier, India, and work and all. Then, when I got this commission (the Indian Institute of Management), the first person I thought of was Kahn. Here was a man, as good as Corbusier. I wanted him to work on this so that I could get a chance to learn something from him. You know the story of how I worked with him.

I have been seeing Kahn all through these years. He is someone who comes from Europe, has a hard life, has a late beginning in his career, seen ups and downs, and talked about the Depression—the way one had to live almost on nothing, not even a shoe-string budget. A lover of classical architecture, of Hadrian, Parthenon, but more the Roman, the bricks, strong qualities of space. Always the hard shadows and this powerful line and all. You could see that this man was trying, and when he talked about an opening, he would make a triangular opening. He would make the opening that would go like this and end into a triangle because those are the ones, which are very ancient, like Egyptian and other openings. I began to see: how does one bring the limits of definition? To give you an example, when I did the School of Architecture in 1962, he said that you should design so that nobody has a chance to rectify it. When you make an angle, you should make it so that there is no way you can say why not twenty-nine degrees and why not thirty-one. So it was that kind of precision that he was looking for, and therefore, it is not the precision of the angle but the precision of the opening itself.

How does one define an opening? It could be five feet; it could be seven feet, it could be 6′6″. It is not modular. It is the other law, which was coming there that, governs his structure and joins at the right place and, therefore, you know where the limit is, and therefore, where the sky is, where the opening is.

So, he was always looking for the proper opening; that is, the proper beginning and the proper end. And, I think it is very important to know how does one end the thing, and how does one begin? Which means what is the size, what is the dimension? How does one decide the dimension of a room? The room has to be of such a kind that you know that it cannot be more or less. That I found more and more when I worked with him on the IIM in Philadelphia and other places, which I never found working with Corbusier.

Which leads me to Dhaka. Both Corbusier and Kahn worked on assembly projects. With your own experience at Chandigarh, how do you see Kahn's Assembly at Dhaka?

Going to Dhaka, a couple of things always struck me there.

I asked Kahn about Chandigarh as soon as he came back from visiting the place, and he said, "I can't describe it." What do you mean? He says, "I am yet to see somebody who knows how to materialize dreams; now, I know there is a man called Corbusier." It is fairly difficult first to dream and then to put it to practice, to draw, and then finally to build and experience that dream. So, what it implies is that he was also thinking about a dream in Dhaka, but in contrast to Chandigarh with its big backdrop, the Himalayas, Dhaka is an absolutely flat plain: teeming mass, no skyline. At that time, the only thing that comes to my mind is the desert of Isfahan. Last year, I was in Samarkand, and I realized that in a desert climate like that, the dome, the octagon, the mass, the building that sits with absoluteness on the ground is important ... the relation to the ground and sky, the scale you cannot miss it from any place. Kahn's Assembly building has some remote connection to that because of the octagon, the openings, and the skyline. So, the struggle, then, is how does one bring the quality of the dome, the quality of the sheen of the mosaic in contemporary terms and, therefore, the transfer comes out in concrete and marble strips? Everybody knows this that the translucent in-between would give away to heavy mass in concrete, like butter in-

between. So, you almost feel that the heaviness is melted in these little white lines.

The triangular openings are coming straight down, the circular openings from Ahmedabad and other places. But the circular openings in a square are much more powerful than a square opening unless it is made in diagonals because the circle wants to defy that boundary of the square frame so that the circle wants to expand like ripples in the water. So, there is a question of the container and the contained. And I think that's what the whole dimension does.

I found the geometry of Kahn connected to his own background plus the Islamic tradition of the geometry. Also, it had this matter of how you make this geometry twist around and make this rotation work as if they are moving continuously inside. It is like a building within a building, but churning all the time. This churning is quite different from the juxtaposition of Corbusier, in which they confront physically and dimension-wise. They are isolated because they are two assemblies and because he was playing the game of columns, of forests, and buildings, which are eccentric.

How does one go back to the source? What happens is that when you talk about the justification for these movements, geometry and all that ... one doesn't know what must be the force behind which really makes it. Then, he is justifying this by locating them, rotating them, but the whole idea of this movement, that this rotunda which moves, how would this building move within, the face which is outside, which is fixed, and the face which is inside, which is going to have discourses, debates? How does it move so that it continuously churns within it and, then, it really discovers something? Almost like the churning of the ocean. This is really what the Assembly is about.

Kahn comes from a classical, materialistic thinking. Violation is not permitted. Corbusier believed [only] in violation, showing a rule between. You would not find a similar concern done in the same way. One is to use a geometry you cannot break, but the moment you say, "I have no geometry," you have no problems of breaking. This is where the whole difference begins to happen. Kahn wanted to break that geometry, but the problem is, having started that geometry, he is finding ways to see that the geometry does not exist. A very tough job, but that is what he was challenging himself with. I think his whole mind was saying that I have to make the laws, and I have to see how far I can go so that out of those laws, I get the eternal truth so that they become transparent. How do you make a law transparent?

I think law has a very coarse attitude. But when the law becomes transparent, it is truthful; it has no limits. Then the law is completely universal. I think this is what Kahn's search was before he left, before he disappeared. He used to come to the house every day when he visited here. We used to have dinner together, almost in isolation, three or four people, my family, and he talked. He said that if Corbusier were alive today he would gradually make a building as simple as possible; his lyricism would make that building so simple that you cannot make it simpler than that—almost reaching the level of the Parthenon but in a much simpler way. Actually, he was not talking about Corbusier; I think he was talking about himself. And, to me, this is what Kahn was trying to do. That's why you have Kimbell, an extremely simple building, against this complex, large building. For him to work in the West is different

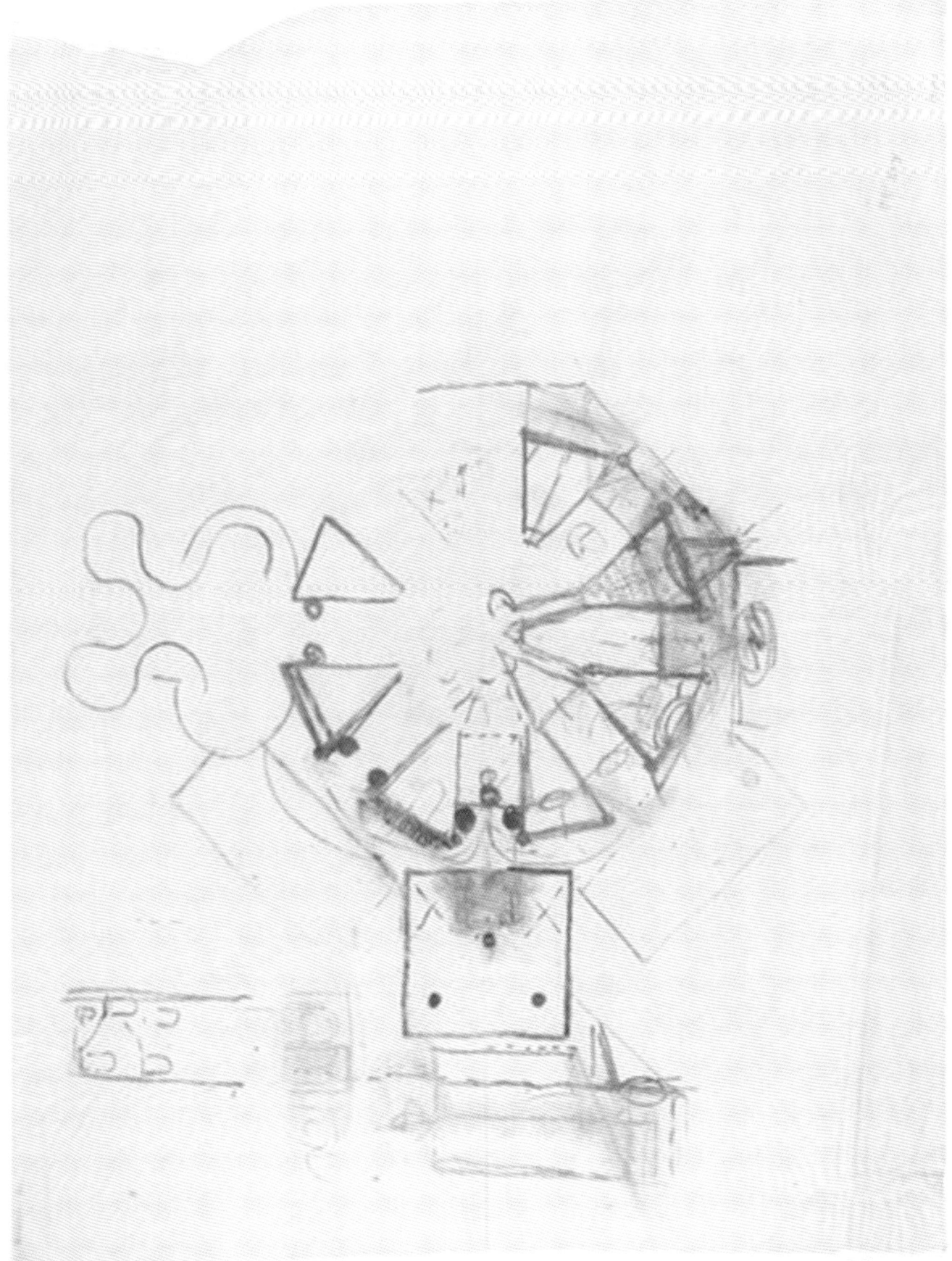

from working in India and Bangladesh, but this is the way he was working, and this is what the great thing is about. His other buildings in Dhaka—hospitals, staff quarters, and all that—are very close to the vocabulary in Ahmedabad. The other thing that is amazing about Dhaka is the pedestal, the steps. Having done this building, and having decided that it will be like that, how do you democratize it? Did he democratize it, because there could be two views? When Aldo van Eyck came to India for the first time in the 1960s, he saw the Assembly and the Mill-Owners' Building, and he mentioned that Corbusier is a great democratic man because he makes the Assembly only thirty centimeters above the ground, so that anybody can walk in without any problem. He doesn't make steps; he doesn't make pedestals so that you have to look up, and the emperor looks down, or the parliamentarians look down. This is Aldo's interpretation of Corbusier, which I think is very correct. Now, here is Kahn, who should have done this building absolutely on the ground, but he raises it to one side, with this huge flight of steps going up—almost awe-inspiring, like the Mughals. Like the Mughal buildings, which have podiums, you have big pedestals and steps going up. But then the scale of the steps and the kind of plaza has that feeling of a bigness, the vast number of people, but the moment you go in, the moment you are inside, you find that the level begins to become very simple and easy. But perhaps this is one area that he would have resolved very differently if Bangladesh were free at that time. Perhaps. I don't know because, when he began the scheme, it was with [General] Ayub Khan. Even though it is in Bangladesh, it is supposed to be the "second capital." Whether he thought like this or not, I don't know. But this question has always created a little doubt in me. Did Kahn think of merging this building, though big in size, with the masses? I think this building has not merged as other buildings have.

I wonder about Aldo Van Eyck's interpretation. The Assembly at Dhaka also scales down in other ways. The plaza level mediates between the ground and building level; and the way the concrete assembly is set with the brick architecture, and the way the whole thing is staggered, is other ways of mediation. From any vantage point, you can see the Assembly, not in isolation, as perhaps the case is with the Assembly in Chandigarh.

I don't know. When you look at the plaza here [at IIM in Ahmedabad], when you look at the entry here, when you look at the relationships, you do not feel you are away from the place. The building is not distanced.

I think, in Dhaka, Kahn wanted to create a distance and relationships. There's a play between creating a distance and then overcoming it, what I have described as a tug between a centrifugal and centripetal force.

That could be interpreted in many ways, but when it is a democratic assembly, people's representatives are there, so people are there directly or indirectly.

It is curious that Kahn had never used the term "democracy." He thought of "assembly."

Kahn did not describe this point; neither did he think [of] it that way. This issue is very significant for me, but leave aside whatever it is, I think once you go there, once you are inside the building, once you look at the spaces, the kind of offices which are located all around, the way you enter and go around, it's a maze but very beautifully articulated. What he also did was not

question certain issues; for example, the mosque, the angle, he took it that way. Corbusier would have reinterpreted it. Kahn is also capable of reinterpretation but the moment was not right. The time that Kahn did this job, and the way the foundations were dug, it was already managed from Islamabad, if I am not mistaken. Therefore, in a majority Muslim country, he did not want to raise those questions.

But the mosque is very vital to understand relationships of the Assembly with the whole complex. As you know, initially, the prayer hall was not attached to the Assembly. It was a freestanding, large-scale structure. Kahn had been studying and working on the mosque for a long time. There were a number of reactions in Dhaka at that time. He was using the mosque as a buffer between the Chief Justice and the parliamentarians. There is the story of a meeting between the chief justice and Kahn in which they were going over a drawing, and the chief justice snatched the pencil from Kahn remarking, I don't want to be with those rogues.

If it were a democracy, the situation would have been different because there would be a direct access, and the people won't be rogues because the [condition of the] ruler and the ruled won't be there.

Absolutely. I see that. Had it been not only a democratic government but, say, the government of Sheikh Mujibur Rahman, it might have wanted the mosque in some other ways.

Not only that, Sheikh Mujib would have said, look, give me a Bangla assembly so that I can have access to people, and let people come to me, or I can go to them. This is where the difference is. Pandit Nehru telling Corbusier, look, I want to shake hands with my people; I am part of the masses. The moment you say that you come out of the assembly, then you are part of the masses. But if a military ruler comes to India, he says, no, I cannot be there. The British have made the Parliament building and the Rashtrapati Bhavan. You have to climb up; you are not easily accessible. What I am saying is if Kahn were there today, it would have been a very different expression because he would have really looked at the people in a different way, not in terms of the relationship of the ruler and the ruled.

If Kahn had to work on this job when he had all his life and not receiving many commissions, and when you meet a dictator where your meetings can be anything, when you have no access the way Corbusier had. Corbusier's access to Nehru or anybody was with absolute freedom. That access was never there for Kahn. In these constraints, the only thing anybody could do was to make these beautiful transparencies of laws; transparencies of light which travel and [are] all pervading, so the illumination comes in. This is where Kahn becomes important at that point, because anybody else would not have thought of light and the rules, which can become transparent. This is where Kahn is great. His buildings around the Assembly, those buildings he made as time went by, those buildings are very beautiful because they are slow, easy, accessible. He tried to compensate [the Assembly] with the buildings he made in brick—the housing, the hostels, and everything else. And the second thing he was experimenting with was a vocabulary that never existed before, and this is the genius of an architect. How does one create a new experience, and how does one invent the language of architecture? Like Corbusier, Kahn was trying to invent his own language, and I think he would have made his language complete after the Mellon Center [at Yale]

View of the Hostel walls.

Wall over belt area

Alternate design for wall openings of the Hostels.

The enclosed garden of the Dining and Lounge counts of the Hostels.

Inside of
outside

Glass in quantities less walls against the light are dark

Glass quantity modified so walls against the light receive light them selves

The light is reflected off walls. A wall against light, thereby this idea is intended of in the hot climate of the assembly buried and Kimbell. The thing that he was talking about last was the freedom, the Buddhahood, the enlightenment. ... Once, he said, he was waiting at the airport, [and] he saw these little *Chitrakatha*, the children's stories; he read those books. There was a book on Buddha, his life story, and of other people. The whole idea of permanence, simplicity, questioning of the issue of life and death—questioning what is the human endeavor. He was also fascinated by Arabian Nights, the man who enjoyed talking about stories, a man who read and told stories, a man who could tell you his dreams through words so that they can materialize in front of your eyes. A man who knew so much rhythm naturally and gradually has to come to this stage. This is where I say he is a yogi because it is not the culture of the West; it was the Estonian, the Eastern Bloc culture, which came back to him, which began to ask him the question, okay, Lou, what else? You are looking for truth; have you found it? You are looking for truth, which is in buildings, but is that what it is? Can you say what the building is about?

So, he always talked about the building, the psyche, what the material wanted to say, et cetera, but what he was really implying was, what is Kahn? What is that he has to do? How does he really behave? In life, he was very simple. I went with him once to buy a shawl for his wife, Esther, and there were some little dots, mango motifs. He said, "No, no. I want plain with one little border." From food habits to buying things, he knew what was superfluous and what cannot be taken away. It was the Shaker tradition, the Quakers, and the same thing continued in his work because he was saying, "Let me see how far I can go. How simple can I be?" He told me once, when I was in Philadelphia, he was doing this competition in Florida and met Eero Saarinen then. They were discussing, and Eero asked, Lou, if you have to make a building, how many materials would you use? So Lou says, I don't know, maybe concrete, maybe something else, maybe gray and white, what do you think? And Eero says I would try to use one, at the most two. It was something that Lou knew, but he remembered again. Minimalism is something else, and that is what you see here.

There is another story that Stanley Tigerman narrates. He is supposedly the last architect Kahn met on his way to New York and to his death. They met at Heathrow Airport. Tigerman was coming to Dhaka. You were saying how in the later stage Kahn was thinking about what he is to be, what he has to do. He is sort of assessing himself in a certain way. Tigerman says somewhat the same thing. They were talking for a couple of hours while they were waiting at the airport. One thing that seemed to bother Kahn was about [the Bangladeshi architect] Muzharul Islam. He was asking Tigerman, why did Muzharul Islam leave architecture for politics? Kahn seemed very disturbed about that, and was saying, "I could never do that." Probably, Kahn was asking, how does someone ultimately relate to society, to a larger whole? What is one's contribution after all?

His trips to India and Bangladesh must have given him another message. That message is very simple. This is a question [that is] probably raised in everybody's mind. There is something in the air, and that is, what is the purpose? What do you leave behind? Kahn was never fascinated by money either, so the question of money is not there. So, if not money, what else? The question that what is left is eternity. What stays? What cannot be questioned will stay. What cannot be altered will stay. What is natural, what will naturally flow, will stay. What is inherent will stay. And, therefore, the Upanishad is talking

about the air, the water, the sky, and then the soul, the moving soul, the non-local mind. This will stay, and that is all pervading. And that is what Lou was always talking about: the psyche. What it is.

I think he was looking for those things always, because, as he says, if he has to find the architectural expression of a brick wall, what is the difference between his brick wall and somebody else's brick wall? Then, he is talking about the slice of light, which comes and just touches that. That means what kind of little vibration the bricks must give or the joints must give, the little projections must give so that the bricks begin to sparkle and smile, so that little slice, that light, that breeze which comes with a fragrance, but it is actually what is. You don't know where the breeze is, and you can't hold the fragrance, either. It is only the sensation that is left, and I think good architects are looking for those sensations. I think that is what is Kahn does. He always talked about silence; he talked about the ruins. To him, finally, it was that meditative silence: How does one make a building, which exists and yet doesn't want to say anything and yet says everything everybody wants to know?

So the building in Dhaka stands there. If you look at them in the evenings, if you look at them in the early mornings, it is almost as eternal as the rocks of the Himalayas. He makes the statement that "I have no Himalayas around, but my buildings stay there as long as this sun rises because it is so simple from the outside, from the distance." How do you make that opening unless you make a circle, that opening from where you see very simple things? Hardly any extra thing has been done, and also, the scale has to do with that. The scale is big. If there were small holes, it won't be the same. They had to be big enough to make them look infinite. The power is in the scale in which he makes the apertures and the box.

I think from that point of view of the base is very important for him. You should go in the early morning and walk around the houses, go around, and then you see this base; it is almost like a banyan tree, which comes up with the roots coming out and covering the whole ground, as if it is all pervading. It is stretching its arms at the ground level, and the ground level stretches far beyond because all the houses are at the same height so that everything becomes part of that, and then this rises up like this.

I was struck by the way of his model making. The buildings always seemed to rise from the clay base. They are not boxes thrown from the top to the ground.

Yes, it was like a mesa. It was very much like a stupa. I would say Dhaka is like a stupa, as in Sanchi.

Before he even started thinking about the Assembly, there was something else that intrigued him. He asked himself two questions: One, how do buildings take their place on this land? And, the other thing, how are buildings to be grouped together? Also, he began to talk of a new way of thinking about architecture, which he called "an architecture of the land." He was saying that for Bangladesh, the primary thing to think about is architecture of the land. In that context, I see his buildings as land-sculpted.

All studies with diagonals, triangles, and geometry really become part of the land, part of the wall. The land and the wall do not change. You see, Wright made a wall and then made

the roof in such a way that the whole wall continued, his studio as a shell, and his other buildings go like this with an inclined wall, and he brings the roofline right up to the wainscot, so the whole building really hugs the ground. Kahn is trying to do it from the ground up, to go up like this, to reverse this.

Here, can we also discuss the importance of water? Before Dhaka, I don't see any significant presence of water in Kahn's work.

In Dhaka, it is the whole question. You are on the plains, and the water is going to be there, anyway, so the Dhaka landscape cannot be without the Ganges, without the rivers around, and so the flooding, the delta, has to be there. It is the reflecting element but also water, an integral part of your culture. The whole of Bangladesh is made of lakes and rivers. To me, it is a country that is floating.

I am curious to know what places he visited in Ahmedabad or elsewhere in India?

He went to Ranakpur. It is a Jain temple about ninety miles from Udaipur. He also went to Abu, the Delawara temple. Delawara is before Udaipur. These are all Jain temples, and Kasturabhai [Lalbhai] had asked him to come with him. The Jain Abu Temple is made of marble, exquisitely carved, translucent. Ranakpur is very geometrical, again in a valley, a solitary temple with an axis and raised plinth with a huge number of columns. You can see the gods from anywhere. When he came back, I asked him which one did he like. He said Ranakpur, and I asked why. He said Abu is very decorative and asked me back which one did I like. There [at Abu Temple], the marble has been totally transformed into wax. You talk of marble as marble; we in India talk of dematerializing things. And I said that when you can spiritualize a matter, it is quite different. I said this body, which is material, has to be spiritualized, and that's what the message is. And he said I didn't know that, but I prefer the other one.

This is really where you asked me a question yesterday: How do I see Kahn as an "Indian" architect? Well, there are only a few great architects who came to the sub-continent, Lutyens, Corbusier, and then Kahn. There are not many like them because people like that are not born every day. But what one is looking for is what is it one can do so that the material really moves, the material begins to become something else. Can we learn about ourselves as a vehicle of the spirit moving, and can we infuse this vehicle into bricks and concrete and stones so that the material also melts away in the process and just emerges as it should be?

And as I told you last night, I invited you here [the Gufa] only because here is one building which I tried to do. You can say that partly, it is an influence of Gaudi; partly, it is from other places, I don't know where, but I feel one is trying to do here is really to infuse things so that finally, you know only the experience, and I think in this building, you get that "Silence," not my other buildings, so what I have learned from Kahn is this search for silence; what I learned from Corbusier is the lyricism; what I learned from Wright is the point of hugging the ground, and what I learned from Gaudi is the great quality of flowing inward and outward.

And so what I am doing really is trying to find these because that's the only way I cannot only pay my respects to them, but I can also learn. Slowly, I am trying to learn the silence, the act of silence through the ruins of Kahn going below ground, going above ground, relating the surfaces.

And then one is still trying to say that in the content of their work that if you still want to get this, then there are these paradoxes in India, in Bangladesh, where different cultures stay together; different religions stay together; you find a mosque and a temple next to one another; you find a big palace and a haveli and shacks together. [There are] people [who] are well dressed and people with no clothes. There is a car, and there is a buffalo on the road. There is a cycle-rickshaw, and there is a jet plane. These are all contradictions that we have accepted. We know that without the disparity, true existence doesn't work. There is no existence without disparity. It is only when we see it in a short span that there is a disparity. Actually, it is the same process; you see only one end, and you see the other one, but [they] depend upon the suitability of one and the other.

It is like an insect; the fly has only one hour of life, and the mountains have thousands of years of life. So, we consider temporary and permanent. It is not there at all. It is all permanent and all temporary because we also go away. So, these are relative terms, and I think if we can learn these from those people that they knew this relativity and felt them, and that's why you will find all the great architectures of the world, including the work of today's masters, you will find there are a lot of things, but the experience is very similar; it touches us the same way as we can smell the fragrance of a flower or look at the mountains or go to the sea. That is because this kind of continuous phenomenon is there; that is what is beautiful. This is the great lesson to me working with these masters, including Bucky Fuller, whom I met several times.

I am finding that there is a thread. They want to find out what will last. What will disappear? How can you make things without a strain? The most important thing is, is there a strain in that building? Is there a strain in that triangle which hits the opening, and, therefore, the opening looks as if it is very natural? In a circle, there is no strain; in a square, there is no strain.

It seems to me, if I am not mistaken, that you are looking at these major figures, especially with Kahn, that he is moving in a continuum, almost autonomous from specific experiences related to [coming to] India and Bangladesh.

Yes, yes … because they are made to sense things; they are made to smell, feel. They don't feel superficially; they feel deeply within themselves. Actually, they are themselves. The whole reason of their being what they are is because they know themselves, and they work within their own self. They are very alive within; we are very alive outside. To them, the body has no meaning because their presence is inside. That's why they are yogis, and that's why they cannot be communicated in a normal way, because they are only manifestations of [what they are doing on this earth]. But manifestations come, as if like a spring, from within. It is a surge, which tells them to do this. It is a manifestation, and they become instruments. That's what Kahn talked about, that's what Corbusier talked about, and that's what Bucky talked to me about: that we are only instruments. And that's what our yogis talk about. It's not man conquering this, man doing this, and man doing that. [That's how normal people talk.] That's why humility becomes very natural to them. You can see one doesn't seek publicity, one

doesn't want things, one doesn't copy … why? Because one is looking within, and he knows everything will be available to him in the long run. To them, the game was continuous.

1994

INTERVIEWS WITH WANG SHU

BUILDING FROM THE HEART
INTERVIEW WITH WANG SHU

Jonathan Louie

In a quest for the most novel, eye catching, and unique forms, it may be a return to techniques of the traditional that offers the most resistance to the sleek highrises littering the Chinese landscape. Recently listed as one of Time Magazine's 100 Most Influential People, an honor that places him amongst other trendsetting pioneers, Wang Shu's ability to transcend the debate between traditional and contemporary practices of design makes him the poster child for the discussion over the future urbanization of the Chinese landscape.

It's through the lens of Alexander Tzonis and Liliane Lefaivre one can look at Shu's work as not directly drawing from the context, but rather thinking of elements being stripped of context and used in unfamiliar ways. Projects such as the Ningbo History Museum, and 66,000 recycled tiles installation Tiled Garden protest the waste of building materials that are often dumped in landfills after short-lived structures are demolished. While others, such as his campus in Xiangshan, rely on studies of techniques outside of architecture, such as traditional landscape painting, to influence spatial relationships at the scale of a campus.

By creating urban artifacts that deliberately "misinterpret" material function, Shu blurs the boundaries between the modern and historical vernacular while charging materials as aesthetic and politically motivated artifacts.

Operating outside of the metropolitan cores in his hometown of Hanzhou in contrast to the globe-trotting Chinese "avant-garde," Wang Shu explores the rich legacy of China's intellectual, sculptural, and architectural history, tying his research closely to a simple formal language that emphasizes regional culture and imperfect craftsmanship. Similar to that of Aldo Rossi, Shu's work oscillates between formal and typological simplicity, while emphasizing material expression to structure the experience of the city we live in.

Wang Shu lives and practices in Hangzhou, China, where he established Amateur Architecture Studio with his wife Lu Wenyu in 1997.

JL

Jonathan Louie: *As an architect you've cast yourself as someone who prefers to practice in the region in which you live. Was there a turning point or event in your career that influenced your perception of architecture? How did you determine your regional approach to design?*

Wang Shu: For Chinese architects, the question is: how can we make a Chinese modern architecture? Not just a modern architecture, but China's modern architecture. It's an interesting question because we do have a Chinese architecture. It's a learned and copied modern architecture from the western world, but there is no relation to our local life.

In school, I did some independent work very early on. For example as a student I worked on my first building, which was finished in 1985, and I designed my first independent project in 1989 [a youth center for a small town in Hainang]. In this way I received professional architectural experience. Although I could do good architecture it wasn't really what I wanted. I realized that it's not just about good architecture, but about the best way to design and to construct. It was a more basic question.

Jonathan Louie teaches at the Syracuse University School of Architecture, USA.

So the 1990s were a very important time. It was a turning point. I completely took myself out of the professional system and took time with workers, questioning materials together with them. I did a lot of renovation work for old buildings. It was a rich experience because any time you design something in this field it's important to see that there are some things that have existed before you. It's not just designing on an empty piece of paper or on an empty site. You have to wonder how you can create something that takes the past and turns it into the future.

When you do a renovation for a building you have to touch the materials. It's not just the materials, but it's the way the materials change with time, the weather, or with peoples' lives. You have to design new things that can co-exist. So now when I design a new building, even on an empty site, my way is very similar to a renovation.

An important aspect of your work is the emphasis on authenticity, recycled materials, and craft. Can you talk about your interests in relationship to the slick mass produced high-rise construction in the China today?

Usually I like to talk about real things, and realities. I prefer to talk about natural materials that aren't artificial. It's not just about an interest in recycled materials. But if you think you are a modern architect or a contemporary architect you should be critiquing reality. Maybe in the next ten years I'll use other kinds of materials. But in the past ten years I felt there was too much demolition and I wanted to propose an answer to that. Of course this is about attitude. On the other side, using this material has led to an architectural way—the craftsman's skills.

Is this a critique of the state of architecture in China?

Yes. In China, I think architecture is important because in modern times it plays a big role. Architects design so many buildings at such a large scale. The size means that it can totally change people's lifestyles. Who gave you this power? How do you think about how you can control and handle this power? What is the meaning to you? Those are very important things. If you just think that you are an engineer and you're going to create a surface for people without thinking about how the surface can change peoples' lives, it could really destroy peoples' lives. Only once did I design a high-rise building [the Vertical Courtyard Apartments in Hangzhou, 2004-2007]. I wanted to approach the design as a high rise building that used many small buildings collected together.

You're talking about the Vertical Courtyard Project in Hangzhou?

Yes. It's a simple idea. I wanted even those people living thirty meters high to still feel like they were living in a small house where they could live around a small courtyard and plant their own trees. From below they can tell people on the ground that "those are my trees and that's my house." It provides an identity for people to feel like it's their own house. It's more than just blank windows in apartment buildings that can't separate neighborhoods. It's a basic right for people.

Your design process seems similar to Chinese Landscape painting. For example, when you drew the Xiangshan Campus in Hangzhou you drew the project all at once. Is this a typical approach?

It's not just an abstract concept to talk about the country. In fact the country includes many things for me. I spent a long time researching traditional landscape painting. It means that you can control a large-scale landscape in a spatial way. The Hangzhou Campus was my test project. It was very successful, but for another project, there may be another way to do it. Every time I like performing different experiments.

It's not enough to say that I have a good education and I know how to design. You should talk about it not as designing something, but instead asking "how should I design?" It's a more basic question. How do you ask the question? The way is more important than the design itself. It's my way, and it's very simple.

What does the Pritzker Prize mean for you and for architectural design in China?

Especially for young architects, this prize encourages them to do more experimental work—because the fact is, it's not easy. In China we have many projects, but only a few good projects. Good architecture is not just design, but I think it's closer to a struggle. It'll give them more self-confidence.

For me, it has another importance. Originally I wanted to stop for two years, to have time with my wife and time to raise our son together. I worked too much over the past ten years. My son is ten years old now, but now with the prize, maybe this means I have to do more things and more design. But I still want to spend more time with my son.

If you keep the feeling in your heart pure, people will like your building. If you really do good design, you will find that your building will smile. Because the building comes from your heart, and it really gets a good feeling from life, and they can feel it. If you just work hard, and worry because you want a good building, people can feel that the building is a little nervous. So it's very important to keep your heart in the right way.

Originally published in *"Architects Newspaper West Coast"* (February 2012).

WANG SHU AMATEUR ARCHITECTURE

An Interview with
Nina Rappaport

Nina Rappaport is an architectural critic, curator, and educator. She is publications director at Yale School of Architecture and editor of the biannual publication *Constructs*, the exhibition catalogs, and the school's book series.

Pritzker Architecture Prize winner Wang Shu, who co-founded Amateur Architecture Studio, with his wife, Lu Wenyu, gave a series of lectures in the East Coast of USA (2013), including one at Yale University School of Architecture. Yale's Nina Rappaport met with him to discuss his approach toward traditional and contemporary materials and construction issues in his work in China.

Nina Rappaport: *I am interested in your decision to work in isolation for ten years, rejecting the life of a contemporary architect to learn traditional crafts and construction*

Wang Shu: This thinking started in the late 1980s, because, at that time in China, young men were looking forward to modern things. They were very patient about Modern architecture. But, in fact, in just a very short time, I started to understand that people don't really think just about the meaning of modernization: it means modern buildings, high-rises, highways, et cetera. But this does not have a real relationship to Chinese life. People think that to have a modern city, they must abandon their traditional lives and buildings, so they demolished the historic Chinese buildings. But I thought, maybe what I learned in architecture school is not right. I found that the traditional architectural system is closer to real thinking about the natural environment, and is totally different from the modern system. I thought that if I really want to understand modernization, the first step is to understand tradition. After I did several projects, including a 1986 high-rise hotel, I understood that it is not just about design skills, not just about concepts, but the important thing is that people can relate to your attitude about life. What is your world vision? What are your real experiences? I realized that if I really wanted to change my experience about architecture, I had to change my life first.

Did you work as an apprentice to a craftsman? Was it about preservation or just learning traditional building skills? And how did you re-orient your work?

At that time, I did a series of small works, really renovations on different kinds of old buildings. It was relating to something that existed before you, so I was constantly reminded of it. It is a different way of designing: you have to think directly about materials, about how to use your new design and materials combined with the old things so they can co-exist.

When you talk about wanting to find architecture closer to nature, do you mean in terms of natural materials or the nature of …

In China, we have a long history of people living with nature. Landscape is more important than architecture. Every time you start to think about architecture, you think about landscape. Large or small scale, you think about how the architecture will mix with natural things. They can't be separated.

What is the attitude of politicians toward saving historic buildings and re-using them in different ways? Are you politically active, or is it too difficult?

Politics is still a very abstract topic. Our traditional way was to recycle buildings and use recycled materials in construction. People used to keep the traditional habit of saving materials for re-use. But around the year 2000, I found the situation changed: people were still collecting old materials, but they no longer used them because they didn't know how to use them in modern buildings. They didn't know how to use them with

Tiles Hill (Hoels for visiting Professors) Photo : Iu Wenyu

214

Ningbo History museum Photo : lv Hengzhong

reason and dignity. So I thought maybe I should show them: starting in 2000, I did 1a 1b to make modern structures. I think it is very important.

How did you work with recycled tiles and bricks for the Ningbo Museum in 2005, and how was it received?

Before the design of the Ningbo Historic Museum, we had done a great amount of investigation on the city and countryside of Ningbo, especially on the construction and application of the local special materials. I found that there are more than eighty different-sized bricks. There are many different tiles—large ones, small ones, thick ones, thin ones. It is not just about materials but also keeping the variety of architectural history. Just talking about traditional buildings is not enough because, meanwhile, everything will disappear. I am interested in how we can use traditional materials and craftsmanship along with modern technology.

But your design ideas are contemporary, especially, for example, the forms of the vertical courtyard apartments in Hangzhou. They are interesting in terms of the variegated setbacks, the upper-level courtyards, and the perforated volumes. Can you describe what inspired them, and how you worked with the developer?

People think good design reflects good reasoning. If you have to use a concrete system, the form must spring from the basic nature of the materials. Carving a traditional shape into the form has no meaning. How invisible can tradition be and still exist in contemporary buildings? The idea is simple: even if you are living many meters high, you can still feel that you live in a small cottage. In your room you can see the ceiling. It is a double-height ceiling. The ceiling controls the vision. You are living in a high-rise building, but you have a two-story vision. The main construction is simple and rational, but around this rational system there are different depths. Every family unit is double-layered, as a duplex with access to sunshine. Every six families share a public courtyard in a social experience, and every family has a tiny private courtyard. We wondered if people would actually use these public courtyards. Because I got the Pritzker Prize, CCTV did a film of me, and the director went to the apartments and found that the public courtyard worked. But the first courtyard: nothing. It was all dust, and no one was using it. The residents were worried it was haunted. We went into another courtyard that was very clean, with furniture and some young students' homework left there. I thought, oh, people are using it! We continued on to the third courtyard, and it was very crowded. I think this means there is hope. It means that architects may have the power to change how people live inside of architecture. You see the potential, and you make the condition, then you just wait for something like this to happen.

But is this happening anywhere else? Or are you one of the few Chinese architects working against the massive wave of demolition and development?

In fact, few architects are talking about this; they are just following the market model. In China, you go to the developer and they say, "Let's copy from the French for luxuries," which has no relation at all to Chinese life. This project makes someone think there is 2a 2b

Would you be able to do another project like this? Does the developer want to repeat it?

No. The client is my friend. He was feeling very honorable about doing this, but, finally, he told me it was the first and last time.

What is it about traditional building that is better in relation to contemporary construction?

Our traditional structural systems were very lightweight; new concrete-and-steel systems are heavy and destroy the land. When a traditional building collapses in the countryside, you can salvage the field and use it to grow vegetables. I think, in the future, we will talk more about a way of doing architecture that is not so solid. That is my interest now. To think about conservation the Western way doesn't work; ours is more a routine of rebuilding things, about a building's life.

How do you incorporate traditional materials while drawing new attention to older materials along with new technology for construction and conservation?

I recently designed a new building in our Xiangshan campus of CAA. I tried to do something to keep the local tradition of earth architecture. Originally, there were many of that type of building in the area; the question was how the tradition could go forward. There is a hotel for visiting professors with a very thick wall of rammed earth and a new wood structure for the roof. It is a very new approach because it is related to tradition, but it is constructed in a new way. It is not just about the traditional experience; it is about the earth, in order to experiment with construction. I am training my students and workers to use traditional materials. If we can do this in cities, it means our rammed-earth building has some spatial value.

How are you continuing this building tradition with your students?

Next year, at the China Academy of Art, in Hangzhou, I would like to train a new group in this type of conservation. In the first two years, we would start with training in brick, stone, metals, and carpentry. We would also have a year of Chinese calligraphy

How do you maintain China's scholarly tradition?

We can still keep the scholarly tradition, but I think this revolution may be the last because all the scholar groups have disappeared. It is a red collision, which means that workers and farmers have some of the highest positions in society, and for the scholars in China, it is bad. After the Cultural Revolution, the old scholar groups disappeared. When you are a scholar, it doesn't mean you are just a professor teaching in a city but that you have some independent attitude within society. You insist on something.

Are there architect-scholars?

Almost none. We just have architect-businessmen.

So you are an architect-scholar?

Yeah. It is really interesting that, from the late 1990s, before I was an architect, I was a scholar. Few people understand what I say.

What is your current focus in this direction?

Now I am doing two things. First, I have projects in cities but in the Chinese garden tradition, which means I want a value system in my buildings that shows people they can have another life. I moved my focus to the countryside, where I want

to leave some beautiful things. In the last twenty years, we have lost ninety percent of traditional cities. Every day they are demolished. People are living in beautiful traditional buildings, and they don't realize their meaning, so they abandon the towns and move to the modern cities. I think it is a very urgent situation in China.

How do you get involved in trying to save the traditional towns in the countryside?

I have been working a long time on this. Maybe this is the most difficult work to do in China. But now that I received the Pritzker, maybe I can have more influence in local government. The government is very powerful in rural China. If you don't have the support from government, you almost cannot do anything.

The interview first appeared in *Constructs* (Fall 2013), Yale School of Architecture. Reprinted with permission. Photographs by Lv Hengzhong.

CAIRO

EVERYTHING NEEDS A REVOLUTION NOW

Frederick Deknatel

In Cairo, there is a street named after the Arab League. It's a grand boulevard that cuts through Mohandiseen, a neighborhood built in the 1950s to house engineers and other civil servants, whose ranks swelled during the 1960s with the guarantee of employment under the state socialism of President Gamal Abdel Nasser. These days, the boulevard is lined with luxury car showrooms, drab mid-rises and fast-food chains, all forming the commercial spine of an upscale area too expensive for most clerks and bureaucrats. Last December, on one of the quiet streets that radiates off the boulevard, I visited the office of an architect named Dina Shehayeb. A professor at the Housing and Building National Research Center in Cairo, Shehayeb also runs her own firm, which focuses on community-based development and the revitalization of historic areas. The deadly street battles of late November between the police and unarmed protesters on Mohamed Mahmoud Street near Tahrir Square had ended, and the attacks on protesters by military police outside the People's Assembly near Tahrir were a week away. Cairo was relatively calm. But in her office, Shehayeb spoke heatedly of a city transformed during the reign of the recently deposed president, Hosni Mubarak.

"We had thirty years of the government pushing us to informality," she said, alluding to Cairo's vast "informal" areas: dense urban districts built without official planning or permits, often in cheap red brick and concrete on agricultural land that once formed the Nile's flood plain. Some two-thirds of Cairenes live in informal areas, the urban reality in a country where the government has never provided enough housing; during Mubarak's three decades of power in Egypt, state assets and land were sold off in a costly dream of turning Cairo's desert outskirts into satellite cities and gated suburbs. But Shehayeb was also talking about Mohandiseen, where someone with money and connections can skirt lax planning guidelines and build a tower on a street of low-rise buildings. "It was governance by informality, articulated and made ambiguous on purpose," she said. "Things were always done with vagueness, uncertainty and contradiction."

Shehayeb then lashed out at the latest master plan for the city, "Cairo Vision 2050," which imagines Egypt's capital as a high-rise delirium modeled on Dubai, with crowded informal areas and neglected Nile-side neighborhoods replaced by glass towers and an abundance of green space. As for the city's "heritage" areas, from its belle époque downtown to its medieval core, home to an unrivaled concentration of historic Islamic architecture, they would become a vast "open-air museum." Drawn up by the General Organization for Physical Planning (GOPP), part of the Ministry of Housing under Mubarak, Cairo 2050 (as it's also known) was promoted as the "strategic urban development plan" for Greater Cairo, the sprawling urban area that includes three governorates, some 17 million to 20 million people and no mayor. Urban management falls instead to governors, often retired generals appointed directly by the president and given the rank of minister. Never made public, Cairo 2050 was presented at conferences starting in 2008, to consultants and advisers like the United Nations Human Settlements Program (UN-Habitat), and to investors in an Egyptian real estate market dominated by Gulf petrodollars.

The plan called for the massive decentral-ization of the capital, one of the densest cities on earth. Ministries and state institutions would move to the desert near New Cairo, one of the satellite cities to the east built under Mubarak, while millions

Frederick Deknatel is the senior editor of World Politics Review. His writing has also appeared in The Nation, The New Republic, Foreign Policy, and other publications.

All photographs by Frederick Deknatel

Birqash
Dhat al Kawm
Mit Halfa
Qalag
Ring Rd
Burtus
Mansuriya
Bahtim
Ausim
Gesr El Suiz
Teraaet El Esmaeliah
Kafr Hakim
Giza
Cairo
Cairo Alex Desert Rd
Kirdasa
Kafr Tuhurmis
Msadak
Tana Hussen
Circular Rd
Moubarak Axis
90 Axis mahmoud Talaat
Maadi
El Fayom - El Wahat Rd
6 October - Wady El Natroun
Abu an Numrus
Shabramant
Tura
El Maady - Bear Gendaly - El Katamia

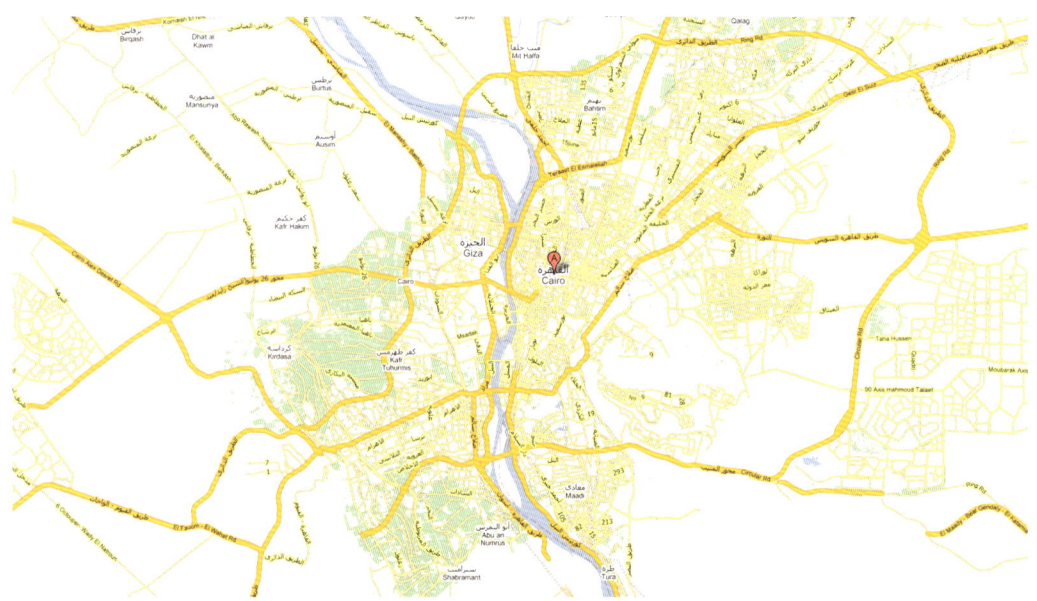

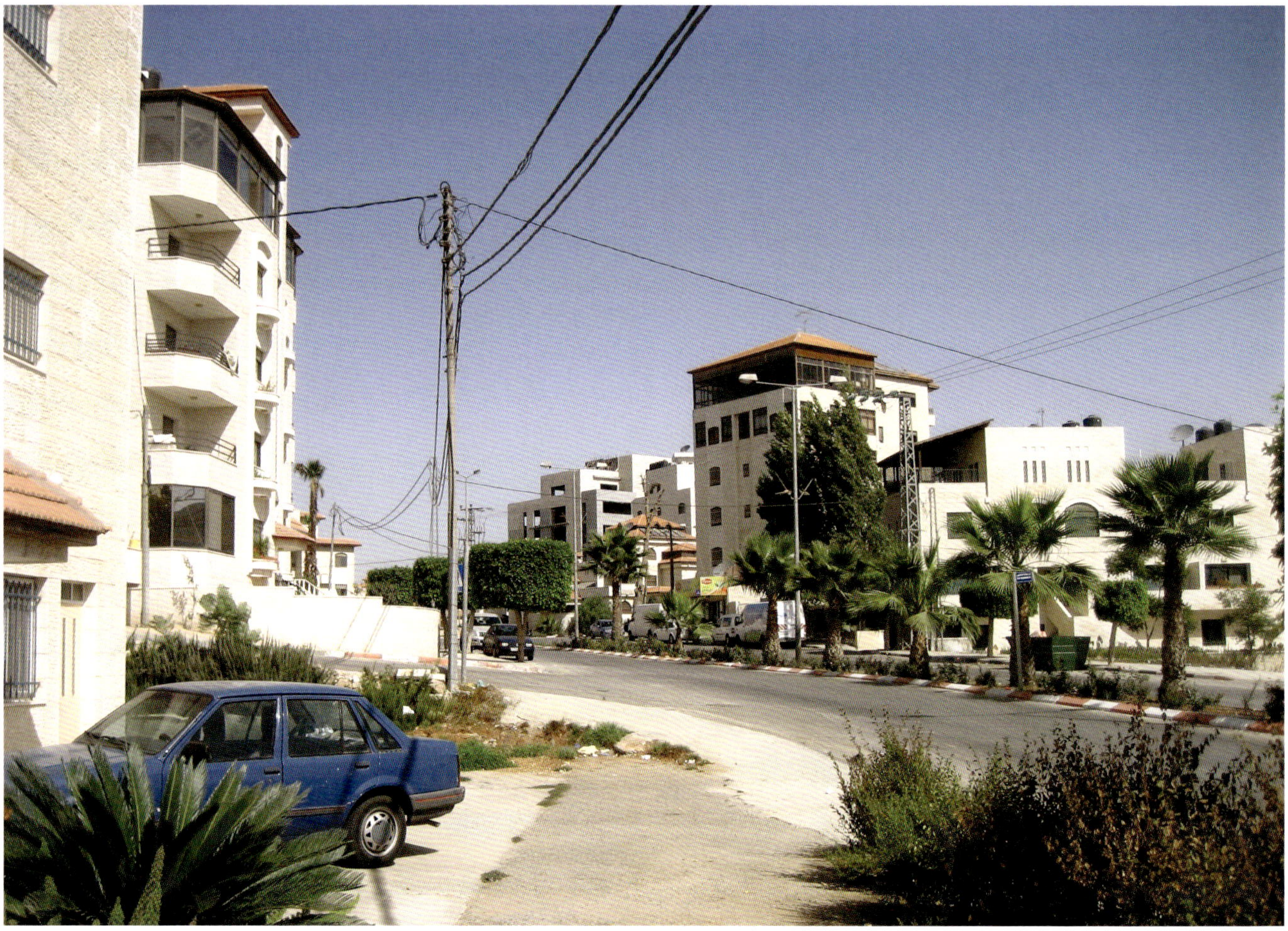

of poor residents living in informal areas would be relocated to housing in an ever more distant stretch of desert. Snippets of the plan soon emerged in the local press. Bird's-eye-view renderings of Khufu Avenue—a runway-size boulevard with dedicated bus lanes running in a line from the heart of Mohandiseen to the base of the Giza Pyramids—convey nothing of contemporary Cairo, a hectic modern capital with major infrastructure, housing and planning needs that is nevertheless depicted by the Egyptian and Western media as a traffic-snarled, smog-choked jumble of slums.

When Mubarak fell during the Arab uprisings in February 2011, Cairo 2050 did not fall with him; UN-Habitat and GOPP have been drafting an update. "It is curious, and an indication of GOPP's isolation, that the organization and its parent, the Ministry of Housing, continue with this work in spite of mounting criticism from both Egyptian and foreign quarters," writes David Sims, a longtime urban planner and economist in Egypt, in a new postscript to his authoritative book, *Understanding Cairo: The Logic of a City Out of Control* (2010). A year ago I met Bassem Fahmy, the project manager of the Strategic Urban Development Plan for the Greater Cairo Region, at UN-Habitat's office in a cheerless tower in Dokki, near Mohandiseen. Leafing through a draft of Cairo 2050 on his tidy desk, Fahmy described the updated plans as tied "much more to reality. You cannot just present nice pictures with perspectives that are unrealistic … kind of like Dubai." He admitted that some of the original plans represented "fantasy work, a kind of marketing," and that certain mega-projects, like Khufu Avenue, were "totally confused. It will not see the light." But the cover of the draft on his desk included a rendering of a huge roadway—much wider than the Champs-Élysées, the planners' self-expressed model—terminating below the Pyramids, along with a few stock images of contemporary Cairo. The revised plans, Fahmy said, "will see the light, after public engagement," and with UN-Habitat as a consultant. He cited questionnaires, focus groups and public presentations at which residents were shown images of the proposals. In the original Cairo 2050 plans, however, GOPP claimed to have consulted 1,800 "key officials, planners, and thinkers" through two conferences, "28 specialized workshops," four symposiums, and four surveys covering between 3,000 and 5,000 households in Greater Cairo.

"This was the promise of a Mubarak presidency: economic prosperity through real estate," says Dina Shehayeb. For her, the corruption of the Mubarak era is far from over, even if Mubarak and his two sons, Gamal and Alaa, now sit in Tora prison, along with the ministers whose prosperity Gamal Mubarak's liberalizing economic reforms had assured. "Those ministers in jail are just scapegoats," she insists, because Cairo 2050 "is about legalizing conflicts of interest and sanctioning personal benefit."

* * *

In June 2012, Mohamed Morsi became Egypt's first freely elected civilian president. An engineering professor and ranking Muslim Brotherhood bureaucrat, Morsi campaigned on a platform tied to the Islamist movement's social justice policies. Officially banned but tolerated under Mubarak, the Brotherhood has built and operated schools and clinics in poor urban areas that the government neglected or abandoned altogether. Like other Islamist parties in the Arab world, it filled a welfare gap in an authoritarian state that had increasingly cut

public subsidies, sold state assets, and otherwise operated a crony economy under the auspices of economic liberalization. The platform for the Brotherhood's political arm, the Freedom and Justice Party, decries the corruption of the old regime, but less so its economic policies. On urban development in its so-called Nahda (Renaissance) Project, the FJP promises to redistribute the population density of Egypt's 80 million to 90 million people and "get out of the Nile Delta valley to new regional growth areas."

What this means in practice is vague, but the promise is consistent with the policies of past governments, which devoted their budgets and resources to alleviating Cairo's demographic challenges by building out into the nearly ninety-six percent of Egypt that is desert. The construction of new satellite cities, beyond the natural borders of the Nile flood plain that bounded Cairo for a millennium, also reflects a broader governmental obsession with massive building programs as social policy. Nasser made huge outlays on modernist public housing blocks, industrial towns in the desert outside Cairo and, most prominently, the High Dam in Aswan—promoted as a sign of Egypt's postcolonial independence and modernization. Nasser's successor, Anwar el-Sadat, shifted the focus of Cairo's desert to housing, where worker communities would rise up in new satellites east of the metropolis; Sadat also tried to turn downtown Cairo into Houston on the Nile, in the words of anthropologist Farha Ghannam, its high-rises either government ministries or American chain hotels.

The pace of Cairo's desert urbanization accelerated under Mubarak, as state land—much of it controlled by the military—was sold to private developers in an era of so-called economic reform that began in 1991, when Mubarak agreed to a structural adjustment program with the International Monetary Fund. On stretches of rocky, barren terrain, Egyptian and Gulf developers raced to build villas, malls, gated compounds and golf courses with names like Dreamland, Beverly Hills, Moon Valley, and Madinaty ("My City"). Meanwhile, closer to the Nile, where most people lived, residents of informal areas bribed local municipal officials in lieu of applying for a building permit, or to gain access to plumbing and electricity. A section of Duweiqa, one of Cairo's poorest shantytowns, collapsed in 2008 in a rock slide that killed 119 people; the area was bulldozed and its residents promised new housing that never materialized. The same year, the World Bank and the International Finance Corporation, in their Doing Business Report, named Egypt the "world's top reformer."

"Financial stabilization and structural adjustment were intended to generate an export boom, not a building boom," Timothy Mitchell writes in *Rule of Experts: Egypt, Techno-Politics, Modernity* (2002). "Egypt was to prosper by selling fruits and vegetables to Europe and the Gulf, not paving over its fields to build ring roads. But real estate had now replaced agriculture as the country's third-largest non-oil investment sector, after manufacturing and tourism." Mubarak turned Cairo's desert cities into a luxury real-estate market, much of it speculative and driven by Gulf investment, which made Egypt's political economy increasingly dependent on the region. According to Adam Hanieh of the School of Oriental and African Studies in London, as of January 2012, half of the twenty-six most valuable real estate developments in Egypt—those worth more than $100 million—were fully owned by Gulf-based conglomerates. In fact, Gulf-based companies held 80 % of the value of all real estate projects under development.

The landscape of a city long defined by its natural desert borders was transformed. A Cairo University thesis by Rania Rashed—cited by Khaled Adham, an Egyptian professor of architecture at the United Arab Emirates University—estimates that Cairo's recent eastward and westward desert expansion under Mubarak totaled some 300,000 acres. Half of the eastern and the western desert, beyond the Pyramids and Sphinx of the Giza Plateau, were set aside for high-end residences, from villas to gated communities. But the building boom extended well beyond Cairo. In 1996, Mubarak launched the "desert reclamation" project of Toshka, a failed scheme to irrigate a vast stretch of desert near Sudan and conjure up a "second Nile Valley" that would accommodate the world's largest farm, to be run by a California agribusiness owned by billionaire Saudi prince al-Waleed bin Talal.

Such mega-projects exemplify what Yale political scientist James Scott calls "authoritarian high modernism," a state-led development logic which presumes that rapid modernization and social order—a shift through industrialization and urbanization—can be realized with sweeping projects imposed by a cadre of planning authorities. Cairo 2050 was the latest such scheme, even if it veered well into fantasy with its costs—not only budgetary, but also social and political costs for the millions it would displace. Sims sees the scheme as an example of the government's "continued penchant for the manufacture of unrealistic dreams."

* * *

Aboul-Fetouh Shalaby teaches urban planning at Cairo University and coordinates the FJP's committee on urban development and housing. Like many Brotherhood technocrats, he has multiple degrees: a PhD from Cardiff University in Wales and a master's in urban planning from the University of Nevada. "I lived in Reno for two years," he told me with delight. When asked about Cairo 2050, he had a ready reply: "It was politically driven for the benefit of certain investors and power groups. It was centered around the very idea of investment and maximizing profit." Shalaby detailed the nature of the police state under Mubarak, mobilized to protect corrupt and exclusive economic interests. "They used the security state to control, impose and force their own ideas and their own urban plan. This is why I call it a businessmen's government."

But immediately after, Shalaby admitted that, despite his criticisms of Cairo 2050, not "everything in it is all wrong." The mistake of the Mubarak regime was not just devising a fanciful urban plan from "a businessmen's government looking for fast revenue," but also concentrating too much on Cairo. "Most of the desert cities were established on the periphery, but were managed together as one continuous urban area," Shalaby said. "This actually caused more burdens on the existing infrastructure. Those settlements were meant to be independent cities, but ended up being dormitory outskirts for the rich. They didn't have any economic basis to be real cities." Shalaby added that the FJP aims to invest resources, "whether private or public sector, to open new developmental avenues outside the congested valley—to establish, in the real sense of the word, new independent settlements."

In his October Paper of 1974, which launched Egypt's economic liberalization and signaled its strategic shift from Soviet ally to American client, Sadat proclaimed: "After all these thousands of years, and in view of the rapid increase in the population and

the new life sought by them, the life of the Egyptian people cannot remain confined to the Delta and the narrow valley of the Nile." Speaking before Parliament in 1996 to launch the Toshka project, Mubarak declared that "the conquest of the desert is no longer a slogan or dream but a necessity dictated by the spiraling population growth. What is required is not a token exodus into the desert but a complete reconsideration of the distribution of population throughout the country." The FJP is upholding these policies. "We're looking at the current existing urban context not to add to it, but to make it less dense," Shalaby told me, "by attracting people outside of the congested valley to the barren desert, to undeveloped areas."

For all of its social justice policies and history of persecution and imprisonment, the Brotherhood presents a prosperous, business-friendly face to Egyptians and the world. Behind the technocrats and professors like Shalaby, who described his party as one of "gradual change," stand the group's millionaires. One of them is Khairat al-Shater, the Brotherhood's powerful deputy and leading financier, who was barred from the presidential election because he served time in prison under Mubarak; another is Hassan Malek, who started a software company with Shater in the 1980s and currently operates the Egyptian branches of major Turkish furniture and clothing chains. Malek drafted the FJP's economic policies, which advocate continued privatization along with the requisite condemnation of the corrupt old regime. Last spring, Shater addressed foreign investors at the American Chamber of Commerce in Egypt with familiar free-market talking points. Ahead of a subsequent trip by executives from nearly fifty American companies last fall, Deputy Secretary of State Thomas Nides—who traveled with the trade delegation to Cairo—told The New York Timesthat the Brotherhood's leaders, focused as they are on deregulation to spur a moribund economy, "sound like Republicans half the time." Nides added, "Our goal is to send a very strong message to Egypt that the government understands it's not just about assistance. It's about growth and business."

The Egyptian Business Development Association, a new 400-member trade group headed by Malek, represents this emerging Islamist business class—men who distinguish themselves from the corruption of the Mubarak era with the language of values, ethics, and revolution. "The spirit of the EBDA is different because it was established after the revolution," said Osama Farid, a co-founder of the group and its head of international relations, in a recent Financial Times profile. The soft rhetoric is the only assurance, however, that the EBDA and other groups like it won't become clubs of patronage and cronyism, replacing Gamal Mubarak's coterie with a larger group of investors and industrialists with close ties to the Muslim Brotherhood and the Morsi government. Farid's career took off with the fortunes of his construction company in the housing boom of the 1970s; the FJP's current development ventures seem linked to his own business concerns. The Financial Timesended its profile by describing him as "filled with passion about building a new Egypt, and eager to talk about ideas to develop the Suez Canal region. He urges the launch of initiatives to jump-start housing construction and create jobs for the country's youth."

This doesn't sit easily with critics in Egypt. The journalist Wael Gamal, in an op-ed in al-Shorouk, a Cairo newspaper, noted that the FJP's electoral platform was the most straightforward in its adherence to neoliberal tenets, as well as the only one "based on attracting billions of dollars in foreign investment for infrastructure projects." Ahmed Mansour, a legal researcher for the Housing and Land Rights Network at the Habitat International Coalition in Cairo, was more direct: "If you look at [the FJP's] urban proposals, they use the same terms that the Mubarak regime used in the past. It's the same urban planning exactly. They have the same vision as the Mubarak regime, copy and paste."

* * *

In 2005, running for re-election in what would turn out to be his last presidential campaign, Mubarak touted an ambitious housing platform even though his victory would be assured in a vote rigged by his ruling National Democratic Party: 500,000 new affordable housing units were to be built in just six years through the National Housing Program, half of them on state land in the desert exurbs of Cairo. But what Egyptians called "the president's promise" catered to the crooked economy overseen by Gamal Mubarak and cronies like Ahmed Ezz, a billionaire steel tycoon and former high-ranking NDP official who ran the Parliament's budget committee. The government contracted real estate developers—the builders of the villas and compounds of Cairo's speculative desert frontier, who formed part of the new economic elite around Gamal—to construct these units. In *Understanding Cairo*, Sims describes attending a 2009 conference on "Affordable Housing in Challenging Times," hosted at the five-star Semiramis Intercontinental by the Ministry of Investment and the Mortgage Finance Authority. Along with glossy brochures for villas, sprawling apartments and "iconic malls that attract the world's top brands," the conference panels addressed subjects like "Moving Down the Price Pyramid" and "Can Good Margins Be Made in the Affordable Housing Market?" Any reference to affordable housing was merely a nod, Sims writes, "a kind of recognition that, in tough times, maybe going a little down-market might find some customers who, in the halcyon boom times of 2006 and 2007, would have been ignored."

In the six years of Mubarak's final term, the houses became another grand unrealized dream, as well as a sop to the construction industry (including Ezz's steel monopoly). The units that were built remain mostly unoccupied, priced far above what most Egyptians can afford and located on a distant patch of desert land accessible only by car (just eleven percent of Cairenes own one, Sims notes). And even "years later, no one's really sure how many of the 500,000 units actually were built," said architect Yahia Shawkat, who runs a blog called the Shadow Ministry of Housing. "I have estimates of anywhere from 60,000 to maybe 400,000 units that are mooted to have been completed."

Yet barely two months after Mubarak stepped down, the Egyptian government, through the holdover minister of international cooperation, Fayza Abul-Naga, announced a new round of public housing to international donors. Called the National Social Housing Program, it was based on Mubarak's plans for a second round of the "president's promise," this time double the size: a million units built in six years, at a staggering annual cost of $3.34 billion and overseen by the Housing Ministry, the Housing Development Bank, and the New Urban Communities Authority (the powerful planning authority that administers the satellite cities. Sims said that NUCA is run like a "secret society"; Shawkat called it a "black box"). Over half of the new program's budget was to come from international donors—an unprecedented amount, higher than any previous

donor-financed program in Egypt. Yet it was promoted as "part of a rescue/stimulus package to help put the Egyptian economy back on track," one that "utilizes the construction sector of Egypt—which is known to spur other economic sectors."

Sims reports that the donors politely demurred, requesting an initial housing strategy with actual details. But the "president's promise" 2.0, quickly dubbed the "million-units program" in the Egyptian media, remained a priority for the transition government. The FJP's new housing minister, Tareq Wafiq, a professor of urban planning at Cairo University who directed the party's housing committee and drafted the urban components of the Nahda Project, has promoted the million-units program as part of a national development plan known as "Egypt 2052," an updated series of regional master plans of which the earlier version—reportedly now referred to as "Cairo 2052"—was a component. ("The revolution added two years," Mansour joked.)

* * *

Ali El-Faramawy, a former senior human settlement officer at UN-Habitat who helped craft the original Cairo 2050 plan, is the million-units program's technical adviser. He also directs the Informal Settlement Development Facility, a fund established with the pledge to upgrade and safeguard informal areas. The ISDF identifies "unsafe" areas that must either be demolished or "redeveloped." So far it has identified over 400 (which house an estimated 850,000 people), and 116 of these are in Greater Cairo, according to Amnesty International. "It is not clear what criteria were used to decide which areas were more 'unsafe' than others," Amnesty reported. "Nor is it clear why only 404 areas were deemed 'unsafe,' given that people in all informal settlements lack security of tenure and usually face other risks identified by the authorities as criteria for designating areas as 'unsafe.'" Amnesty commended the motives behind the ISDF but warned that it was "being developed and implemented in ways that fail to respect the human rights of residents" through forced evictions, upon which plans like Cairo 2050 depend.

Some of the areas deemed unsafe in Cairo are located in Boulaq Abul Ela, a historic Nile-side neighborhood and former port that housed a palace of Mohamed Ali Pasha in the nineteenth century. Today, its crumbling buildings are home to thousands of poor families, a picture of government neglect in the shadow of the glass towers that front the river—among them the Cairo World Trade Center and its adjacent Hilton hotel, and the Nile City towers, a joint Egyptian-Saudi development that includes shopping malls, a movie theater, corporate offices, and a Fairmont hotel. Nile City's Egyptian developer was Orascom Construction, part of the huge Orascom holding company run by the billionaire Sawiris brothers—Nassef, Samih, and Naguib—who founded the secular, free-market Free Egyptians Party in 2011. Under Cairo 2050, this line of towers would expand to absorb Boulaq and transform it into the Maspiro Central Business District, named for the nearby Maspiro state television building, with gardens stretching along the Nile. The threat of eviction has lingered since the towers went up. Last summer, after Egypt's highest court dissolved Parliament, the governor of Cairo ordered an eviction notice for the area's "shack-dwellers," to be carried out by police.

In 2008, the year the ISDF was established, Mubarak's rubber-stamp Parliament passed a new Unified Building Law (UBL), which introduced to Egypt the concept of "land readjustment," a term that UN-Habitat promotes as a means of improving infrastructure and services through the regularization of land tenure in informal or unplanned areas. When applied to the "upgrading" of informal areas as outlined by the ISDF, however, land readjustment can mean the wholesale replacement of urban fabric and the displacement of residents, with the 2008 planning law providing the legal framework. The law expanded a previous eminent domain decree from 1990 on "Expropriation for the General Interest," permitting the government to seize private properties—most often in informal areas—for "works of general interest," from roads and infrastructure to anything broadly defined as serving the public good. The law allows "compulsory land acquisition" and provides compensation to displaced residents, though the Egyptian media are full of stories of Cairenes who were relocated to substandard public housing in the desert and never given full compensation.

The UBL also established the Supreme Council for Urban Planning and Development, directly under the office of the prime minister, "with membership from all concerned ministries and authorities." The council has a greater role in planning, but allows no effective public participation. Since its inception, it has been responsible for, among other self-interested regulations, attempting to establish a new law on the sale of state land in the weeks before the uprising. Under the proposal, four bodies would be responsible for administering and developing such plots, including the council itself along with the State Land Authority, the State Land Protection Authority and "any official with legal jurisdiction over the land in question, such as provincial governors."

In December 2009, Prime Minister Ahmed Nazif, who oversaw the most feverish pace of privatization during Mubarak's final presidential term, expanded the definition of "works of general interest" to include all building removals from informal areas classified as unsafe. "Forced evictions are justified under 'compulsory land acquisition' for public use. But whose public use?" Yahia Shawkat asked. "And which public? That's always an issue. How you get these laws passed, and how you get compulsory purchase orders, has to be changed. They need to happen on a much more transparent, much more relevant level." Shawkat sees the ISDF and a plan like Cairo 2050 as the government's solution to a saturated real estate market. Having overbuilt the desert outskirts—along with the Mediterranean coast, on land also controlled by the military—the GOPP and its consultants are now eyeing central districts, either near the Nile or near valuable historical sites. The obstacle, to the government planner, is that most of these districts are informal, long neglected and home to thousands of underserved poor residents. "They are only profitable if you raze them," Shawkat says.

* * *

Two major Egyptian institutions, the Ahly Football Club and the Ministry of Culture, loom over the southern end of Zamalek, a leafy island in the Nile in central Cairo. The ministry occupies an enclosed compound that stretches across the narrow half-mile island. The Cairo Opera House, built in the 1980s with Japanese aid, commands the fenced-in area, which is home to the drab architectural expressions of a swollen bureaucracy: the Supreme Council of Culture, the Cultural Development Fund and the Palace of Arts. What was Cairo's exhibition grounds in the 1920s has become the quiet campus of the state's cultural buildings, spread among a parking lot caked with sand and paved walkways with little shade, and rarely opening their doors to the public.

Last winter, at the cafe on the steps of the Supreme Council of Culture, I met Mohamed El Rashidy, the technical director of a ministry-led restoration scheme known as the Historic Cairo Project, which sought to revive Cairo's crumbling medieval core by turning it into "an open-air museum." The project centered on al-Muizz Street, the qasaba (or traditional commercial and ceremonial spine) that cuts through the urban fabric and is named after the tenth-century Fatimid founder of Cairo, the Caliph Muizz Li Din Allah. The area known as Historic Cairo, a UNESCO-designated world heritage site, is just under four square kilometers of the city's foundation to the east of the Nile. It is home to an unrivaled concentration of medieval Islamic architecture, much of it lining al-Muizz, along with an estimated 310,000 people, many of them poor, some living three to a room.

Among architects and urbanists in Egypt, a so-called "open-air museum" conjures images of Luxor, where the former governor, Samir Farag, along with the Supreme Council of Antiquities, a branch of the Ministry of Culture, has tried to unearth and reconstruct a 2.4-kilometer "Pharaonic avenue" lined with pedestals thought to be the bases of sphinxes. The modern nineteenth-century town was developed over the so-called Avenue of the Sphinxes, along with nearly every settlement and civilization since Pharaonic times. The only way to restore the avenue was to raze the town and displace its residents, which the authorities did with bulldozers—and then promoted the removal as a public good. The American architectural firm Abt Associates designed the original plan for the "restoration of the Avenue of the Sphinxes," which will connect the Luxor and Karnak temples. Farag, a former chairman of the Cairo Opera House, opined that the project would turn Luxor into "the largest open-air museum in the world" by 2030. When asked by Time about the protests from displaced residents, Farag replied: "It was very difficult to convince the people that this master plan is for the sake of them."

Rashidy described the Historic Cairo project in the words of Farouk Hosni, the longtime minister of culture (and Hosni Mubarak's longest-serving minister), who recently joined the ranks of ex-ministers and officials charged with corruption: "When you look at al-Muizz Street from an airplane, Hosni said, you only see a narrow line. We need to expand that small line." And so, for the last dozen years of Mubarak's rule, al-Muizz Street was dug up by workers from the state's largest construction companies, such as the Arab Contractors, a partially state-owned giant that seems to build everything in Egypt, and Wadi al-Nil, which is operated by the General Intelligence Services, otherwise known as the Mukhabarat.

With the power of a presidential decree, the Ministry of Culture was allocated an unprecedented budget for the project: an estimated 1 billion Egyptian pounds (over $150 million) to restore al-Muizz's Islamic monuments, and also to lower the street to its original level, repave it, replace a sewer system, and renovate other buildings along the street, which became a pedestrian-only zone. But there was a problem: the contractors specialized in poured concrete, not painstaking preservation work, and they were criticized for hasty, careless restorations of the 800-year-old mosques, whose entrances were affixed with marble plaques commemorating the patronage of Mubarak, first lady Suzanne Mubarak and the governor of Cairo. The new,

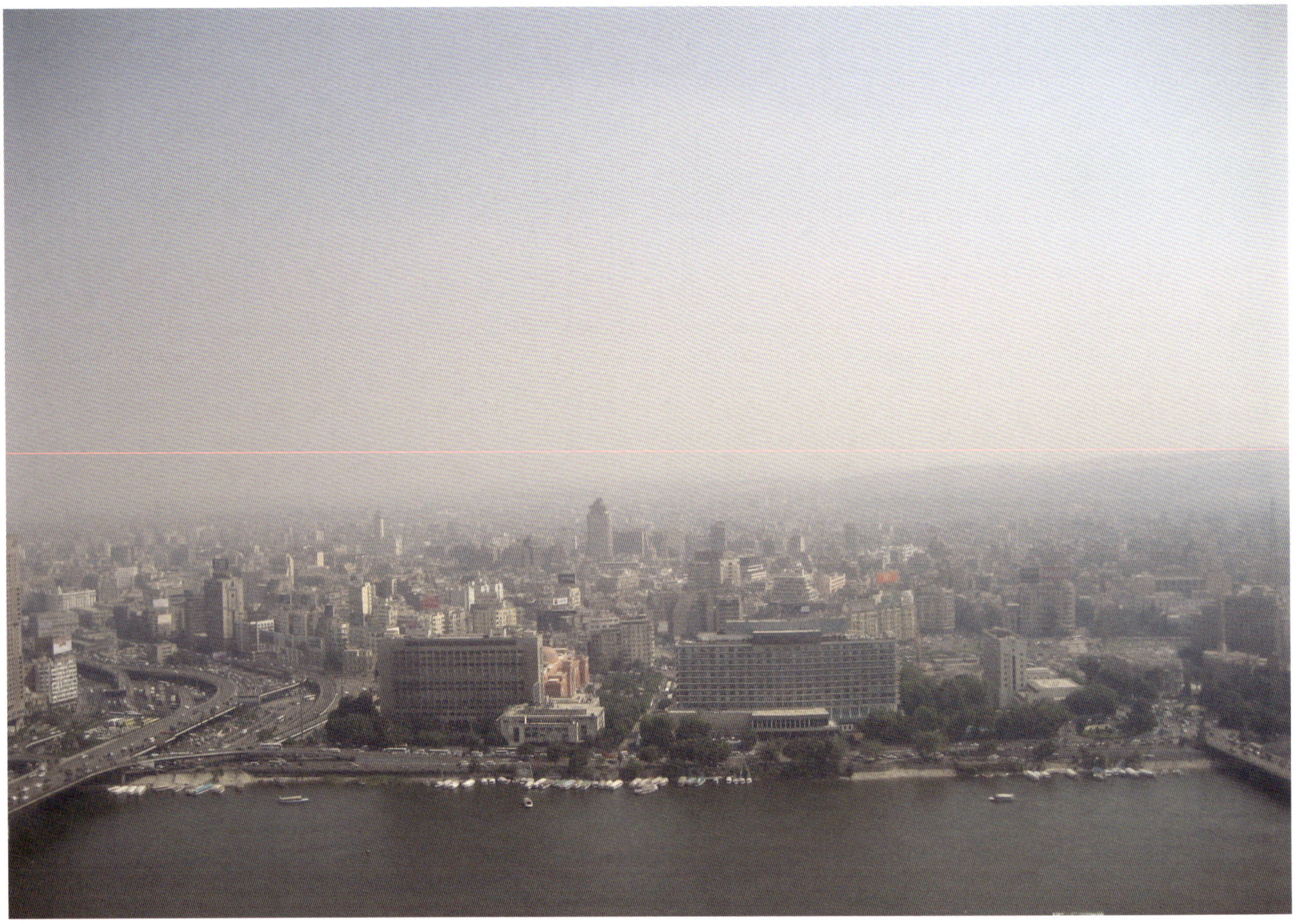

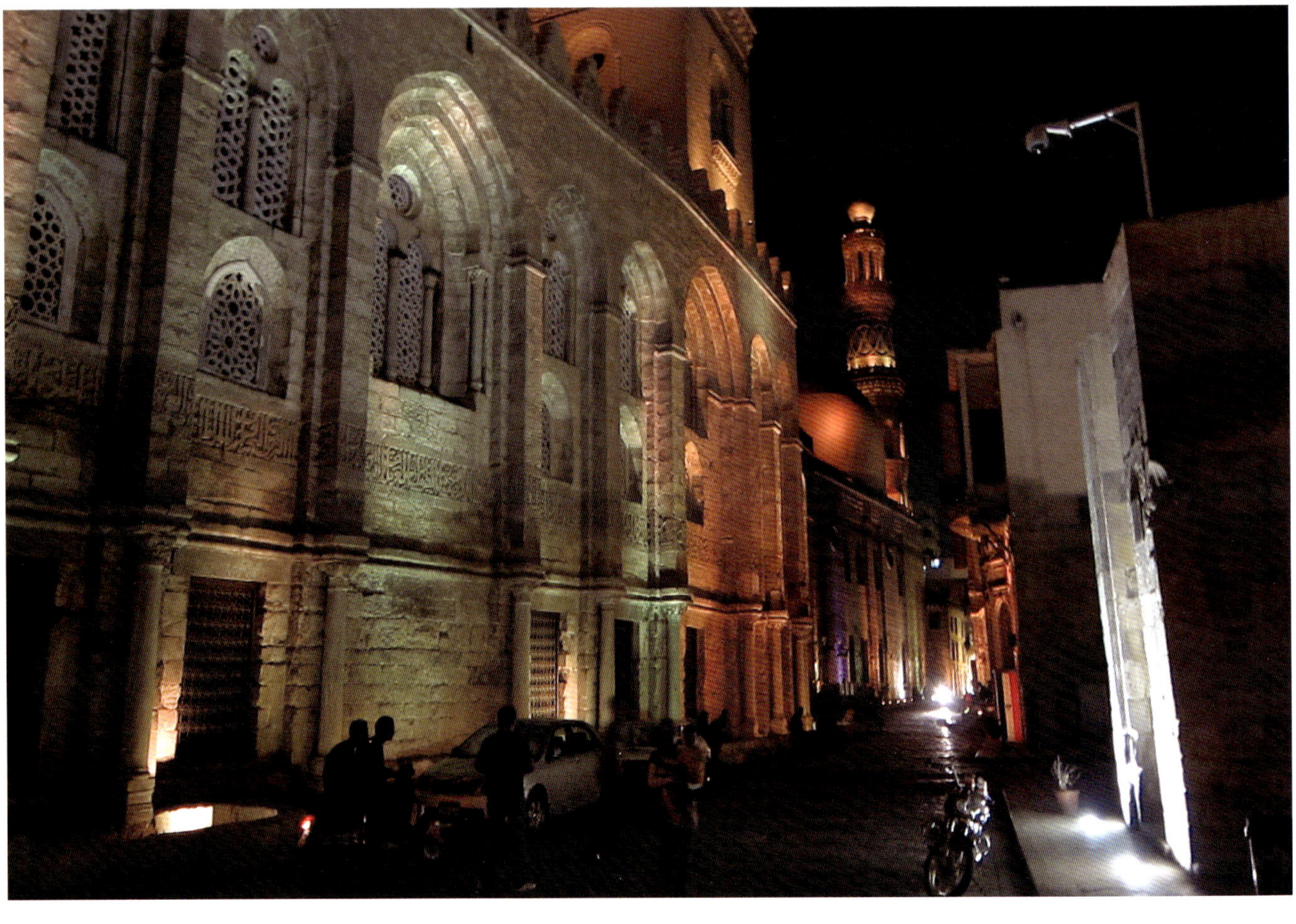

"revitalized" al-Muizz Street officially reopened in 2010, in a ceremony attended by the first lady, the sidewalks aglow with recessed orange and purple Italian lighting. "To revitalize this street is to revive authenticity and to resurrect it is to save the true meaning of civilization," Hosni declared in the introduction to a ministry publication on the project, which transformed a row of monumental Mamluk mosques and mausoleums into urban lanterns.

"The project was tailored for contractors attached to the government, and only open and competitive for companies with a huge capitalization," said Nairy Hampikian, an architect and preservationist who was one of the project's consultants, speaking to me at a Francophone cafe in upscale Heliopolis. May al-Ibrashy, another architect on the project, whom I met outside the northern city walls beyond al-Muizz, said, "There was no transparency, as with most things in Egypt." There were limits to the questions a consultant could raise about the project on-site. Referring to Wadi al-Nil, the Mukhabarat company, Ibrashy said, "You can't really criticize them, can you?"

As in Luxor, the open-air museum didn't put out the welcome mat to everyone. The urban businesses catering to the poorer workers who moved into Historic Cairo since the flight of the wealthier residents in the 1960s—carpenters, wholesale fruit and vegetable sellers, and small metalworkers—were pushed out to make way for tourist cafes offering more shisha than its residents could have wanted. The museum has walled out of the neighborhood certain people and livelihoods, and it reflects the practice of architectural preservation in Egypt, with its narrow focus on "monuments"—the government's favored term for valuable historic buildings. Inherited from the colonial era, the term suggests buildings devoid of local use, to be protected from Egyptians and preserved for the visiting tourists. But after the eighteen-day uprising that ended Mubarak's presidency, the tourism industry took a nosedive, and the economy with it. Throughout 2011, al-Muizz Street was quiet, especially the shisha cafes (although the cars returned, since the police who enforced the pedestrian-only zones were gone). Needless to say, the Muizz project, with its huge but opaque budget and administration, was never open to public participation or review.

When asked about this, Rashidy took a drag of his cigarette and said simply, "The people are benefiting," then quickly repeated the mantra. It wasn't a dodge so much as a stark reminder of how the Egyptian state, from its urban planners in the Ministry of Housing to preservationists in the Ministry of Culture, views the management of a metropolis like Cairo and many of the people who live in it. Shawkat expressed this institutional attitude another way: "To the government planners, it's actually much better to work in the dark, outside of the public scope, and get something done—and then say, well, they're doing it for the greater good."

The update of Cairo 2050 that UN-Habitat is drafting with GOPP continues to endorse this perspective—and even includes on the cover of its draft document a photograph of al-Muizz Street illuminated at night, along with a rendering of Khufu Avenue. The draft promotes the Historic Cairo project as an initiative "to upgrade El Moez [sic] street and transform it into a world-class open museum." Three photos of the street glowing at night match those that appear in glossy Ministry of Culture publications. The transformation of al-Muizz into a pedestrian

zone and open museum, according to the draft, "was carried out in coordination with the inhabitants of the area."

* * *

The chief slogan of the popular uprising that brought down Mubarak—"The people want the fall of the regime!"—was coupled with three basic demands: bread, freedom, and social justice. These were not just a rallying cry to get people into the streets, but a concise, elegant platform for the essentials that a new government must provide. The Mubarak regime had treated state budgets and assets—among them, the military-controlled land that underwrote Cairo's desert transformation—as private portfolios. Urban control came to mean not just the deployment of the security forces to contain protests, but a network of governing, planning and business interests that grew wealthy building Mubarak's Cairo.

Mansour at the Habitat International Coalition is part of an emerging group of housing rights activists who argue that little has changed since the uprising. "Housing is not just a commodity or a commercial good," he told me. "It is a right. It's a social good. So urban planning should be a social good, too. You are planning for people's lives, not for a particular category of people at the top." The urban nature of Egypt's revolt might seem apparent with every reference to Tahrir Square, but Tahrir itself does not capture the role of the state's urban planning and development policies in producing cities of extreme social and spatial disparities. "It's top-down for a reason," Shawkat said. "If you look at something like Cairo 2050—if people got in and wanted their way, or wanted their rights, then you'd never have it the way that they're doing it."

Mohamed Lotfy at Amnesty International cautioned against dismissing Cairo 2050—as well as the kind of socially destructive urban development that it represents—as simply an artifact of the old regime. "Even if they realize ten percent of it," he said, "that would be catastrophic for many, many people." For her part, Dina Shehayeb recalls that even during the presidential campaign, candidates like Amr Moussa, former secretary general of the Arab League, spoke of plans for a Maspiro Central Business District. "We need to have a revolution in the universities, in planning education, in urban planning and architecture faculties as it is taught and practiced," Nairy Hampikian insists. "Everything needs a revolution now."

This article appeared in the January 21, 2013, edition of *The Nation*. All photographs by Frederick Deknatel.

HONG KONG

REFLECTIONS ON THE CITY OF DISAPPEARANCE

Susan Ingram and
Markus Reisenleitner

This article originally appeared as Susan Ingram and Markus Reisenleitner, "The Identity-Producing Spaces of Hong Kong: Reflections on Ackbar Abbas's City of Disappearance."*spacesofidentity* 8.1 (2008) and is indebted to Ackbar Abbas's seminal work *Hong Kong : Culture and the Politics of Disappearance* (Minneapolis: University of Minnesota Press, 1997)

Postcolonial Hong Kong—city and special administrative region, home to regional migrant workers and global souls, one of southeast Asia's key entertainment and financial centers, and one of the Pacific Rim's key traffic and communications hubs—presents glimpses of the future of urbanity under the conditions of intensifying and accelerating global flows of traffic, people, and communication. Hong Kong has been described as the "international Home Page of a city."[1] It is "Asia's world city" according to its own advertising, a city "on fire" according to film critics,[2] a paradigmatic "generic" city in Rem Koolhaas's understanding, a city that political, economic, and social transformations have rendered so thoroughly malleable that it resists and reasserts temporality and locality in unique ways. Yet it is precisely this malleability that generates complex spaces that are in themselves unique, and therefore profoundly local.

Hong Kong's specific ability to defy homogenizing descriptions, characterizations, and explanations breathlessly conjuring up visions and paradigms of the future of cities and the experience of global urbanity has motivated this essay on our diverse and often difficult-to-reconcile visions of Hong Kong—visions that draw their power to impress and produce place, meaning, and memory from the constant juxtapositions of seemingly irreconcilable vantage points separated by spatial, physical, and symbolic barriers. In this article, in some ways a piece of life-writing, we reflect on the experience of no longer living there.

During our five years in Hong Kong (2001–2006), we experienced the city from a myriad vantage points: from air-conditioned shuttle trains and the crowded streets of the "new towns" (planned satellite cities, mostly in the New Territories); from superhighways connecting shopping complexes and the pedestrian overpasses that guide the flows of crowds; from hermetically sealed-off hotel and apartment rooms that command dieu-voyeur vistas of Hong Kong's landmark skyline; and from the green-and-white ferries that for decades have been used to steer through the bustling harbor traffic. Our reflections take their cues from Michel de Certeau's work on heteronomous second geographies and focus on the unstable, interstitial, marginal spaces of Hong Kong's urbanity between global visual ambiguity and the persistence of place in local visions, between the suspension of physicality in non-places and the topographies created by bodies firmly grounded in the heat, smells, and pollution of the sometimes obscured but never quite disappearing material city.[3] Just as de Certeau attends to indigenous voices,[4] we pay attention here to Hong Kong's indigenized spaces and how they have informed, deformed, fed, and weaned the incursions of global space since 9/11—years no longer characterized by the cultural turmoil of the heady handover period, but also years that have seen their own share of commotion, from SARS to demonstrations against mainland encroachments on political rights and the WTO (we have noticed with alarm from afar how those encroachments seemed to have intensified in the past few years).

While these memorable political events deserve, and have produced, their own analysis, our focus here is on the

Susan Ingram is Associate Professor in the Department of Humanities at York University, Toronto, where she is affiliated with the Research Group on Language and Culture Contact. She is the general editor of Intellect Book's Urban Chic series, the co-author of the volumes on Berlin and Vienna, and the editor of the World Film Locations volume on Berlin. A past president of the Canadian Comparative Literature Association, her research interests revolve around the institutions of European cultural modernity and their legacies.

Markus Reisenleitner is Professor of Humanities at York University. His research focuses on the imaginaries of mobility, community, fashion and style. Publications include *Wiener Chic: A Locational History of Vienna Fashion* (Bristol: Intellect, 2013; co-authored with Susan Ingram), *Historical Textures of Translation: Traditions, Traumas, Transgressions* (Vienna: Mille Tre, 2012; co-edited with Susan Ingram) and *Urban Imaginaries in the Asia-Pacific* (Interasia Cultural Studies Special Issue, Vol. 9:4: Routledge, 2008; co-edited with Meaghan Morris and Caroline Turner).

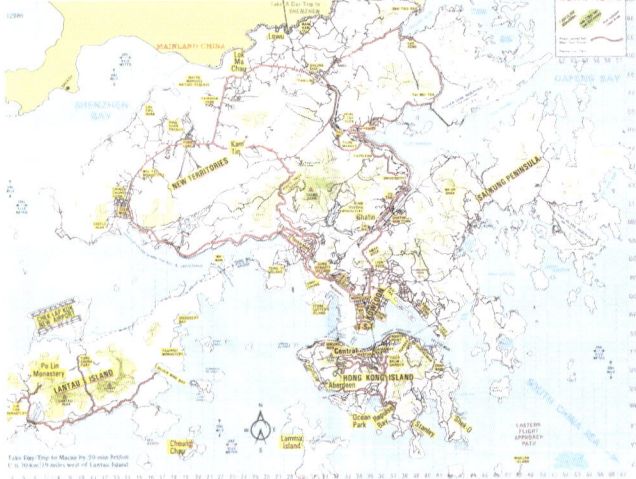

secondary: the discontinuities between Hong Kong's inexorable march towards global urbanity and the contingencies of daily negotiations that give meaning to the moving through, and making a home in, a space that remains, literally, local in several dimensions.

One invariably arrives in Hong Kong in a daze. Whether it be the millions of bleary-eyed international travelers who land every year at Chek Lap Kok,[5] with its airy 1930s airport-hanger design by Norman Foster, which opened in 1998 replacing the dive-bomber approach between the rickety Kowloon skyscrapers at the old Kai Tak, the plans for whose refurbishment currently include a cruise terminal, a multi-purpose stadium, a metropolitan park, and several housing units, or whether it be the millions of eager mainlander visitors who swarm through the rather worse-for-wear checkpoint at Lo Wu (whose numbers have increased dramatically since the introduction of the "Individual Visit Scheme" in 2003): arrival in Hong Kong is discombobulating, distended. One never really arrives but rather is whisked onwards, funneled through spaces of dislocation into the bright, shiny compartment of an airport express or light-rail transit (KCR/MTR), remaining in a state of suspension, looking down on the rabbit warren of streets or up at the bamboo-like beehives of housing estates, endless container terminals, and the hulking, rusted carcasses of factories.

One looks in vain for landmarks of orientation outside. Too similar are the endless rows of high-rise housing estates and office buildings, only distinguished by a state of relative dereliction that indicates, in a climate less kind to man-made than human façades, an age of more than five years; few other traces of the city's history and grown structures survive. In this ultra-new city, orientation happens virtually out of necessity, on futuristic LCD screens within the air-conditioned spaces of movement that trace one's progress and announce, in three languages (English, Cantonese, and Putonghua), the next stop.

Hong Kong poses enormous challenges to, and rewards for, any sense of orientation one might have. Hapless newcomers who have to rely on their own urban survival skills to get outfitted for their multi-matchbox-sized apartments in gated communities recommended and paid for by employers have several means at their disposal for reaching the necessary destinations that provide for staples and daily needs, destinations found mostly in secluded local shopping centers, which house post offices, clothing and shoe chains, modest department stores like Jusco, competent appliance and electronic stores like Fortress and Broadway, Watson's pharmacy, which sells an impressive array of skin-whitening products and over-the-counter birth-control pills, the delectable Wellcome grocery chain, the welcoming Deli France coffee-shops, and conveyor-belt Genki Sushi places, in front of which there invariably seem to be queues. Tucked away beneath or inside housing estates, these maze-like mall-complexes teem with clumps of dawdlers driven from the closeness of the quarters above so that those on determined missions for pillows and bed-sheets have more to navigate than cacophonies, smells, and perpetually changing construction sites. Local or not, one never quite masters the blueprint, the overview of those mazes; rather, one accustoms oneself to following routes through them. There is little possibility of, or reward for, flaneuring in the malls of the New Towns. What reward there is in the smoothness of movement that knowing a locale affords, and the community this makes you part of. In the New Towns, there is no serendipity effect of just finding things randomly; flows are regulated, not by architectural

All photos: Masudul Islam & Farhana Rashid

design but by local knowledge, the stuff conversations are made of, and not being part of them makes you a stranger on shakier footing than most.

Unlike the local malls, which service the housing estates that sprout up from peripheral metro stations and other transportation hubs and tax the senses of the uninitiated, the shopping centers at the top of the hierarchy, which radiate from the swish Landmark in Central (the central part of Hong Kong Island where, according to local advertising, "people move faster"— presumably because they know their way), offer the decorous comfort of luxury liners. Bookended by the elegant Pacific Place at Admiralty and the swimming-pool-like Times Square in Causeway Bay, with the stately, QEII'ish Harbour Center in Tsim Sha Tsui and the latest addition, the phallic IFC, staring each other down across Victoria Harbor, and Festival Walk in Kowloon Tong with its indoor skating rink, multiplex, restaurants, and university providing added value to the north, these interestingly geodesic, often curvaceous, sparkling surfaces envelop unsuspecting visitors and guide their frictionless ascent towards the most highly sought of the global brands.

Lifestyle beckons from every polished window and over-attentive shop assistant to a wider range of clientele than the global souls contractually housed in the boutique quarters in the soaring towers above would imagine, and the inconspicuous but ever-present security detail assures that no one engages in anything but consumption, even if only vicariously. It is here that one finds flaneurs, although hardly ever solitary ones. Rather, aimless gliding hand-in-hand along the polished floors of upscale shopping centers seems a favorite pastime of romantic young couples. As long as one is swathed in air-conditioned solace from the inhospitable stickiness outside, the difficulty of finding exits doesn't present itself as something in need of solution, on the contrary: the comfort of strangers in these spaces is provided by the illusion that you can spend your whole life there, connected to a global world whose operations are reassuringly mediated by the consumable homogeneity of brands and the very clear social order and stratification they have come to indicate.

Transportation in Hong Kong can be daunting, especially for more out-of-the-way locales, such as registries, immigration offices, the Ikea that used to be in Tsuen Wan but is now in Kowloon Bay, or its more upscale local cousin, G.O.D. ("Goods of Desire"), which also opens and closes outlets with off-putting regularity. While heading into Central means the comfort of air-conditioned double-decker buses or standing in a deep-frozen tube that invariably runs on schedule, those on local routes in the New Territories make do with open windows and soothing cell-phone chatter, and are spared the incessant background of Canto-pop TV-advertising on the Samsung screens installed in their upholstered long-haul counterparts.

Whether on a shorter or longer trip, neophyte bus passengers feel compelled to surreptitiously watch their seatmates do their nails, their makeup, their homework, practically everything except their laundry, and thus avoid having to negotiate linguistic politics with either taxi drivers (green for local, red for Central) or souped-up mini-bus drivers. Buses and the underground are obviously not private space, but seasoned passengers do their best to make them such on their one-hour-plus commutes to and from ten-hour-plus work-days: by screening out the shared sounds (if they are not on their cell

Photo: Masudul Islam & Farhana Rashid

phones, everybody from toddlers to grannies has their MP3-player headphones firmly in place) and shared views of each other (by either watching the TV spots on the flatscreens or catching up on the shut-eye that a local pride in four-hour nights cannot provide at home). Hong Kong may be a city in which people rarely stop moving (even if this movement is sometimes unexpectedly slow, especially on foot); but this movement is not merely the faceless flow of urban strangers through a major global communication hub. Spaces have also been created for rest, moments of privacy, and personal communication that offer a respite from the relentlessness of the flows that determine people's work lives.

If anyone ever looked out of the buses' windows, they would see the other possibilities to create privacy on the road: the chauffeured Mercedes, Rolls, and Jaguars with tinted windows (or the more modest Saabs, Volvos, and Nissans without tint or hired driver) that overtake the buses and the endless rows of container trucks on the steep inclines of Hong Kong's major highways. Only those in the right-hand driver's seats actually themselves driving through the concrete jungle of overpasses, the tunnels and roundabouts with their polysemic possible outcomes can't avoid looking out at the ghostly scenery of dramatic backdrops, bridges and shanty-towns. Watery, white cotton-batten backdrops are also visible from the air-conditioned apartments that are smaller than hotel rooms, and the windows of both are often tinted green or blue to give the illusion of clean air. Rather than immersed, one constantly feels the presence of these invisible partitions that keep at bay the particles that make one's eyes sting, one's throat scratch, and the skin of more sensitive break out in itchy red blotches. These uncomfortable physical sensations are difficult to reconcile with the cinematic visuality of a city whose constant mutations exceed thresholds of perception and produce breaktaking, if cliché, backdrops.

Yet there are occasions designed to provide fixes of the great outdoors. A weekend activity as popular among Hong Kongers as shopping is hiking, which exists mainly in three forms: training, competition, and family outing, the latter of which is expansive enough to include the previous two and picnic-barbecuing. In addition to the hyper-urban living conflagrations and the many lively villages that continue to mark festivals with communal bowl dinners, forty percent of Hong Kong consists of official conservation areas, country parks and nature reserves with breathtaking hiking trails. Websites and books about hiking in Hong Kong have sections on "Hazards," "Staying Alive," and "Better Safe than Sorry,"[6] awakening childhood memories of weekends consisting almost exclusively of windswept peaks, gravelly slopes, and other marathon, vertiginous challenges. Hong Kong's trails are not intended for a leisurely stroll after a heavy main-meal of the day, as in the European spa tradition; nor is any attempt made to make nature accessible, by car or secured trails, in the North American way. Hikes here can easily last ten hours in terrain otherwise accessible only by helicopter, and hikers are seriously outfitted in gear obtained from outfitters in the same shopping centers that cater to the luxury needs of the brand-conscious, and equally branded. Patina is as gauche on the trails as in Central; hand-me-downs are only for the hired help, or to be donated to the mainland.

Hiking in Hong Kong may not be about an introspective Romantic vision of a mystical closeness to nature that Western academics have analyzed, critiqued, and scorned for a long

time; however, like Western visions, it is thoroughly mediated by culture. It is not the culture of industrial urbanization that drives many Hong Kongers up the hills and sharp peaks while remaining unfazed at the sight of their harbor shrinking under the onslaught of land reclamation in the form of highways and skyscrapers (rather than waterfronts as entertainment hubs). Hiking is exertion with a goal. It is self-improvement captured in mini-gadgets that measure pulse rates, time and distance and generate curves that visually resemble those charts meant to communicate the supposed pleasures of economic growth, and despite the designer boots and competitive aspects, it can be strangely enjoyable in a profoundly solipsistic, physical, and entirely unromantic way.

While on Sundays the extensive network of trails in the high hills thus transforms into a catwalk for Hong Kong families with phenomenally good conditioning, Central reveals a part of Hong Kong's population that is otherwise almost invisible. Filipino and Indonesian maids have Sundays off (regulated by law like everything else in their employment relationship), and they congregate in choice quasi-public spaces deserted by the office crowd on their only day off (Saturdays are still considered workdays in Hong Kong). Whether they inhabit the small, non-air-conditioned chambers off the kitchens which serve as vestibules to even smaller spaces containing a toilet and shower, and which raise an apartment to middle-class respectability while alleviating the need for kitchens to be equipped with hot water, or share cramped quarters in ethnically marked boarding-houses, all are as relieved as the mall-dawdlers for a space free from goals.

Perhaps most striking about Hong Kong is its elemental quality, its utter vulnerability in the face of the life-threatening natural elements that periodically assail it. Typhoons, pollution, and viruses: despite its sparkling pockets of sanitized sterility, there is nowhere in the SAR that can truly be considered a safe space, which is why Ackbar Abbas underscores that Hong Kong exists: not as a "third space" that can be located somewhere; not as a neither-nor space that is nowhere; not even as a mixed or in-between space, if by that we understand that the various elements that make it up are separable.[7]

Staying on in Hong Kong for more than a few weeks or months necessitates venturing into, and getting familiar with, at least a few of those disjunctures, the routes carved out by local knowledge; and Hong Kongers themselves usually get by with knowing the routes they need and not bothering about finding new ones. In Hong Kong, almost everybody is a relatively new arrival anyway, the feeling of being lost in the city a generation or two away at most, and this exponentially increases the need to know your own neighborhood. For most, dwelling in this world city, and experiencing oneself as part of a global urban environment, is facilitated and mediated by very close quarters. Social difference determines whether one is physically stuck in these quarters, in this city, exposed to global flows solely via technology and media, or whether one has the financial, social and passport means to connect those quarters to the international flows that generated them. As Ackbar Abbas has noted: the cosmopolitan today will include not only the privileged transnational, at home in different places and cultures, as an Olympian arbiter of value. Such a figure, it could be argued, has too many imperialistic associations. The cosmopolitan today will have to include at least some of the less privileged men and women placed or displaced in the transnational space of the city and who are

Photo: Masudul Islam & Farhana Rashid

trying to make sense of its spatial and temporal contradictions: the cosmopolitan not as a universalist arbiter of value, but as an arbitrageur/arbitrageuse. This is arbitrage with a difference. It does not mean the use of technologies to maximise profits in a global world but refers to everyday strategies for negotiating the disequilibria and dislocations that globalism has created. Arbitrage in this sense does not allude to the exploitation of small temporal differences but refers to the larger historical lessons that can be drawn from our experiences of the city.[8]

For all strata of society the daily experience of globalism is paradoxically delimited by the narrow confines of a housing estate, a gated community with all-inclusive facilities, or a boutique apartment, enabling survival in the urban complexity that dazzles any sense of orientation.

[C]osmopolitanism must take place somewhere, in specific sites and situations—even if these places are more and more beginning to resemble those "non-places" that French anthropologist Marc Augé has argued characterise the contemporary city. In a non-place, "one is neither chez soi nor chez les autres." Like the city, Augé's non-place must be understood not literally, but as paradox: a non-place is far from being nonexistent. Rather, it is a result of excess and overcomplexity, of a limit having been exceeded. Beyond a certain point, there is a blurring and scrambling of signs and an overlapping of spatial and temporal grids, all of which make urban signs and images difficult to read. The overcomplex space of non-places means, among other things, that even the anomalous detail may no longer be recognisable as such because it coexists with a swarm of other such details. This means the anomalous is in danger of turning nondescript, in much the same way that the more complex the city today, the more it becomes a city without qualities. The cosmopolitan as urban phenomenon is inevitably inscribed in such non-places and paradoxes.[9]

From this we can literally see the complexities of urban spatial experiences in this multi-tiered city as instances of localizing global flows for which one needs a particular skill-set to navigate. These skill sets make Hong Kong very real; they produce, for everybody, the specificities of the local, of routes mastered, places appropriated: they produce memory and affect. "Arguments about the ways mental maps are incomplete, distorted, and schematized are significant and should be remembered, but they nevertheless fail to grasp people's emotional dynamism, in part seen in the constitutive ambivalence of many, if not all, spatial practices."[10] Because Hong Kong implants itself as a kind of holographic sensation on its inhabitants, it is neither a non-place nor generic. Once one has become a cultural arbitrager, it is remarkably easy to leave Hong Kong, perhaps because one never really does.

Notes

[1]Pico Iyer, *The Global Soul: Jet Lag, Shopping Malls, and the Search for Home* (New York: Knopf, 2000), 85.
[2]Lisa O. Stokes and Michael Hoover, *City on Fire: Hong Kong Cinema* (London, New York: Verso, 1999).
[3]Michel de Certeau, "The Politics of Silence: The Long March of the Indians," in ed. B. Massumi, *Heterologies: Discourse on the Other* (Minneapolis: University of Minnesota Press, 1986), 225-233. We are grateful to Elena Siemens for providing us with the impetus to consider Hong Kong in this light.
[4]R. Terdiman, "The Marginality of Michel de Certeau." *The South Atlantic*

Quarterly, 100: 2 (2001), 399-421.

[5]cf. http://en.wikipedia.org/wiki/World's_busiest_airports_by_passenger_
traffic#2007_final_statistics

[6]cf. http://www.hiking.com.hk/english/ and http://www.hktrampers.com/
index.php/en/

[7]Abbas, *Hong Kong,* 143.

[8]Ackbar Abbas, "Cosmopolitan De-scriptions: Shanghai and Hong Kong,"
Public Culture, 12:3 (2000), 777.

[9]Ibid, 772-773.

[10]Steve Pile, *The Body and the City: Psychoanalysis, Space, and Subjectivity*
(New York: Routledge, 1996), 28.

Upper akcalaan, 1974

TURGUTREIS NOW

FROM A VILLAGE INTO A TOWN

Suha Ozkan

In 1974, under the leadership of Richard Plunz from Columbia University, Suha Ozkan and Selahattin Onur from Middle East Technical University, Ankara, a pioneering architectural anthropology study was conducted on three villages on the Aegean coast of Turkey. The villages of Akçaalan, Karabağ and Karatoprak had only then been recognized as a "town" with municipal management and became "political." The contemporary condition and history of fifteen families were surveyed in reference to their houses and the community. Following the first survey, repeated surveys were conducted by Richard Plunz and the team at Columbia University. Many academic presentations in international fora of vernacular architecture were prepared by Plunz and Ozkan. The outcome of 1974 and successive surveys are about to be published. This article reviews the development and the status in the present day.

Turgutreis is a town that used to be active only for a couple of months, after which the whole peninsula would hibernate for the year. Following our initial survey in 1974, an unprecedented transformation to the Bodrum Peninsula surged, one that Turgutreis shared.

The unassuming, calm, farming, sea-faring, and sponge-diving population was unaware of the changes that were in store for them in the upcoming years.

Being a place of exile for "soft" criminals, the Bodrum Peninsula remained inaccessible until the 1970s. With the building of the Milas-Bodrum highway and the Bodrum Airport, accessibility both nationally and internationally, became very convenient and the attraction of Bodrum grew in leaps and bounds.

In post 1970s when there was an ensuing boom of "second residences" in Turkey, Bodrum Peninsula was most subjected to this insurgence of affordable second homes. Inexpensive pieces of uncultivated, barren land on the seaside became attractive places to build. The primary focus was holiday homes. Over the years as owners became older, many of these developments turned into places for retirement. The owners were mainly the employees covered by the Social Security Council, and had access to existing credit mechanisms. However, soon after, they were followed by people coming from salaries across a wider spectrum, in all sectors of the workforce. While the only condition was to be organized communally as a cooperative, nevertheless in only a matter of time, mass completion of two to three bedroom flats or tiny villas. It took years and sometimes more than a decade to complete, depending on the cash flow to augment of the partial credits. Every setting in Western Anatolia with a view to the sea was a candidate to take part in this massive influx of construction.

While the other towns like Didim, Kuşadası, and Marmaris on the Aegean Coast witnessed the same intense development of irresponsibly promoting apartment blocks, the Bodrum Peninsula endorsed a novel approach by carefully implementing controlled construction rights. A maximum of two stories were allowed, with specific restrictions on lengths of continuous facades, on facade colors, and even on proportions of openings. Building codes of this nature, yielded a uniformity of scale and texture which was not taken seriously in other towns. As a result, other places are now suffering from a substantial lack of a "Mediterranean identity."

Luckily, the politicians and decision makers were willing to listen, direct, and preserve what they could within their powers. There were respectable personalities who could be persuasive

Dr Suha Ozkan is an architect and architectural theorist, and the former Secretary-General of the Aga Khan Award for Architecture. Working from 1982-2007, he helped establish the Aga Khan Award as one of the premier architectural institutions of the world dedicated to the recognition and celebration of work of highest excellence. Dr Ozkan is also the Founding President of World Architecture Community. Educated at the Middle East Technical University and the Architectural Association, Dr Ozkan was also involved with a number of universities and institutions including METU, the UIA, the United Nations Centre for Human Settlements and the Hassan Fathy Institute. He is the author of a number of books on contemporary architecture.

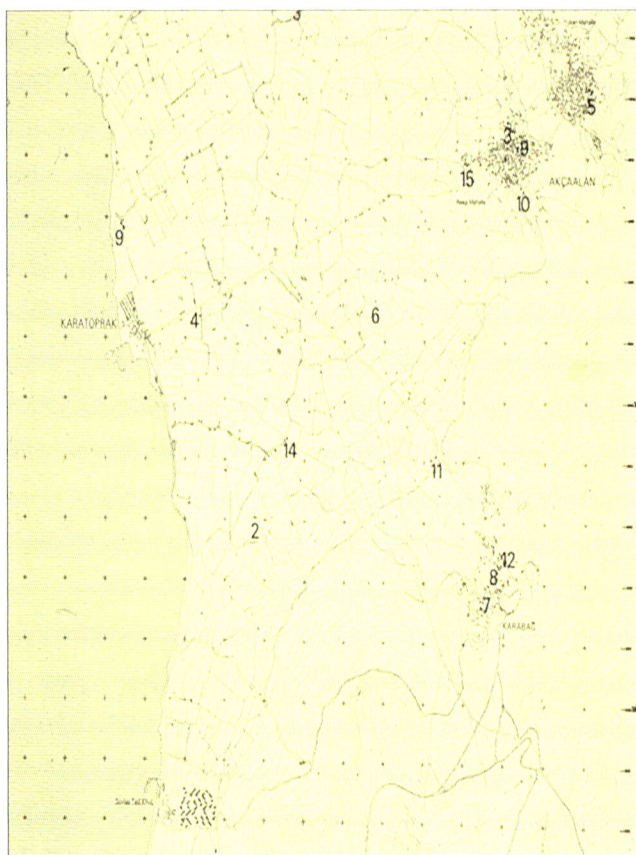

General Plan of Turgutreis, 1974.

Ahmet Ertegün (1923-2006).

with local political leaders. The easiest and least risky strategy was to reinforce the sensibility of the indigenous vernacular architecture and to encourage its derivatives. Among these respectable personalities were the late Ahmet Ertegün. Ertegün is Turkey's claim to a tremendous leadership in the music industry, primarily in the United States, and subsequently, world-wide. When Ertegün decided to have a guest house in Turkey, his selection of Bodrum to purchase two modest town houses took many by surprise. When he could have built a new Californian mansion, his decision to combine and restore the old houses was a neoteric idea in the mid 1960s. His selection of the architect was also important influence. Architect Turgut Cansever is known as a pioneer in perpetuating cultural values in architecture without compromising contemporary needs and technologies. At the time, he was an architect unparalleled in the race. The Ertegün house was completed in 1968, and received the Aga Khan Award for Architecture in 1980 in the first cycle of the award. The decision was perhaps foreseeable, but a lesson for all. Ertegün's preference of the traditional setting, and Cansever's impeccable restoration and creative combination of the two houses, sent a message of Bodrum's capacity as an effete, culturally aware society. In time, not only the Ertegün family but notable figures like Elle Fitzgerald and Mick Jagger stayed there, and presented through the media, the importance of Bodrum's prominence.

Simultaneously, Bodrum was also the home in exile for Cevat Şakir Kabağaçlı, a Cambridge graduate in archeology. He also became a famous novelist under the pen name of Halikarnas Balıkçısı ("fisherman of Halicarnasos"). His book was on the life of the former pirate turned Ottoman Admiral, Turgut Reis (Dragut, 1485-1565). Even though written as a fiction, it is perhaps the most reliable literary source on the Mydos area and on the life of Turgut Reis. It was in the memory of Turgut Reis that the three villages of Karatoprak, Karabag and Akçaalan were combined and re-dedicated as Turgutreis. Cevat Şakir, as well as archeologist Azra Erhat, developed a persuasive thesis that the ancient Greek and Eastern Roman civilizations developed their most urbane culture, not in their main homelands, but on the western shores of Anatolia. Ancient Ephesus, Bergamon, Didyma, Priene, and Miletus are the substantive proof of their assertion. Ancient historians, like Heredotus of Halicarnassus and Homer of Troy, support this idea.

It's also important to mention that Zeki Müren, perhaps the most admired singer and composer in contemporary Turkish music, also chose Bodrum as his late and last residence. Müren purchased his house from Fatma Mansur, one of the most eminent sociologists in Turkey. In 1972, Mansur authored the very significant study called "Bodrum." All these personalities made significant contributions to the lasting cultural and architectural values of Bodrum, and brought awareness of the importance of protecting its cultural assets.

Turgutreis, with its vast agricultural land together with soft planning regulations became an important attraction for investment. In 1967, seven years before our initial survey, the general population's interests were to be able to enjoy modern municipal services. However the main center, Karatoprak, did not have sufficient population to be declared a municipality. They merged with Karabağ and Akçaalan in order to reach the 2000 resident minimum in order to legally qualify. Consequently, Turgutreis with a population slightly more than 2000 of the three precincts that we surveyed in 1974, evolved into a city comparable in population to Bodrum which had historically been the principal regional center. Today, Bodrum has 34,000 permanent residents, while Turgutreis competes with about 25,000 residents.

In 1965, Tuğrul Akçura, Dündar Elbruz and Sevgi Aktüre from Middle East Technical University (METU) conducted an urban survey in Bodrum with their students, similar to our study with Columbia University and METU nine years later. Based on this earlier study, Akçura subsequently volunteered to devise ground rules for new building in Bodrum and the whole Peninsula. Akçura's report became the construction manual prescribing "How to Build." This manual permitted low-rise, high-density construction that emulates the centuries' old vernacular tradition of building.

Politics

When we were there, the founding Mayor Hüseyün Süzen had been elected for five consecutive terms, until 1977. The members of the Municipal Council had an overwhelming majority of Center Right Adalet Partisi (Justice Party). Only sporadically, Center Left Cuhuriyet Halk Partisi CHP (People's Republican Party), gained a maximum of three seats in a nine-member Council.

In 1984 elections Turgut Özal's Anavatan Partisi (Motherland Party), which was in line with the Global liberalism of Ronald Reagan and Margaret Thatcher, enjoyed the majority with three members from the Party with nationalist political dictum. That was the first term when the present Mayor Mehmet Dinçberk was elected and re-elected for three terms until 1999. The members of the Municipal Council had the majority of ANAP's liberal convictions. In 1999, Ali Server Yazgan from the same party won the elections with six out of nine members in the Council, and served as mayor for two terms.

In 2009, Mehmet Dinçberk transferred to CHP. He won not only mayoralty, but also gained 9 seats out of 11 of the expanded Municipal Council. What was a political victory of CHP, became a robust support for contemporary aspirations of the lands of tourism. This victory was an alarming choice where almost all seaside towns reacted to the dominating religious agenda of the present Government's policies. In order to remedy this change, the present government passed a law and gave Metropolitan status to Muğla Province. The forthcoming will dictates a central inland management, and everyone is anxious to see what will happen in next elections in 2014.

Planning bylaws in Turkey allows development of large, privately owned, land parcels by the order of municipal councils. To restrict development is not realistic as there are pressures from the local politics and profits. However, registered forest and cultivatable farmlands are exceptions. Today in Turgutreis, after the craze in construction, to observe many tangerine groves intact and functioning may be the only consolation. Although, some of them remain because they are well protected by fencing, they are abandoned as agricultural estates. The only hope is that the construction restrictions can somehow remain in force. It is worrisome to observe even in the nearby Gümüşlük (Myndos) new construction has been creeping in, despite the fact that a majority of the land is restricted to "zero construction" codes, and has been officially dedicated as an "archeologicalpark".

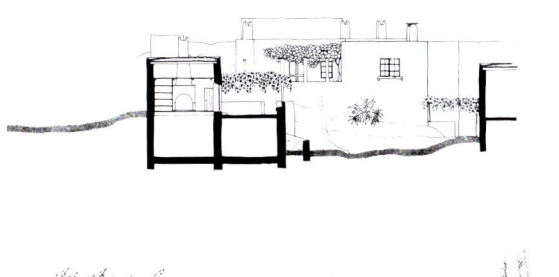
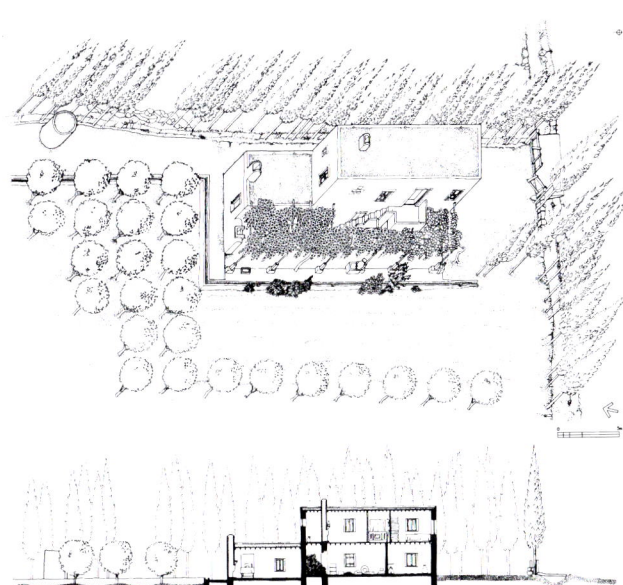

Survey drawings from *"TURGUTREIS IN 1974"* Report.

Photographs and drawings of Ertegün House.

In spite of it all, Bodrum remains identifiable by its abundance of tangerines that are sui generic—heavily aromatic, and full of seeds. They remain available in markets from street sellers even during the winter months. This venerable fruit named after "Bodrum," in fact, comes primarily from Turgutreis where there is an abundance of water and cultivatable flatland. Shockingly, the price can go down to 25 USD cents a kilogram in the stalls. Alarmingly, when we compare this low price with the high value of the land for development and the huge effort of labor and resources put into the production perennially, whether the activity of growing tangerines is even sustainable becomes questionable. What is even more dismaying is the amount that the farmers are getting in return is so minimal. One hopeful experience during the recent years is the return of a beloved fizzy aromatic tangerine drink which used to be called "Myndos Gazoz" back in the kiosks and on the shelves. After having disappeared for more than three decades, Myndos from the 1970s is now back again, a heartening harbinger signifying that everything is not going to be lost.

The insatiable demand to own a holiday destination in Bodrum region led to a horrendous overbuilding. Given that most of the holiday homes are vacant for the majority of the time, they give the impression of a "ghost town" except during the summer months and for some prolonged school holidays. The municipality of Turgutreis, however, evolved into a real town with its own resident population consisting mainly of retirees. The life there is vivid year around, bringing all kinds of amenities for a town of its size.

When we surveyed Turgutreis in 1974, we had the impression of a pressing demand for construction and development, however we never predicted or even imagined it could reach to the present magnitude. In 1974, there was not any branch or agency of any bank for conveying payments we needed to use prepaid checks called "Blue Checks." Today almost every bank has a branch in Turgutreis. There were no hotels. Our only option was the Plaj Pansiyon that we rented entirely and exclusively for our use as we were the only visitors in town. Today, there are more than fifty hotels with three to five star ratings. There are numerous websites dedicated to promoting for holidays in Turgutreis. These range between 40 USD to 150 USD per night, but not more. Back then, there was not a single pharmacy. Today there are ten pharmacies. The only place to buy food and daily necessities were the small shops where one could only find durable, packaged, and bottled goods. Shelf life was more important than substance. The groceries had to resist the slack period of no sales. Today the megastores like Migros, Tansaş, and Carrefour make Turgutreis a shopping destination catering to a larger hinterland including İslamhaneleri, Gümüşlük, and other surroundings.

The local youth of 1970s was deprived of even junior high school education in their hometown. With the exception of university education, today the opportunities are offered at every level from pre-school to high school. There is also a coveted, special high school in Turgutreis.

The Marina at Turgutreis is now a berthing place, serving the national yachting community, offering services that are high in demand. The Classical Music concerts every year places Turgutreis on the international cultural agenda. The Cultural Centre, sponsored by benevolence of Şevket Sabancı, is on the opposite side of the Marina and is a focal point for local culture, history and art, propagated among various interest groups.

Turgut Cansever (1921 – 2009).

Changes

Turgutreis had always an urban setting that was controlled by successive master plans. Soon after our presence in 1974, the Master Plan for Turgutreis was authored by Yıldırım Parlar, proposing vast land to be opened to urban development along the roads to Akyarlar, Akçalan, and Gümüşlük. Even within the confines and restrictions noted earlier, wide avenues with service and parking facilities on the edges were proposed as a condition of contemporary urbanization. The Parlar plan was approved in 1976 and implemented soon after. In return, the scale of Turgutreis had been transformed. The old scale, even from two decades ago, became nothing more than a memory. The efforts of the Municipality, however, in not planting generic urban trees but domestic tangerine, orange, and lemon trees, at least help us reminisce our presence on the edge of the Aegean with nostalgia of the bucolic scene.

There have been two revised plans in 1987 and 1995 which foresee a total 2200 hectares of planned area for development. The dynamics of change necessitate partial or local planning amendments. These partial plans are under the authority of Municipal Council. So far more than 300 partial plans have been approved. These cover more than double the planned area of Turgutreis and reach 5000 hectares including conserved archeological, protected agricultural, and natural areas. The partial planning process also included Gümüşlük which was under the municipal jurisprudence of Turgutreis until 1999.

Population

In Turkey, the population threshold to have a municipal organization is 2000. Turgutreis reached this level in 1965 by combining Akçaalan, Karabağ and Karatoprak villages as one urban entity in which the former villages became precincts. Until 1975, the population remained around 2100 with a balanced male and female population.

The population growth indicated twenty-five percent growth and reached 2500 in 1980. The population growth went on steadily but much more than the national urban growth. In 1990, the population doubled that of 1970 with 4500 residents, and in the year 2000 went up to 8500 then Turgutreis became a popular destination especially for retirees with 12,600 in 2007, 15,500 in 2008, 16,500 in 2009, 17,900 in 2010, and 19,200 in 2011. The present population exceeds 20,300 according to the local census of 2012. In short, the resident population shows increase ten times of what we had surveyed. Needless to, as remind as an affordable second homes, the summer population can grow to estimeted 2,00,000.

Drinking water came to Turgutreis in the form of public fountains in 1970 and piped distribution to houses started in 1972. Following that electricity came in 1974. The infrastructure for sewage collection and treatment started to be laid in 1987. It took seven years until 1994 to be completed and operational.

The road between Turgutreis and Bodrum was compacted gravel until 1976 when it was improved into an asphalt covered village road. Recently, it is a busy highway with separate double-carriage lanes. The bus terminal was built in 1984-1985.

Tangerine Orchard.

Turgureis Marina, 2012.

The wholesale fresh food, fish, and vegetable market was opened in 1977. It was the same when Turgutreis constructed Fishermen's Refuge and the main Plaza of the town. The growth of tourism demand for souvenirs and other paraphernalia urged the Municipality to build an organized trade for the merchants and Touristic Arcade was built in 1992. The following year the new City Hall was built.

Among the most important highlights of growth is the interest of two large capital groups. Benevolent members of the Sabancı Family donated some charitable investments like a school, a cultural center, and an urban recreational area. In 2002, Şevket Sabancı Park was inaugurated. In no time, it became the main "breathing and recreating" area of Turgutreis as she was getting more and more fearful of her future prospects. Later, Hayırlı Sabancı High School was donated in 2004. In the recent years, 2011 and 2013, the town is proud to have Şevket Sabancı Cultural Centers. The municipality plans to have a permanent display and conservation of the documents of our "Turgutreis 1974" study.

On the other hand, Turgutreis had become a magnet, not only as a charitable exercise, but for a commercial venture with strong cultural components. Dogus Group, owning a bank and distribution setups for vehicles, invested in Turgutreis Marina, which became operational in 2002. Dogus Group has a genuine interest in classical music and organizes yearly festivals that make Turgutreis the cultural hub of the country.

In 2012, Turgutreis Marina hosted the 8th of the D-Marin symphonic concerts. As for years, Marina Concerts have been thrilling experiences for music lovers who came to Turgutreis from long distances. Of the many notable musicians, Jose Carreras was there; Carreras is almost as old as the authors. Who would think a celebrity philanthropist like Carreras would come to a totally unknown Aegean town when he was twenty-eight years old? The winds and the waves of the Aegean took his singing as the message of Turgutreis to the rest of the world, one that is not the same for young Turgut, full of love of seas and exploration.

We continue to be mesmerized by the changes, and recall the four decades of transformation with wonder. However, when we examine the facts and figures of the growth and transformation since 1970s development of Turgutreis, the steady growth and political choices in every respect are apparent.

PORTFOLIO
BUILDING
BANGLADESH

Bangladesh played a critical role in the history of mid modern architecture but it is a poorly narrated story. Even earlier, a major architectural idea emerged from Bengal/Bangladesh that eventually became a global paradigm of dwelling: the bungalow. The production and circulation of the bungalow type followed the nineteenth century English adaptation of the *bangla*, the rural hut of Bangladesh, as a climatic paradigm. As an intersection of ecology, sociology, and technology, there was much to learn from the primal bangla hut—a machine for living in a hot-humid milieu. A techno-utilitarian aspect generated from the diminutive bangla hut subsequently informed the content of "tropical architecture," and its metrics of comfort and wellbeing.

Early modern architecture in Bangladesh, in the works of the pioneering modernist architect Muzharul Islam (1923-2012), was framed primarily by meteorological and ecological themes, befitting topics of the tropics, and an utilitarian ethic that coincided with post-colonial nation-building. Through the initiatives of Muzharul Islam and others, examples of a "tropical modernism" were realized in the 1950s and '60s in the works of Constantin Doxiadis, Robert Bouighy, Paul Rudolph, Richard Neutra, Stanley Tigerman, and others. This was an early version of sustainable ethic that combined climate, ecology and functionalism in which an argument for "regionalism" was couched in a climatic logic—angle of the sun, direction of the wind, and measures of thermal comfort.

Next to Chandigarh, Dhaka played a key role in the evolution of modernism towards more humanistic dimensions. Louis Kahn was a critical interlocutor in that turn. His engagement with some of the taboo topics of modernism—landscape and geography, spirituality and sacrality—found inspiration and reciprocal significance in Bangladesh. While the robust geometry of Kahn's Capital Complex has received greater attention from architects and critics, with some hesitant acknowledgment of architecture's psycho-spiritual dimensions, a landscape theme in architecture has remained largely opaque.

Bangladesh's hydro-geographical terrain changed Kahn's own attitude towards the relationship between architecture and landscape. It's a lesson Kahn adopted in his inimitable way and then abstracted as a broader philosophical principle that traveled to his other works. It is to Kahn's meditation on "how the buildings are to take their place" on the wetlands of Dhaka that one may locate a new wave of geography-responsive architecture.

Despite being a small nation of 57,000 square miles, Bangladesh contains diverse (hydro-)geographical zones, each one claiming a distinct sociological and architectural scenario. From a precarious war-torn nationalized economy in the 1970s, Bangladesh has been able to make a turnaround despite a wobbly infrastructure and fractious governance. With much of the economic growth driven by shifts in global manufacturing to low-cost countries, a *New York Times* article notes that "the trend, which began turning parts of Asia—notable China—into manufacturing hubs in the 1980s and 1990s, has started to take root in Bangladesh" (2012). At the same time, aid dependence and trade deficits in Bangladesh are down, and indicators of social progress, such as maternal mortality, nutrition and sanitation, etc., are rising.

An architectural formation refracted by climatic parameters and affected by transnational idioms continues down to this day as a norm; it has well served architects increasingly engaged in

Photo: Mohammad Tauheed

the fruits of a liberalized and globalized economy. Conducted mostly in urban areas, new projects are mobilized for a growing corporate culture with its "international standard," rising middle class aspirations, and grand scale state operations. Ehsan Khan's "Glass House" tower in Dhaka, Mustafa Khalid and Mohammad Foyez Ullah's Grameen Phone office in Dhaka, Vitti Architects' Krishibid Auditorium in Dhaka, and Patrick Rozario's Aarong Centre are examples of an architectural sophistication in executing complex programs for new urban types. In the residential realm, Rafiq Azam's hyper-articulated apartment complexes, Enamul Karim Nirjhar's textual houses and Salauddin Ahmed's meticulously crafted buildings provide instances of new dimensions to urban domesticity.

If architects in Bangladesh were to take on a distinctive challenge today, it will have to be around a (hydro-)geographic theme. While many successful practices are able to prove their forte in dealing with new global and urban types, it is to the gentle but persuasive wave of landscaped themed projects that one must turn to for a new phase.

Modest-scaled detached structures tucked among foliage and ponds, in the larger background of rivers and ricefields, provide a perennial image of the Bengali landscape. Such a scenario seems apt for a theoretical understanding of architecture as part of an environmental continuum. Going beyond the picturesque relationship between building and landscape, a new design intelligence is needed to address contentious and critical issues of the deltaic landscape: climate change, flood and flux, agricultural milieu, and social imbalance generated by the flux. Responding to the alluvial land, Kahn had earlier intuited that in Bangladesh one is required to be a "land architect." While Kahn did not work out the idea systematically, he did indicate an architecture whose language will be conditioned by the physics of the delta—the mutuality of land and water, the malleability of earth, and precariousness of dwelling.

An attitude of archaeological humility and geological impulse was noticeable in Raziul Ahsan's SOS Children's Village in Bogra (1994). An earlier project for now, the SOS Village remains a remarkable essay on placing and siting where buildings sit effortlessly with the land without having to cry out "look, I am architecture ... ," and yet offer a rich variety of spatial experiences.

In an example apart, Kashef Mahbub Chowdhury's Friendship Center in Gaibandha suggests land modulation as an architectural strategy in which a matted building complex with pavilions and courtyards is enframed by an "embankment" to keep the flood water out. Built on a flood-plain as a training center for people living in vulnerable areas, the project speaks of a new landscape-form even if it presents with the embankment a subdued opposition to the surrounding flood-plains.

Various projects, from social engagements to architectural and quasi-architectural creations, indicate new, innovative responses to the aquatic terrain. Bypassing the conventions of city generated forms, these projects are "soft" by their nature and comportment, and suggest a new language of quietude and commitment to social betterments.

A correspondence between boats and buildings seems to be an obvious answer to the diluvial delta. For his much featured educational and social program with floating schools

Mohammed Rezwan converted boats into classrooms that ply to where the students live if they are unable to come to school. Solar powered electricity and computer based education support the arrangement. Yves Marre and Runa Khan, of Friendship, have contributed considerably to restoring the disappearing culture and technology of boat building. In an economic environment in which developmental programs are dictated by the norms of a "dry" culture, a renewed attention to boats goes a long way. Springing from the deep riverine culture of the delta, in which boats have played a key part, restoring and reintroducing some of those beautiful boats may bring about a new ethic and appreciation of water-based practices.

For a special school on a flood-plain outside Dhaka, Saif Ul Haque has created a floating but anchored platform on which simple bamboo woven walls and roofs form a series of classrooms. Unfazed by volumetric flamboyance, the architectural language is one of restraint and adaptation. For a modest arrangement, the school is an important experiment on how to deal with the flux of water and not push it away, and how to carry on life when the water arrives.

Khondaker Hasibul Kabir has been carefully crafting a language of landscape arrangement in which ecology is the fundament of an aesthetic operation. In his "getaway" outside Dhaka, called "Jolo-Jongol," Kabir has composed a cooperative landscape in which all elements participate in a delicate symphony, with none overwhelming the other. Buildings—more like lean-tos —become deliberately non-descript and unassuming as if they had been either always there or on the verge of dissolution; they straddle the edge of a wetland in precarious poise. In his now demolished "bamboo platform" in a slum in Dhaka city, Kabir arranged a similar situation in which an almost invisible architecture, garden, and community assembly sent a quiet challenge to the city's rowdy building culture.

Anna Heringer and Eike Roswag's "hand-made" school in Rudrapur indicated a new direction and commitment for architects willing to be involved in Bangladesh's rural environment; the much publicized project set up an inspiring model for young architects. Marina Tabassum's Panigram resort indicates another direction and commitment for working in the rural milieu. Considering that the language of the Bengali building vernacular has always been one of restraint and accommodation with the landscape, the mud huts of Panigram with their raggedy thatch roofs are alluring because of a reference to the perennial image of the delta with a tilt towards the slightly unusual. Jalal Ahmed and Kashef Mahbub Chowdhury's different projects for the rehabilitation of people living in vulnerable areas, and community driven works such as the "Jogen Babur Math," speak of extending both the geographic and social scope of architecture in Bangladesh.

KKA

[image at top of page]

Friendship Bangladesh (Runa Khan, Syed Wasama Doja & Anika T Karim)
Friendship Boats
Various Areas from Northern & Southern Regions, 2002-Ongoing

Bangladesh is the most densely populated deltaic plane in the world where rivers dominate the livelihoods of the people. Similar to constructing buildings in this delta, the art of building boats has always been deeply rooted in socio-cultural traditions. This Bengal delta once boasted the largest fleet of wooden riverine boats that approached a million. While sea-faring boats in the Bay of Bengal reflected foreign influences in design, the boats navigating through the river waters inland remained free from such influences.

Commencing operations in 2002, Friendship Bangladesh was created as a value-based organization that serve the developmental aims of the most deprived communities of Bangladesh. The cultural preservation sector of the organization has started a program in preserving and promoting the ancient art of making riverine boats. The preservation work involves the creation of perfectly accurate miniature versions of the boats that also go on exhibition, nationally and internationally, allowing people to view these works of art. Friendship has recruited the last of the master craftsmen who belong to the long and proud line of boat artisans to make these boats. As they are preserving this important heritage, they are also training the next generation of carpenters. Annie Montigny, research director, Museum national d'Histoire Naturelle notes: "These river boats deserve, more than anything else at present, urgent attention and development. The skills of the boat-building artisans are disappearing, and must be saved."

Mohammed Rezwan (Shidhulai Swanirvar Sangstha)
Floating Schools for the Children
Districts of Natore and Pabna, Ongoing
(Three months to build each school-boat)

Twenty million people in Bangladesh live in villages that are only accessible by boat. With no consistent supply to electricity and other resources, people suffer from reliable access to education, healthcare, and information. All of these problems are acute especially in the remote Chalanbeel region where many of the inhabitants are landless laborers. With the only access to the area through rivers, school attendance remains poor along with the shortages of teachers. Shidhulai Swanirvar Sangstha, a local charity, provided the solution to Chalanbeel's difficulties through a portable and water-based response. A fleet of boats was designed to use on-board solar powered electricity offering a range of services in the classrooms and libraries. They operate computers, mobile phones, and even battery charging stations for the portable solar lamps. In the evening, educational films are shown to the laborers who have spent all day working in the fields. New services have been introduced such as solar powered early flood warning devices, floating flood shelters and floating gardens. This project with its educational programs brought about confidence in the villagers; a resident put it eloquently, "After this library came to our village, we started to believe in ourselves."

Marina Tabassum Architects
Panigram Eco Resort
Taherpur, Jessore, 2011

Planned as a key destination resort, Panigram will be completed by June 2017. Considering the unique beauty of rural Bengal, the client approached the architect with the idea of an eco-resort that will give guests an authentic experience of rural Bangladesh. Located on the bank of river Kopotaksha, the site is surrounded by farmlands where life moves at a slower pace. The architect felt that it would be "a crime to invade this silence with the roaring noise of architecture ..." The project was seen as an opportunity to bring back the lost belief in the wisdom of the land that lead to crafting a building tradition over hundreds of years. Studies conducted on nearby villages revealed techniques of building with mud in which women were mainly responsible on the maintenance and decoration of the mud houses. When engaged in conversation with the architect, the village elders showed an encyclopedia of information. Although mud is an entirely new material for the architect, with the combination of local knowledge and a language of architecture that is of the land, the project progressed steadily.

Marina Tabassum Architects
Bait ur Rouf Mosque
Faidabad, Uttara, Dhaka, 2012

The mosque attempts to trace the lost glory of Bengali architecture but by presenting a contemporary expression. Located in the northern expansion of Dhaka, in a fast growing community of lower middle income families, the mosque is flanked by roads on west and south, with a 670 sq.m. (7,200 sq.ft.) of area that creates a thirteen degree angle with the axis of the Qibla.

Three volumes were introduced, one inserted within the other to create sequence of spaces. The outer most volume is a 22m x 22m (75' x 75') square of 8m (25') height situated parallel to the road creating the main façade of the mosque. This façade was conceived as a screen and breathing wall for the hot humid climate. A cylindrical volume is inserted into this outer most volume that facilitates the rotational axis of the prayer hall simultaneously formulating light courts on four sides. All ancillary functions such as the entrance courts, ablution and toilet facilities, Imam's office and stairs are located within the space created by the outer square and cylindrical volume. While the prayer hall is in concrete, the outer part is a load bearing brick construction. The main prayer hall is a column free space, 15m x 15m (50' x 50') in square and 10m (35') in height. Intricate terracotta works in the form of jaali (screen) gives porosity ensuring ventilation and controlled light. The rapidly urbanizing nature of the project site demanded an internalized space that also enhances the use of light as a spiritual element.

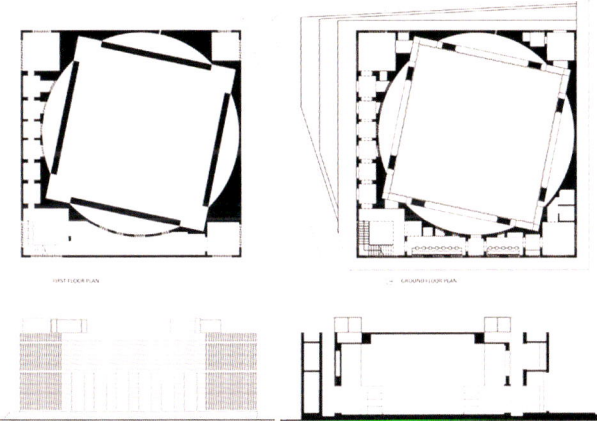

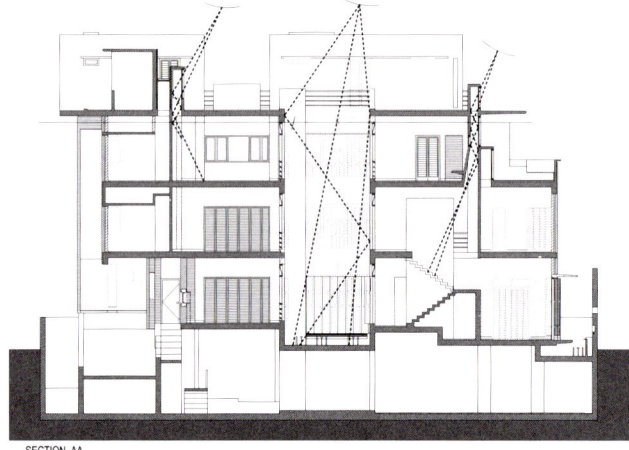

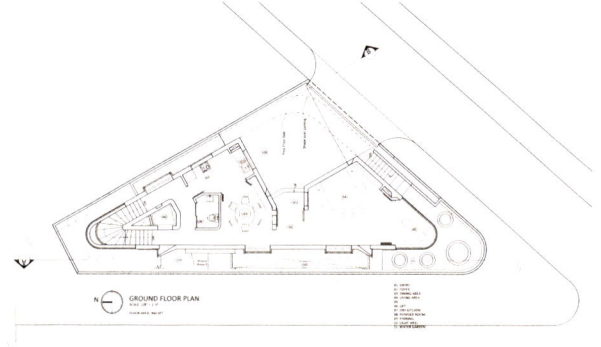

SECTION AA

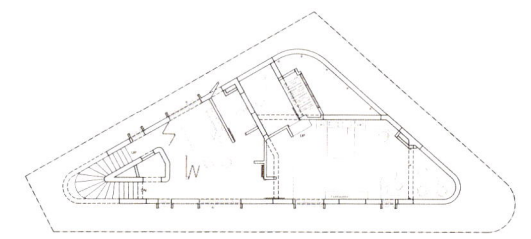

Atelier Robin Architects (Salauddin Ahmed)
Karim Residence
Bashundhara, Dhaka, 2010

The work represents an interpretation of modern-day living with rich cultural values in the realm of domesticity. Designed for a site that once claimed its stability from a soft wetland, Karim Residence is a three-storied residential building that has a highly modulated and overlapped relationship between the exterior and interior, and between depth and height. The undulated floor plate at the ground level and punctuations through the floor plates at various levels are a reminder of an unsettling relationship with the claimed ground. With the ground too soft to receive any building challenge, the response was to push the foundation deep into the ground. To make users understand this condition, natural light was brought in through some of the punctuations deep into the cave-like spaces. The project attempts to transcribe the temporality of life and living through the material construct: Brick to contain the overlapped spaces, reinforced concrete to give it structural stability and timber to define the openings toward the context of the house. With its 134 doors and pulled out veranda from the core to the outer skin and beyond, the residence testifies to its intention of being a part of a larger fabric in which all architecture dwells.

Atelier Robin Architects (Salauddin Ahmed)
Ishtiaq Residence
Nikunjo, Dhaka, 2016

The adversarial shape and size of the site was a challenge in accommodating the program for a comfortable layout. In response to the site, the building received a triangulated shape; despite the tight corners, interior spaces allowed for fresh air and generous ambiance. The outer expression of the building was more an abstraction than a literal expression of the interior. Peripheral walls were clad with timber and punctuated with large windows whenever required, creating a series of curious threshold between the insider and outsider. In its three levels above the ground and the basement below, the residence offered three bedrooms, with their required ancillary spaces; living room with a comfortable veranda, family space, dining space, large working kitchen, roof top garden, and a water garden around the property.

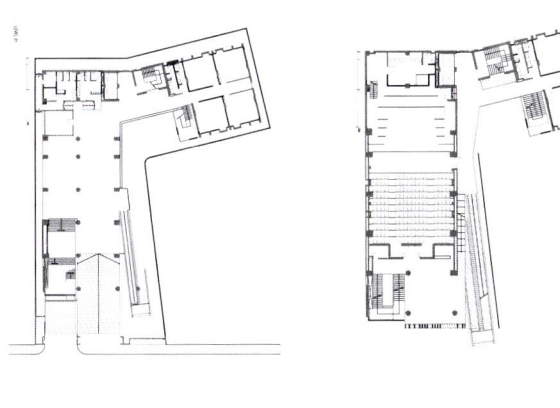

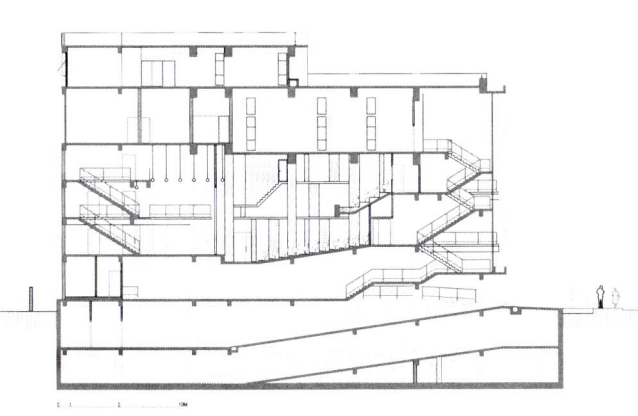

Ehsan Khan Architects
Bangladesh Mohila Samity Complex
Natak Sarani, Baily Road, Dhaka, 2015

The objective of Bangladesh Mohila Samity (Women's Association) is to provide and empower destitute women through vocational training, legal support, leadership training, and activism. Located at Baily Road in Dhaka, it is also a popular hub for theater activists and enthusiasts. Over time, the activities of the association expanded and the existing facility could not meet new demands. Plans for the redevelopment of the premise for present and future needs include theaters (one with 250 seats and the other one with a 100 seat experimental hall), conference facilities, offices, and training facilities for the institution and a primary school. The ground floor of this project may be considered as an extension of a sidewalk, acting as a "chattor" (a gathering space). Women and children will use the space at day time, while cultural aficionados will take over from the late evening into the night. The vertical circulation through ramps, bridges, and voids, link the street with the decks and galleries of the theater. The façade of the building is a combination of heavy masonry brick walls, concrete fins and curtain walls.

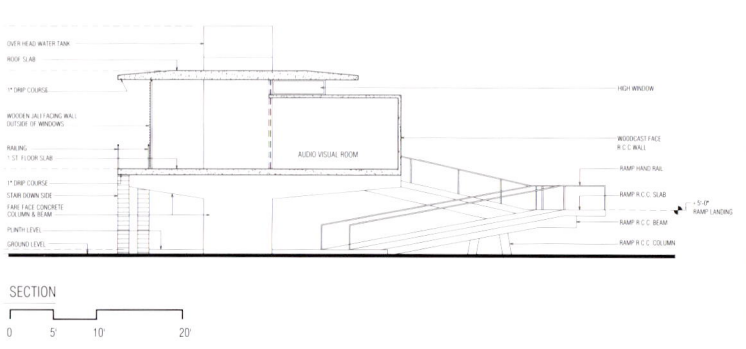

SECTION

0   5'   10'   20'

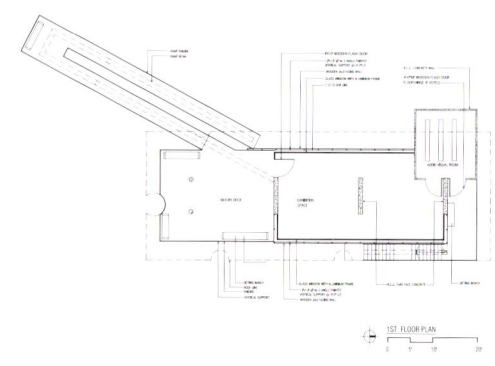

1ST. FLOOR PLAN

VITTI Sthapati Brindo Ltd (Principal Designer: Ehsan Khan)
Nishorgo (Interpretation Centre)
Mochuni, Teknaf, Cox's Bazar, 2008

"Nishorgo" as the environment implies the natural conditions of land, air, and water, in which people, animals, and plants live with "life." Upon investigating the site and its setting, the approach for this project involved preserving nature and life by "unleashing the backdrop to cherish its sanctity rather than an intervention, and sparing nature more than an improvisation." In such a place one will become a "'beholder' (rather) than an interpreter." Proposed activities at the Center are placed in layers of reinforced concrete platforms floating on structural walls, liberating the ground. This allows water to flow through the ground layer during the monsoon season while placing the visitor on a heightened level to experience the surroundings. The creation of a pavilion-like shelter reveals the plasticity of its materials and construction technique. To approach this building, one has to go through the strips of walkways leading either to stairs or to ramps, exploring the transition in continuous mode. A composition of openings framed and louvered by wooden lattice envelope the cantilevered slabs. The interior has arrangements for interpretive exhibits and a screening and briefing theater.

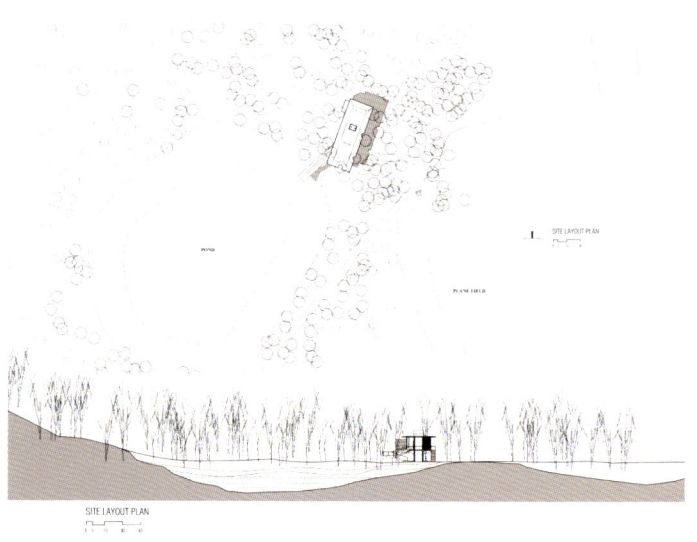

SITE LAYOUT PLAN

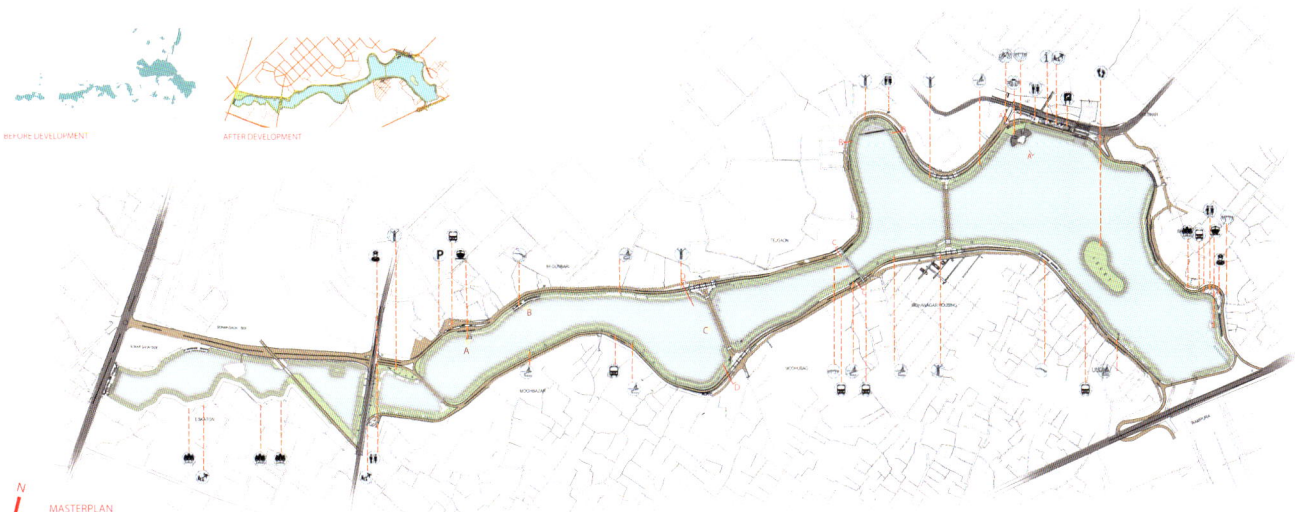

BEFORE DEVELOPMENT   AFTER DEVELOPMENT

N
MASTERPLAN

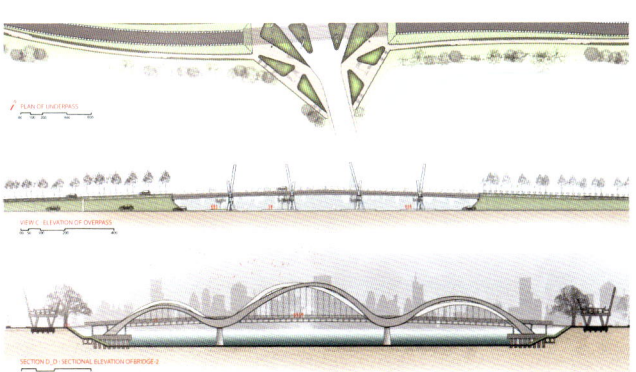

PLAN OF UNDERPASS

VIEW C ELEVATION OF OVERPASS

SECTION D_D SECTIONAL ELEVATION OF BRIDGE 2

VITTI Sthapati Brindo Ltd
(Iqbal Habib, Ehsan Khan, Ishtiaque Zahir Titas)
**Integrated Development of Hatirjheel Area Including
Begunbari Khal (Canal)**
Dhaka, 2013

"Integrated Development of Hatirjheel Area Including Begunbari Khal
(canal)" was primarily conceived as a wetland restoration project to
safeguard a large part of Dhaka from flash flood. Eventually it became a
comprehensive urban renewal project promoting transport connection,
vehicular traffic, water retention during monsoon, waste water
management, and civic facilities. This project hopes to restore and
conserve the floodplain environment and the waterfront legacy from
illegal encroachment that has occurred over the years. By preserving
the low-lying floodplain areas of Hatirjheel, there has been an increased
retention capacity for storm water runoff flowing from the surrounding
catchment area. It also facilitates east-west connection with the existing
road network between several major north-south urban corridors
through the use of expressway, local roads, and walkways around
the canal. The construction of recreational facilities and landscaping
through the employment of infrastructural and landscape components
includes viewing decks, children's play area, floating gardens, floating
walkways, an amphitheater, information center, and an assembly point.

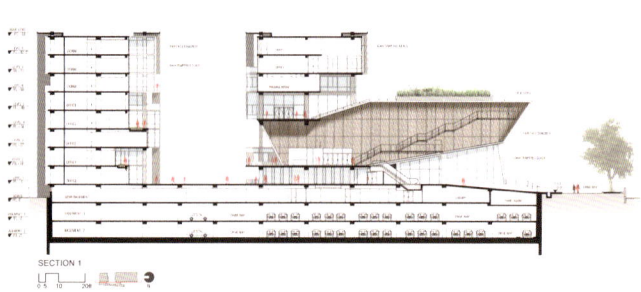

VITTI Sthapati Brindo Ltd (Ishtiaque Zahir Titas)
Krishibid Institution of Bangladesh
Khamarbari, Dhaka, 2014

The Krishibid Institution (KIB) is a national organization dedicated to promoting the farmers of this rich, agriculture based country. Varied programs for the complex are distributed in two blocks: public and private. The private zones houses the institution's office, a training center with class rooms, dormitory facilities, club facilities with a swimming pool, and rentable offices, while the public zone has a 1,000 seat auditorium, a 500 seat multipurpose hall, a 300 seat projection gallery. All are connected and separated by means of plaza, bridge, courtyard, etc. The master plan of KIB tried to recall the unique landscape of Bangladesh with its distinctive pattern of agricultural land division with its colors of varying crops, and traditional building courtyards. Courtyard have been used at KIB to create both a barrier and connection. Taking advantage of natural resources, the project also adopts climate responsive approaches. Passive design methods ensure natural sunlight, flowing of the southern breeze, and shaded western façades reduce the load on air-conditioning and electricity. The project also employs the principles of recycling, reduction, and reuse in terms of water management and energy efficiency that includes the recycling of grey water and rain water harvesting.

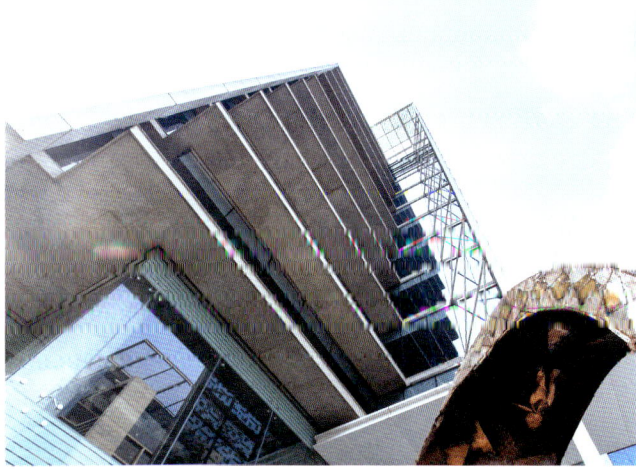

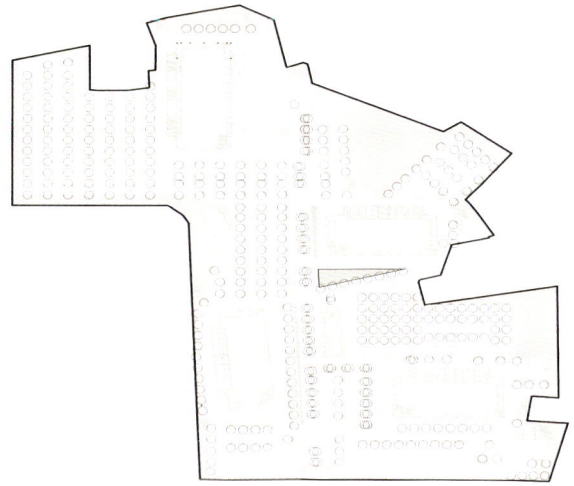

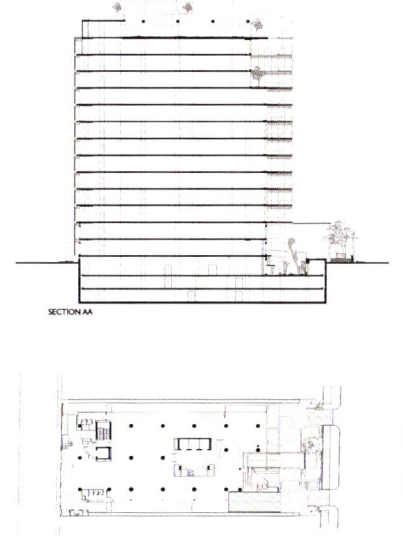

SECTION AA

Volume Zero Ltd (Mohammad Foyez Ullah)
International Convention City Bashundhara (ICCB)
Bashundhara, Dhaka, 2015

The Convention Center is a gateway to the satellite township of
Purbachaal at Dhaka's eastern periphery. The civic oriented initiative
introduced the concept of a multi convention hub in an urban
response to ever-growing needs of an emerging metropolis. Spread
over seventeen acres of reclaimed territory, the Convention Center is
an ensemble of four modular halls along with auxiliary functions such
as mosque, retail outlets and office spaces form the various nuclei of
ICCB. A single loop traffic management against a spacious central spine
manages parking facilities for over 2000 cars at a time. The individual
halls are placed in an oasis of greenery to allow dedicated domains for
a multitude of events simultaneously. The volume of each of the halls
forms a pure rectangle with the exterior envelope layered by glazing
panels encasing a pre-engineered structural skeleton.

Volume Zero Ltd (Mohammad Foyez Ullah)
Simpletree Anarkali
Gulshan, Dhaka, 2015

"Simpletree Anarkali," an office building, is a purist architectural
response to the usual chaotic urban fabric of Dhaka. Planes emerge out
of the base of the structure and fold within and outside generating its
volume. Concrete accentuates the clarity of transparent glass planes
that forms the exterior envelope. The forecourt with a generous
setback presents a curated landscape embellished with waterscape and
sculptures by celebrated artists. Each of 1020 sq. m (11,000 sq. ft.)
floor plates is a rectangular base supported by a central and peripheral
service spine, allowing corporate addresses efficient customization.
"Simpletree Anarkali" also sets a strong sense of environmental
responsibilities by conserving water and electricity, and implementing
environment sensitive construction methods (derived from LEED pre-
certification in the gold category).

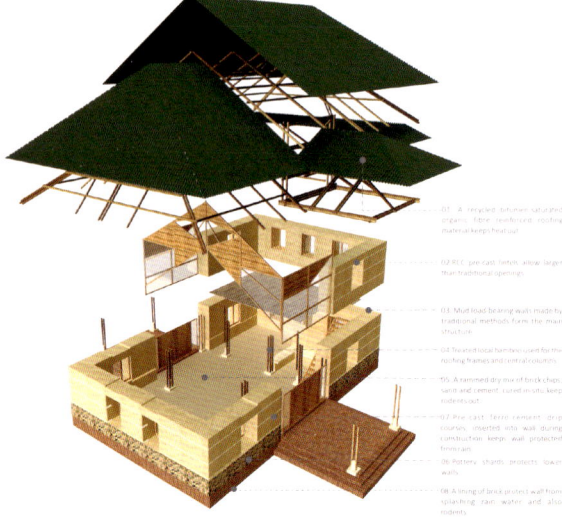

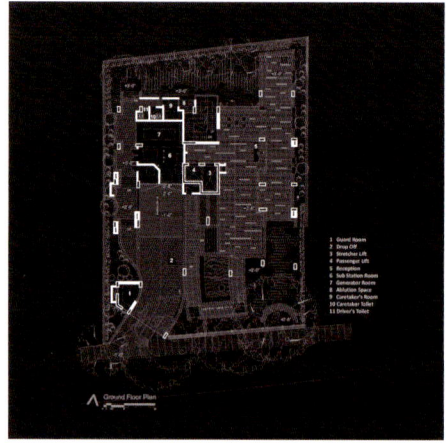

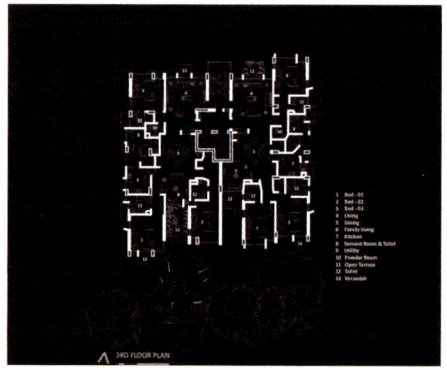

ARC Architectural Consultants (Nahas Ahmed Khalil)
Matir Bari
Sarabo, Savar, 2009

Making mud-wall buildings remains a way of building in rural Bangladesh, but is limited largely to lower income groups. With increasing income, an overwhelming tendency for people is to exchange mud-wall structures for corrugated iron sheet, and then brick-walled structures. Thermal comfort within mud-wall houses is much better. Durability of mud-walled structures is also high but requires regular maintenance. Pitched roof-forms with low overhanging eaves are traditional responses to keeping water off walls during rain. The focus for this project was devising details to protect mud-walls with minimum intervention, at low costs, by using locally available materials, and by allowing current practice and practitioners of mud walls to easily adopt new details.

ARC Architectural Consutlants (Nahas Ahmed Khalil)
SPL Aakash Prodeep
Banani Residential Area, Dhaka, 2014

Due to severe lack of open urban spaces in the city, a challenge is to provide a pleasant view for an average urban plot in Dhaka. Since there are very few open playfields and water bodies, it becomes necessary to create internal views within the in-between spaces of buildings and roads. With the introduction of Floor Area Ratios (FAR) in the building code (since 2008), it has become possible to provide an "oasis" at different levels of a building that residents can enjoy. Based on this idea, SPL Aakash Prodeep is designed as a 45 m (150') high building with views from verandas in the lower floors towards the ground level landscaping and vegetation while views from verandas in the upper floors access areas created by alternating conditions.

SHATOTTO (Rafiq Azam)
Imran Residence
Uttara, Dhaka, 2015

Following vernacular principles in design, using locally available materials, both natural and crafted but with modern amenities, the Imran Residence addresses the theme of home in the tropics within "traditional modernism." Bearing in mind people are imprisoned within their concrete homes in the burgeoning city, the Imran Residence presents a long green veranda that spans outwards from home, creating the feeling of wandering away from it. This multi-storied family residence has a lawn placed in the south-west corner on the ground floor and steel-bridges leading to gardens on each level. Wooden louvers on the west façade act as an element for privacy and hide the mechanical units. The duplex unit starting from the first floor comprises of internal wooden steps leading to the upper floor consisting of the bedrooms. All other levels have a one unit apartment. The two upper floors accommodate the party hall surrounded by a grand terrace, a gym, garden, and sitting room.

SHATOTTO (Rafiq Azam)
South Grace
West Raza Bazar, Dhaka, 2013

Built on a small site of 300 sq m area, South Grace is an eight storied residential apartment. The orientation of the site was a crucial factor as the spatial planning tried to maximize winter insolation. Taking advantage of southwest orientation, each apartment has ample solar exposure allowing the vines to grow in their garden beds, providing a beautiful green cover on the exteriors. The first five floors of the building have typical residence with small verandahs. The bedrooms of the sixth floor residence have been adjusted to yield a lawn and a paved terrace. The seventh floor of the building has a community hall with a landscaped patio to let the inhabitants of the building interact and socialize. Exposed concrete is used for its climatic sensibility. With extensive landscaping and greenery covering considerable portions of the façade, the building appears as a vertical garden in the high density settlement that also draw birds and butterflies.

Synthesis Architects (Patrick D'Rozario)
BRAC – Aarong Commercial Center
Sector # 3 Uttara, Dhaka, 2010

This project is a contemporary and comprehensive flagship store for the country's leading fashion house, Aarong. With "aarong" meaning a traditional village fair, the design evolved around making people from different places and ages be attracted to the place to participate in a festive atmosphere. A drama of horizontal free flowing spaces has been translated into vertical arrangements. The nine storied Brac-Aarong Center is divided into two parts: continuous interlinked spaces create the flagship store up to the fifth level. The first three floors with triple height glazed façade allow maximum visibility to attract people. The rest of the levels accommodate functional activities with a 5 m (16.9') high canopy on the roof along with an open sky terrace for multidimensional outdoor activities. The Aarong floors are connected with a lofty internal processional stair continuous with a six storey high wall offering a crafted journey.

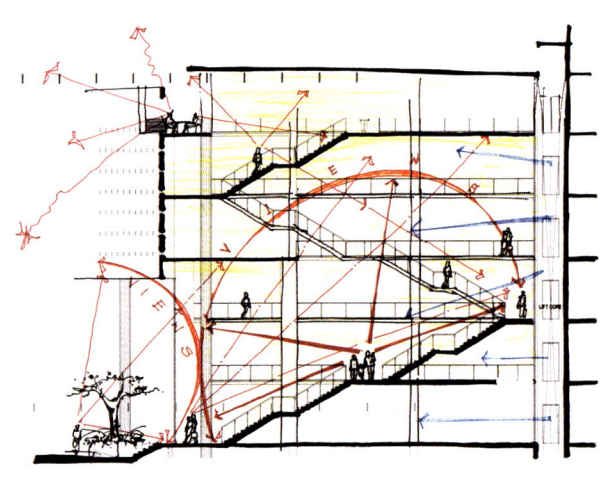

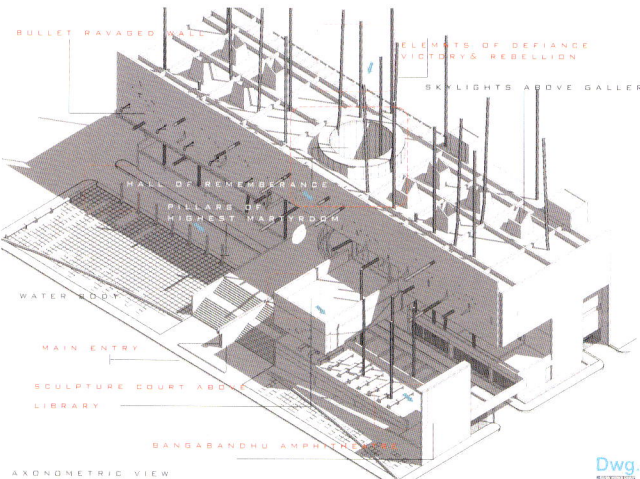

DWG (Tanzim Hasan Salim)
Liberation War Museum
Sher-e Bangla Nagar, Dhaka, Ongoing

The nine month long Liberation War of Bangladesh culminated in victory and independence in December 1971. The challenge for designing a Liberation War Museum was in representing all chronological events in a unified way under one single roof. While it was easier to convey the factual part of the narrative, representing the spirit of the independence for various generations was a greater challenge. A ceremonial entry to the museum guides visitors to the circular water body depicting the "flame of eternity." Bullet marks as signs of the war depict the exterior through which light falls in the gallery. The inner side of the wall in the upper level gallery carries the names of martyrs. Vertical column-like elements punch through the gallery literally celebrating the mood of victory. Artifacts of the war are displayed below nine light shafts. There is the chamber of remembrance in the heart of the museum where a dark space is lit by circular light from above.

System Architects (Enamul Karim Nirjhar)
Nina Kabbo (office)
Tejgaon, Dhaka, 2013

With Bengal's longstanding history of writing political slogans on city walls, the office building "nina kabbo" acts as a tribute to Bengali language, culture and literature in which writings play an important part. The architect proposed that: "Even though architecture is not a performing art, it plays a strong role, in stimulating social, cultural, and psychological impressions." The architect also wondered if architecture can instigate sensitivity in a violent world. The office building displays poems from twelve eminent poets of Bangla literature, sculpted on its facades and drawn into the interiors. Natural light illuminating the linear atrium in front of the lift lobby creates a visual connection through all floors. The water and green feature along the sitting areas have been designed to encourage public interaction. Elimination of visual boundaries links the neighboring people to the constructed space.

System Architects (Enamul Karim Nirjhar)
"Jeebon Anondo" Residence
Nikunjo, Dhaka, 2014

Portraying the unity and bond of togetherness amongst the family members in a celebration of life, "Jeebon Anondo" (the joy of life) is a residence designed for a family of seven on a small plot of land in Dhaka. With the intention to visually connect different parts of the house and its residents, varying sizes of circular punches have been made into the inner facades keeping a decent level of privacy at the same time. The perforated ceiling lets in light inside the house adding up to the interplay of light and shadow. Doors, passages, windows, and stairs of this residence were designed with consideration for the special needs of a particular occupant. With four levels to this residential complex, the basement is dedicated to family entertainment and gym, ground floor for drop off, welcome foyer, and parking. The first floor contains the dining and living spaces while the second floor contains all family bedrooms.

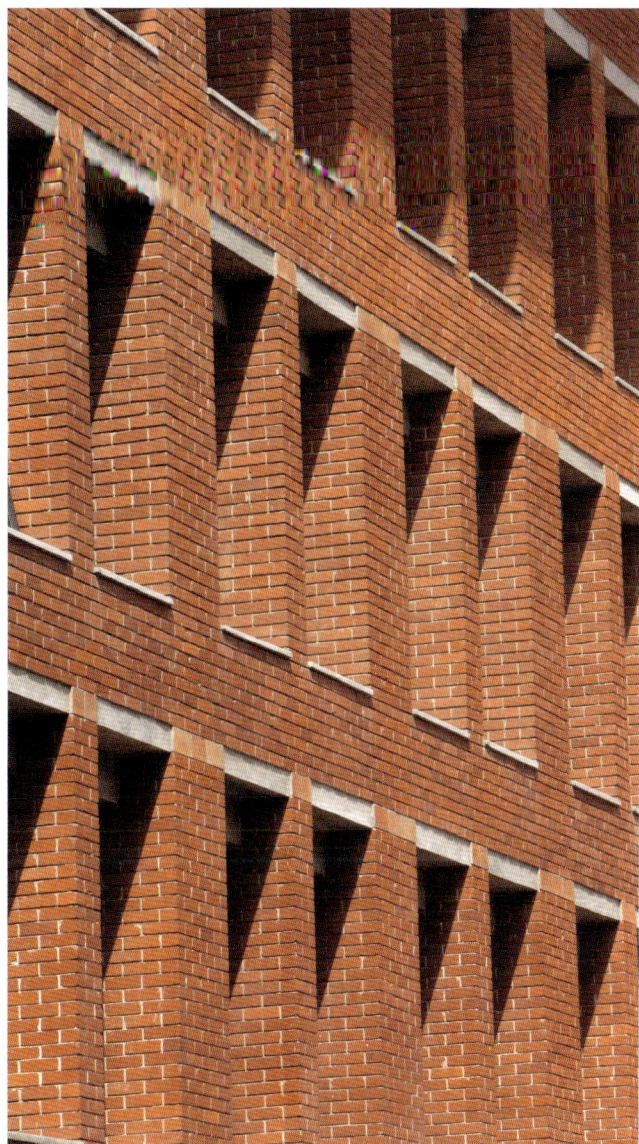

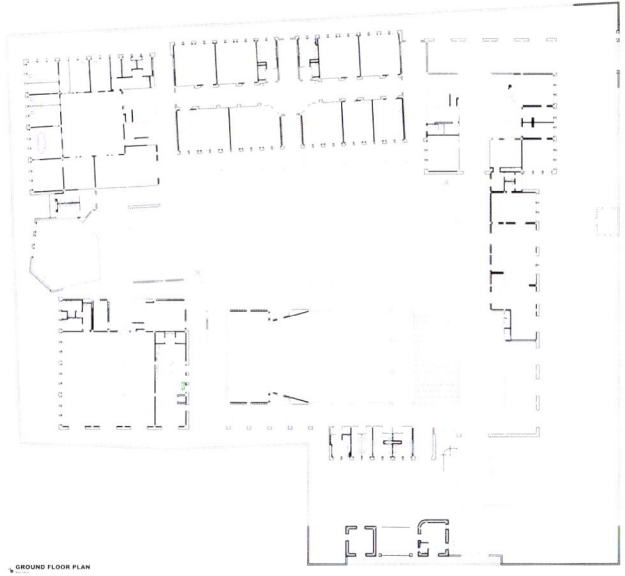

GROUND FLOOR PLAN

Bashirul Haque & Associates
East West University
Aftabnagar, Dhaka, 2012

A minimalist approach and an innovative use of local materials were adopted for the design of this academic complex for a new university. Located in the midst of the rapidly growing metropolis, the complex consists of a large courtyard surrounded by three academic buildings and a student center. Classrooms, lecture galleries and a library constitute the academic buildings. The student center has auditoriums, a canteen, gym facilities, a bookshop, and a club. A separate administrative building houses office spaces, car parks, a cafeteria, and a publication area. The interior of the building complex is illuminated by a skylight revealing the interchanging scales for various activities. The placement of functions and differences in height are positioned according to the requirements for natural ventilation, light and shadow.

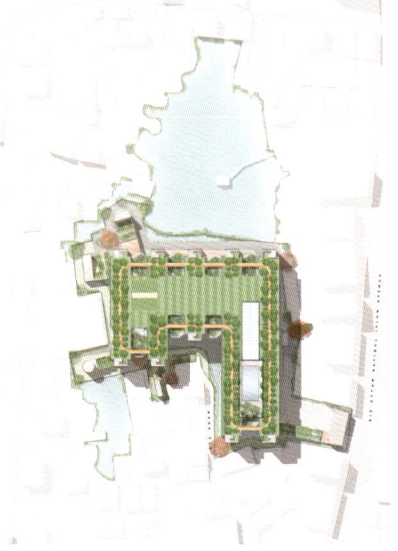

WOHA (Wong Mun Sum & Richard Hassell) and
Local Architect (J.A. Architects Ltd)
BRAC University
Merul Badda, Dhaka, Ongoing

Sited near an urban lake, the new BRAC University presents an
innovative and sustainable inner city campus by exemplifying tropical
design strategies in response to the hot, humid, and monsoon climatic
conditions of the region. Drawing inspiration from the Sundarbans,
which have separate ecosystems above and below tidal level, the
main design strategy was to create two distinct programmatic strata
by floating the academic component (Academia) above the lake and
revealing a Campus Park below, reflecting the synergistic coexistence
between mankind and mangrove. The Academia occupies the upper
nine floors, consisting of the university administration, building services,
and student union spaces such as the library, canteen, fitness centers,
clubs, faculties, and lecture theaters. On the roof top, there is a large
recreational sky park, an open playing field, a 450m running track, a
swimming pool, and a cricket pitch overlooking stunning views of the
lake and the city.

Surrounded by a bamboo garden, the Campus Park is the public
interface of the university. This quadruple volume space features a
series of commercial and retail units within the close proximity of the
main entrance and drop off. It houses an exhibition gallery, a 700 seat
auditorium, a multi-purpose hall for major campus events. There is
also an adjoining amphitheater arena, faculty guest house, and female
student dormitory. Linking these facilities is the brick-paved Campus
Lake Promenade on a water edge that has outdoor bistros and mini
jetties.

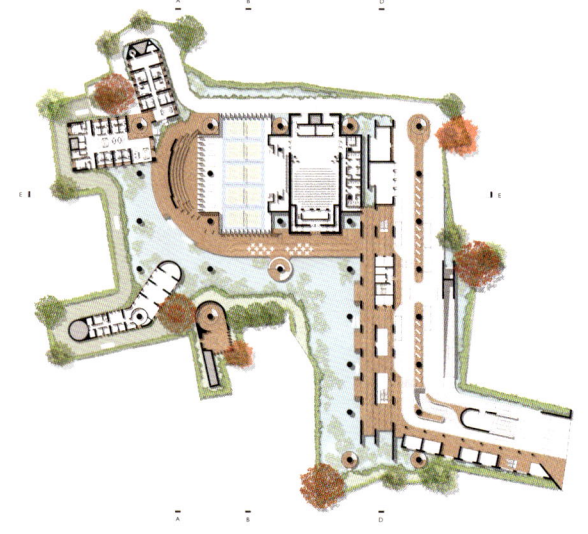

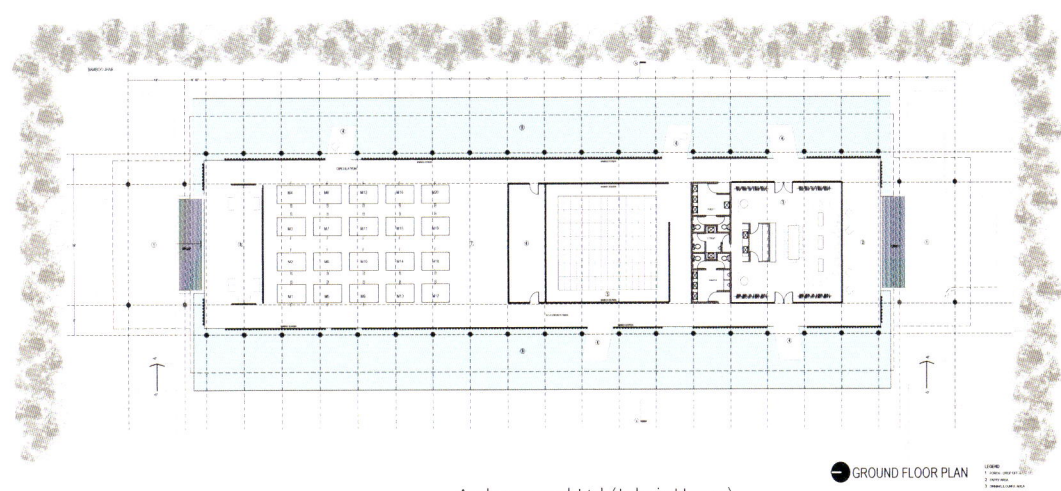

GROUND FLOOR PLAN

Archeground Ltd (Jubair Hasan)
Shuttle Loom Shed for Amber Denim
Rajendrapur, Gazipur, 2015

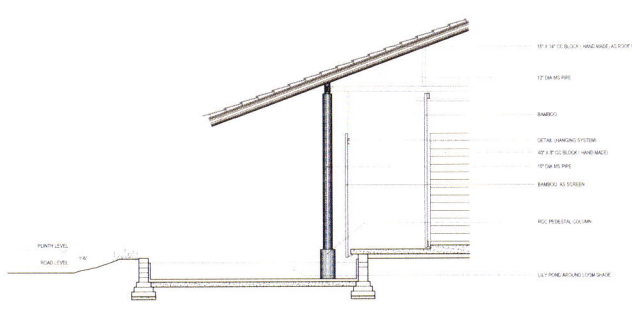

DETAIL SECTION 01

Shuttle Loom Shed was inspired by traditional houses in Bangladesh built in minimal yet effective ways. Those houses show a genuine sensitivity toward nature, climate, and the needs of the people, even though constructed by individuals with no formal architectural training. The Shed Building is located within a factory premise in Gazipur outside Dhaka. The layout has been kept as open as possible to house several loom machines, a buyers' lounge, a dining for the workers, toilets, and a prayer space. A low cost budget was implemented throughout the project. The operating costs of the building were kept minimal by introducing a water body, bamboo screen, high ceiling, and other vernacular elements. These were installed to reduce electricity costs by eliminating the need for air conditioning and artificial lighting, but still making the space naturally cool and comfortable to work in.

URBANA (Kashef Mahbub Chowdhury and Marina Tabassum)
The Liberation War Museum and Independence Monument
Suhrawardy Udyan, Dhaka, 2013

The Liberation War Museum and Independence Monument project was
won by URBANA through a nationwide competition in 1997. The site
is extremely historical: On March 7, 1971, the Bengali people united
under the leadership of Sheikh Mujibur Rahman, following his address
on the site, towards the fight against the oppressive military rule of Pakistan. Once again, it was on this ground, on December 16, 1971, the
Pakistani army accepted defeat, and a sovereign Bangladesh was born.

With the duality of joy and sadness brought in the same platform, the
Independence Monument and Liberation War Museum had to deal
with a paradox—celebration of freedom and liberty gained through
selfless sacrifices. Above ground, the Plaza is organized as the forum
of celebration. At the center of this plaza, water converges in the
middle of a circular pool and falls through the void. A ramp, guided
by a long thick wall, leads one into the underground portion of this
complex. Here the subterranean functions encourage contemplation—
memory embedded in the heart of the earth. The museum, library,
and the research center that embody the history of struggle, torture,
and genocide are displayed in the black exhibit zone. Eventually, one
discovers the central chamber where there is a water column appearing
as an open wound—a column of tears. One is then ushered through
the ramp again to the plaza to discover the Tower of Light, a symbol of
freedom and aspiration.

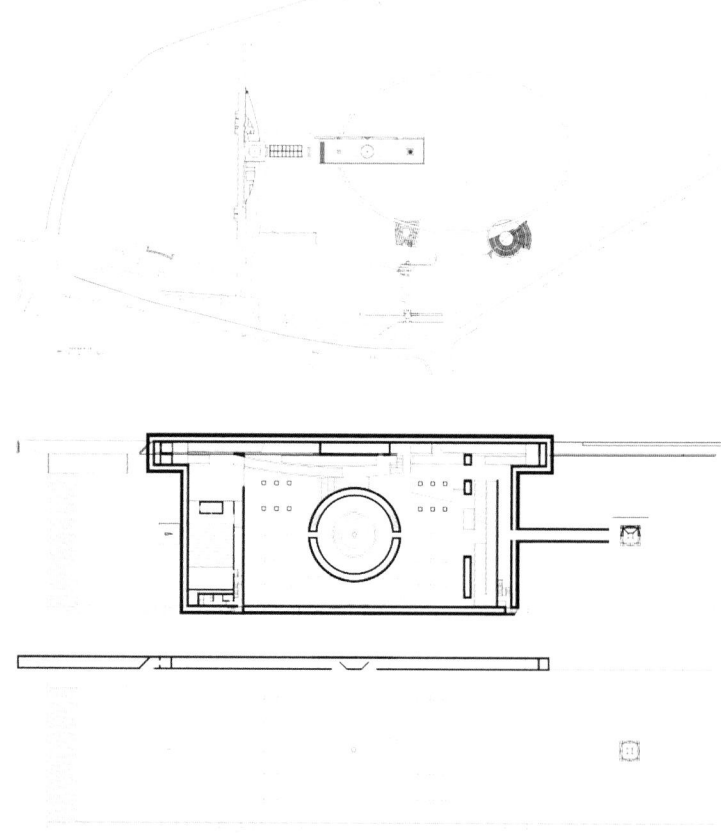

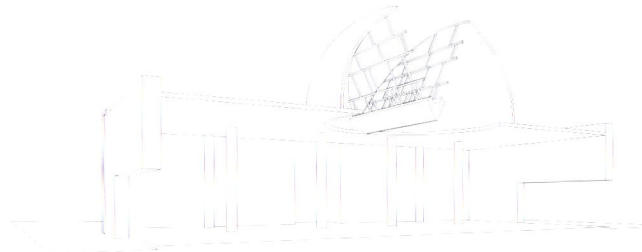

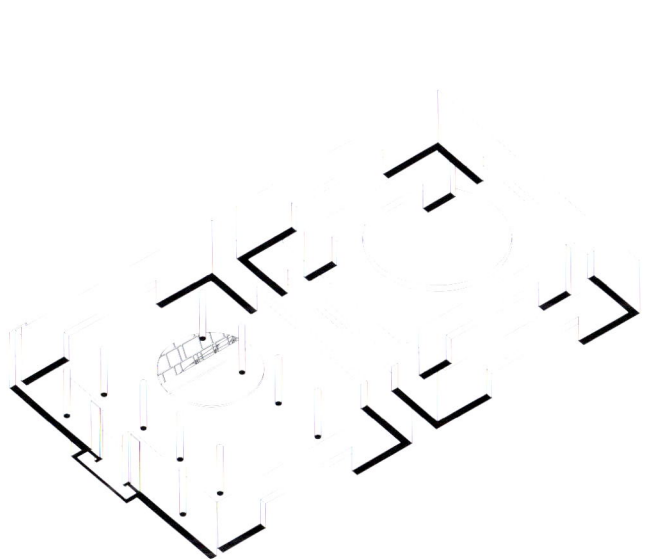

URBANA (Kashef Mahbub Chowdhury)
Chandgaon Mosque
Chittagong, Bangladesh, 2007

The design of the Chandgaon mosque consists of two identical cuboid volumes, one being the traditional courtyard in front of the mosque and the other being the mosque itself. The courtyard serves as spill-over area during larger congregations. The design pivots around the tension between the horizontal elements (earthbound) such as the low, wide openings for the gathering of worshippers, and the vertical elements (spiritual) such as the zenith of the circular opening and the cut-dome. In the front court, the visual connection through expansive apertures to the surrounding landscape is offset by the circular disc of the sky above. The cut-dome of the main mosque, in contrast to a traditional dome, expresses a non-spanning character and also brings in daylight. At night, the light from the mosque works like a beacon in the locale. More than a place of worship, the design attempts to reinterpret the traditional elements of a mosque and create a gathering space for the community.

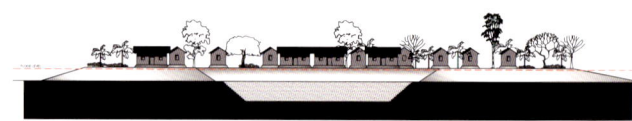

URBANA (Kashef Mahbub Chowdhury)
Raised Settlements
Various Locations in the Jamuna River Network, Northern Bangladesh
six projects, 2011

In northern Bangladesh, the Jamuna River that comes down from the Himalayas is ten km wide in places, that change course every so many years, eroding and creating sand banks in its wake. In monsoon season, flood waters become like a sea and submerge many households on the river islands. The landless people of the area continue to live on rooftops or temporary platforms in the water, without healthcare or hygiene and risking the lives of their children. People in these liquid landscapes live with the water instead of fighting it. The architect's intention was to design with the flow of the river and create a settlement through a self-help and interactive process involving those affected by flooding almost every year. As a self-help initiative, the project involves those affected to create an adjacent raised "plinth," instead of raising individual houses by 2.5 m (8'), where the entire village is shifted to remain above highest recorded flood level of that area. The "food-work exchange" program means the villagers were paid to work on their own plinth, thus simultaneously creating temporary jobs.

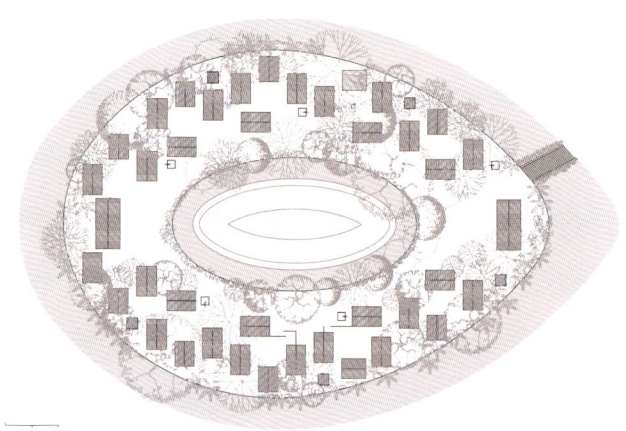

The design resulted from the study of maps and aerial observations of river islands, whose "comet" shapes, are formed by the flow of water and alluvial deposits. The teardrop shape of the island has a pond in the middle that can hold rainwater and be used for a fishery. The master plan of the settlement was prepared by studying the wisdom of placement of houses and courtyards in traditional villages. The villagers were however given the freedom to not follow the drawings: an interesting result was that many villagers did follow the master plan—accepting to build from drawings perhaps for the first time in their lives.

Shareq Rauf Chowdhury, Nur-e-Dipha Shamima Muttaqi,
Iftekhar Ul-Haque
Rishipara Mandir Paathshaala
Naryanganj, Dhaka, 2013

As part of an education program initiated by two friends, Christopher
Lee Hesse and Mark S. Fave, who wanted to give back to Bangladesh
after staying there for several years, the Rishipara Mandir Paathshaala
was conceived as a traditional outdoor school in the Bengal region.
Using local artisan craftsmanship, traditional, and modern forms
of intermediary and indigenous technologies have been explored
in this project. Bamboo has been used to revive the traditional
environmentally-friendly methods of construction. Previously, the school
had only one classroom built of corrugated iron sheets with minimal
openings allowing inadequate light and ventilation; it was expected to
cater to the learning needs of eighty-five children aged six to fourteen.
The new building has three classrooms and a library room running
in two shifts to accommodate approximately ninety-eight students.
The total site was 12 m (38') by 9 m (28'). At the initial stage, design
workshops were held with the community to promote a sense of
ownership with the design, construction and future maintenance of the
school. A "Paint Your Own School" workshop was held in which the
children drew on the walls to increase their level of involvement with
the project. Neighbors also contributed their specialized skills such as
making mats and bamboo light shades.

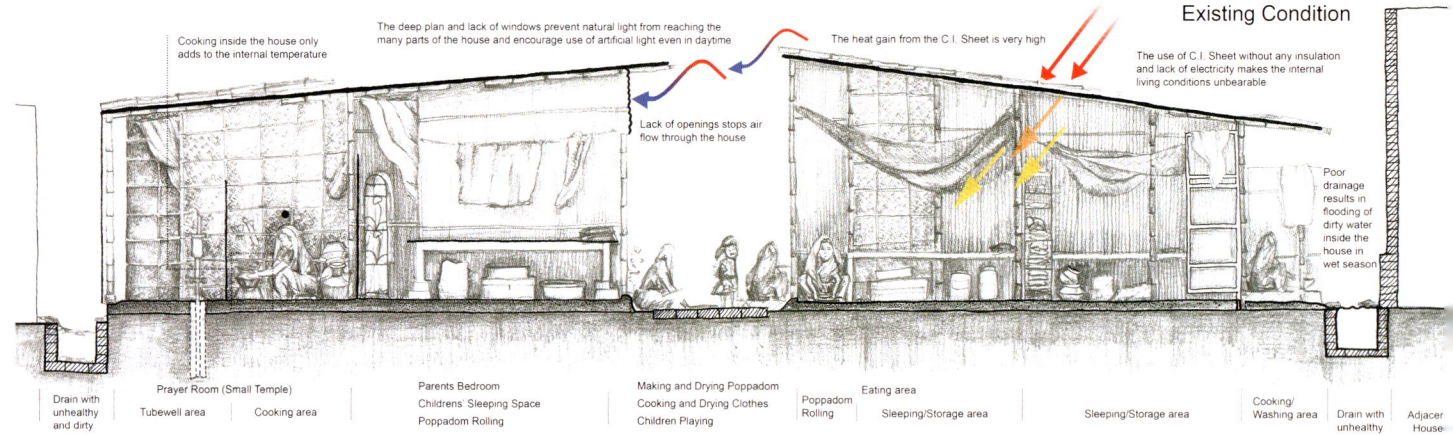

Existing Condition

Cooking inside the house only adds to the internal temperature

The deep plan and lack of windows prevent natural light from reaching the many parts of the house and encourage use of artificial light even in daytime

The heat gain from the C.I. Sheet is very high

The use of C.I. Sheet without any insulation and lack of electricity makes the internal living conditions unbearable

Lack of openings stops air flow through the house

Poor drainage results in flooding of dirty water inside the house in wet season

Drain with unhealthy and dirty	Prayer Room (Small Temple)		Parents Bedroom	Making and Drying Poppadom		Eating area		Cooking/	
	Tubewell area	Cooking area	Childrens' Sleeping Space	Cooking and Drying Clothes	Poppadom	Sleeping/Storage area	Sleeping/Storage area	Washing area	Drain with	Adjacen
			Poppadom Rolling	Children Playing	Rolling				unhealthy	House

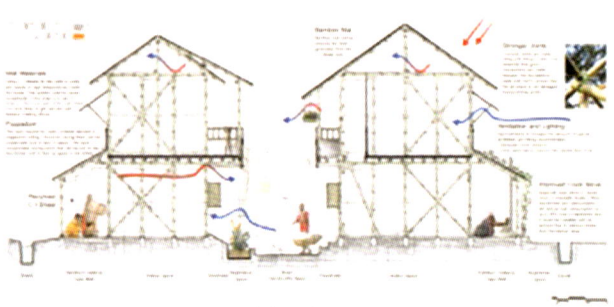

Collective of Professionals and Community Participants
Jogen Babur Maath Low-Income Housing
Jogen Babur Maath, Dinajpur, 2011

Jogen Babur Maath is an informal settlement of 500 families. Situated approximately 2 km from the town center of Dinajpur, this low-income housing pilot project was undertaken by a team of volunteers, mainly architects and engineers, who worked together with the community, local artisans and builders for an NGO, Simple Action for the Environment (SAFE Bangladesh). The design team included John Arnold, Ishita Alam Abonee, Shareq Rauf Chowdhury, Mahmuda Alam, Marianne Keating, and Samuel Stephens. The team from the community included Azit Roy, Apu Chandra Roy, Porimol Roy, Pulin Roy, Bikash Roy, Folik Dash, Tushar Kanti Roy, Uzzal Roy, Delowar, and Masud. This driving idea for the project was to promote architecture as a process. To enable the low-income community to take control of their housing choices, a group of volunteers guided the community through a design workshop, to make informed decisions to solve their problems using available resources. Consciously integrating intermediary techniques with the existing construction practices in the region, the aim was to promote the community's self-reliance by training them into informed local builders, craftsmen, and house owners. The benefits of using the techniques were also demonstrated to the wider community through workshop and jatra (folk theater). One of the challenges of promoting traditional building material was the social stigma of poverty and low social status associated with bamboo and mud as most households aspire to own a brick or "pucca" house. The construction of the additional houses using these materials beyond the pilot project signifies the growing trust and confidence in the techniques promoted through the demonstration.

Anna Heringer and Eike Roswag
METI Handmade School
Rudrapur, Dinajpur, 2006

Located in the in the village of Rudrapur, in the north of Bangladesh, this two-storey school was described by the architects as being "hand-made by local craftsmen, pupils, and teachers together with a European team of architects, craftsmen, and students." Inspired by a regional practice, the use of earth and bamboo as building materials draws on creating self-confidence and maintaining sustainability while improving on the existing techniques through training local laborers, schoolchildren, and teachers during the construction process. Highlighting process in architecture, the project is a compelling example of rural architecture in Bangladesh that represents a return to the principles of sustainable ecological design in promoting socially effective enterprise.

The ground floor, with its thick earth walls, has three separate classrooms and cave-like spaces at the rear, while the upper floor in contrast is porous and airy, with a flexible space made of latticed bamboo. The play of colors, whether it is through the use of sarees as canopies and curtains or by painting the door blue with names of the schoolchildren hand-written in white color, creates a creative reincarnation of traditional designs.

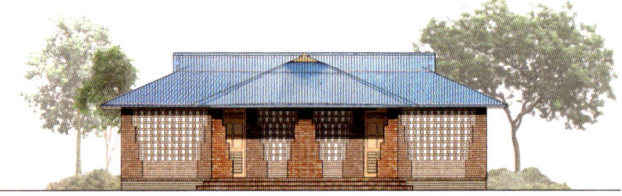

J.A. Architects Ltd (Jalal Ahmed)
Cluster Village Development
Pascim Belkar Char Village at Gaibandha district, Rangpur, 2009

Four "cluster village development projects" are a response to a resettlement program known as "Disappearing Lands: Supporting Communities Affected by River Erosion." Launched in April 2004 by Practical Action Bangladesh, the project targets people from villages located in the north-eastern region of Bangladesh at the confluence of two major rivers, Tista and Brahmaputra, in areas vulnerable to river erosion and flooding.

The project was developed based on a number of initial consultations with local communities to develop a model addressing the issues of the displaced communities. The land for the proposed villages was selected by the NGO in cooperation with the local administration and public representative. Layouts of the villages were based on local tradition of clustering houses around courtyards due to their extensive use by the villagers for different activities like drying food grains, cooking, and vegetable gardening as well as social activities. Each cluster has two types of housing, depending on the size of the household with a livestock shed. There are other amenity buildings within each cluster that includes, a community hall, a non-formal school, a mosque, a community shop, a communal cattle shed, communal toilet, and formal gateway into the village. As the beneficiary communities have no cultivable lands, alternative livelihood options were generated through homestead and floating vegetable gardening during flood seasons, and, pumpkin cultivation in barren sand bar and livestock rearing. The project also demonstrated a comprehensive and participatory disaster risk reduction model for the district.

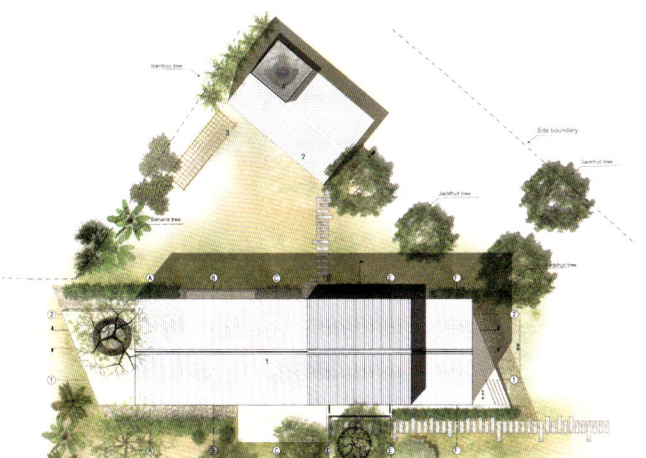

C Purlin 100x50x20
I section 100(8)x100(6)

J.A. Architects Ltd (Jalal Ahmed & Shahnawaz Bappy)
Shuborno Dighi
Sreepur, Gazipur, 2014

"Shuborno Dighi" is a vacation home for a client who wishes to spend his retired life in a village away from the bustling city. Considering the intensity of the surrounding greenery and brown color of the soil, colors of nature were expressed through the design. As the client had a limited budget, locally available materials where explored. With mud building is common in the area, rammed earth construction technique was used. Palm woods and local bamboo were also used extensively in this building. An open deck provides a breath-taking view of the surrounding nature. With minimal disturbance to the site, the ground floor was elevated so that natural vegetation remains intact. Existing trees were also preserved to keep the house within natural surroundings.

Saif Ul Haque Sthapati
Arcadia Education
Char Algee, Keraniganj, Dhaka, 2016

The Arcadia Education Project presented a particular design challenge
primarily present in this region that involves inhabiting the floodplain.
This relocated preschool building provided the architect with an
opportunity to improve on traditional practices and offer something
new and innovative. Since the site is underwater one third of the year,
different options were studied to consider something amphibious that
was also a reinterpretation of a stationary raft. This experimental project
accommodates diverse conditions of the changing aquatic landscape.
By respecting both land and water, decisions were made to proceed in
a cost effective way with easily available materials. The substructure,
designed for floatation, uses steel drums on bamboo framing while
the rest of the structure uses bamboo. The shape of the site supports
a linear design that comprises of four rooms of the same size, three
to function as classrooms and training rooms during different times
of the day, while the other is used as an office. A pantry and toilet
are all connected through a corridor. The structure has withstood one
monsoon during construction and awaits its complete assessment the
following year.

Schilder Scholte Architects (Gerrit Schilder Jr., Hill Scholte)
Pani Community Centre
Makurtary, Rajarhat, 2010

The Dutch foundation Pani commissioned the architects to design an educational building in the northern region of Bangladesh with the goal to "improve the hygiene and work on education, reduce child mortality, and ensure economic independence." Spurred by ideological motives and knowledge sharing, the architects accepted the assignment pro bono. Apart from the local materials, craftsmanship and skills, the architects realized that an environmentally friendly building contributes to the community in a significant way by improving the hygiene and providing employment and education. During the design process, attention was focused on locally available materials and weather conditions. Bamboo, hand-shaped brick, mango wood, reused steel, local mortar, and wafer-thin recycled corrugated panels are the main materials used. The drive was to encourage locals to become aware on the basic principles of sustainability and durable building concepts. Close to zero electricity or fossil fuels were used during construction. Some biomimicry elements are put on the test here. In order to minimize the use of insecticides, the color light blue and yellow were applied in hues that are specifically disliked by insects.

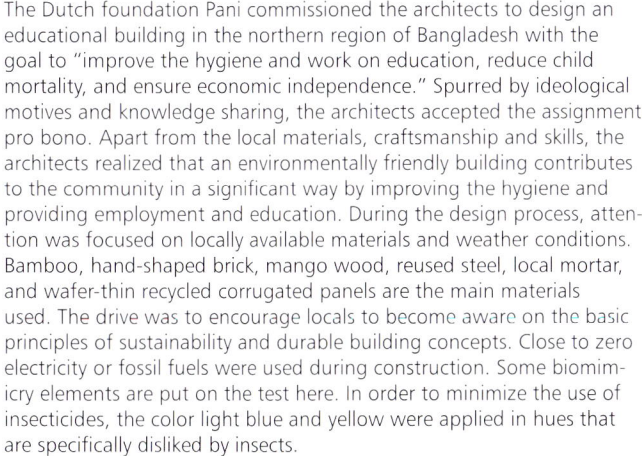

Khandaker Hasibul Kabir
Ashar Macha
Korail Basti, Dhaka, demolished

Architect Khandaker Hasibul Kabir lived for many years in Korail known otherwise as an informal settlement in the middle of Dhaka. He built a small bamboo platform with a garden known as "ashar macha" or platform of hope. The platform served as a community space for the slum children to gather there, tend garden, and find purposes denied to them. It is non-descript space that is both radical yet humane demonstrating what is possible in a condition of adversity. Kabir describe this endeavor as "a 'happening' in rhythm with an ecologically informed garden design, in which the macha acts as a seed of generative aesthetics providing for children a lesson in producing future spaces of well-being." With no major funding or investment, this platform has provided fresh air and greenery for the larger Korail residents.

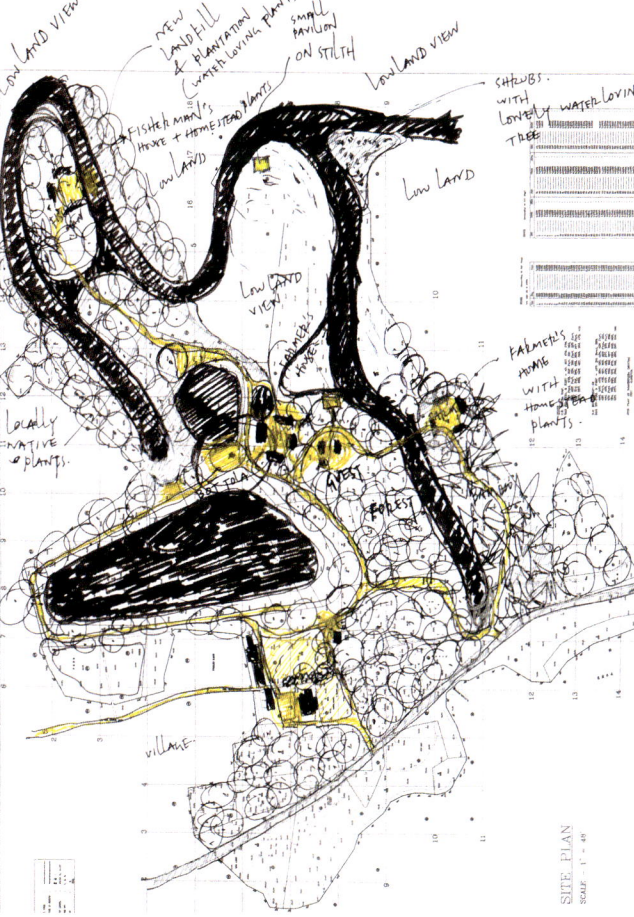

Khandaker Hasibul Kabir
'Jol Jongol' Pubail Retreat
Demur Para, Gazipur, Ongoing

Pubail retreat was designed based on a philosophy that on the site a "constant learning process of protecting a small jungle, wetland, and a habitat for beings other than humans" will take place. The site has been divided into three zones: Nature is the first zone (jungle) where human interactions are restricted. "Nature comes naturally," is the prime idea for this area where "not doing" is more effective than "doing". A complex process within a natural habitat prevails there which people will appreciate from a non-anthropocentric point of view. The buffer-zone is organized not for staying in but for passing through or crossing by the wildlife and human beings. A human first zone ("bashati") is where human activities are prioritized over nature. Architecture, agriculture, and other day-to-day activities (material and spiritual) are in tune with diurnal and annual climatic rhythms. Existing and borrowed elements and ideas from nature are nurtured from an anthropocentric point of view. It is a place built by local craftsman with rapidly grown renewable building materials.

BENGAL FOUNDATION

Bengal Foundation is a private trust that began its journey in the late eighties by the chairman and founder Abul Khair. The main objective was to conserve tradition and allow diversity through evolution and growth from within that could uphold a positive image of Bangladesh by disseminating information about its cultural wealth.

After more than two decades of its establishment, the Foundation has been enriched by an enlightened body of creative thinkers. The organisation's work now encompasses many forms of visual, performing, and literary arts. Bengal Foundation set up three art spaces in Dhaka—Bengal Gallery of Fine Arts, Bengal Art Lounge, and *The Daily Star* Bengal Arts Precinct. It has also established the Safiuddin Bengal Printmaking Studio, the country's largest and finest equipped workshop. To pay homage to the illustrious painter SM Sultan, Bengal Foundation has facilitated the SM Sultan Bengal Art College in the artist's hometown. In order to promote local crafts, Bengal Foundation has focused on the revival of natural dyes through its crafts outlet Aranya. Work has begun on the country's first and largest private contemporary arts and crafts museum in the outskirts of Dhaka in order to create a venue for a collection of more than 5,000 artworks by old masters and contemporary painters.

Much of the Foundation's work involves organizing local and international events, such as exhibitions, festivals, concerts, talent-searches, art camps, and workshops. Bengal Foundation also organizes, annually, the largest classical music festival in terms of number of performers on a single stage, audience capacity, and duration of the program in Dhaka, Bangladesh. The Foundation pursues the policy of making its events free to all. Recognizing the fact that film and visual media are extremely powerful, and attempting to encourage young and talented filmmakers, the Foundation has established the Bengal Cinema Development Forum to support movies by young filmmakers.

Bengal Foundation also publishes musical recordings, catalogs, books, and journals. In 2011, Bengal Foundation and renowned Italian publisher Skira joined hands to produce the "Great Masters" and "Contemporary Masters" series on Bangladesh art. The same year the Foundation facilitated Bangladesh's maiden participation in the prestigious Venice Biennale. To encourage a wider readership in the international audience and to promote writers from Bangladesh, Bengal Foundation has entered into publishing in both Bengali and English. The country's presence in such international events and publications is gradually making a difference in the way Bangladeshi art is perceived in the West.

In 2015, the Foundation set up the Bengal Institute for Architecture, Landscape, and Settlements with an aim to bring about effective social and environmental changes. This was followed by the Gyantapas Abdur Razzaq Bidyapeeth that allows researchers and serious readers to access Professor Razzaq's outstanding collection of books. Professor Razzaq, Mr. Khair's uncle and mentor, is a National Professor, and the inspiration for kindling the beginning of Bengal Foundation.

"WE MUST BE ABLE TO LEAVE SOMETHING CONCRETE FOR FUTURE GENERATIONS. I THINK I CAN SAY THAT UNDER THE AEGIS OF BENGAL FOUNDATION, WE HAVE BEEN ABLE TO GIVE SOMETHING BACK TO THE PEOPLE IN TERMS OF THE ARTS AND CULTURE BUT I FEEL A PRESSING NEED TO DO SOMETHING MORE FOR A LARGER SOCIAL, ECOLOGICAL, AND SPATIAL IMPACT."

Abul Khair

In 1971, when Bangladesh gained independence, it was a small country with a population of about 60 million and with a lot of challenges. At that time, food had to be imported. Now some forty-five years later, population has expanded to about almost 160 million and yet we no longer have to import our staple food. The governments and various NGOs are working mostly in rural areas towards alleviating poverty and increasing the standard of life and living. Institutions like BRAC and Grameen Bank are known worldwide for their micro finance initiatives for the underprivileged.

Great success has been achieved in reducing infant mortality, increasing life expectancy, achieving women's education; BRAC has about 50,000 primary schools all over the country so that all children have access to basic education. Remittance of almost 17 billion dollars per annum are sent by people who have gone to work abroad after much struggle; this is a big boost to the national economy. With the rise in the garments manufacturing sector, the empowerment of women has also increased. Of near 6 million people working in that sector, about 5 million are women.

We, at Bengal Foundation, are doing our part and have been working with the various aspects of the arts for the last twenty-six years. We work to endorse, encourage, and promote the arts in all its forms for an increased awareness and appreciation, as well as create a knowledge base. At Bengal, we strive towards producing enlightened and erudite minds. My uncle and mentor Professor Abdur Razzaq, who was known as "gyantapash" (saint of wisdom), used to say that land and the country's rivers and waterways are the biggest assets, and if we wish to do something for the country, for the people, we must work with these assets.

While Bangladesh is definitely on the rise as a developing country, there are a few factors which seem to be holding us back. Space is a big issue. With our current population at 160 million, and with a projection of 250 million or so in the next fifty years, we have to be prepared for a better utilization of our land. I now realize more than ever how prescient my uncle's wisdom has been in proposing that the arrangement of rivers and land is the clearest way to tackle the challenges of population and its demands.

Muzharul Islam, a pioneer in architecture in Bangladesh, would always speak of the need to "re-design" Bangladesh but unfortunately he did not leave any written guidelines on how to accomplish that. To accommodate people and improve the living conditions we must re-design (for a lack of a better word) the whole of Bangladesh. One first step could be to reorganize rivers and canals, and consequently land, both for transportation and for trade and commerce. Settlements and residential areas could be organized by working with the shorelines and flows of rivers and waterways. Agricultural land needs to be preserved through special land use acts. It is possible that out of the 56,000 sq. miles of Bangladesh, the population could be redistributed within 20,000 sq. miles.

We have taken a few initiatives in that direction. Bengal Institute for Architecture Landscape and Settlements was set up to study, investigate, and imagine new prospects for a land and water rearrangement for Bangladesh. Prominent architects, planners, and thinkers from Bangladesh, and beyond, have joined us in this initiative. For creating a new and energetic environment for exchanging ideas, in which renowned architects from all over can learn about Bangladesh and its

prospects, and architects in Bangladesh can see different work and ideas, we have organized major symposiums: "Engage Dhaka" in 2015 and "Architecture Now/Next" in 2016. I now look forward to the publication of LOCATIONS. I imagine it to be an international forum for flourishing of architectural and urban thinking that can give new directions for the kind of challenges countries like Bangladesh face.

My own regard and passion for architecture have also played a role in making preparations for the future. We already have architects doing the necessary research work, and once we complete the actual plan for a re-designed Bangladesh we will give it to the government, as well as open it for public opinion. Our objective is not necessarily to carry out the actual work but rather show that it can be done with our own resources.

We must be able to leave something concrete for future generations. I think I can say that under the aegis of Bengal Foundation, we have been able to give something back to the people in terms of the arts and culture but I feel a pressing need to do something more for a larger social, ecological, and spatial impact. If we are able to carry out some of the ideas we are pursuing, I am confident that within the next ten years Bangladesh will become a country people will want and opt to live in.

Abul Khair
Chairman, Bengal Foundation.

"A NEW "ARCHITECTURAL INTELLIGENCE" IS NEEDED THAT IS MORE ABOUT "PLACE-FORM" RATHER THAN SPECTACULAR OBJECTS. DEVELOPING THIS DESIGN INTELLIGENCE REQUIRES A NEW KIND OF KNOWLEDGE BASE, TRAINING, AND ORIENTATION THAT WILL UNCOVER THE ORIGINAL INTIMACY BETWEEN ARCHITECTURE, HABITATION, AND LANDSCAPE."

Kazi Khaleed Ashraf

TOWARDS A NEW ARCHITECTURAL INTELLIGENCE

BENGAL INSTITUTE FOR ARCHITECTURE, LANDSCAPES AND SETTLEMENTS

Operational since July 2015, with the support of Bengal Foundation, Bengal Institute for Architecture, Landscapes, and Settlements is providing an intellectual platform for imagining and shaping the futures of the environment. Realizing that the environment is the "life-world," and conversations on the environment need not be confined within academic or professional universes, the Institute is committed to bringing issues of contemporary architecture, cities, settlements, and landscapes not only to participants in its various programs but also to a larger public audience.

Established as a transdisciplinary forum, Bengal Institute is engaged in improving the conditions of environmental learning, practice, and knowledge. In generating a critical, creative, and humanistic dialogue, the Institute proposes an integrated approach to the arrangement and rearrangement of the environment that includes architecture, landscapes, and settlements. Programs of the Institute integrate architectural and design research, investigation of cities and settlements, and the study of larger regions and landscapes.

Bangladesh is the primary focus of the Institute's programs and initiatives. With the aquatic-geological formation—in flux—and projected consequences of environmental changes, the organization of land, water, and settlements takes on an urgency that is unique to Bangladesh. The delta formation brings to the foreground the intimate relationship among architecture, habitation, landscape, and sustenance. At the same time, the Institute considers Dhaka city as a critical site for new architectural and urban design thinking.

Realizing that professions focused on the built environment can be catalytic agents for effective social and environmental change, Bengal Institute takes a longer view of the architectural task. No single discipline or profession can address environmental challenges, especially when that involves the consequences of emerging urbanisms, rapid technological shifts, and radical economic and sociological transformations. Bengal Institute proposes that the architectural task should extend its sights to the intellectual, ethical, and creative issues facing the futures of human habitats. In this regard, a new "architectural intelligence" is needed that is more about "place-form" rather than spectacular objects. Developing this design intelligence requires a new kind of knowledge base, training, and orientation that will uncover the original intimacy between architecture, habitation, and landscape.

Bengal Institute promises unique learning programs by bringing outstanding thinkers and practitioners to a common stage in Dhaka. Programs offer opportunities to both fresh and established professionals, and young faculty, in developing their interests and imaginations, as well as their obligations to the new environmental task.